The Moneylenders of
Late Medieval Kyoto

The Moneylenders of Late Medieval Kyoto

Suzanne Gay

UNIVERSITY OF HAWAI'I PRESS

HONOLULU

01 02 03 04 05 06   6 5 4 3 2 1

Library of Congress Cataloging-in-Publication Data
Gay, Suzanne Marie.
The moneylenders of late medieval Kyoto / Suzanne Gay.
p.   cm.
ISBN 0–8248–1929–2 (cloth : alk. paper)—ISBN 0–8248–2461–X (pbk. : alk. paper)
1. Banks and banking—Japan—Kyoto—History.   2. Bankers—Japan—Kyoto—History.
3. Credit—Japan—History.   I. Title.

HG3330.K962 G39 2001
332.1'753'0952186—dc21   2001027572

University of Hawai'i Press books are printed
on acid-free paper and meet the guidelines for
permanence and durability of the Council
on Library Resources.

Designed by Deborah Hodgdon

Printed by The Maple-Vail Book Manufacturing Group

To James, Emily, and Jeffrey

Contents

List of Illustrations   ix

Acknowledgments   xi

Introduction   1

PART ONE
THE SETTING: KYOTO'S EARLY YEARS AND MEDIEVAL RESIDENTS   9

PART TWO
THE LIVES OF THE MONEYLENDERS   35

Chapter One   The Business of Lending Money   37

Chapter Two   Overlords   56

Chapter Three   Transcending Subordination   90

Chapter Four   Responding to Siege   127

Chapter Five   Urban Affairs   172

Chapter Six   The Fate of the Moneylenders
in the Early Modern Period   201

Conclusion   211

Appendix   225

Notes   237

Bibliography   285

Index   297

Illustrations

Medieval storehouse   38

Sake peddler   43

Woman *sake* brewer   44

Woman moneylender suffering from obesity   46

FIGURES

1. Medieval Development of the *Machi*   25

2. Multiple Taxation of the Moneylenders   99

MAPS

1. Layout of the Ancient Capital of Heiankyō   12

2. Medieval Kyoto, before the Ōnin War   14

3. Brewer-lenders in Medieval Kyoto   42

4. Major Guilds in Medieval Kyoto   60

5. Ōnin War Damage to Kyoto   153

6. Post-Ōnin Kyoto   159

Acknowledgments

Kuroda Toshio and John W. Hall, my two mentors, each had a profound influence on this study. They shaped my approach to medieval history as a combination of people and the processes they create. Professor Kuroda inspired me with his vision, originality, and infectious enthusiasm for history and the people in it. Professor Hall was instrumental in expanding to a western scholarly cohort, with focus and discipline, the lively and challenging study of medieval Japan. I regret that they are no longer here to enliven our field.

Umata Ayako, Niki Hiroshi, and Hayashima Daisuke, in succession, gave me patient and valuable help reading and interpreting primary sources. They also introduced relevant secondary works, apprising me of the range of scholarly views of the moneylenders. I also appreciate greatly the hospitality over the years of the Department of Japanese History and the Historical Archives at Kyoto University, in particular Professors Asao Naohiro, Ōyama Kyōhei, Fujii Jōji, and Ms. Noda Emi.

At various stages of this study, many individuals have offered me valuable advice. The following list is by no means complete, but these scholars' input was especially valuable: Wakita Haruko, Takahashi Yasuo, Tabata Yasuko, Shiga Setsuko, Wakita Osamu, Nishio Kazumi, Julie Nelson Davis, Wendy Kozol, Anne Walthall, Hitomi Tonomura, and Mary Elizabeth Berry. I also appreciate the helpful suggestions of the readers of the manuscript. Any errors are of course solely my own responsibility. At a crucial stage, Hosoya Masahiro of Dōshisha University provided me a serene work space with a view of Shōkokuji's bamboo grove.

I am deeply grateful to Patricia Crosby, editor of the University of Hawai'i Press, for her combination of encouragement and patience. Likewise, Masako Ikeda and Cheri Dunn, also of the University of Hawai'i Press, were efficient and ever helpful. Barbara Folsom copyedited the manuscript with a light but deft touch. Bill Nelson produced the graphics.

Financial support was provided for this project at various stages by the Japan Foundation, Yale University (Sumitomo Fellowship), Social Science Research Council, Oberlin College, U.S. Department of Education (Fulbright Fellowship), and the Associated Kyoto Program.

Finally, I thank my husband, James C. Dobbins, who believed all along that this project would come to fruition, and encouraged me persistently to that end.

Introduction

THIS IS A STUDY of a group of people, residents of medieval Kyoto, who brewed *sake* and lent money for a living. Demand for credit was strong in medieval times, and available from a variety of sources. From about the early thirteenth century, *sake* brewers dominated secular moneylending in the city.[1] Under the direct or indirect control, first of Enryakuji, the great Buddhist monastery on Mount Hiei, and later of the Muromachi shogunate, they numbered in the hundreds in the late medieval period (approximately 1350 to 1550). Flush with capital from brewing and a constant flow of interest income, they were seen by the elites as a reliable and plentiful source of tax income.

The moneylenders occupy a significant niche in medieval history for their economic function and because, as wealthy and influential townspeople, they were major players in Kyoto's culture and society. Through their multitude of activities, including moneylending, *sake* brewing, self-governance, and self-defense, and also as participants in a new secular culture of urban commoners, they had dealings with all groups in society. Hence their lives touched the diverse elements that made up the fabric of medieval Kyoto. They experienced firsthand many of the profound changes that occurred over the course of the medieval period as traditional hierarchies gradually weakened. In the process these commoners, because of their economic leverage, found themselves in a temporary ascendancy, flourishing as wealthy and prominent townspeople.

There were other moneylenders in medieval Kyoto besides the brewers. Specialist pawnbrokers sometimes offered credit on a small scale in return for pawned items, as did bean-paste merchants and lenders who computed interest on a daily basis. For the most part these were individuals with small lending capacity. In contrast, the brewer-lenders of this study, with their wealth derived from brewing, their numerical strength, and their powerful overlords, constituted a cohesive commercial bloc.

Clerical moneylending was also widespread in the medieval period at Enryakuji and other temples like Tōji.[2] In the latter half of the medieval period the *gozan* Zen monasteries, although relative newcomers to the business, engaged extensively in moneylending at low interest rates with shogunal protection.[3] Most *gozan* lending was fairly large-scale, from one Zen temple to another, to the shogunate, or to secular moneylenders, including those of this study. Zen lending was in a different category from that of the brewer-lenders, for it required access to a monastic agent, rendering such loans out of reach to the ordinary person seeking credit.[4] *Gozan* lending declined with the Muromachi shogunate, its protector. This study will examine the activities of the brewer-lenders with occasional reference to these other moneylending entities, individual and institutional.

The twelfth through sixteenth centuries, labeled "medieval" by Japanese historians following the Western model, were more than a static time between ancient and early modern.[5] They saw the gradual rise to dominance of the warrior class with its own governing mechanisms; the complete permeation of Japanese society by Buddhism, which produced a unique Buddhist-Shinto worldview as well as an array of lay-centered faith sects; a transformation in the nature of property holding; and the emergence of an urban economy and culture. The latter came to full flower in the late medieval period, the focus of this study, beginning approximately with the establishment of the Muromachi shogunate in 1336 and extending to the dismantling of the medieval order in the late sixteenth century, a process keenly felt in Kyoto when Oda Nobunaga destroyed Enryakuji in 1571.

Most of the moneylenders' activities described here took place in the latter half of the medieval period, a time of dynamic upheaval. Peasant invasions, some of them large-scale, were repeatedly visited upon Kyoto; the ten-year Ōnin War brought devastation and long-term change; the Lotus leagues, religious cells of townspeople, dominated city life until they were crushed; and finally the political and economic order was redefined in such a way that the moneylenders' favorable niche was obliterated. Often the destructive aspects of this period are emphasized, reflecting the concern, perhaps, of elite record keepers who saw their world being threatened. To moneylenders, however, though upheaval could bring destruction, it could also present business opportunities as credit became more essential than ever. More fundamentally, upheaval became the catalyst for social change. As moneylenders and other commoners took the opportunity to distance themselves from their overlords while never making a complete break, they increasingly lived as autonomous townspeople. Thus these centuries were years of transformation, especially for wealthy commoners like moneylenders.

The medieval period in Japan was characterized by a social structure that encompassed the elites—temples, aristocrats, and warriors—as well as most peasants and merchants in complex hierarchical arrangements featuring not only dominance and subservience but also varying degrees of mutual benefit. In the agricultural sector these were expressed through the estate system with its layered rights to land, into which the local warrior class gradually insinuated itself. In the commercial sector the same hierarchy found expression through guilds or guildlike arrangements, which, like the estate system, featured overlords drawing income from the commoners below them in return for monopoly rights and other forms of protection. Early in the medieval period, such overlords tended to be aristocrats and religious institutions; the Muromachi shogunate joined their ranks as an overlord of late medieval Kyoto's commercial sector. To the very end of the medieval period, even as traditional rights to agricultural and commercial income were being successfully challenged elsewhere, long-standing vertical ties prevailed, if tenuously, in Kyoto, the capital and focus of this study. Commoners like moneylenders functioned outside of these relationships in their activities as townspeople even as they continued to function well within their hierarchical boundaries in other respects. They gradually evolved into secular townspeople and played a leading role in the life of the city. At the same time, however, these moneylenders remained tied to the medieval hierarchical order. As a result, they benefited richly from their position in the middle for as long as the medieval order lasted, but as a group they did not survive its decline. Credit was to become the preserve of other merchants in the early modern period.

At the same time medieval society was hierarchical, it was also, at the top, plural. Multiple overlords, sometimes with overlapping claims, competed and coexisted. These elites—emperor and imperial family, aristocrats, temples and shrines, and the warrior newcomers—came to a loose and sometimes uneasy accommodation. The resulting "order," which was often disorderly, featured no single entity in medieval Kyoto that could accurately be labeled sole ruler, as many enjoyed parts of rulership. Traditionally, the medieval period has been characterized as belonging to the warrior, with the aristocracy and religious establishment in an inexorable decline.[6] Another characterization of the medieval authority structure that is particularly apt for medieval Kyoto posits group rulership: elite families or family-like entities such as temples, aristocrats, and warriors with interests rooted in the estate system and therefore coinciding generally, cooperated to preserve their "order" as much as they competed against one another.[7] According to this theory, these elite groups, called *kenmon* (a medieval term meaning houses of authority and power),[8] fall into three broad categories: the aristocracy, including the emperor and imperial house, the Buddhist-Shinto religious establishment, and the leading warrior houses. Each group had its own function: aristocrats to serve as civil officials with their expertise in state ritual, temples to protect the state spiritually, and warriors to defend the state militarily; together they constituted the medieval Japanese "state."

The *kenmon* theory is by no means airtight: even its originator, Kuroda Toshio, applied it mainly to the Kamakura period and saw it as moribund after the Ōnin War.[9] It has been criticized for exaggerating the remaining influence of court and temples. It has also been pointed out that the very term "medieval state" (*chūsei kokka*), though also used in other characterizations of the medieval period, is contradictory: the authority structure of the medieval period was so diffuse and decentralized that it can hardly be called a "state."[10] But to the extent that in practice the medieval authority system was fluid and plural in nature, then the *kenmon* theory is a useful one, for it recognizes fully the importance of all the elite players on the medieval stage without pushing any of them into the wings prematurely. Its impact has been broad, particularly in bringing the role of the medieval emperor into fuller focus and in shedding light on the pervasive role of religion in the society, not only in a spiritual sense but in economic, political, and institutional terms as well.[11]

The *kenmon* characterization applies particularly well to medieval Kyoto, both from the perspective of commoners like the moneylenders and as an explanation of elite dynamics. Even beyond the Ōnin War and well into the sixteenth century, with most of Japan under warrior domination Kyoto functioned under multiple elites whose interests often clashed but who remained dedicated to the preservation of the order that served them so well. In the area of landed wealth, this order took the form of the traditional estate system; in commerce it meant the estate's parallel, the guild (*za*) system. Thus the elite overlords, whether aristocrats, warriors, or temples, tended to accommodate one another. As the period wore on, their commoner clients with economic leverage, like the moneylenders, also tended to be accommodated as they pressed for more benefits within the resilient and flexible system. Ties to the overlord remained but could often be manipulated to enrich and empower subordinates. The entire latter half of the medieval period was one of complex, overlapping jurisdictions and challenges thereto. These intensified after the Ōnin War, and irregularities abounded: taxation by multiple overlords, frequent incidental levies, evasion of taxes, and bribery in return for exemptions. A fragile equilibrium prevailed in which the overlord arrangement yielded less income than before for the competing elites at the top, who for their part could offer their clients less substantial protection. As will be shown, the moneylenders of this study, though taxed at frequent intervals, for the most part thrived in this state of affairs.

The behavior of overlord institutions was often internally contradictory, featuring formal, institutional practices alongside quite different, informal, even personal practices of its individual officials. Probably present all along, by the late fifteenth century these contrasting behaviors became more starkly evident. On the one hand, the overlord institution behaved according to long-established, formal procedures through its house organization, procedures that were marked by hierarchy and documentation: levying taxes and in return protecting clients through monopolies, lawsuits, force, or political pressure. Especially when in decline, however, an overlord's individual members informally behaved otherwise, profiting personally through irregular practices like bribes. Even the imperial court and the Muromachi shogunate displayed both types of behavior. Both used their administrative powers to enforce order and to adjudicate disputes in the city. At the same time, however, and sometimes in ways that actually conflicted with their official role, their members informally enriched themselves. As city administrators, for example, court and shogunate were concerned that the toll stations on the roads leading in and out of the city not overcharge or proliferate in number to the extent of impeding commerce. But officials within both the court and shogunate at times set up their own toll stations as a source of private income.[12] As a result, in dealings with commoners especially, overlord rule could be arbitrary, lacking consistent adherence to precedent. To commoners, this presented anomalies: both privileges (like exemptions and monopolies) and restraints (especially taxation, at frequent and irregular intervals) were visited upon anyone affiliated with an overlord. But in great measure because of the continuous income provided by these informal practices, the overlords of medieval Kyoto maintained some control over commerce after their hold over distant estates had loosened. This arrangement offered something for everyone, and a wily commoner like a prominent moneylender could sometimes evade its arbitrariness.

The term "commoner" is used in this study primarily in reference to the economic consequences of nonelite status in the medieval hierarchy: clients were required to pay taxes to their overlords whether they were involved in agricultural or commercial activities (or both, as was increasingly the case in the medieval village). They are called commoners, as opposed to the elite recipients of those taxes, including temples, shrines, aristocrats, and warriors. ("Taxes," in late medieval times usually paid in cash rather than in kind, is used here in preference to "dues," "imposts," and a range of like terms. Taxes are defined here simply as payments, regular and irregular, by commoners to those at the other end of the social hierarchy.) Compared to most medieval commoners, moneylenders were well-to-do. They both paid taxes and, in their role as tax farmers, received a cut of taxes, so it could be argued that they were not true commoners at all. It is perhaps most accurate to think of them as advantageously poised at the top of the commoner class. As the period wore on, particularly in the post–Ōnin years, from that high perch they learned to manipulate the tottering overlord arrangements to their advantage.

The term "overlord" is used here to refer to the elite recipients of commoners' taxes. An overlord could be male or female, a warrior, an aristocrat, a temple, or another institution like the imperial court. The term is chosen in preference to others like "proprietor" and "patron." Ownership being its most fundamental attribute, "proprietor" is a misleading descriptor of the nature of the elites' authority. "Patron" for its part implies benevolence, protection, and paternalism. While these elements were present in some cases, for the client there was also quite a sting to the arrangement. In not acknowledging the predatory nature of the elites' authority, therefore, "patron" is an inadequate term. "Overlord" is the most inclusive and descriptively accurate term for medieval elites who operated from a position of acknowledged privilege. This is not to imply that subservience was the whole story in commoners' relations with overlords: especially as the medieval period wore on, individual wealth and a more secular outlook allowed some flexing of commoner muscle, as will be shown.

A study of the moneylenders must acknowledge the major presence of the monastery Enryakuji, which, through its network of subordinate shrines, dominated Kyoto's commercial sector as tax-absorbing overlord for the first half of the medieval period. Gion, Kitano, and Hie Shrines received taxes from the brewer-lenders in return for protecting their monopolies. The Enryakuji affiliation also gave the moneylenders a privileged clerical status that enhanced their position among the townspeople. A modicum of religious erudition gained through actual monastic training, however brief, may have contributed to the impressive cultural attainments of some moneylenders. The success of the moneylenders as Enryakuji's affiliates is a powerful reminder of the institutional and spiritual pervasiveness of religion in the medieval world. The Muromachi shogunate from the fourteenth century placed some limits on Enryakuji's ability to dominate commerce, though the extent of the decline is far from clear. An uneasy accommodation existed between the shogunate and Enryakuji, both of which were dependent on similar arrangements for commercial income, and neither willing to confront the other directly. The historical record yields evidence that Enryakuji moved over but not out to accommodate the shogunate in Kyoto.

The Muromachi shogunate singled out the moneylenders as a major source of commercial income. This study is therefore also about the shogunate as it functioned in Kyoto. Utilizing the existing overlord system to gain some control over commerce, the shogunate showed flexibility in adapting to existing conditions. It was protean: Ashikaga Yoshimitsu's Bakufu, with its comprehensive and expanded reach, was not "typical" any more than was Yoshihisa's in retreat. This quality, as much as its limited ability to dominate the country, accounts for the difficulty historians have in characterizing it convincingly as the governing authority of late medieval Japan. The Muromachi shogunate was a very narrowly based institution, but in Kyoto it was public administrator and adjudicator, even in decline. Its presence, like that of Enryakuji, profoundly shaped the moneylenders' lives.

This study presents two somewhat overlapping stories: that of the moneylenders as they made their way in the world of the overlords and that of the moneylenders as townspeople. The former is characterized by the conventional use of mostly official sources, in most cases approached credulously. Ulterior motive in their composition is rarely presumed, and some degree of compliance or enforcement is assumed, perhaps unwarrantedly so. It should be acknowledged, however, that these sources reflect the overlords' wishful thinking as much as reality, which was never so neat. Cracks and weaknesses in the system, discussed in Part 2, can be readily discerned even in the overlords' own version of reality. The other narrative, that of the moneylenders as townspeople, is limited by the fact that there are no extant records of a moneylending house. This is a group of people whose experience was recorded in fragments, almost incidentally, by others. Thus their story by necessity is based on many of the same sources as the first narrative, but skeptically, recognizing that their purpose was not to reveal the details of the lenders' lives per se, and that they do so only grudgingly. Overlords were interested in moneylenders as a source of income, and their records reflect this one-dimensional concern. The moneylenders, however, saw their lives quite differently: credit transactions, *sake* brewing, neighborhood self-defense and administration, and extensive cultural pursuits occupied their days, into which the overlords' demands also intruded. The second narrative attempts to convey this ground-level perspective. Each conveys part of the moneylenders' experience; both explain their prominence in medieval Kyoto.

Part One

The Setting

Kyoto's Early Years

MEDIEVAL KYOTO EVOLVED gradually on the site of the ancient capital, Heiankyō. Although transformed in many respects, the medieval city still bore a physical resemblance to the earlier metropolis and remained home to the same group of elite residents. Moneylenders and other merchants had more shallow roots, for the city was originally designed for administrative not commercial purposes.

Kyoto was made Japan's capital in 794 in an attempt to solve political problems in the previous capital, Nara. The move from Heijōkyō (the ancient name for Nara) to Heiankyō was part of an effort by Emperor Kammu to assert the primacy of his segment of the imperial lineage group, the Tenji line. Another factor in the move of the capital was the friction between the civil aristocracy and the powerful Nara Buddhist establishment.[1] Determined to revive the traditional method of governance by bureaucrats, which had given way in recent decades to heavy clerical involvement, the reform faction seized its chance in 770 and Kammu was made emperor, ending the dominance of the Temmu line. Attempts were begun to move the capital. After a crisis-ridden decade at Nagaoka, Kammu selected another site to the northeast and moved there in 794. This was the capital of Heian, later to be known as Kyoto.

Kyoto was well placed. It occupied a natural point for trade at the intersection of the San'in highway from the northeast and the east-west Tōkaidō route. Moreover, topographical features met the traditional requirements for a Chinese capital: surrounded by mountains on three sides, with one protective peak, Mount Hiei, in the inauspicious northeastern corner, the site could be considered naturally fortified.[2] Furthermore, because Kyoto was on the northern, most elevated edge of the Yamato plain, its rivers lacked the often destructive force of those in a lower location like Nara.

Like Nara before it, Kyoto was based on the familiar checkerboard pattern of Chang-an, the capital of Sui and Tang China (Map 1). Although the Japanese version was smaller, it contained many of the features of the Chinese model: a large palace enclosure in the north-central section of the city containing the emperor's residence and various grand halls for administrative offices; an imposing main gate, Rajōmon, in the south, from which led a broad avenue, Suzaku Ōji, through the middle of the city north to the palace; official east and west markets; and broad east-west avenues intersected by narrower north-south streets dividing the city for administrative purposes into small square units. In keeping with Kammu's anticlericalism, the Buddhist presence in the city proper was intended to be

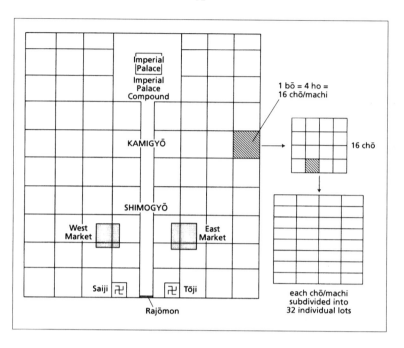

Map 1: Layout of the Ancient Capital of Heiankyō

limited to two major guardian temples, Tōji (east temple) and Saiji (west temple), on either side of the great entrance to the city. The aristocracy occupied the northern or upper section of the city, while the southern or lower half, later to be the commercial sector, was at first but sparsely inhabited by artisans and craftsmen. South of Gojō, the fifth major east-west avenue, the city gave way to agriculture.

Kyoto in its early centuries was surrounded by no huge wall like that of Chang-an, except for a low one on the south; a small earthen embankment may have encircled the rest of the city. Even today, however, Kyoto bears the mark of the continental plan in its symmetrical street layout. But in later centuries Kyoto failed to develop strictly according to this model. Apparently due to the swampy condition of much of the western side, only the eastern half of the original site was actually inhabited, and the southern portion of that was sparsely populated for several centuries. Efforts were made in 825 to encourage the development of the western side by giving its market a monopoly on certain items like cloth, but to no avail.[3] Even Saiji, the western guardian temple, declined, its buildings destroyed by fire one by one and never rebuilt, with the pagoda finally burning in 1233. Its counterpart, Tōji, flourished with the rest of the east side, as it became a stronghold of esoteric Buddhism in the Heian period.

The emperor moved to Kyoto in 794, marking the founding of the city, but building continued. Each age contributed its share of structures, renewing and extending the city constantly. The Fujiwara family, which monopolized the regency from the late tenth century, constructed elaborate residences that also served as administrative centers. The palace of the reigning emperor fell into disrepair from the late eleventh century, as the office of retired emperors (*In no chō*) dominated politics, and the area east of the Kamo River as far as the hills was settled with imperial temple-residences, starting with the imposing Hosshōji, retired Emperor Shirakawa's base, in 1075. Retired emperors favored this area for their own palaces and retirement temples, and encouraged the construction of other temples there as well.[4] Thus, while the city as a whole moved eastward and took on a notably religious character—Kammu's original intentions notwithstanding—the western half remained sparsely populated until the early decades of the twentieth century.

Kyoto has been known by several names. The word *Kyōto* consists of two characters with a slight difference in meaning, together denoting the capital city.[5] *Kyō* was a suffix for capitals in the ancient period (Heian-kyō, Heijō-kyō, etc.), and under the ancient government system it referred to the place where the emperor's residence was located. The ideograph *to* means the population center—the city—where the emperor permanently resides. Initially named Heiankyō (Capital of Peace and Tranquillity), the city acquired various nicknames over time. In 818 Emperor Saga dubbed the eastern portion (Sakyō) of the city "Rakuyō" (Ch. Lo-yang), and the western portion (Ukyō) he called "Chōan" (Ch. Chang-an), a felicitous application to one city of the names of the two great ancient Chinese capitals.[6] Because the western portion of the city remained relatively uninhabited, "Chōan" was seldom used, and the city as a whole was popularly referred to as "Kyōraku" or just "Raku." With the move of administrative offices to Shirakawa and Toba during the period of dominance by the retired emperors in the late Heian period, "Heiankyō" fell out of use, and "Kyōto," which first appeared in documents in 988, became a common term for the city, including the Shirakawa vicinity east of the Kamo River and the area of the Toba Detached Palace to the southwest.[7]

From the tenth century Kyoto gradually began to take on a long, narrow shape, centering on the eastern half of the original capital layout (Map 2). In the medieval period, it became common to refer to this as "Rakuchū" ("within Raku"), as distinct from the area surrounding the city, "Rakugai" ("outside Raku"). "Rakuchū" extended from about the Kamo River in the east to Suzaku-dōri (in the vicinity of present-day Ōmiya and Senbon-dōri) in the west, and from Kami Onryō-dōri in the

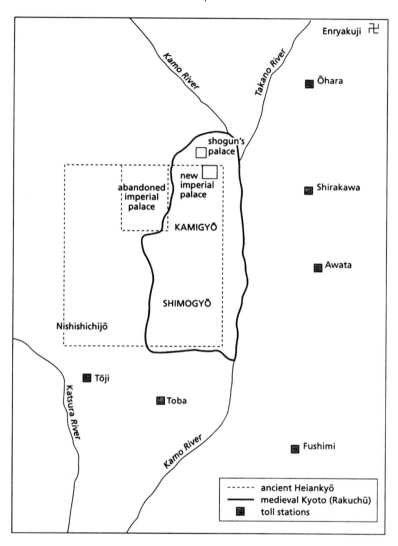

Map 2: Medieval Kyoto, before the Ōnin War

north to Gojō in the south. The area outside these parameters was called "Rakugai," and included the eastern suburbs, the southwestern districts of Otokuni, Otagi, part of Kadono, and the southern district of Uji. "Rakuchū Rakugai" was a common medieval term for Kyoto and its outskirts, but in reality it hardly referred to a static area: "Rakuchū," in particular, was a constantly changing area as population and commerce waxed and waned.

During the Heian period, administration of the entire capital area fell under the control, first, of the Capital Office (*Kyōshiki*) of the imperial government. Its duties included recording the population through a household registration (*koseki*) system and policing the city. The latter function was absorbed by the Bureau of Capital Police (*kebiishichō*) in the tenth century as the offices of the old civil administration atrophied generally.[8] Established by Emperor Saga in 816 outside the original civil government structure to control lawless behavior in Kyoto, the Bureau of Police became the only police force in the city with comprehensive public authority as the court and aristocratic families assembled private armies in the eleventh century. The scope of its duties gradually expanded: surveillance, arrest, policing the streets, collection of stolen goods. With their close knowledge of neighborhood life, Bureau members came to control aspects of commerce in private arrangements deriving from their public authority as city police. In the late Heian period, market activity shifted from the official east and west markets to large intersections along Sanjō, Shijō, and Shichijō avenues, areas not under the direct jurisdiction of the Capital Office. Although the Bureau of Capital Police kept a branch office in each ward of the city, in practice, given its responsibility for crime control, its activities tended to concentrate on market areas, places where people congregated and therefore where crime was most likely to occur. Thus Bureau members rubbed elbows regularly with merchants, and in time offered them monopolistic as well as police protection in return for regular payment. As will be seen, it was an easy step for the Bureau to move from policing of the market areas to an active role in commerce as overlord when the medieval guild system began to take shape.

In the mid-twelfth century, warriors began to assert themselves and street battles punctuated city life. From about 1156 the warrior leader Taira Kiyomori dominated Kyoto from his headquarters in the southeastern Rokuhara district, keeping the imperial court under surveillance, policing Rakuchū, and regulating the activities of warriors of western Japan. Marauding by criminals and monks, famine, and numerous natural disasters accompanied political disintegration. A great fire in 1177 destroyed about one-third of the city, including the imperial palace.

After the defeat of the Taira in the Gempei Wars of 1180–1185, the new shogun, Minamoto Yoritomo, posted a representative called the *Kyōto shugo* in the city. Nominally his duties included policing Kyoto, but in practice the Bureau of Capital Police continued in its accustomed role at the neighborhood level.[9] Except in cases involving warriors, crime control for a time remained the responsibility of the Bureau of Capital Police.[10] After the retired emperor Gotoba's unsuccessful attempt to restore impe-

rial rule in 1221, the Kamakura shogunate, determined to keep the imperial court under close surveillance, upgraded its Kyoto office to a deputyship (*tandai*) located at Kiyomori's former headquarters at Rokuhara. Shogunal forces under the deputy took a more active role in the defense of
the city, including guarding the major roads into the city. One long-term
contribution of the deputy was to make the city neighborhoods secure by
instituting regular patrols and guard stations at major intersections, where
bonfires were kept burning to reduce nighttime crime.[11] The Rokuhara
headquarters served as a place from which to conduct shogunal (e.g., warrior) affairs in central and western Japan and at the same time to keep a
watchful eye on reigning and retired emperors. Kamakura Bakufu rule was
primarily by and for warriors, particularly the vassals of the Minamoto
family. Aristocrats were bound by their own legal code, and commoners
did not fall under the purview of a specific legal system. City life went on,
therefore, and the Rokuhara deputy did not administer Kyoto with a heavy
hand or involve himself with commerce.

Kyoto originated as a planned city, not built on the site of a preexist-
ing town of any importance or size. Several familial groups had dominated
parts of the plain before the capital was moved there; they appear to have
been absorbed into Kyoto's imperial officialdom. It has been said that the
concept of "urban community" did not appear in Asia because Asian cities,
being primarily centers of state administration, lacked the political
autonomy of European cities.[12] This characterization, although inappro-
priate for medieval Kyoto, is somewhat apt for the ancient city insofar as
its social and economic development followed the establishment of the
offices of the central government there and remained in its shadow for a
time. Under the ancient system of government borrowed from China, in
principle all land belonged to the state, which was to parcel it out on an
equitable and regular basis to the cultivators who worked the land and
submitted tax and corvee to the state. Nonagrarian laborers, at least in
theory, also worked at the behest of the government. They included craftsmen and artisans who produced goods and services needed by the government and its officials. There were also some stipended facilitators of
government and estate taxes-in-kind who transported and exchanged goods
for the city's elite residents. Although this theoretical description of commoners' relations with the state was from the beginning an ideal intended to bolster imperial authority, it describes with some accuracy the
workings of a planned capital city: except for officialdom, in the beginning Kyoto was populated mainly by such workers and by peasants. No
extensive commodity market existed in the early city: goods were produced

mostly for the needs of the civil aristocrats and not for trade. Before the Heian period was over, however, entrepreneurial impulses began to prevail among such workers and a merchant class emerged, catering to the needs of aristocrats, for personal profit.

With the rise of a new, private type of control of land and resources from about the tenth century, the conditions necessary for the development of a market economy began to emerge in the Kyoto area. Religious institutions and aristocratic families became overlords of landed estates from which they derived income. Estates in the Kyoto area, where the elites were heavily concentrated, tended to be under their direct but loose control. The proximity of the overlords prevented the emergence in central Japan of the strong local estate manager found in more peripheral areas; he was usually a warrior whose collection of taxes could be exacting and severe. In the Kyoto area, on the other hand, peasants asserted some control over the collection and transport of estate taxes to overlords in the city. They resisted the arbitrary collection of taxes, generally paying fixed, yearly taxes limited to two forms, a standard annual tax (*honnengu*) usually paid in rice, and a tax rendered in labor or goods (*zōkuji*). (Commutation was widespread before the fourteenth century.)[13]

More than their counterparts in peripheral areas, well-to-do peasants of central Japan, an agriculturally productive region, altered their activities to take full advantage of the market economy. The typical estate of the Kyoto area in the fourteenth century was prosperous: crops were diversified, often for their cash value; double- and even triple-cropping was common; improved methods of irrigation and fertilization produced a surplus; and peasants were typically involved in subsidiary occupations such as handicraft production. Some engaged in commercial activities like moneylending to the extent that it became their main occupation. The economy was doubly stimulated, by overlord demand and consumption, and also by the management and distribution of commodities in abundance by small peasants instead of local managers.[14]

In general the peasants of central Japan prospered by participating in the commodity market, while peasants on the periphery tended to be occupied with subsistence. But during the fourteenth and fifteenth centuries a split occurred within the peasant class of the central region, with those on the bottom held in their place by the harsh taxation and unforgiving moneylending practices of those on the top. Thus, although Kyoto area peasants in general enjoyed a decent existence, in practice some were very disadvantaged while others thrived.

With the decline of the ancient civil government and the growth of a market economy, Kyoto emerged in the medieval period as the political, cultural, and economic hub of the country—far from the sterility of a planned administrative city. Ancient Kyoto has been termed a "city without citizens," an officials' city, in which most of the land was still used for agriculture, with a small population of service workers.[15] By the twelfth century, however, a transformation had occurred: artisans produced commodities and merchants marketed them; they paid taxes to aristocratic and religious overlords in return for monopoly privileges and exemptions from government taxes.[16] In medieval times Kyoto was a thriving commercial center of manufactured goods and wealth derived from estate taxes as well as from local industries. The smaller north–south side streets of Kyoto, unnamed when the city was founded, took on popular names reflecting the types of goods and services concentrated there: brocade, armor, oil, salt, needles (for acupuncture), and the like.[17] Moneylenders provided credit as cash came into use. The social fabric of the city was enhanced, with urban commoners adding significantly both to its population and to its cultural ambience.

At the end of the twelfth century Kyoto was upstaged politically by the establishment of the shogunate in Kamakura, but it continued to be the economic center of Japan and the home of the traditional elites, including the emperor and major religious institutions, and therefore of the estate system. The transition to medieval times included the conversion of more land from agricultural to residential use as the population began to rise, a gradual waning of the power of the aristocracy, a growing warrior presence, further expansion of the city to the south of Gojō and east of the Kamo River, and a move away from agriculture toward commerce and industry by the city's commoner inhabitants.[18] Medieval Kyoto boasted all the features of a metropolis: it was the site of the declining imperial government and extensive markets, headquarters of the country's religious establishment, and a cultural hub. Unlike many of the world's ancient capitals, Kyoto successfully made the transition to the medieval age as the country's metropolitan center.

Kyoto's Medieval Residents
Relationships and Living Patterns

IN THE *KENMON* RULE by multiple elites, the social hierarchy consisted of competing and cooperating elites: aristocrats led by the emperor, warriors whose leader was the shogun, and the clergy. The emperor was not only the central figure in the aristocracy, he was at the apex of the *kenmon* order, subordinate to no one. Specifically, he proclaimed laws, performed court ceremonials, and throughout the medieval period continued to monopolize the important function of the appointment and dismissal of officials. Though exercise of imperial authority was increasingly circumscribed by the rising warriors, at its most profound level it was always closely tied to religious and ceremonial aspects of the office, the significance of which cannot be disregarded in a medieval context as easily as in modern times. The medieval emperor, even as a small figure retreating into a series of palaces and borrowed residences, possessed an aura of sanctity and authority; he was not replaceable by any other entity in the political order. Aristocrats supported the emperor as court officials, even as the real power of the civil government atrophied. They also held landed estates in a private capacity, and some brokered lucrative overlord arrangements with commercial groups. The glory days of the Heian period may have been long over, but aristocratic wealth and privilege proved quite durable.

Ashikaga Takauji founded the Muromachi shogunate in 1336. Relative latecomers to Kyoto, the Ashikaga warriors fundamentally changed the power balance in the city by establishing their headquarters there. Unlike the Kamakura shogunate, which had maintained only a limited presence in Kyoto, for a time the Muromachi shogunate made Kyoto the very base of the warriors, who were primarily a provincial phenomenon. Despite their military capabilities, however, they were not able to have their way in Kyoto completely. In the medieval balance of multiple elites, both the aristocracy and the religious establishment continued to be forces to contend with. Nevertheless, the warrior impact on Kyoto was soon evident. The Ashikaga and their supporters were not merely the latest rulers to arrive in the city. The important functional difference between them and the other elites was based in part on their military capacity: city administration, including adjudication and the enforcement of law and order, often involved the use of force, or at least the threat of force. Their application of existing warrior legal conventions to a broader social spectrum was also a significant factor in their ability to administer the city.[19] Eventually the Muromachi shogunate came to adjudicate disputes not involving warriors: two aristocrats, for example, or an aristocrat and a temple might turn to the shogunate as the only entity whose authority carried enough weight to decide a dispute.[20] By the early fifteenth century the shogunate, like the imperial court in earlier times, was recognized as the city's administrator.

Thus the Ashikaga, founders of the Muromachi shogunate, fulfilled well their warrior mandate as defenders of the state, within the *kenmon* order.

By the late fourteenth century the imperial court had lost most of its administrative authority over commerce, and over the city as a whole, to the Muromachi Bakufu.[21] The shogunate adopted a stance toward the court and aristocracy that was more protective than confrontational, if sometimes deliberately negligent. One of its earliest actions was to order that their Kyoto lands, which aristocrats had abandoned or been driven from in the fighting of the 1330s between the northern and southern court factions, be returned to them.[22] Offices of the ancient civil government continued to exist and to be filled, but increasingly as no more than hereditary sinecures providing income on a private basis. This is not to say that the court and aristocracy were powerless: as one segment of the ruling class, their continuing prominence was based both on their expertise in cultural matters and on their real, though declining, ability to command economic resources—namely, landed and commercial sources of income. But in Kyoto the court's administrative authority was limited largely to official appointments and ceremonials.

The late medieval fate of the imperial accession ceremony, the *daijōe*, provides an important example of how the shogunate dominated the imperial court.[23] No longer able to collect the substantial sum needed to stage the ceremony, the imperial court turned to the shogunate, and in doing so ceded a large measure of control over its own affairs. By the middle of the fourteenth century, only a few years after its founding, the Muromachi Bakufu took control of collection of taxes for the ceremony. This also included the right to grant exemptions to the tax and the right to determine the budget for the ceremony. A procedure was followed: first an imperial agent would request funds of the shogun's Board of Administration (*mandokoro*), which would then direct its tax agents to collect the funds through a variety of levies—a tax on the city's brewers, estate taxes, provincial taxes (*tansen*), and taxes on houses (*munabechisen*) and frontage (*jiguchisen*) in Kyoto. Thus during the Muromachi period imperial accession occurred only with the oversight of the shogunate. The large amount allotted for the ceremony, 3,000 *kanmon*, suggests that the court's position was not thoroughly debased. By the mid-fifteenth century, however, the amount actually collected to finance the ceremony fell far short of the figure budgeted for it, as much a sign of the shogunate's growing inability to collect taxes from the provinces as an indication of further decline in the imperial institution itself. The ceremony was canceled altogether during the Ōnin War and not revived until the seventeenth century. The imperial court, therefore, continued its ceremonial functions in the Muro-machi period, but its real power had so declined that it no longer con-trolled the financing of its most important ceremony. Thus the warrior government recognized the spiritual authority of the emperor and offered him protection tantamount to control of his finances.

Warrior influence in Kyoto extended beyond the political and mili-tary arenas. The warriors avidly patronized the arts with a fervor rivalling that of the aristocrats.[24] And in the area of culture the Muromachi shogun bowed to the traditional aristocracy as expert authorities. An early example was the shogunal declaration of 1346–1349 that aristocratic regulations would be the standard for dress for economic reasons, and no one was to dress above their status.[25] Shogun Yoshimitsu's patronage of the arts in particular produced a hitherto unknown cultural diversity. Some of this was due to the willingness of low-ranking aristocrats and wealthy com-moners to contribute their talents to warrior-sponsored cultural activities that the exclusive and highest-ranking aristocrats would not have per-mitted.[26] In this way warriors exerted a liberating influence on culture, allowing give-and-take between members of different classes and produc-ing a rich hybrid culture to which even commoners like the moneylenders contributed.

By medieval times Buddhism and its institutions had pervaded Japa-nese society thoroughly and profoundly. The medieval Buddhist establish-ment encompassed both Buddhist temples and Shinto shrines. Shinto had become so thoroughly absorbed into Buddhism institutionally and to some extent even doctrinally, not to mention in the popular mind, that it is use-ful to think of the two collectively as the religious estate of the medieval period.[27] The medieval Buddhist establishment consisted of both elite and popular forms. The former included mostly temples and shrines dating from about the ninth century when the private control of land under the estate system began to spread. The Tendai school's Enryakuji on Mount Hiei, the Shingon temple Tōji, Gion Shrine near the heart of the commer-cial district, and the more recent Rinzai Zen monasteries (*gozan*) were the most representative of the Kyoto religious elite. The latter, a relative newcomer, lacked the vast landed and commercial wealth of the others.[28] The actual amount of land controlled by the religious establishment is hard to estimate, but it has been said that overlordship of more than 60 percent of the estate land in the country was held by religious institu-tions in the late twelfth century.[29] This figure had declined somewhat by the Muromachi period, but was still high in the Kyoto area.

In addition to their economic power, Enryakuji and Tōji represented the institutionally dominant, elite, orthodox Buddhism of the time. In addition there were the popular faith movements, often referred to as "Kamakura Buddhism." (Though they first appeared in the Kamakura period, they did not take root as dominant institutions until the latter half of the medieval period.) Zen enjoyed a large number of adherents among the warriors and commoners. The Time (Ji) and Lotus sects, while drawing members from all classes, were more representative of the townspeople's religious leanings toward faith and salvation teachings, and they stood outside the elite power structure. Whether elite or humble in character, religion and religious institutions pervaded the society, culture, values, everyday awareness, and worldview of the medieval Japanese.

Unlike the imperial court and the aristocrats who eventually cooperated with and became partially dependent on the Muromachi shogunate, the religious establishment held powers of moral suasion and coercion with which the warriors could not easily compete. As mentors of the rulers and spiritual protectors of the state, the major temples played an important political role that could not be dismissed by the shogun. In economic matters as well, the religious establishment asserted itself persistently throughout the medieval period. In the Kyoto area in particular, the large temples and shrines defended their interests so aggressively, often with armed force, that they could not be ignored. Still less could they be disciplined: a major attack by the shogun, the military defender of the state, on the religious establishment, the spiritual protector of the same state, would have been hard to justify.

Emblematic of the medieval rivalry between warriors and religion was the uneasy accommodation between the Muromachi shogunate and Enryakuji, the great monastery on Mount Hiei. The Enryakuji monks were particularly disturbed by the ascendancy of the Zen sect in tandem with its warrior patrons, and the rising influence of both at court. On the day of a memorial ceremony for Emperor Godaigo at the Zen temple Tenryūji in 1345, for example, the monks of Enryakuji descended into the city in a gesture of defiance, threatening to bring the portable shrine used for transporting the Shinto deity of the mountain in ritual processions. This was a favorite tactic of intimidation, for the presence of such a sacred figure in mundane space like city streets was enough to arouse awe and unease in the populace—a threat to civil order, in the view of the shogunate. On the one hand, the shogun responded with his own threat: to confiscate Enryakuji's holdings if the shrine was brought down the mountain. On the other hand, Emperor Kōgon refrained from attending the ceremony, thus reassuring Enryakuji that the court was not entirely in the pocket of the shogun.[30] The monks backed down. A few months later, another great ceremony was held at Tenryūji, with the shogun and his major vassals in attendance in an impressive show of the warrior presence in the city. This time the Enryakuji monks did bring the portable shrine into Kyoto. No sources indicate that the shogunate mobilized its forces in retaliation, and it is recorded that when the shrine passed in front of the warriors, they extinguished their bonfires, put down their arms, and did not attempt to resist the monks by force.[31]

Quite a different shogunal reaction was forthcoming in 1368 when, nominally in protest against the construction of the main gate of Nanzenji, another prominent Zen temple in Kyoto, the Enryakuji monks again carried the portable shrine into the city in a show of force. This time the shogunate met the challenge by dispatching its troops, including major vassals, to take up key positions in the city, including the point where the shrine would enter Kyoto and at Gion Shrine, a powerful subsidiary of Enryakuji.[32] Enryakuji's influence in Kyoto declined somewhat during the fourteenth century, but throughout the medieval period its monks caused periodic disruptions in the city that the warriors were hard put to quell. Enryakuji's control of commerce in Kyoto was equally tenacious, as described in this study. Only in the sixteenth century, when the warriors destroyed the multifaceted ruling order and asserted themselves as sole rulers, was the religious establishment attacked head-on. Oda Nobunaga's audacious destruction of Enryakuji in 1571 was the most symbolically momentous step in this process.[33]

In actual practice relations between religious institutions and the Muromachi shogunate varied greatly, because the "religious establishment" was not a monolith and because all elites rubbed shoulders to some extent. For example, the shogunate had close ties to the Zen *gozan* network of temples and even regulated its internal affairs, including particularly attempts to control the indecorous behavior of monks,[34] to an extent unprecedented in warrior rule. Warriors had close ties to other temples as well: the Shogun Yoshinori, for example, served as abbot of Enryakuji before becoming shogun. In general, however, the shogunate kept its distance from the religious establishment's internal affairs. The main exceptions were cases involving commerce, debts, or property that threatened order in the city, and these resulted in a great deal of shogunal interference, for a temple's internal affairs typically included a wide range of economic activities, as will be seen in Part 2.[35] For the most part, these activities continued after the founding of the Muromachi Bakufu, with the latter in the limited role of regulator.

The elites thus far described were only one part of medieval Kyoto society. Commoner townspeople made up about half the population of Kyoto and produced the goods and services that fueled the economy.[36] Although they never attained full governing powers like their counterparts in some late medieval European cities, at times and usually by default they exercised control over trade and important aspects of self-governance, including self-defense. Their significance in the city is clear from the large number of shogunal laws that pertain to commerce in Kyoto and from the fact that Bakufu law deigned to consider them beneficiaries.[37] In the fifteenth century they also came into their own as participants in a distinctive urban culture.

The lives of the commoners revolved around neighborhood and occupation. The latter was usually organized in guilds known as *za*, discussed in Part 2. Neighborhood life, from self-defense to sewage disposal, was ordered in a small, self-governing institution called the *machi* or *chō*.[38] Square blocks of land, these were the city's original basic administrative units; their inhabitants in the southern portion of the city were mostly merchants and craftsmen. When the situation demanded it, they communally took charge of local matters.

Although originally devised for the administrative convenience of the rulers, the *machi* developed over the centuries in accordance with the living patterns of its residents, the townspeople.[39] When Kyoto was founded, the entire city was divided, on paper, into these neat blocks, each about one hectare in area. Four *machi* comprised a ward (*ho*) and four wards a sector (*bō*) (Map 1). Officials were appointed to head both wards and sectors, which, with the *machi*, constituted the building blocks of urban administration. The breakdown of this neat division of land first occurred within the *machi* themselves. Many had been divided into four rows of eight oblong lots (thus the name *yongyō hachimon*—four rows, eight gates) each measuring fifteen by twenty meters with a narrow road for local access running north–south through the middle of the *machi* (Figure 1a). The reason for this subdivision was that state regulations prohibited anyone below fourth rank in the aristocracy from building a gate opening onto a major street.[40] Commoners' egress, therefore, had to be from the inside of a *machi*. This halved division of the *machi* gave it the nickname *nimen-machi*, or two-sided *machi*.

As might be expected, real use of land did not correspond to this neat division, and plots of irregular dimensions proliferated within *machi*. In some areas, especially the west and south, Kyoto simply lacked the population necessary to fill the original grid, and locals occupied and used the

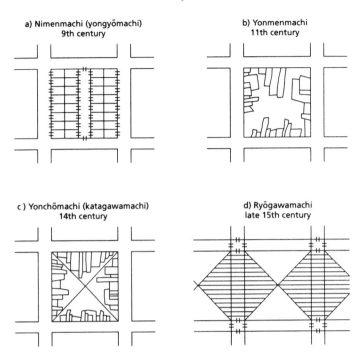

Figure 1: The Medieval Development of the *Machi*

land mainly for agriculture. Temples and aristocratic mansions could easily take up entire *machi*. In lower Kyoto especially, populated mostly by commoners, as early as the eleventh century many *machi* had lost their symmetrical appearance, with lots of varying sizes fronting on one of the four sides of the *machi*. Hence the *yonmenmachi*, or four-sided *machi* (Figure 1b), a much more utilitarian configuration, displaced the earlier two-sided *machi*. (Evasion of the frontage tax, *jiguchisen*, was one motive behind these irregularly sized lots: those with small entries were especially valuable because their taxes were low.) The area in the center of the *machi* became a backyard of sorts for the residents, space used communally for laundry, cooking, bathing, and toileting. (The communal toilet was a wooden fixture placed over a hole. Sixteenth-century Europeans commented favorably on the sanitary conditions in Japanese cities: waste was removed regularly, as a prescribed *machi* activity.)[41] Several wells could usually be found in the *machi* "backyard."

By the mid-fourteenth century, this configuration had become formalized into the diagonally subdivided *machi*, called *katagawamachi* (*machi* on one side of the street—Figure 1c). This pattern reflected the reality that a community is more naturally formed among those facing a common street than among those inhabiting the same block of land but facing in opposite directions. This diagonal subdivision was approximate: there were not necessarily any physical demarcations such as walls or fences in the interior of the *machi*. From about this point commoners developed a separate consciousness of themselves in these organized units of urban living. Concurrently, their identity shifted from the image conveyed by a term favored by some historians to characterize the early medieval townspeople, *"Kyōwarabe"* (originally referring to city residents under the public jurisdiction of the Capital Office), to *"machishū,"* residents of *machi* who were involved in commerce and were possessed of a strong communal sense of responsibility for matters of daily living, such as self-defense.[42] The trend was carried to its logical conclusion for defense purposes about the time of the Ōnin War, when gates erected at either end of the street were closed at night and during uprisings to afford the residents security. As a result, those facing each other along the street formed a natural community, and this late incarnation of the *machi* was referred to as *ryōgawa-machi* (literally, *machi* on both sides of the street, Figure 1d). This medieval evolution of the *machi* was not imposed from above, as had been the case when the city was laid out, but was a natural outgrowth of indigenous living arrangements.

The emergence of neighborhoods as social units at major intersections where commercial activity was concentrated could be seen as early as the late Heian period. The first such *machi* was located at the intersection of Machikōji (now Shinmachi-dōri), then the main north–south street, with the major east-west avenue, Shijō.[43] In other words, although one function of roads originally had been to divide city land into square blocks, as commerce flourished the roads themselves gradually became the core around which neighborhoods developed. Names of *machi* were designated at intersections in the fourteenth century.[44]

Trade organizations, the guilds described in Part 2, were not entirely independent of the neighborhood: *machi* with numerous residents who were members of one guild tended to be dominated by that guild. Thus *katagawamachi* sometimes evolved because members of the same trade group lived on the same side of the street; conversely, *ryōgawamachi* could develop if members lived opposite one another.[45] There was a tendency for shops selling the same product to be clustered in one area, proximity apparently being preferred by trade group members. Dish shops (from Heian times the people of Kyoto customarily ate on pottery), fish shops, cake shops, ink and brush shops, fan shops, lacquer shops, and others were clustered by type.[46] Thus the membership of *machi*, a residential social unit, often reflected trade or occupation. The combination shop-residence form of architecture was widespread in medieval *machi* inhabited by merchants.[47] Living quarters were located in the rear of the house, while the room in the front was used for display of goods or transaction of business. Many merchant houses had a large front window covered at night by a wooden shutter that could be folded down in the daytime as a shelf for the display of goods.[48]

In spite of growing commoner autonomy in the *machi* neighborhoods, medieval townspeople did not own the land they lived on. Rather, they paid rent to an aristocratic or clerical landlord.[49] In cities as in the countryside, control of land conformed to the custom of layered rights seen in the estate system. Each plot of land had an overlord, usually a temple or an aristocratic family, to whom the resident submitted a fixed sum of cash, typically on a semiannual basis. Called *yajishisen*, this was a sum calculated according to the amount of frontage and therefore alternatively called a frontage tax (*jiguchisen*). It applied to both residential and cultivated land in Kyoto. Another form of residential tax called *munabechisen*, an incidental but in fact frequently levied impost, was calculated according to the number of roofbeams in a building rather than the amount of land it occupied.[50] Over the course of the medieval period the relationship between overlord and resident gradually became contractual in nature, like that of landlord and tenant, as the townspeople gained autonomy. Nevertheless, because overlord holdings in Kyoto were scattered rather than concentrated, in disputes townspeople had to take on the overlord one-on-one, not as a neighborhood group. This tended to give the overlord, with his prestige and resources, a distinct advantage.[51] This was not the whole story, however: as the population of Kyoto grew, from about the twelfth century commoners also encroached onto public land, using the edges of the extremely broad thoroughfares of the ancient city rent-free, both for living space and for cultivation.[52] As a result of this land-use pattern and the declining power of the civil government to do anything about it, the broad, straight avenues of the ancient city gave way to the meandering, narrow streets of medieval times. In the late medieval period, moreover, townspeople constructed houses directly over canals, creating more tax-free living space and a more congested environment.[53] A portion of the city's residents, therefore, was beyond any overlord's ability to tax.

The lives of the townspeople, only dimly visible now, appear to have been lively and colorful. Their dress, in the case of the wealthy, could run to the garish, including gaudy folding fans, silk clothing, and swords with gold and silver ornamentation.[54] Their working garb was sober, however: they usually wore simple cotton kimono, often knee-length for ease of movement, with an apron and sometimes a loose jacket, and went barefoot or wore straw sandals.[55] Commoners of all types except the outcastes wore their hair pulled into a chignon on top of the head. Women at work often pulled their hair back into a ponytail at the nape of the neck. Wearing a hat was considered something any adult would do, except outcastes, whose heads were swathed in white cloth. Public baths were of either the steam or hot-water variety.[56] In the illustrated screens of Kyoto, men are portrayed as the main patrons of these establishments; most commonly people bathed by the bucket method in the *machi* backyard.

A wide variety of entertainment was available to the townspeople. Noh was patronized by them after the Ōnin War.[57] That gambling was a favorite pursuit is perhaps less surprising.[58] On a simpler level, people enjoyed pets: birds and insects kept in cages were especially common; dogs led on leashes by children can be found in illustrated screens as well.[59] (Animals shown with commoners are usually on a leash or perched on a shoulder; those with aristocrats and warriors are usually being hunted. Cockfighting and hawking were also elite pursuits.) Puppeteers and performing monkeys found an eager audience on the street. The monkey was a most familiar animal to the medieval Japanese: believed to be inhabited by a protective spirit, monkeys were often kept in front of stables to protect horses from disease.[60]

Religion, from formal temple adherence to popular practices, had a pervasive influence on the lives of all of Kyoto's residents. Although many of the moneylenders of this study had religious names and were affiliated through monastic and guild ties with Enryakuji and its subsidiary shrines (see Part 2), like other medieval people they were eclectic in religion, and in some cases belonged to more than one temple simultaneously. The Lotus Sect attracted townspeople in late medieval times; its appeal may have derived in part from its emphasis on the Buddhist doctrine of *genze riyaku*, benefit in this world. Yanagiya, Kyoto's largest *sake* brewer and a prominent moneylender, was a convert to this sect. One Komiyama Shungan, a silk merchant known as the richest person in late medieval Kyoto, belonged to both the Zen and Pure Land schools simultaneously.[61]

Street life was enlivened by religious observances. In the late medieval period, with the spread of popular Buddhist movements, a dance called the *nenbutsu odori* was added to the commoners' celebration of the Buddhist festival of the dead, observed in the summer. It was performed in a circle at major intersections, with flute and drums in the middle of a ring of dancers wearing black aprons, holding wooden clappers, and chanting the name of the Buddha. The dance took on an air of uncontrollable if subdued hysteria that the authorities found disturbing—the shogunate banned it once and aristocratic diaries mention it disapprovingly.[62] The dance fell by the wayside with the devastation of the city during the Ōnin War, but it was revived later, reaching its height of popularity in the mid-sixteenth century.

Popular devotions also abounded among the townspeople. The gods of fortune were especially revered, in the hope that they would bring material success.[63] Indeed, they were the very embodiment of the get-rich spirit of the times. In every house there was said to be a wooden statue or picture of Daikoku and Ebisu, who promised wealth and comfort in the here and now. At its extreme, this spirit of the times manifested itself in the worship of money.[64] In hard times, such as the years following the Ōnin War, hysteria based on popular religious beliefs could sweep the city. In 1483 a rumor spread that sixteen or seventeen good fortune gods in the guise of women from Sakai had entered Kyoto just as fifty to sixty gods of poverty in the form of men with nightingales and chickens on their heads departed Kyoto for Sakai. These "sightings" were widely hailed as an auspicious sign of recovery from the Ōnin War.[65] (What they signified for Sakai, though, was probably not so auspicious.) There was no end to outlandish stories about the gods of good fortune. In 1490 one disguised as a thief was said to have entered a rich man's house, so for a time everyone eagerly anticipated a visit by a thief. Also in 1490, an image of Daikoku on display at Tōji appeared with his usual bag but without his mallet and bale of rice. Worshippers thronged to view this as a great miracle. The allure of these gods to commoners is understandable: in an era dominated by religion, merchants would be most attracted to the deity who promised prosperity.

At the bottom of medieval society were the outcastes (*hinin*), many of whom were concentrated in Kyoto. The origins of this group are obscure: there was a class of "lowly persons" in the ancient legal code, but they are generally distinguished from the medieval outcastes.[66] The Japanese abhorrence, generally associated with Shinto, of the impurity connected with death intensified in the Heian period, when it was extended to animals as well as humans; this was roughly simultaneous with the emergence of a social class of outcastes with characteristic professions.[67] Beggars, lepers, the deformed, the crippled, criminals, the indigent, prisoners, traveling entertainers, some mendicant monks, riverbank dwellers, the sick in general (because of their proximity to death), and any others who were excluded from their communities and lacked binding ties may have drifted into the outcaste class.[68] Some, like mediums, diviners, yin-yang specialists, fortunetellers, street musicians, and exorcists, may have been held as much in awe as disdain for their perceived magical qualities.[69] Outcastes could also be found in occupations that took them into areas despised or abhorred by others: some, like leather workers and butchers, handled animals; others disposed of night soil; but many had a purifying function, namely, of cleansing defiled space.[70] In Kyoto, many outcastes worked in such a capacity for temples and shrines in guildlike arrangements, cleaning the precincts and handling dead bodies in funerals and cremation. Outcastes who remained outside of such social arrangements lived a solitary existence, supporting themselves by begging.

Because they tended to work primarily for large institutions like the court, temples, and shrines, whose taboos were especially strong and therefore needed their services most, outcastes were more numerous in Kyoto than anywhere. By the early eleventh century, the hillside below Kiyomizu-dera on the eastern side of the city was an outcaste neighborhood, conveniently located near both the overlord Kiyomizudera and one of the city's cremation sites, Toribeno.[71] Outcastes are ubiquitous in illustrated screens of Kyoto, their heads swathed in cloth. One of their main congregating places was the banks of the Kamo River near Shijō. (Riverbanks, because of their susceptibility to flooding, lay outside the city's tax structure and, besides being a safe haven for the indigent, were something of a medieval "stage": for entertainment and relaxation, for executions, for battles.) In 1070 the outcastes' access to the section of riverbank belonging to Gion Shrine was formalized by the emperor as a legal right in return for performing certain duties shunned by most people because of their defiling properties: handling the dead at funerals, participating as combatants in skirmishes between temples, cleaning the streets, keeping order during the Gion festival, and the like.[72] In other cases, outcastes involved in leather work and night soil collection may have been banished to riverbanks to prevent them from coming into contact with and thus defiling ordinary people.

The Bureau of Capital Police was a major employer of outcastes in Kyoto from the eleventh century until its functions were absorbed by the Muromachi shogunate in the fourteenth century. Not only were the outcastes important in keeping order in the city, but more fundamental to the nature of their debased status was their role in fulfilling the Bureau's mandate to control defilement in a society obsessed with purity. Commonly this purity fetish is understood in a ritual sense, but it extended to the mundane as well, including ridding the city of criminal elements and cleaning the streets. The outcastes, by virtue of their despised status, were uniquely suited to such tasks and hence were vital to the Bureau of Capital Police. Conversely, the Bureau has been characterized as "historically having the greatest influence on the formation and development of the medieval outcaste system."[73] The Muromachi shogunate, as part of its administration of Kyoto, absorbed the functions of the Bureau of Capital Police and placed "riverbank dwellers" (*kawaramono*)—outcastes, in most cases—under the jurisdiction of low-ranking officials (*kodoneri* and *zōshiki*) on its Board of Retainers.[74] This strongly suggests that outcastes performed similar functions for the shogunate as for other elite groups.

There were public baths in Kyoto used exclusively by outcastes, whose debased status is poignantly clear from the low value attached to the land upon which the baths stood. In a long-running land dispute between the temple Honnōji and the aristocratic Nishibōjō family, for example, a small strip of land on the corner of the parcel claimed by Honnōji was carefully exempted from the litigation in all relevant documents because it was used as a bath by outcastes.[75] The implication is that such land was not even worth considering.

Outcastes pursued a variety of occupations. Some were employed as the lowest-ranking members of temples and shrines (*inujinin* or *tsurumeso*), as guards, cleaners, and to bully tardy debtors and other enemies. In screens they are often depicted wearing persimmon-colored robes, but when on guard duty they were hard to distinguish from warriors: wearing armor, carrying swords, a quiver on their backs and arrows on their shoulders, they presented a fierce appearance.[76] Though despised, they were not uniformly poor, and some were in lucrative professions. Others were gardeners, entertainers, performers, and teachers of art forms like the tea ceremony, dancing, *koto*, *shakuhachi*, and recitation.

Many outcastes in medieval Kyoto were attracted to the Time (Ji) movement of the Pure Land school of Buddhism, some temples of which were located near the Kamo riverbank. By taking the "-ami" suffix designating priesthood in this sect, they were able at least nominally to escape their class and enter the priestly ranks. Some members of the sect, which enjoyed shogunal protection, were involved in cultural activities. The Zen'ami family of garden designers, for example, traced their origins to a butcher who had become a Ji sect priest.[77]

Such were the people of medieval Kyoto. It is logical to wonder about the size of this population. Reliable figures are hard to come by, and great fluctuations occurred over the centuries due to famine, fire, and warfare on the one hand, and peace and prosperity on the other.[78] In the Heian period Kyoto may have contained 90,000 to 150,000 people.[79] The population of the city dropped with the unrest and natural disasters of the twelfth century but was on the upswing by the fourteenth century, when it may have numbered 100,000 people.[80] This figure is reached by unsatisfying methods, however: dividing the citizenry into classes and coming up with an approximate figure for each. The aristocracy, including the imperial family, members of the civil nobility, and their servants, may have numbered 10,000. The warrior population, that is, the entire Muromachi Bakufu including the shogun, shogunal troops (2 or 3 thousand), shogunal officials, over 20 military governors (shugo) and their entourages (200 to 300 troops each) who maintained residences in Kyoto in the early part of the Muromachi period, plus the relatives and servants of all of these, is put at 30 or even 40 thousand. Temple and shrine records suggest that the membership of the religious establishment exceeded 10,000 by the fourteenth century. The total of these elite groups was about 50,000, but this figure may be high: the calculation of the number of warriors seems especially inflated and likely decreased as the Muromachi shogun's real power declined. (During the Ōnin War, many military governors and their entourages left Kyoto and returned permanently to their provincial bases.) The number of townspeople, about 50,000, is based on particularly gross calculations: in the absence of detailed population records, it is simply estimated that there were about 10,000 households of common people, with each containing an average of 5 persons. Hence the figure of 100,000 commonly given for Kyoto's population in the fourteenth century. Most likely it is an overestimation; even so, ancient and medieval Kyoto, if not large cities by modern standards, were quite sizable by world standards of the times. Given the heavily rural distribution of premodern societies, Kyoto was also a large city in proportion to Japan's total ancient and medieval population—perhaps ten million in the late Heian period and eleven million in the fourteenth century.[81] The great destruction of the Ōnin War caused Kyoto's population to drop drastically for a time.[82] Thereafter the city actually became more densely populated than before the war, however, squeezed into a bipolar configuration, with upper and lower Kyoto constituting two separate communities.

Like war, famine struck frequently, with drastic effects on population. In cities like Kyoto, one season of bad weather could mean famine in a matter of months, for the food supply was not sufficient to tide over large numbers of people. Nine very large famines occurred in the medieval period, four of them in the fifteenth century.[83] There was a strong chance, in other words, that at least one major famine would occur in the lifetime of any inhabitant of medieval Kyoto. Most are attributable to weather, their effects in some cases aggravated by war.[84] Record keeping did not extend to systematic corpse counting during famines, but some anecdotal evidence suggests how high the toll could be. For example, during a major famine in 1460, a priest in northern Kyoto was reputed to have had 84,000 miniature stupas made, which he placed on corpses as a pious Buddhist act. Depending on the version of the story, when he finished his mission of mercy he was said to have exhausted his supply of stupas. During the same famine, a priest from Kiyomizudera reportedly officiated at a mass funeral for 2,000 victims at the Gojōzaka Bridge.[85] Although the record is inexact, famine and other natural and human disasters countered medieval advances in agricultural productivity, and the population waxed and waned accordingly.

Part Two

The Lives of the Moneylenders

Chapter One

The Business of Lending Money

Moneylenders of unknown number do a flourishing business; the
wealth of the country is all in their storehouses.
—Fujiwara Teika, *Meigetsuki*

THE POET'S DIARY notation of the early thirteenth century suggests there
was already a large community of moneylenders in Kyoto. A burgeoning
demand for credit was met by these merchants, primarily through the
medium of coinage imported from China. Some started as storehouse
keepers (*mikura*) for aristocratic families and gradually extended their
activities to include moneylending.[1] Others began as creditors like pawnbrokers offering small loans and in time added the safekeeping of valuables to their services. As pawnbrokers, these small-scale moneylenders
were regarded as reliable not only because of their sturdy storehouses
but because in the event that items were stolen they would compensate
the owner.[2] Even during a large peasant invasion of the city in 1441, for
example, the aristocrat Fujiwara Tokifusa, who lived in Kyoto's outskirts,
recorded bringing his valuables to a moneylender in the city for storage,
fearing that the shogun's forces would be unable to protect him.[3] The
more successful of this type of moneylender offered another convenient
service: handling not only storage but receipt and disbursement of an
overlord's tax income, some of it in kind. Moreover, accustomed as they
were to dealing in cash, in hard times these lenders would grant loans exceeding the debtor's worth, and in good times would pay interest on cash
entrusted to them, like a bank. The most prominent among them were
employed by the imperial court and aristocratic families not only as

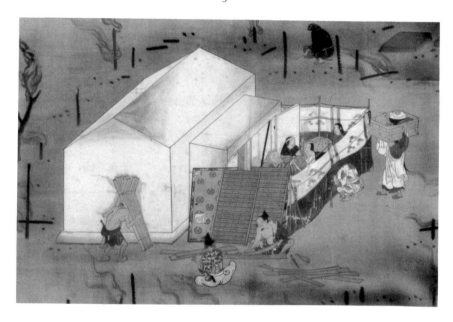

A medieval storehouse. After a fire destroyed their main house, a fourteenth-century Kyoto family takes shelter temporarily in their sturdy storehouse, like those used by moneylenders. Detail from *Kasuga gongen genki,* collection of Tokyo National Museum. Reproduced with the permission of the Tokyo National Museum.

creditors but as managers of property. Moneylenders themselves sometimes borrowed capital on which they paid interest and in turn loaned out to others, presumably at higher rates of interest.[4] To satisfy customers with a large appetite for credit, medieval lenders, most of them only family operations, had to have a large and steady source of capital, and sometimes brewing alone may not have sufficed. The source of loans to moneylenders was likely to be Zen temples or other wealthy townspeople.[5]

Moneylenders begin to appear in documents from 1234 as "*dosō*," after their sturdy fireproof earthen storehouses erected to safeguard pawned items.[6] (That such a practice was not seen in the Heian period may have been partly a function of architectural limitations: Heian storehouses were simple structures made of wooden boards that any family might have. The word "*dosō*" appears for the first time in the Kamakura period, indicating a sturdy building with earthen walls.) The storehouse usually had a porch-like entrance with a thick outer door and an inner wooden lattice door, making penetration by fire or thief difficult.[7] The moneylenders' activities gradually expanded to include the functions of primitive banks, and they became a common fixture of everyday life in medieval Kyoto. In addition to lending money, they stored and protected cash and valuables in return for a deposit fee. They also managed their patrons' landed income, performing such services as tax farming and transporting goods from distant estates.[8] Some of them managed shogunal finances.[9] The greatest moneylenders even helped finance the fourteenth- and fifteenth-century trade missions to Ming China, providing capital for ships and goods for export.[10] "Pawnbroker" or "moneylender" may be too modest a term for an occupation that embraced so many functions. "Financier" or "financial house" is perhaps a more suitable word for the larger *dosō*. Nevertheless, it was through their moneylending activities that lenders large and small had the most impact on medieval society in general, both as providers of capital and as subjects of taxation.

The main source of capital for moneylenders often came from another line of business. Zen monasteries had institutional wealth to draw on, but individual lenders used the proceeds from the production and sale of a commodity—*sake*, primarily. The popularity and, presumably, lucrative nature of their product is attested to by their large number, about 350 in the early fifteenth century. In good times and bad one can assume that *sake* consumption remained constant and the brewers enjoyed a steady, high income. Purveyors of bean paste, although fewer in number, were also moneylenders. The moneylenders of this study, however, were so intimately connected with *sake* brewing that sources commonly refer to them as brewer-lenders (*sakaya-dosō*).[11]

From the thirteenth century the brewer-lenders were affiliated with the monastery Enryakuji, medieval Kyoto's most powerful religious institution, either directly or through one of its subsidiary shrines. Typically they were low-ranking monks of Enryakuji and townspeople, complete with clerical names. Although they became increasingly secularized as the medieval period wore on and as new lenders joined their number, their dual status as merchant-priests remained significant: it enhanced their prestige as townspeople and gave them an edge over other commoners in the eyes of elites like the shogun. In return, they had to pay taxes to Enryakuji.

Lending currency at high rates of interest in return for land or valuables (art works, clothing, armor, tea ceremony utensils, etc.) as collateral, moneylenders found customers among not only peasants and townspeople but aristocrats and warriors as well. Larger moneylenders did a great volume of business: for example, in 1420 the storehouse of the lender Hōsen burned, destroying its contents, including three hundred kimono stored there as collateral on debts.[12] As a result the lenders were conspicuously wealthy by the fifteenth century, the quintessential rich commoners of the time.[13] Much of their wealth was in the form of land acquired through usurious practices. Peasants who found themselves in financial straits commonly put up land or their rights to land as collateral.[14] If the debt was not paid off in a given period of time, the lender could confiscate the land, and the peasant would become his tenant, paying him yearly dues. Peasant resentment against the moneylenders exploded repeatedly in the fifteenth century in the form of uprisings focused mainly on Kyoto.

The most complete available list of the brewer-lenders is dated 1425–1426.[15] It reveals that the overwhelming majority enjoyed clerical status at that time. Of 347 names, 256 (70 percent of the total) are clerical, most with a seal attached, while 61 (18 percent) are lay. Among the clerical lenders ten to twenty were highly successful throughout most of the period, and their names recur in sources over the centuries as their businesses flourished and they forged important political connections. Of the lay lenders on the list, most are youth names, suggesting young men at a preclerical stage, while a few, like "Sparrow" (*suzume*) and "Snake" (*hebi*), may be whimsical trade names. Eight others are province names, perhaps indicating the origins of the lender; one, Rai, may have been Chinese, and another, Goun, a Korean, or perhaps they were Japanese with exotic trade names. Three names are of women; two, Shōani and Hōshōni, are nun's names, suggesting widowhood. Most likely they were either childless or their children were still too young to take over the business. The third woman, Memeko, may be an example of an independent woman entrepreneur, unusual in documents if not necessarily in reality. Ten names are like those found among adherents of the Time (Ji) sect; these individuals could have had such sectarian inclinations and still have been connected to Enryakuji, for plural sectarian affiliation was not unusual in the medieval period. Or they could have been lay adherents of this popular form of Pure Land Buddhism. At any rate, the many clerical names suggest that the majority of these moneylenders had an Enryakuji affiliation, and most of the rest possibly assumed priestly status as they grew older. This changed over time: after the Ōnin War there was a decline in the number of moneylenders with an obvious Enryakuji affiliation. The 1425 list, then, describes a diverse group, but their most striking difference was economic: from 5 to 10 percent of the group, the clerical names that endure over time, were highly successful, wealthy merchants. The others had more modest operations and in hard times attrition was high. Thus, although in matters of taxation and other collective activities it is appropriate to speak of them as a unit, in local prestige and in cultural pursuits there were drastic differences among them.

Sake brewing, the source of capital for much medieval moneylending, was perfected during the medieval period. Techniques for making *sake* from rice, malt, and water existed in Japan from at least the fifth century, but prior to about the eleventh century commercial breweries were rare.[16] Presumably this was because *sake* brewing, or more correctly fermentation, was a simple operation that could be done in the home.[17] During the late Heian and early Kamakura periods, however, with the spread of a market economy and the adoption of more sophisticated techniques of fermentation, *sake* began to be produced as a commodity, especially in the cities of Kyoto, Nara, and Kamakura.[18] Kyoto's early prominence in the *sake* industry can be attributed in part to the large amounts of rice coming into the city as estate taxes.[19] Many merchants dabbled in small-scale brewing as a sideline.[20] Brewing on a large scale, however, was an expensive operation requiring a large initial investment; moneylenders who needed an outlet for their accumulated wealth could establish breweries and thereby become even wealthier. Conversely, successful brewers had reserves of cash to lend. Regardless of the initial causal relationship, by the fourteenth century *sake* was one of the main products of Kyoto and brewer-lenders were well established institutions constituting the bulk of the city's individual moneylenders.

With so many competitors, the successful brewer needed not only a good head for business but a distinguished brew as well. *Sake* was produced once a year, during the cooler autumn and winter months, for the fermentation process took place at low temperatures. The *sake* made in medieval Kyoto was cloudy, called *nigorizake*. Kyoto area casks usually had a capacity of 2 or 3 *koku* (one *koku* = 180 liters). Small brewers produced about 40 *koku* per year, large ones about 200 *koku*. Most breweries were small family operations, but the giant brewer Yanagi had 600 casks and boasted the best *sake* in Kyoto–at least, he charged twice the going rate for it. Yanagi, which means willow, took his name from the material used to make his casks, storage in which reputedly produced a *sake* of high quality.

By the early fifteenth century there were about 350 such moneylender-brewers in Kyoto, most of them concentrated in the commercial heart of the city between Sanjō in the north and Gojō in the south, Muromachi in the east and Higashi no Tōin in the west (see Map 3).[21] A few were sprinkled throughout the aristocratic northeastern sector of Kyoto and in outlying areas like Saga. Some were clustered around Kitano Shrine in northwest Kyoto, and Gion Shrine's moneylenders could be found east of the Kamo River near the shrine. (Kitano and Gion Shrines were subsidiary institutions of Enryakuji, as explained below.) Proximity to the over-

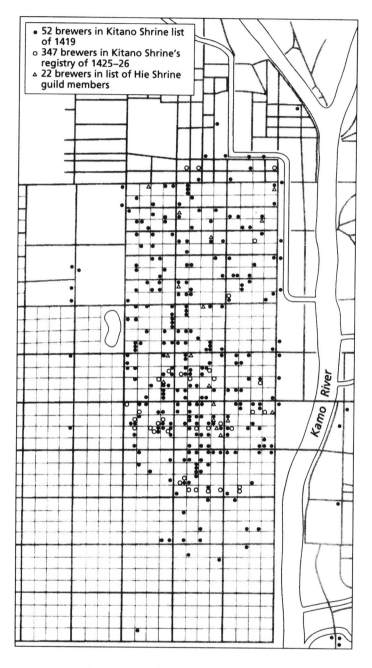

Map 3: Brewer-lenders in Medieval Kyoto (derived from Noda, "Chūsei Kyōto," pp. 43–44)

Sake peddler. Detail from *Haseo kyō sōshi,* collection of
Eisei Bunko Museum. Reproduced with the permission of
the Eisei Bunko Foundation, Tokyo.

lord may have determined location for some; access to a plentiful source
of water was also helpful for *sake* production.

Not until late medieval times was the retailing of *sake* physically separated from the production site. Early methods of transport and packaging
were unsuited to moving large amounts of liquid, so most brewers simply
sold their *sake* on site. Thus each region developed its own distinctive *sake.*
Small amounts were sold in the vicinity of the brewery by peddlers carrying two wooden buckets attached by a rod on the shoulder. A scoop was
used to ladle out the liquid.[22] In the thirteenth century, production of the
malt-like fermenting agent (*kōji*), which, after rice and water, was the
main ingredient in *sake*, was monopolized in Kyoto by the brewers affiliated with Kitano Shrine and sold to other city brewers. After the Ōnin
War, as the production and retail aspects of the business began to take
place at separate sites, small *sake* shops could be found in Kyoto separate
from breweries.[23]

Moneylending and *sake* brewing were family operations on a modest
scale for the most part, and sources suggest indirectly that women may
have participated in the brewing end of the enterprise. Although female
participation in brewing became taboo from about the mid-Edo period, it

Women *sake* brewer. Detail from *Shichijū ichiban
shokunin zukushi utaawase,* collection of Tokyo
National Museum. Reproduced with the permission
of the Tokyo National Museum.

has become a commonplace among Japanese historians to say that *sake*-brewing was women's work in medieval and ancient times.[24] This probably derives from the fact that before the Heian period Shinto female shrine attendants made *sake* for ritual use as part of their duties.[25] It is far from clear, however, that *sake* for general consumption was produced specifically by women in ancient times. There is a good deal of evidence, on the other hand, that women participated in the medieval enterprise of *sake* brewing in various capacities. There is a female character in the *Nihon ryōiki* who makes a good income producing *sake*; in the Kyōgen play *Hakubogazake,* a woman both makes and sells *sake*.[26] The existence of women *sake* brewers may also be construed from the 1510 Muromachi Bakufu threat to punish both male and female *sake* brewers who violated currency regulations.[27] Tax documents indicate that the delivery of taxes from brewers to the imperial court's Distillery Office in the 1510s was a woman's job.[28]

Art-historical sources also suggest that women participated in the *sake* business. One scroll depicts a woman *sake* peddler.[29] Another, depicting aristocrats competing in a poetry contest dressed, for fun, as people from various mundane occupations, features a woman as a maker of malt and another as a peddler of *sake*, carrying a bucket along with a ceramic container.[30] (The latter may also indicate that there were many very small *sake* establishments in the city barely able to eke out a living, whose addresses do not even appear on lists of brewers.)[31] In this handscroll the general prevalence of women in the retail stage of various businesses, including sellers of kimono sashes, fish, and rice in addition to *sake*, is also striking, suggesting a gender division of labor along production and retail lines.[32] *Sake* production required some lifting of heavy containers and thus may have been more difficult for women.

Given the frequently opaque nature of medieval sources regarding commoners and women, these constitute persuasive evidence that women and men may have both made and sold *sake* and malt.[33] The general absence of women's names from brewer rosters is not itself an indication of either women's involvement or lack of it. As in the records of craftsmen like potters and of peasant landholders, by the Muromachi period a woman's name was recorded only in cases in which there was no male head of household.[34]

There is some evidence that women played an important role in moneylending as well. Excluded by the ancient civil law code from most aspects of public life, including even from rosters of land and business holdings, women may have thereby been as much freed to pursue mercantile activities as restricted from other activities. Women sometimes served as storehouse keepers for aristocratic and warrior families, and this occupation may have paved the way for medieval careers in moneylending.[35] The disease scroll (*Yamai no sōshi*, late twelfth to early thirteenth centuries) depicts a woman moneylender who suffers from obesity, considered a disease of the rich.[36] Women lenders pursued debtors through lawsuits to the Muromachi shogunate.[37] The 1425 list of brewer-lenders discussed earlier includes the names of three women. And in the sixteenth century the missionary Luis Frois commented with surprise on Japanese women's literacy, their right to hold property, and even on instances of women lending money to their own husbands.[38] Taken together, these cases suggest that women did participate in medieval moneylending.

The moneylenders were most appreciated by the elites, however, not for the quality of their *sake* or their skills in managing finances, but for their ability to generate taxable wealth. A malt tax was exacted by Kitano

Woman moneylender suffering from obesity, a "disease" of
the rich. Detail from *Yamai no sōshi*, collection of the Fukuoka
Municipal Art Museum. Reproduced with the permission
of the Fukuoka Municipal Art Museum. Photography by
Fujimoto Kenhachi.

Shrine from its moneylenders, while others generally paid a product tax
based on the number of casks in their breweries.[39] Separate taxes were
levied on usury, calculated according to the number of items held as collateral by a moneylender at a given time.[40] The credit function of the brewer-
lenders made them widely indispensable to the medieval economy. Their
prosperity made them prime targets of taxation by various overlords.

Moneylending Practices

Moneylending was the central activity of the brewer-lenders and an indispensable part of the monetized economy of the Kyoto area in the medieval period. Details of the process—moneylending in practice—are somewhat obscure because records of individual enterprises do not survive.
These were not kept by the overlord but by the enterprise itself, which

besides being susceptible to fire, bankruptcy, looting, and other destructive forces, notably lacked any motive to preserve its documents beyond a few years. Indeed, to close out a loan receipts were routinely destroyed. Only from the Edo period did documents at a nonelite level of society begin to have a reasonable chance of survival.[41] Thus the way to detect the particulars of moneylending is to infer from other sources. Especially helpful are shogunal regulatory edicts, many of which concern the moneylenders and their activities. Starting with the assumption that such decrees were primarily ad hoc and reactive—that is, a response to abuses and excesses that led to repeated invasions of the city by peasant leagues—rather than long-term policy aimed at shaping events positively, one can then extrapolate from the content of the regulations the minimal reality of moneylending in practice. For example, if a law forbids a particular activity, then one can assume that that activity in fact occurred, perhaps on a large scale and almost certainly on a regular basis. If it had not, there would have been no necessity for a law. (One cannot necessarily assume that the activity ceased as a result of the Bakufu edict. Enforcement is a separate issue altogether, and less frequently addressed in sources.) Similarly, if a law outlines minimally acceptable activities, such as rates of interest, then one can assume that it was common to exceed those limits, though by how much one cannot say. Thus an analysis of Muromachi Bakufu regulation of the moneylenders can reveal at least the general contours of moneylending practices.

A person seeking a loan brought to the moneylender an item of property or, especially in the case of peasants, documentary evidence of rights to land. The lender then determined the duration of the loan period and the rate of interest according to the type of item proffered. Next the lender took the item (or documentation, in the case of land) as collateral, placed it for safekeeping in his storehouse, and presented the debtor with the cash loan and a receipt (*azukarijō*) on which was written the terms of the loan. The same information was entered in the lender's ledger.[42] For at least some loans, a formal contract (*shakusho*) was written.[43] The money was carried away in the form of strings of copper coins (in the *mon* denomination, one hundred per string; ten strings equaled one *kan*); large loans might be denominated in a mix of currencies, silver and copper.

A shogunal decree of 1431, the first attempt to regulate moneylending practices, reveals the basic components of a loan arrangement—the types of articles offered as collateral, the duration of a loan, and interest rates.[44] Silk goods could be held for up to twelve months and arms and armor up to twenty-four. After that the moneylender could claim the article if it had not been redeemed (e.g., if the interest had not been paid). It would appear, therefore, that in 1431 warriors and aristocrats were seeking loans, and that their collateral was being confiscated in a matter of months when interest was not paid. Commoners may well have been experiencing the same problem—the invasion of the city in 1428 by peasants demanding debt amnesties strongly suggests it—but this shogunal law does not appear to address their interests.

In Bakufu decrees of 1459, the list of regulated collateral items was enlarged and refined to include many more items and rates of interest, as follows:[45]

> 12 months at 5% monthly interest (plus the month in which the loan was granted): silk, brocades, books, musical instruments, furniture, miscellaneous
>
> 20 months at 6% monthly interest: trays, tea ceremony utensils, vases, incense burners, metal objects
>
> 24 months at 6% monthly interest: weapons
>
> 7 months at 6% monthly interest: rice and other grains

In 1520 the list was expanded even further to include many other items:[46]

> Same terms as miscellaneous: horse-riding gear, screens, sliding doors, including lumber, acupuncture needles, lily bulbs, lacquerware, rugs, straw mats, animal skins, cattle carts (cattle were accepted as collateral for non-interest-bearing loans), apothecary mortars, Buddhist ritual objects, inkstones, writing tables, medicines, mirrors, nail files, spades, hoes
>
> Same terms as flower vases: bells, iron vessels, bronze tea containers (for use in tea ceremony)
>
> Same terms as rice and other grains: foodstuffs, vegetables, fish
>
> Same terms as silk: gold brocade, satin damask, Chinese textiles
>
> Same terms as musical instruments: masks used in *sarugaku*, banners, Buddhist altar decorations, bunting, altar cloths, gold brocade curtains
>
> Same terms as armor: various types of swords, spears, hilt ornaments, metal rods attached to sword sheaths, cords attached to sword sheaths and handles, leatherwear
>
> Same terms as tea implements: bowls, dishes
>
> Same terms as metal objects: temple bells/gongs

Same terms as furniture: *sake* bottles and servers, decanters, pots, metal hoops, cleavers, knives

Men or women pawned into servitude: The recent debt amnesty does not apply to them.

These terms were reiterated by shogunal decree in 1530 and 1546.[47]

These lists are useful for what they suggest about actual moneylending practices. One starts with the assumption that the items found on the Bakufu lists reflect common practice—that such articles were normally used as collateral for loans—and that it is the periods of entrustment and the interest rates which were modified by the shogunate to coax moneylending practices into a range more acceptable to debtors. It is clear from the articles listed that at least by 1459 a wide range of people in the society were seeking loans. Clerics offered as collateral ritual objects, banners, trays, bunting, altar cloths, gold brocade curtains, bells and gongs. Warriors hauled in weapons of all sorts and attached ornamentation, armor, horse-riding gear, tea ceremony utensils, and anything else lying around the house from vases to nail files. Aristocrats were bringing in silks and brocades, trays, musical instruments, books, furniture, tea ceremony utensils, inkstones and brushes, lacquerware, and all manner of household goods. Wealthier commoners had tea ceremony utensils, screens, musical instruments, calligraphy implements, and maybe a vase or a rug to pawn for a loan. But almost anyone could come up with straw mats, animal skins, nail files, spades, hoes, iron vessels, fish, vegetables and other foodstuffs, dishes, pots, cleavers, and knives. Merchants and craftsmen put the tools of their trade in hock: apothecary mortars, medicines, writing implements (used by calligraphy teachers and professional scribes), acupuncturists' needles, lumber, lily bulbs, cattle carts and cattle, and actors' theatrical masks.

It would appear from the wide range of items on these lists, then, that people of all classes borrowed money by custom, by necessity, or by a combination of both. Living on credit, even on harsh terms, was a way of life in late medieval Kyoto. (It would also appear that moneylenders needed capacious storehouses!) Warriors did not receive special treatment: in contrast to the Kamakura Bakufu, the Muromachi shogunate did not specifically protect warriors who fell into debt, perhaps because it had become so commonplace to seek a loan in the monetized economy.[48] Still less were aristocrats and even members of the imperial family shielded from the necessity to borrow money. Imperial Prince Fushimi Sadafusa, for example, in 1437 was asked by the court to return a sword entrusted to him three years before by the emperor. Embarrassingly, he had pawned it and was unable to come up with the cash necessary to redeem it. The prince, rather than threatening or cajoling the moneylender, persuaded the imperial court, which insisted that the sword was needed immediately, to advance him the necessary cash (5,000 *hiki* or 50 *kanmon*, a very large amount) to redeem the sword.[49] Similarly, in 1454 Nakahara Yasutomi, a mid-ranking aristocrat, needed a ceremonial garment for a ninth month observance at court. He had pawned it earlier to a moneylender, and unlike Sadafusa he had the cash to get it back but—alas!—the moneylender had closed shop for the time being as a result of recent peasant invasions of the city, and Yasutomi was unable to get his robe back.[50]

The rationale behind assigning certain items specific interest rates and loan periods may have included factors like perishability (i.e., grain could only be entrusted for seven months), durability (clothing would wear out before metal objects), and long-term value (weapons, to warriors). In the 1520 list, food including fish is placed in the grain category, though it is hard to imagine even dried fish being worth much after seven months! (Most likely the creditor consumed such items immediately, replacing them with fresh ones when redeemed by the debtor.)

It is a sobering fact that debtors had only a matter of months, not years, before forfeiting their collateral if they neglected their interest payments. Equally harsh were interest rates, routinely exceeding 60 or 70 percent annually, sometimes by a large margin.[51] Indeed, a certain arbitrariness characterizes much of medieval moneylending, suggesting that high demand gave lenders the upper hand. Most sobering of all is the mention of men and women pawned into servitude. Not only is this proof that human beings were used as collateral for loans, but that it was not illegal to do so. In this decree, the shogunate merely declared that debt amnesties did not apply to this form of collateral. Presumably, therefore, such people became the moneylenders' property when the period of entrustment was up. They may have become servants or continued as cultivators of fields taken over by moneylenders. No mention is made of the status of such people, and one wonders if they were outcastes, hereditary servants (*genin*), or children. Nowhere is the period of entrustment or the interest rate specified for human collateral. Perhaps they were like oxen—so useful that they were accepted as collateral for interest-free loans.

An entirely different but very large category of moneylending was done in exchange for rights to land, especially agricultural land, as collateral. In this case, peasants, not city people, were usually the debtors, and creditors were commonly village moneylenders—wealthy peasants and local estate managers. But the Kyoto moneylenders also did business with peasants, and thus were the main targets of peasant fury in the fifteenth-century invasions of Kyoto. Such loans were characterized by longer duration than those granted in return for goods: a twenty-year statute of limitations was in place in the Muromachi period, as will be seen below, though enforcement of it was probably not rigorous.

In response to peasant demands, the Muromachi shogunate issued debt amnesties delineating applicability according to the nature of the loan. These decrees provide a convenient summary of widespread methods of lending money to peasants, although they do not specify interest rates. Peasants usually put up cultivator rights to land as collateral for a loan.[52] (Such collateral land was called *shichikenchi* or *shichiken shoryō*.) According to some shogunal decrees, if the debtor did not repay the principal, the loan would be considered paid off and the land returned when he paid the creditor interest in the form of harvests (*honmotsugaeshi*) or cash (*honsengaeshi*) equal to twice the principal.[53] In this decree, the shogunate put the brakes on moneylenders' excesses; it would seem that creditors commonly required debtors to continue paying interest beyond twice the amount of the loan. The 1440 decree was apparently not effective in limiting the excesses of the lenders, for a huge peasant invasion of Kyoto took place in the following year.

Other types of agricultural loans were devised to escape nullification should a debt amnesty occur. The creditor, needless to say, insisted on imposing such terms, but as the shogunate began to issue conditional debt amnesties (*buichi tokuseirei*, discussed further in the context of *ikki*, below) in the latter half of the fifteenth century, even debtors colluded with moneylenders to avoid the necessity of paying the shogunate this "amnesty tax." One type of disguised loan was called *urikishinchi*, in which the transaction was written up in two ways: as a sale of land and as a donation at half price.[54] Thus on paper it did not appear to be a moneylending transaction, but this "bargain sale" was in fact a loan totaling half the "price" of the land. Another common category was *nenki kokyakuchi* or *nenkiuri*, land "sold" for a predetermined period, usually ten years, after which it would revert to its owner.[55] This too was a type of loan, with the land serving as collateral and its yield (harvests) as interest payments.[56]

A final category of land-based transaction involving moneylenders was land sold in perpetuity (*eitaibaitokuchi*, *eitaibaibaichi*, or *eiryōchi*). In return for land, the seller, usually a peasant, received cash from a buyer, usually a moneylender, who might be a wealthy villager or a resident of

Kyoto. Often but not always the seller remained on the land to cultivate it, as a tenant. This was a primary form of land accumulation by medieval moneylenders, and generally debt amnesties did not apply to this type of transaction.[57]

In reviewing these categories of agricultural loans one is struck by the high degree of risk compared to loans backed by goods, however expensive. Land was, after all, the peasants' source of livelihood, precious in its renewability. Once it was confiscated by a creditor, however, peasants either lost access to it or, more commonly, became tax-paying tenants on what had been their own land. That the shogunate attempted to impose a twenty-year term on such loans indicates perhaps how difficult they were to pay off: peasants were dependent on the harvest, and by definition peasants seeking loans had little surplus to cushion their existence. If bad weather and crop failures could bring on famine quickly, they could also make default on loans inevitable. From this perspective, then, it is hardly surprising that peasant frustration periodically erupted into violence.

A less quantifiable aspect of indebtedness was the moneylender's attitude toward the debtor. It was harsh and relentless: creditors seeking repayment of principal would go after tardy debtors for decades, and even dun the descendants of deceased debtors.[58] An anecdote from a collection of stories illustrates well the cavalier unfairness of moneylenders.[59] A carpenter went to a moneylender to redeem his tools. When the lender got them out of the storehouse, the carpenter noticed that one, or perhaps its wooden handle, had been eaten away by a rat. He demanded to be charged less interest. The lender went to the storehouse, killed the rat, brought it back, and flung it down before the debtor, saying: "Here's the culprit who was in the storehouse gnawing on your tool. Have it out with him, if you like." The incensed debtor took his case to the shogunate, and the official in charge, renowned for his ethical character, ruled against the lender and ordered his house and possessions confiscated and handed over to the debtor. The story's main purpose is to honor the memory of the official, Taga Takatada, a late-fifteenth-century member of the shogunate, but the depiction of the moneylender makes it clear that they were regarded as ruthless and without scruples.

The shogunate periodically attempted to curb the moneylenders' excesses but at other times supported them. This inconsistency kept debtors uncertain about recourse. In 1425, the shogunate forbade moneylenders to hire agents, perhaps outcastes, to collect debts for them and enjoined them to use shogunal channels instead.[60] In 1430, however, the Bakufu sought to protect moneylenders by setting strict limits on debt payment schedules because moneylenders were concerned about absconders. Regarding the debts on which no interest had been paid, at the ten-year point twice the principal must be paid; if more than ten years, three times the principal.[61] Similarly, three years later the Bakufu stipulated that debts could be pursued for up to twenty years, though at the ten-year point twice the principal and after ten years four times the principal was to be repaid.[62] (This is not, strictly speaking, a statute of limitations, for the decree merely says that it does not apply to debts outstanding for more than twenty years.) In 1436 the shogunate favored the debtor by decreeing that the number of times a creditor could dun a debtor was limited to three in 150 days, after which the matter was to be handed over to the shogunal Board of Administration, thus taking it out of the hands of the moneylenders.[63] In principle at least, this established a procedure for the pursuit of bad debts, protecting the debtor from coercion by the creditor. On the other hand, in the same decree of 1436, the shogunate refers to the lending of money itself as a "service [done] out of kindness," a turn of phrase that emphasizes the responsibility of the debtor.[64] Somewhat later, in 1466, the shogunate was clearly watching out for the debtor: it tried to limit dunning by decreeing that when twice the principal had been paid in the form of interest, the debtor was entirely off the hook and the debt became null and void.[65] A balance had to be struck between the extremes of allowing defaults to the extent of denying moneylenders a profit and a debt payment schedule so harsh that its fulfillment was beyond the capacity of most debtors. Shogunal policy moved between these two poles, depending on factors like peasant invasions of the city and the level of tax revenues from moneylenders. Left to their own devices without Bakufu intervention, the moneylenders, of course, would have imposed the harshest loan terms.

For the debtor, risk was not limited to the ability to pay. Moneylenders sometimes absconded with collateral, claiming theft or loss. Although it is hard to imagine this as a widespread practice, as it would destroy a lender's reputation for safety and reliability, there were many lenders and many people seeking credit in medieval Kyoto; shogunal decrees inveighing against the practice, furthermore, suggest that it was a common occurrence. In this area the shogunate came down squarely on the side of the debtor, making it clear that the moneylender was responsible for pawned items. If stolen, the lender was to compensate the debtor at the level of twice the principal, unless the debtor was in arrears on interest payments, in which case compensation would be limited to one and a half times the principal.[66] Any lender who fled was threatened with punishment; an overlord who covered for such a lender would be required to repay the principal. Such stiff penalties, if enforced, were a negative incentive to money-lenders to safeguard collateral items properly. Similarly, the period of en-trustment specified in the lists of collateral items set clear bounds on exactly when the moneylender could claim an item of collateral.[67] How all this legislation can be interpreted to illuminate actual moneylending prac-tices depends heavily on where one stands on the likelihood of any reg-ular official enforcement. At the very least, moneylenders claimed collat-eral as their own often enough for this to be an issue frequently brought to the attention of the Muromachi shogunate.

To some extent moneylending posed risks to the creditor as well. While it is easier to pity the debtor, ultimately there was only so much a money-lender could do to get his money back. In 1425 the Bakufu warned against the practice of Kyoto-area moneylenders, in their loans to commoners, "donating" loan contracts to great temples and shrines or otherwise having third parties collect outstanding debts for them.[68] Violators were threat-ened with severe punishment—a sure sign that there were violators. This law suggests that the moneylenders were having large institutions—over-lords—help them collect loans because as individuals they were not up to it. (Otherwise, the sale of loan contracts would not have been a partic-ularly attractive option for the creditor.) Not only peasants but towns-people in Kyoto pleaded poverty in cases of dilatory debt repayment; in response the shogunate warned them that they would not be allowed to enjoy debt amnesties.[69] Another risk to creditors came from within: money-lenders' employees absconded with collateral often enough for the shogu-nate to threaten them with punishment.[70] The risk inherent in lending money was minimized in cases in which lenders demanded a guarantor in order to close a loan; if the debtor went bankrupt, the creditor was pro-tected to the extent that the guarantor was legally responsible to repay the loan in full.[71] And finally, moneylenders could be victims of violence: three times in Bakufu law it is stipulated that "females must come peac-ably in the daytime" to redeem collateral after a debt amnesty, implying that violent nighttime "redemptions" by males occurred as well.[72] Peasant invasions of the city demanding debt amnesties, described below, also spe-cifically targeted moneylenders. In spite of these risks, however, money-lending was a lucrative pursuit, as is suggested by the large number of lenders and their importance to overlords as taxpayers.

Frequent peasant invasions of Kyoto and shogunal regulations con-cerning usury suggest that moneylending routinely took place on terms favorable to the creditor and harsh toward the debtor. Indeed, interest rates were so high and periods of entrustment of collateral so short that one wonders what proportion of debtors avoided confiscation of their collateral if not ultimate default on the principal. Perhaps the rationale behind the moneylenders' methods was to get what they could out of the debtor as quickly as possible. Autonomous merchants neither reined in nor thoroughly protected against default by their overlords, moneylenders could play fast and loose, as the market would bear.

Chapter Two

Overlords

UNTIL ABOUT THE EARLY SIXTEENTH CENTURY most Kyoto merchants, like the moneylenders, were not independent agents. Rather, like most peasants, they were members of occupational groups bound by prescribed obligations to overlord families, temples, and warriors. In return the overlord was expected to bestow patronage: exemption from other taxes and monopoly protection from competitors. (The monopoly protection extended to the brewer-lenders was on *sake*, not on moneylending; the overlord may have been helpful in dunning tardy debtors as well.) How effectively patronage was in fact bestowed depended on the overlord and the time. It seems to have diminished over the course of the medieval age, especially after the Ōnin War. To the moneylenders and other commoners, the overlord was for the most part an annoying intrusion from above, an ever-present if not primary feature of life. Moneylending and *sake* brewing were central, along with general aspects of life in an urban neighborhood. Like static in the background was the need to keep the overlord satisfied. The moneylenders paid their taxes as necessary and otherwise lived their lives as merchants and as townspeople. When they could, they charged their customers to the limit, avoided taxes, played overlords off against each other, and generally maneuvered around them whenever possible. Nevertheless, the overlord presence was an unavoidable fact of medieval life, and deference to him was an ingrained habit.

Already in the late Heian period aristocratic families and religious institutions in Kyoto had become the overlords of nonagrarian occupational groups of merchants and craftsmen. This arrangement was essentially the commercial equivalent of their role as estate overlords.[1] In return for exemption from the taxes levied by the civil government, the groups submitted taxes privately to their aristocratic or religious overlords in the form of commodities or services, and later cash. This relationship was the basis for a control mechanism similar in function and organization to the medieval European guild. It was the main channel through which the medieval Kyoto elites, including the Muromachi shogunate, sought to derive income from the commercial sector. From the Kamakura period, the economic life of the central cities of Japan, notably Kyoto and Nara, was defined to a great extent by such guilds, among which were the moneylenders.[2]

Guilds of the early medieval period were composed of people sharing a trade, and could include merchants, artisans, entertainers, or those involved in transportation. They have been labeled "service guilds," because their most distinguishing feature was service rendered to their overlords.[3] The first appearance in sources of such a guild was in 1092: a group of woodcutters in Yase, north of Kyoto, received the right to sell firewood in Kyoto in return for cutting timber and bearing the palanquin for their overlord, the religious retirement villa Shōren'in. Other early service guilds included Tōdaiji's swordsmiths' guild, formed around 1118; a group of Kyoto leather workers, probably outcastes, active by 1153; and a *sake* guild from about 1183 which rendered *sake* to its overlord, Genpukuji in Nara.[4]

The word *"za,"* the most common term for these guildlike arrangements, literally means seat, and may have derived from the practice of assigning members special seats at the overlord's ceremonial functions or of reserving a space for them at specific markets.[5] Some guilds were granted stipendiary lands rather than tax exemptions in return for providing goods and services to the overlord. As guild members began to sell their surplus on the market, these lands became superfluous and were disposed of, for the most part. But the overlord's protection, in the form of monopolies, monopsonies, and exemptions from tolls and other taxes, could be helpful to a guild's successful operation, in some cases even through the late medieval period. By the thirteenth century there were also rural guilds in the provinces organized on the same principles. Some of them answered village needs, while others participated in the Kyoto-centered national market. But central Japan, especially Kyoto with its intense degree of commercial activity, remained the locus of most guild activity (see Map 4).

From about the fourteenth century a gradual change occurred in the character of the guild—namely, trade or business aspects became more prominent than service to the overlord.[6] The overlord–client relationship became more contractual in nature, offering the latter autonomy in his commercial activities. Some of these were entirely new guilds whose members shared the same occupation and who had moved as a group into cities from nearby villages or who operated in cities as peddlers, for example, even as they continued to live in their villages. In other cases, former "service" guilds evolved into "trade" guilds as the overlord's protection became less necessary and, sometimes, meaningless. In the early fourteenth century, for instance, the imperial court began to levy a business tax on certain commercial groups, including brewers. Though not always successful in collecting this tax, the court imposed it regardless of the prerogatives of the guild overlord, whose ostensible purpose, in the eyes of his clients, was to protect them against just such additional imposts. Likewise, the Muromachi shogunate, as will be shown, imposed its own tax on the moneylenders in the late fourteenth century. Their original overlord, Enryakuji, was not able to extend its protection adequately to ward off a new tax by the shogun.

The distinction between service and trade guilds is an important and real one separating the guilds of the early and later medieval periods, but it should not be drawn so sharply that the importance of the overlord to the trade guild is discounted altogether. As trade guilds emerged with monopoly powers, the strongest of them were able to crowd out all competitors, but their ability to do so depended in part on the relative strength of the overlord to grant and ensure tax exemptions and monopolies.[7] In principle, the protective role of the overlord was still important: it offered the guild protection against intimidation by other ruling elites and minimized competition from other merchants. In addition, overlords could be called upon to help settle disputes between the guild and outsiders, while the guild controlled internal matters itself.[8] In practice, however, and especially after the Ōnin War, overlord protection was not necessarily comprehensive or effective. In addition, from even before the Ōnin War, overlords were finding themselves at a loss as to how to control their clients. The new type of guild still paid taxes to its overlord, but it was increasingly autonomous, negotiating the amount of taxes and exacting special privileges, such as monopolies on the production and sale of commodities, and monopsonies on raw materials. For some guilds, such as that of the powerful oil merchants of Ōyamazaki, these monopolies were extended to include whole provinces or more. Thus the role of the overlord continued to be useful to merchants when the overlord was powerful enough to extend meaningful protection; at the same time, guild members sought to escape taxation, sometimes successfully, as often as possible.

In principle if not necessarily in practice, relations among trade guild members were equitable and horizontal.[9] All members participated in the selection of officers, who served one-year terms, and all were subject to guild rules. Whereas the service guild had functioned to the overlord's benefit, the more autonomous trade guilds could concentrate on internal matters. Profits from shared ventures were distributed among members. Guild regulations delineating members' responsibilities and duties became customary law during the fifteenth century and were widely codified during the early sixteenth for use in lawsuits against proliferating nonguild merchants who were challenging the monopolies of the guilds.

The guild, then, was to commerce what the estate system was to land: an organization peculiar to the medieval period through which the overlord laid claim to the fruits of labor of a group of merchants or craftsmen in return for monopoly protection and exemption from taxation by other authorities. Guild members originally accepted subordinate status to their overlords as a necessary condition for protection, but in later centuries they attained autonomy or near-autonomy, operating increasingly from a position of strength, as protection dwindled.

By the late fifteenth century there were forty-four guilds in Kyoto, thirty-one with aristocratic overlords, seven under the protection of religious establishments,[10] and the remaining six presumably controlled by the Muromachi shogunate. The single most powerful and economically significant of these groups were the brewer-lenders, who made up the bulk of the non-Zen moneylending establishment in Kyoto. Their guild was never called a *za* but went by the term *yoriaishū*, or council, in its dealings with Enryakuji, the overlord, and bore the main characteristics of a *za*. Other guilds included those handling salt, paper, clothing, textiles, dying, weaving, cotton, thread, silk glossing, fresh fish, dried fish, salt-cured products, and so on. Guilds had strict agreements among themselves concerning the types of goods and services offered by each, and the areas in which they could be sold. For example, the salt-cured products guild once brought suit against a fish guild that had sold salted fish in Kyoto, a violation of their agreement concerning the type of goods each was allowed to sell there.[11] Sometimes guilds were located near their overlords (like Kitano Shrine's malt guild) or near raw materials. The largest concentration of guilds was in the central downtown area between the north–south Muromachidōri and Aburanokōji between Sanjō and Gojō.[12]

As guilds became securely established and their monopoly rights extensive in the fifteenth century, commerce in Kyoto became more and more an exclusive activity, closed to outsiders. Guilds refused to recognize the rights of nonmembers, and they limited membership to keep production low and demand high.[13] As a measure of their increasing autonomy, guilds were successful in demanding that both traditional overlords and

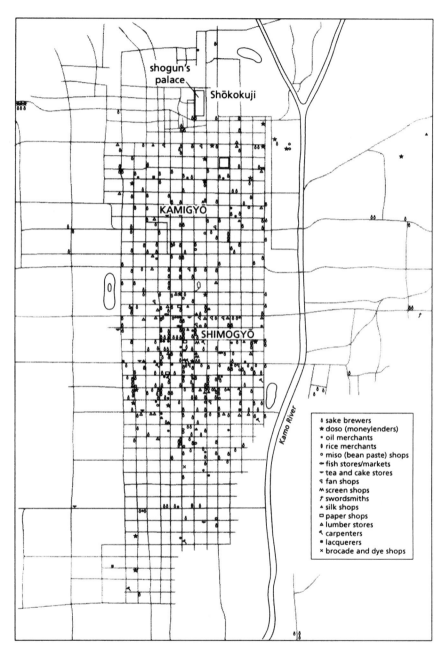

Map 4: Major Guilds in Medieval Kyoto (derived from map insert, *KR*, vol. 3)

the shogunate accept taxes from them in a lump sum.[14] In the process, the method of collection became an internal guild matter. The overall effect of these restrictive measures was to make the guilds ever more exclusive and autonomous, both of those who tried to tax them and of those who tried to compete with them. But just as the established guilds were beginning to seem unchallengeable, the resurgence of commercial activity in the late fifteenth and early sixteenth centuries following the Ōnin War brought into Kyoto a large number of nonguild merchants and artisans from the surrounding areas seeking to take advantage of the reviving urban economy. The old guilds, their ranks depleted from the ravages of the war, could not prevent the newcomers from creating their own guilds, or even from operating completely outside the guild system. Some of the new guilds competed successfully with established guilds for religious or aristocratic patronage in order to garner monopolies.[15] The death knell for the medieval guild was rung in the late sixteenth century when powerful regional lords, in order to establish control over their domainal economies, abolished the special privileges of the guilds and appointed their own merchants (goyō shōnin) to oversee commercial activities in their domains. In Kyoto, meanwhile, powerful individual wholesalers (ton'ya) began to buy up the monopoly privileges of some guilds, establishing themselves as independent enterprises.[16] The waning power of the medieval commercial overlords like Enryakuji and the shogunate made this development possible; consequently, guild privileges gradually became meaningless.[17]

The Japanese za has inevitably been compared to the European guild. Similarities can be found in organization and function, but in addition to the relatively stronger position of the overlord in Japan, there was another important difference: guilds in Japan never united into federations to form the self-governing organ of cities, as in Europe.[18] Guild members in Japan were organized by profession, not necessarily locale, so they could be scattered geographically, making constant solidarity on a neighborhood basis difficult. Instead, the machi, the neighborhood unit discussed in Part 1, served as a unit of limited self-governance. The resilience of traditional arrangements, offering some benefits both to overlords and to their clients, precluded broad-based self-governance.

The Enryakuji Network

By the early fourteenth century about 80 percent of the Kyoto moneylenders—those examined in this study—were affiliated with Enryakuji either directly or through one of its shrine subsidiaries.[19] Although it is not thought that most of these moneylenders lived a monastic lifestyle, it was within Enryakuji's complex organization that they emerged as successful entrepreneurs, and at least some of them remained there until the end of the medieval period.[20] Thus the functioning of Enryakuji and its affiliate shrines was relevant to aspects of the moneylenders' lives. As for Enryakuji itself, that its control of commerce in Kyoto exceeded that of any other overlord, especially in the early medieval period, bespeaks its significance in the medieval economy.

Founded by the monk Saichō in 788 as Hieizanji on the highest peak looming over what would soon be Kyoto, Enryakuji was designated the headquarters of Tendai Buddhism in Japan in 805, after which Saichō spent nearly a year studying in China.[21] In 818 he established an ordination platform at Enryakuji, making a dramatic split with the Nara Buddhist establishment, which had hitherto monopolized ordinations in Japan. Saichō's prominence as a religious figure brought the monastery to the attention of the Kyoto aristocracy. Enryakuji received its permanent name in 823, when the emperor officially designated it a spiritual protector of the nation (*kokka chingo*), making the monastery a political ally of the state, complete with stipend. Henceforth, Enryakuji could be considered to embody both public authority and the prestige of religion. Its location in the inauspicious northeastern corner of the city of Kyoto also made its protective powers much sought after by the political authorities.

Mount Hiei itself, where Enryakuji is located, had been regarded for centuries as home to a protective mountain spirit called Ōyamagui. In the 660s Emperor Tenji ceremonially moved Ōyamagui from the peak to make room for a Yamato *kami*—an ally, in spiritual terms, of Tenji's government. Ōyamagui was given a new home at the eastern base of Mount Hiei, called Hie Shrine. (The pronunciation of the shrine's name changed to Hiyoshi during the medieval period.) The two institutions were inextricably linked, with Hie acting as the protective shrine of Enryakuji and Enryakuji serving as administrative head of Hie Shrine, overshadowing it both physically and institutionally.[22] The close tie between the two extended to economic matters, including moneylending, to the extent that in some respects the two could be considered one institution. From the thirteenth century, the moneylenders in their guildlike council (*dosō yoriaishū*) were affiliated with Enryakuji itself; at the same time they held a subsidiary rank (*jinin*) in Hie Shrine, to which they paid regular taxes. When Enryakuji monks engaged in displays of protest and intimidation in Kyoto, it was one of Hie's portable shrines that they carried into the city.[23]

During the tenure of the head priest, Ryōgen, in the latter half of the tenth century, Enryakuji's organizational structure took form. Three separate complexes—east, west, and Yokawa off to the north—comprised the main centers of the monastery. Under each were several "valleys" (*tani*) or subordinate temples, numbering sixteen in all. In addition, from the late Heian period aged or infirm monks were allowed to live at the more temperate base of the mountain in houses called *satobō*, each affiliated with a "valley." Most of these were located in the vicinity of Sakamoto near Hie Shrine, and some became substantial structures, as even ablebodied monks, many of them with wives despite the Buddhist requisite of celibacy for monks, took up residence in them and gathered their spiritual disciples and flesh-and-blood progeny around them. In the medieval period there were as many as three thousand of these affiliate residences, each with its own particular body of religious teachings and property held and inherited with the *satobō*. At times during the medieval period, Enryakuji's spiritual and material power revolved as much around these structures as around the monastery proper on the mountaintop.

As aristocrats and members of the imperial family began to enter the monastery in the ninth century, using it both as a religious haven and as a basis for establishing hereditary retirement villas (*monzeki*) for religious purposes, conflicts became rife within Enryakuji. In 858 an outright schism occurred, with the losing faction reestablishing itself at Onjōji (popularly known as Miidera) south of Enryakuji overlooking Lake Biwa.[24] Hence Enryakuji would often be referred to as *sanmon* (mountain gate), as opposed to Onjōji which was called *jimon* (temple gate). The keen rivalry between the two temples continued throughout the medieval period, often resulting in bloodshed and extending to economic affairs. But Enryakuji itself was hardly a bastion of internal tranquillity. Quite the contrary: strife among the various camps on the mountain was endemic, and to sort out loyalties and rivalries is often impossible. For some of the medieval period the abbot of Enryakuji and therefore of Tendai Buddhism in Japan was based not on the mountain at all but at Shōren'in, an Enryakuji retirement villa in eastern Kyoto.

From about the fourteenth century the monks on the mountaintop began to dictate monastic affairs as a group, and the abbot often found himself under attack, sometimes even physically. In some conflicts no single party could clearly be said to represent Enryakuji. It was not uncommon for a monk to aggrandize himself at the expense of others in the monastery. For example, several Enryakuji monks living in a *satobō* in Sakamoto erected a new toll station on the shores of Lake Biwa in 1471.[25] Everyone passing by was obliged to pay, including religious pilgrims ascending the mountain and also merchants transporting Enryakuji's estate income—that is, its food. The situation so aggravated the monks on the peak that they denounced and then attacked the offending monks at the eastern base of the mountain. Although one speaks monolithically of Enryakuji vis-à-vis its Kyoto moneylenders, it was in fact hardly a monolithic institution, however formidable it appeared to outsiders.

Only in conflicts with other institutions did the Enryakuji monks display a modicum of solidarity. A long-standing rivalry with Kōfukuji in Nara, in particular, produced many altercations between the two monasteries. Kiyomizudera, Kōfukuji's subordinate institution in Kyoto, often acted as its proxy in battles there, sending its outcaste lackeys into battle against Enryakuji's forces. Religion was not necessarily at issue in these conflicts; indeed, in the medieval period the control of land loomed large for any group. Disputes over rights to even small pieces of land could rouse the monks to battle. This may have been unseemly behavior for individuals who had supposedly devoted their lives to religion, but two factors make their behavior somewhat understandable. First, Enryakuji was inhabited strictly by consumers, producing nothing itself.[26] In other words, all food and goods necessary for daily life had to be brought in from the outside. Given its remoteness and height, and therefore its susceptibility to isolation, ready access to income was a necessity, and in the medieval period that often meant aggressively asserting control over land. The second factor to be considered in the behavior of the monks is that by the Kamakura period many of them had offspring, if not living on the mountain itself, then at its base in a *satobō*. Matters of property become matters of inheritance when the next generation is a factor. Though sexual union and therefore marriage were still officially proscribed in orthodox Japanese Buddhism, they were in fact widespread, and this may partially explain why on so many occasions the concerns of the clergy were not entirely spiritual.

Enryakuji's considerable wealth was based originally on its vast landholdings, acquired in several ways. From about the tenth century, property holding began to take on a private character in Japan. Enryakuji, in one sense a public authority by virtue of its official status as a spiritual protector of the state, nevertheless began to accumulate land privately in the form of estates, scattered parcels of arable over which the monastery held overlord rights. Its old state stipend also took the form of rights to land, called *kokugaryō*, designated by the state for local officials. In addition, it was not uncommon for aristocrats entering the monastery to bring some rights to land with them. Thus Enryakuji's lands were held by various elements within the monastery. In the eleventh and twelfth centuries, its aggregate landed holdings reached considerable proportions: including those of Hie Shrine, Enryakuji's estates numbered over three hundred and were concentrated particularly in Ōmi province directly to the east, as well as in Yamashiro to the south. The rest extended northeastward throughout the Hokuriku region, namely the provinces of Echizen, Wakasa, Mino, and Kaga. Enryakuji's notorious "warrior-monks" (sōhei) first appeared at this time to defend the monastery's claim to its lands.[27] Some of Enryakuji's estates were extremely large: there were seven major Enryakuji estates in Ōmi in the Kamakura period, and one of them, overseen by Shōren'in, yielded 520 koku per year, huge by medieval standards.[28] By the early thirteenth century, Enryakuji was even attempting to extend its reach into western Japan, in the hope of seizing some of the profits of trade with the continent.[29] Enryakuji's estates were administered by its low-ranking monks (santo) and lay officials (kunin). On many of these estates a branch shrine of Hie could also be found complete with shrine personnel appointed by Hie, bolstering overlord control with an added religious presence. Unquestionably, Enryakuji had gone far beyond accumulating land merely for its monks' subsistence; it was now one of the major overlords in Japan.

Over the course of the medieval period, local warriors made incursions onto the lands of the traditional overlords. Sometimes they were helped in this by the shogunate. In 1352, for instance, the Muromachi Bakufu instituted a practice known as hanzei, in which half the income from estate lands was to go to warriors.[30] Ostensibly a temporary measure to tide over the shogunate's supporters as they continued their struggle against the forces supporting the rival southern court, this tax became permanent, and was interpreted broadly to mean that warriors took over half the actual land of estates. This measure opened estate gates to local warriors, and even though the shogunate made constant attempts to curb their excesses, it proved devastating to the income of many traditional overlords, halving it at a stroke. Included in the 1352 decree were estates in Ōmi, Mino, and Owari, all areas of extensive Enryakuji holdings. Presumably, then, Enryakuji's real holdings were diminished at this point. On the other hand, in 1368 the Muromachi Bakufu specifically exempted from hanzei land under the total jurisdiction of an overlord (ichien chigyō), an apt description of Enryakuji's control of many of its estates, so it is likely that Enryakuji continued to control many of its holdings as before.[31]

Because of the preponderance of landholdings to the east of Enryakuji, much of the monastery's estate income had to be transported across

Lake Biwa and then up the mountain by way of the entrepôt town of Sakamoto.[32] The monastery's income from the west, including commercial income from Kyoto, could be handled through the other Sakamoto, an entrepôt at the western base of Mount Hiei, in the area of Yase northeast of Kyoto. It was important for Enryakuji to establish control over these vital checkpoints of transport as well as over the lake pilots and packhorse drivers who carried the goods, and the routes over which the goods passed. The latter were controlled through the maintenance of toll barriers at strategic points. Katada, for example, on the western shore of Lake Biwa at its narrowest point, was firmly under the control of Enryakuji during the medieval period. Toll income from Katada was large because all goods —not only Enryakuji's—from Hokuriku estates bound for Kyoto had to pass that point.

The lake pilots and packhorse drivers had organized guilds affiliated with Enryakuji. Strikes by these drivers were an effective means of getting the attention of the medieval authorities, since the drivers not only controlled goods going to Enryakuji but those bound for Kyoto as well. In the Muromachi period, moreover, they commonly purchased the goods they transported, reselling them upon delivery. Thus their role took on the entrepreneurial aspect of middlemen. As will be seen later, it was the packhorse drivers who fired the opening volleys in some of the largest attacks on the moneylenders in the fifteenth century. Confrontations between them and their overlord, Enryakuji, increased as the medieval economy expanded and, therefore, as control over them became ever more important to Enryakuji.

In the mid-fourteenth century the Muromachi shogunate challenged Enryakuji's control over the Lake Biwa toll points, ordering them dismantled as a hindrance to travelers.[33] There being no evidence of enforcement, however, it is not clear if the edict took effect. Even as its estate holdings decreased from the fourteenth century, then, Enryakuji found ways to remain a key player in the medieval economy, exploiting its ties to commerce and thus continuing its prosperous existence within the context of the burgeoning economy.

Oversight of this economic activity was provided by Enryakuji personnel at various levels. The monks were organized into three general ranks that defined their role and function within the monastery. In the highest rank were monks whose lives revolved around religious matters per se: meditation, prayer, the study and teaching of religious texts and other traditions. They had their own cliques within the monastery, often centered at the *satobō*. They tended to be men drawn from the imperial family and from the upper ranks of the aristocracy who entered the monastery in childhood and worked their way, ideally, through twelve years of formal learning. The abbot of Enryakuji was chosen from this group. The second rank of monks usually lacked the illustrious pedigree of the first; those who were of aristocratic stock had failed to prove themselves worthy of that rank during their years of training and were demoted. In the beginning they acted as servants of the first group, but from the late Heian period they assumed control of the administration of the monastery and even of religious services as the higher-ranking monks became embroiled in factionalism.

The lowest-ranking group of monks were called *santo*. They handled the daily, mundane affairs of the monastery. In the medieval period they usually had wives and became increasingly secularized, until by the fifteenth century they commonly lived either in Kyoto or Sakamoto, dressed as lay people, and were only distinguishable as priests by their Buddhist names. Though some among even the highest rank of monks engaged in moneylending in the medieval period, it was the *santo* who were heavily involved in this enterprise. Starting in the late Heian period as lenders of seed rice to peasants for the spring planting, these monks and their counterparts at Hie Shrine moved into cash lending at rates of 2 to 5 percent monthly.[34] This lowest rank of monks constituted Enryakuji's most palpable link with the outside world. In administrative matters, prominent *santo* were designated envoys to the Muromachi shogunate, the imperial court, aristocratic families, and other temples. They also acted as high-level envoys to Enryakuji estates, overseeing the collection of yearly dues and resolving disputes. The *santo* formed the bulk of the notorious "warrior monk" forces augmented by outcaste subordinates in disputes with other temples. Through their military prowess some became landed overlords in their own right. Thus, although their status within Enryakuji was low, the *santo* could be individually wealthy and powerful. In fact, by the late Kamakura period the *santo*'s moneylending within Enryakuji was becoming a threat to the monastic hierarchy: rights to land and other property put up as collateral was passing into their hands and out of the possession of their frequently defaulting clients, the higher-ranking monks.[35] The most prominent of Enryakuji's Kyoto moneylenders probably hailed from the *santo* originally. For example, a moneylender-tax agent for Hie Shrine in the late fifteenth century referred to himself as "following in the lineage of the *santo* Enkaku."[36] Some, on the other hand, may have been townspeople who by virtue of their involvement in moneylending were granted nominal priestly status as *santo*.[37] The total number of *santo* in the medieval period cannot be reliably estimated, but given their broad role as support personnel to the monastic complex, it is likely that they outnumbered the other two groups. Total Enryakuji clerical personnel is thought to have numbered in the thousands, although it probably fluctuated over the course of the medieval period.

There were other personnel in Enryakuji's network. In considering Enryakuji's role as a comprehensive medieval authority (*kenmon*), it is appropriate to include the shrines under the monastery's control. Enryakuji presided over a network that included, first, Hie Shrine at the eastern base of the mountain, as explained above. Later, Kitano and Gion Shrines in Kyoto became affiliated with Enryakuji. Founded in 876, Gion's full name, Gion Kanjin'in Gionsha, indicating both a shrine to a *kami* (Gionsha) and a Buddhist temple (Gion Kanjin'in), reflected the perception of religion as a single unified sphere, prior to its arbitrary division into two religions, Buddhism and Shinto, in the modern period.[38] In 974 Gion Shrine's affiliation was transferred from Kōfukuji to Enryakuji, marking the beginnng of long-standing antagonism between the two temples.[39] This change meant that Gion's head priest became directly subordinate to the head abbot of Enryakuji and was even to be appointed and retired from office along with Enryakuji's head abbot. From then on, Gion's connection with Enryakuji was close and proceeded from the highest levels. For its part, Kitano Shrine dates from the mid-tenth century when it was founded to appease the vengeful spirit of the exiled poet-statesman Sugawara Michizane. A combination shrine and Tendai temple (*gūji*), Kitano was also under Enryakuji's umbrella, if more tenuously than Hie and Gion. Its legendary history (*engi*) was written by a Tendai monk appointed to the shrine.[40] A handful of the brewer-lenders of this study were located in the neighborhood of Kitano, their overlord, while others lived near Gion, whose yearly festival was financed by their taxes. Hie Shrine, as well as Enryakuji itself, had established an overlord relationship with these merchants earlier. For the Kitano brewers, who became specialist malt producers, the location near the shrine in the upper portion of the city may have offered proximity to a good water supply. In the case of Gion, the area west of the shrine by the early medieval period was developing into the main commercial center of the city, an ideal site for moneylenders. In medieval times Enryakuji zealously protected the commercial interests of these shrine affiliates, as will be seen.

Low-ranking functionaries of these shrines (*jinin*, alternatively pronounced *jinnin*), subordinate to the head priest, were originally responsible for miscellaneous support services related to religious ceremonies or to the administration of the shrine.[41] With the great increase in shrine lands from about the tenth century, many new *jinin* were appointed. Their functions included the administration of the shrine's landed and commercial interests, policing shrine property, and performing guard duty during religious ceremonies. In the latter capacity military prowess was valued highly, and many *jinin* regularly participated, alongside their temple counterparts, in clashes between religious institutions. The frequency of these conflicts in medieval times is attested to in decrees issued by the various authorities in Kyoto prohibiting such behavior. Other *jinin* had managerial and entrepreneurial skills. The rank was also bestowed on affiliated merchants, including the brewer-lenders, who in return paid taxes to the shrine.

It is thought that early *jinin* had a strong clerical character, living at the shrine with access to the shrine's sacred objects such as portable shrines, powerful symbols of religious authority useful in conflicts. Later *jinin* appointees commonly lived as lay people, in their own dwellings. From the Kamakura period, for example, estate officials on shrine lands throughout Japan were sometimes designated *jinin*. Even well-to-do peasants and members of the local overlord class could be appointed to this rank, giving them, in effect, an extra, religious dimension of authority. Other *jinin* were lay people involved in commerce, including money-lenders, in the Kyoto area organized into guilds. Thus the *jinin* label came to encompass a wide variety of functions and individuals both within a shrine and in the greater society and economy. A common term in the medieval period, it imparted to its holders an authentic if low-ranking status within a religious institution, and thus afforded them protection and a measure of prestige in lay society.

The temple equivalent of *jinin* were *kunin*, the lowest-ranking members of Enryakuji itself; by the medieval period they were usually lay people who held a temple rank distinctly lower than that of *santo*, the third-level monks.[42] *Kunin* often joined ranks with Gion and Hie *jinin* in the Kyoto area to further Enryakuji's interests. They also performed duties in far-flung areas, such as overseeing the collection of estate taxes, acting as messengers to estates or to other institutions, taking coercive action against recalcitrant debtors, and a variety of other miscellaneous chores. *Kunin* usually lived in the general vicinity of their temple and sometimes formed guilds whose overlord, the temple, offered exemption from various taxes borne by other commoners. In return for paying yearly dues, they could depend on Enryakuji for protection from taxation by other elites in the society and for support in debt collection. Among these various monastic groups the moneylenders of this study had *jinin* designations, mostly from Hie Shrine; in addition, the most prominent of the moneylenders were *santo* of Enryakuji. *Kunin* were sometimes employed by *santo* to assist them, but they were apparently seen as disruptive by the authorities in Kyoto.[43]

At the very bottom of the Enryakuji organization were Gion Shrine's *inujinin* (dog *jinin*), a derogatory term for a despised class of shrine functionaries who performed tasks disdained by others.[44] Another term for them was *tsurumeso* (bowstring-selling monks), indicating their probable origins as *jinin* craftsmen who lived in the vicinity of Kenninji making bows and arrows, successors to the craftsmen of the ancient period who produced military paraphernalia for officials. Members of the outcaste class, *inujinin* were found at many shrines, but those of Gion Shrine were especially well known. Awarded the position of funeral attendants by the emperor in 1031, they performed this important function for the shrine. In 1070 their importance was recognized by Emperor Gosanjō in the form of a grant of the land along the Kamo riverbank between Shijō and Gojō near the shrine. In addition to assisting at funerals and burials, the *inujinin*'s duties included cleaning and guarding Gion Shrine, policing the shrine precincts, and acting as bailiffs or process servers in shrine disputes. In time they monopolized these functions not only for Gion Shrine but for the entire area of downtown Kyoto near the Kamo River, as employees of the Bureau of Capital Police.

To Enryakuji, acting through Gion, its branch shrine, the *inujinin* were a useful cat's-paw in any dispute calling for coercion. The centuries-long rivalry between Enryakuji in Kyoto and Kōfukuji in Nara, for instance, was frequently carried to the streets by such outcastes attached to Gion Shrine (representing Enryakuji) and Kiyomizudera (representing Kōfukuji).[45] They may have functioned as a police force for the moneylenders, forcibly collecting outstanding debts and dunning tardy debtors. Just as easily could they have been called upon to turn on the moneylenders if the latter were in arrears in their taxes to the shrines. Neither the imperial court nor, later, the Muromachi shogunate was able to prevent completely the terror tactics of these agents. Their favorite ploy was borrowed from Enryakuji's monks, their bosses: to carry a portable shrine into Kyoto, rampaging through the streets as they went, breaking into debtors' homes and terrorizing the occupants. Sometimes they would leave the portable shrine on the land of a debtor, or even in the streets. The presence of such a sacred object in an unsanctified place created an atmosphere of anxiety and unease stemming from fears of retribution by the *kami*.

Some of the monks of Enryakuji were involved in moneylending even early in the medieval period. The same applied to its subsidiary shrines: by the middle of the twelfth century, for example, there were *jinin* of Hie Shrine involved in the lending of grain at high rates of interest to provincial officials in return for land as collateral.[46] The grain being used as capital was from the shrine's yearly tax revenues, and the prestige of the shrine was useful in intimidating debtors to pay up promptly. During the unrest of the late twelfth century, there was much lending of currency at high rates of interest to aristocratic and warrior overlords by individuals of lower status. The author of the *Genpei seisuiki*, a late Heian period chronicle, grumbled that there were altogether too many people using Enryakuji's authority to lend money and enrich themselves, even taking inflated sobriquets with an aristocratic ring and appearing to be functionaries of Enryakuji.[47] The Kyoto brewer-lenders generally were *jinin* of one of the affiliated shrines, while some held *santo* or *kunin* rank at Enryakuji itself.[48] It cannot be proven definitively, but logically the *santo* had religious roots and evolved through moneylending into merchants, while the others were more likely brewer-lenders first, who later sought or were pressed into a temple or shrine affiliation. In either case, Enryakuji's reach into commerce was long.

In an incident occurring in 1213, some Enryakuji moneylenders utilized a tactic that was to become a trademark.[49] The deputy *shugo* of Echizen Province formally protested to the imperial court about the harassment of his deputy, Kaneyori, by some moneylenders affiliated with Hie Shrine, Enryakuji's subsidiary. He demanded that they be made to cease. The lenders then asked Enryakuji to apply pressure to the court, which subsequently ruled in favor of the lenders and levied a punishment on the debtor Kaneyori. Still not satisfied, the lenders went back to Enryakuji, claiming falsely that the court had decided to strip them of their shrine rank and to punish them. In response, the monks of Enryakuji threatened to bring Hie's portable shrine down the mountain and into the city. The court replied with a decree from the office of the retired emperor (an *inzen*), denying that the lenders would be stripped of rank. This incident vividly demonstrates the remarkable power invested in the portable shrine, mere threat of whose movement could fill people with fear and dread. By their Enryakuji affiliation, then, the moneylenders could influence the outcome of litigation.

By 1278, the Kyoto moneylenders, most of whom were Hie *jinin*, formed a guildlike council called the *dosō yoriaishū* for their dealings with Enryakuji, the overlord.[50] Communal aspects like collective control of paddy land put up by debtors as collateral and the sharing of profits and forfeited collateral are sure indications that this guild already had strong internal cohesion not dependent on overlord support.[51] In return for paying yearly dues, these moneylenders could count on the Enryakuji "syndicate" to protect them from taxation by other elites and to give them support in the form of monopolies on the production and sale of *sake* and assistance in collecting outstanding debts. More abstractly, the awesome authority of Enryakuji implicit in their clerical status, even if nominal, enhanced their stature in the eyes of their customers. Their power to obstruct litigation proceedings, as in the 1213 incident described above, also derived from their Enryakuji connection. Conversely, Enryakuji protected its clients from intimidation or taxation by other powerful elites who might have found them an easy prey. Overlord taxes may well have been a reasonable price to pay for such powerful protection. Membership in the Enryakuji guild was, for these moneylenders, a combination business license and protection racket in which membership was compulsory but, at least in the early medieval period, worthwhile.

To observers of medieval Europe or the Islamic world, the deep involvement of a religious institution like Enryakuji in moneylending—indeed, moneylending at usurious rates—may seem curious. Unlike Islam or medieval Christianity, Buddhism does not specifically prohibit usury; on the other hand, among the forty-eight minor precepts of Enryakuji's Bodhisattva vows is a prohibition of clerical involvement in commercial activities. Nevertheless, temples—not only Enryakuji—were commonly in the business of moneylending in medieval Japan. Presumably they not only had the resources but may have been considered more trustworthy than laymen. They also charged lower rates of interest. The exact origins of Enryakuji's involvement in moneylending are obscure, but they were most likely related to its accumulation of land and involvement in commerce from the late Heian period.

There were precedents in China for moneylending by religious institutions which shed some light on the Japanese example. It is known, for example, that at least from the late fifth century some of the large monasteries of China were involved in pawnbroking.[52] Relevant to the example of Enryakuji's moneylenders was the common practice in the Southern Sung for wealthy laymen to form partnerships and open pawnshops on monastery grounds. In so doing, they evaded a type of property tax from which monasteries were exempt.[53] The government put a stop to this in 1201 by ending the tax exemption. The arrangement, while it lasted, was similar to that of the Kyoto moneylenders and Enryakuji: they received a type of protection from the monastery by placing themselves—in this case, physically—within the monastic institution.

Other forms of moneylending by temples, such as mutual finance associations consisting of several dozen temple adherents, were common throughout China, and the Chinese temple was the locus of a good deal of moneylending activity. Japanese monks like Saichō, the founder of Enryakuji, no doubt had occasion to observe these practices while studying in China and perhaps came to view them as a normal part of the monastic scene. Enryakuji's tolerance and even encouragement of this violation of the Buddhist precepts contrasts sharply with its persecution of individual monks accused of defying other precepts, such as those proscribing meat and sexual relations. Moneylending, though it may have been forbidden by religious precepts, did not constitute a challenge to Enryakuji's authority, as did the activities and teachings of such clerics as Hōnen and Shinran who broke away from the establishment in the early medieval period. Clearly, to a powerful institution like Enryakuji, certain religious violations, especially when committed in defiance of religious authority, were considered worse than others.

Until the fourteenth century Enryakuji had few rivals in its control of the moneylenders. The Kamakura shogunate's concern with moneylenders extended only to protecting its warriors from the lenders' excesses. A favorite ploy of moneylenders in general in the thirteenth century was to force warriors to appoint them to local managerial posts on nearby estates. In response to such abuses, the Kamakura shogunate attempted to protect its warriors and their lands, and indirectly to place some limitations on moneylenders. In 1239 it prohibited military estate stewards (jitō) from appointing moneylenders as tax agents, thus hoping to prevent them from taking warrior land as debt payment.[54] The following year stewards were forbidden to sell or mortgage land to nonvassals or to commoners, presumably also to prevent moneylenders from chiseling away at vassal holdings.[55] In 1267 the shogunate allowed its vassals to recoup defaulted lands by paying up late, and also flatly forbade any more land sales by its vassals.[56] In 1284, the Kamakura Bakufu issued its first debt amnesty for vassals in northern Kyushu, devastated by their hollow victory in the Mongol invasions.[57] In 1297, the Kamakura shogunate canceled the debts of all its vassals.[58] These debt amnesties, though not aimed specifically at the Kyoto moneylenders, were precursors of what was to become a major part of Muromachi shogunal policy toward them in later centuries. But the Kamakura shogunate was concerned mainly with limiting the abuses of the moneylenders toward its own vassals, and even at that was only partially successful. Indeed, the 1297 debt amnesty was canceled in 1298, signifying insufficient shogunal strength "to defy the dictates of a monetized economy,"[59] in contrast to overlords who eagerly participated in it through the guild system. The Kamakura shogunate did not concern itself with commerce in Kyoto. In any case, it posed no serious threat to Enryakuji's claims on the moneylenders.

The Kamakura shogunate took a similarly ineffectual stance regarding *sake* brewing, the other occupation of the Kyoto moneylenders. Far from benefiting from it financially through a tax, as the Muromachi Bakufu later would, the Kamakura shogun attempted to prohibit commercial brewing altogether, banning the sale of *sake* during a famine in 1252. (The rationale here was that any rice going toward *sake* production was being denied to hungry people.) A subsequent survey of homes in Kamakura, a city of modest proportions, revealed 37,274 *sake* casks. The shogunate ordered all but one per house destroyed and banned *sake* markets in the provinces; its ban on *sake* brewing for retail purposes became standard policy, if largely honored in the breach.[60]

THE IMPERIAL COURT

The imperial court, on the other hand, imposed a small malt tax on the Kyoto brewer-lenders from about the middle of the Kamakura period. The Distillery Office (*mikinotsukasa* or *zōshushi*) was originally a court office responsible for supplying *sake* to the emperor for ceremonial use.[61] At first an annual tax was collected by the governors of twelve provinces and submitted to the Distillery Office; it became harder and harder to collect in the unrest of the late Heian period and all but stopped thereafter. In 1226, for example, no tax was forthcoming from eight of the twelve provinces. The Distillery Office had to find another source of income, therefore, and pounced upon the flourishing brewer-lenders of Kyoto.

In 1240 the Distillery Office requested permission of the imperial court to impose a tax of one *shō* (1.8 liters) of *sake* on each brewer of east and west Kyoto, most of whom were already taxed by Hie Shrine, part of the Enryakuji network.[62] The request was rationalized by pointing out that other offices of the imperial government were now taxing commercial groups in Kyoto.[63] Permission was not granted, perhaps because the court did not want to antagonize Enryakuji, and the Distillery Office was urged to obtain income from its traditional sources in the provinces.[64] Nevertheless, later events suggest that the Distillery Office did not give up attempts to extract a tax from the brewer-lenders: in 1302, for example, the retired emperor directed the malt producers to pay an incidental levy.[65]

Friction between the imperial court and Hie's brewers spilled into the streets on at least one occasion. Subordinates of Hie Shrine got into a street fight in 1302 with another powerful commercial group, the court palanquin bearers, and Hie Shrine's portable shrine was damaged. Blaming the Hie group for the damage, the court ordered them to bear the cost of repairing the portable shrine. Enryakuji opposed the order, but the Bureau of Capital Police collected a special tax from the Kyoto brewer-lenders for that purpose anyway.[66] On another occasion, in 1305, the imperial court, apparently irked by the brewers' nonpayment of taxes, took the harsh step of banning the sale of *sake* in Kyoto.[67] (It is not known whether the ban was enforced.) But the brewers' Enryakuji tie (via Hie Shrine) paid off sometimes: when a Distillery Office tax ostensibly for the reconstruction of Hie's portable shrine was levied in 1313, for example, 280 brewer-lenders affiliated with Enryakuji were accorded a special exemption by the court.[68]

In 1322, by order of Emperor Godaigo, a *sake* tax was declared a sinecure of the Distillery Office, to be enforced by the Bureau of Capital Police.[69] Brewers subordinate to Hie Shrine opposed the tax, and it is not clear to what extent and how regularly it was actually collected.[70] The brewers were unhappy to be taxed by two overlords; at the end of the fourteenth century they were to come under triple overlordship, as the Muromachi shogunate began to tax them as well.[71]

The Distillery Office was administered by an aristocratic family, the Nakahara. As the office itself atrophied, the small imperial malt tax on *sake* became a private arrangement with the Nakahara in the position of overlord, albeit a weak one. They nevertheless maintained a tenuous hold on the relationship until late medieval times, as will be seen.

In addition to the Distillery Office, the imperial court's Bureau of Capital Police exercised some separate control over some of Kyoto's money-lenders. A part of the civil government, in commerce the Bureau behaved exactly as an overlord, within the guild system, though its activities were formally considered among the duties of office.[72] As explained in Part 1, the Bureau kept offices in each of the city's wards. Hence its judicial and police authority—its responsibility for the inhabitants' security—was close and direct, like those of a sheriff, involving prosecution of criminals, enforcing imperial decrees such as those requiring heads of households to deliver "wastrals" (illegal residents) to the police, presenting the main Bureau office with necessary proof when citizens' documents needed to be replaced, enforcing proper procedure during litigation, such as timely court appearances by residents, and so on. These local Bureau officials often employed personal retainers to perform such activities, yet another case of official duty executed through a private relationship.

During the eleventh and twelfth centuries Bureau members had formed close neighborhood ties in their line of work, especially in market areas. Establishment of a merchant clientele was the next logical step as commerce expanded. In this way some moneylenders came under the protection of the local Bureau official in a guild arrangement that was an extension of the official's duty to protect the residents. During the thirteenth century this became a direct tie between guilds and the central Bureau office, as its local branches atrophied. Some of the guild members also served as personal retainers of Bureau members, performing public duties for them. There were fifty-five moneylenders affiliated with the Bureau of Police, somewhat less than 20 percent of all Kyoto's brewer-lenders.[73] Like Enryakuji's agents, Bureau members collected taxes from their clients and in return carried out the forceful collection of debts and the private seizure and confiscation of mortgaged property of debtors. Such "private" sources of income were considered to be the Bureau members' stipends in return for the execution of official duties.[74] In the medieval period, however, the distinction between public and private can be a difficult one to draw.

During the early medieval period, then, the Distillery Office and the Bureau of Capital Police, two traditional imperial offices, both derived revenue from the moneylenders. Enryakuji may have been the ultimate overlord of nearly all the moneylenders of Kyoto, but this did not exclude the imperial court from claiming some jursidiction. Competing overlordship became more complicated, however, with the establishment of the Muromachi shogunate, a new warrior government, in the city in 1336.

THE MUROMACHI SHOGUNATE

The coming of the Muromachi Bakufu to Kyoto in 1336 signaled changes for the city, and although guilds continued to function, the shogunate's claims on commerce had a profound effect on Kyoto's merchants, particularly the moneylenders. Forty percent of all Muromachi Bakufu laws pertain to moneylending, a good indication of both the importance of credit in the monetized economy of Kyoto and the extent to which the shogun realized that and took advantage of it. Indeed, the Muromachi shogunate's keen interest in commerce, and especially in the money-lenders, was in contrast to the Kamakura shogunate's general noninvolvement in the monetized economy of the late thirteenth and early fourteenth centuries, on the one hand, and the Tokugawa shogunate's relative aloofness from urban commerce, on the other.[75] By the early fifteenth century the Muromachi shogunate had become an active overlord of commerce in Kyoto.

Considering its limited control over the rest of Japan, the Muromachi shogunate's active interest in commerce, especially the moneylenders, may seem in hindsight only logical; at the time it was a venture into territory unknown to warriors. The shogunate may have specifically decided to follow the example of the imperial court, including policies of Emperor Godaigo, in taxing commerce. It is more likely that the example of many traditional overlords, including the court and temples, taxing commercial groups in Kyoto seemed a good one to follow. At any rate, from the end of the fourteenth century the shogunate began to tax the moneylenders formally. This coincided with the conclusion of the north–south court conflict and with the regime of the third shogun, Yoshimitsu, who significantly expanded the authority of the shogunate. From then on the Bakufu could concentrate on consolidating its powers and extending its reach to embrace aspects of commerce, especially moneylending.

A range of Kyoto merchants was eventually taxed by the shogunate. Of these, the moneylenders were the single most important group, and their numbers expanded somewhat over the years to include newcomers to the trade not in the original Enryakuji group. Other prominent merchants and craftsmen paid shogunal taxes as well. The bean paste (*miso*) guild, whose members also dealt in moneylending, was a source of income for the shogunate.[76] Control of the rice guild came under the overlordship of members of the Board of Retainers, as it absorbed various functions and prerogatives of the imperial court.[77] The same was true of the swordsmiths' and fan makers' guilds.[78] (Both fans and swords were important items of export in the trade with China, and for that reason the shogunate singled out those guilds as its own.)[79] Swordsmiths, fan makers, and silversmiths, along with the oil merchants of Ōyamazaki and the Kitano malt producers, may even have welcomed shogunal overlordship to protect and extend their monopoly rights as the market expanded and demand increased. In addition, shogunal overlordship could sometimes give a guild an advantage in litigation.[80] In the area of commerce, at least, it is appropriate to characterize the shogunate as a successful late medieval overlord.

The Muromachi shogunate did not set its sights on commerce immediately, however. Its takeover of Kyoto may be divided into four stages: military conquest; the imposition of order through routine policing of the city; the establishment of judicial authority; and, finally, taxation of the commercial sector for shogunal income.[81] Absorbing the functions of the

Bureau of Capital Police was vital to the success of the first two stages and may have facilitated the fourth stage to some extent, for Bureau members had long-standing ties as small-scale overlords to some commercial groups. Until the dispute between the northern and southern court factions and their warrior surrogates was resolved in 1392, the Bureau of Capital Police continued to exist, if with increasing tightening of shogunal controls.

Secure administration of Kyoto also entailed oversight of the seven roads leading into the city.[82] Originally established by the imperial court for military purposes, toll stations on these roads became a source of income for aristocrat-officials in various bureaus of the civil government, eventually evolving into private sinecures of their descendants.[83] In Muromachi times these were four: the Yamashina, Mibu, Higashibōjō, and Kikutei families.[84] The new shogunate as city administrator allowed toll income to continue to go to the traditional recipients, but its officials guarded the entrance points to the city and sometimes also built toll stations for their own personal income. (Hino Tomiko, the wife of Shogun Yoshimasa carried this practice to excess in the late fifteenth century when her toll stations at the seven routes into the city brought her a large income.) Temples and shrines also erected these stations when they needed an infusion of cash. If allowed to get out of hand, the proliferation of these stations could cause the roads leading into Kyoto to become fairly clotted with barriers plaguing commercial traffic.[85] This would eventually cause commerce in the city to stagnate, and the Bakufu, like the imperial court in earlier times, periodically had toll stations dismantled or at least ordered those controlling the stations to stop impeding the flow of traffic by collecting excessive taxes.[86] Nevertheless, late-fifteenth-century toll revenue has been estimated at nearly four times that of the 1330s, providing an easy source of income for elites whose landed income was drying up.[87] Even within the shogunate, individual interests sometimes clashed with administrative policy.

The shogunate's first concern regarding the moneylenders was not to tax them but to resuscitate them as the backbone of the city's economy after the unrest of the 1330s. Article six of the *Kenmu Shikimoku*, the legal code of the Muromachi Bakufu, called for the revival of the moneylenders, many of whom had been forced out of business during the fighting.[88] Promulgated in the hope of encouraging a return to normalcy in the city, this measure was also an early indication of what would become a general shogunal policy of encouraging commerce. Interest in the moneylenders as a source of revenue was yet to come.

As city life stabilized and the economy revived, the shogunate next ventured into the area of regulating moneylending practices. In 1346 it condemned "unjustified parties" who were swindling loan contracts from their rightful owners and intimidating debtors with them.[89] (Judging from the large number of shogunal attempts to regulate moneylending, such extreme practices by lenders apparently swung in and out of control.) The shogun's Board of Administration was to see that this activity ceased, according to the decree, indicating either a new policy or some previous involvement by that organ in the regulation of the moneylenders.

The Muromachi shogunate did not claim for itself the limited areas of commerce that were traditionally the preserve of the imperial court. The Distillery Office of the imperial court remained in the hands of the aristocratic Nakahara family as a hereditary sinecure. This arrangement was confirmed as a sales tax on malt during the 1360s and was collected regularly, usually with shogunal acquiescence.[90] In 1368 the court informed Shogun Yoshimitsu and Enryakuji that the Nakahara family had permission to collect this tax broadly, from "*jinin* of Kasuga Shrine living in Kyoto" and "*jinin* of Hie Shrine."[91] The shogunate occasionally showed a lack of regard for this arrangement, however: in spite of strenuous protests from the Nakahara, Shogun Yoshimitsu ruled in 1387 that Kitano Shrine could claim from its small group of malt-producing brewers the tax that had previously gone to the Distillery Office.[92] In 1393, on the other hand, the Muromachi shogunate confirmed and thus stabilized the now modest Distillery Office tax on the brewer-lenders as a whole.[93]

Ashikaga Yoshiakira, later to become the second shogun, set a precedent for shogunal taxation of the moneylenders by levying an irregular tax for special purposes on them in 1352.[94] On a wartime footing, as the fighting in the continuing rivalry between the northern and southern court factions temporarily intensified, the shogunate was no doubt eager for additional revenue. Until nearly the end of the century, however, taxes were levied on moneylenders only on an arbitrary, ad hoc basis. Still, Yoshiakira's tax was an important precedent. In 1356 and again in 1380 the shogunate, through the imperial court, granted a tax exemption to a group of moneylenders.[95] The very fact that the moneylenders were seeking exemptions suggests that the shogunate was levying some taxes on them, or perhaps exacting forced loans from them.[96] In 1371 the shogunate taxed the moneylenders substantially for expenses surrounding the succession ceremony of Emperor Goen'yū.[97] Brewers each paid 200 *mon* in cash, while moneylenders were charged the large sum of 30 *kan* per storehouse. The moneylenders could expect such incidental levies on occasion, especially for imperial ceremonies, but for the shogunate to be the entity actually levying the tax was another important precedent.

As it began to show an interest in the moneylenders as a source of income, the shogunate also challenged Enryakuji's high-handed habit of interfering in Kyoto life on behalf of its moneylenders. In 1370, the Bakufu in its capacity as city police denied Enryakuji's right to deal with tardy debtors on its own and ordered Enryakuji's agents to stop harassing the inhabitants of Kyoto.[98] The shogunate decried the fact that the abbot of Enryakuji had simply ignored the emperor's previous admonitions and warned that continuing violence would be considered an imperial offense, with perpetrators to be arrested and punished by the shogunate. (This incident simultaneously calls attention to the new role of the Muromachi Bakufu as imperial protector, in effect, and to the weakness of the emperor vis-à-vis Enryakuji, whose abbot had treated the emperor with contempt by ignoring him.) Whether the shogunate enforced this decree is unclear, but it represented a claim, on paper at least, to police jurisdiction over Kyoto—that is, the responsibility to quell violence in the city, formerly a domain of the court.

Again in 1386 the shogunate prohibited Enryakuji's marauding agents from seizing and confiscating Kyoto homes and persons (in arrears), and specified the Bakufu's judicial system as the only legitimate channel for such grievances.[99] "Committing violence in Kyoto where there are many people" is cited as particularly heinous. Any shrine priests—probably of Hie, Gion, or Kitano—involved in the disruption were threatened with arrest and imprisonment, and were warned that their case against tardy debtors would be dismissed if they resorted to violence while it was pending. In its early years, then, the Muromachi Bakufu went on record as being firmly opposed to violent means of settling disputes and, even more importantly in the long run, claimed to be the city's judicial authority.

As in other areas of shogunal administration, however, enforcement and compliance should not automatically be assumed to have followed on the heels of decrees. On the contrary, the very frequency of shogunal attempts to control Enryakuji's agents may well be an indication of the difficulty in bringing them to heel. Furthermore, it is important to note that in neither decree was the shogunate attempting to infringe on Enryakuji's authority to tax the moneylenders but was simply endeavoring to bring peace to the streets of Kyoto.

The shogunate's relationship with Enryakuji was not, moreover, wholly adversarial. The Bakufu appears to have lent support when Enryakuji's institutions needed it. In 1372 the Bakufu levied a provincial tax (tansen) to rebuild Hie Shrine's portable shrine, and imperial lands were not exempted from the tax.[100] A similar measure in 1379 raised funds to re-build the portable shrines of Hie, Gion, and Kitano, all major entities in the Enryakuji network.[101] Not only are these measures persuasive proof of the shogunate's ability to tax broadly for nonwarrior purposes, but they also hint that Enryakuji's institutions in Kyoto were taken very seriously as part of the ruling order.

Five laws issued in 1393 mark a watershed in shogunal policy toward commerce in Kyoto. They are of great importance and deserve careful scrutiny because they express the intention of the third shogun, Yoshi-mitsu, to derive revenues on a systematic basis from commerce, in par-ticular from the moneylenders. Translated below, the laws have been variously interpreted as epochal in their denial of Enryakuji's right to tax the moneylenders or as simply a successful attempt by the shogunate to establish itself as a regular taxing authority by taking a portion of the moneylender's wealth without denying Enryakuji its share.[102] In any case, they heralded a fundamental change in the moneylenders' lives, both as taxpayers and as townspeople.

Laws regarding Moneylenders and *Sake* Brewers in and around Kyoto

ITEM: Functionaries of temples and shrines and those in service to an over-lord shall lose their special privileges [tax exemptions] and will be taxed as are others.

ITEM: Those who on some pretext go against this law (e.g., do not submit the tax) will be dealt with in accordance with the law by the [Bakufu] tax agents. If there is some difficulty, the Bakufu will wait for the agent's report and then instigate arraignment proceedings. Part [of the guilty money-lender's confiscated property or the penalty fee] will be used by the Bakufu, and part will be designated for temple or shrine rebuilding costs.

ITEM: This tax will be 6,000 *kanmon* allocated to cover the annual operating expenses of the Board of Administration. The tax will be collected on a monthly basis, and even if there are emergency [shogunal] expenses, the moneylenders are perpetually exempted from incidental levies by temples, shrines, or the Bakufu.

ITEM: Regarding taxation in the intercalary month: since the total yearly amount is already determined, there will be no additional tax.

ITEM: Regarding the malt tax of the [imperial] Distillery Office: since ancient times this has been an important tax and it will not be affected by this law.

There are to be no transgressions against these articles. It shall be so conveyed. By order [of the shogun], it is so decreed.

Meitoku 4 [1393]/11/6   Saemonnosuke
Minamoto no Ason

[seal of Kanrei Shiba] Yoshimasa[103]

The first item has been interpreted both as a denial by the Bakufu of the right of the traditional religious and aristocratic overlords to tax the moneylenders and as a claim to that right for itself.[104] In fact, however, in this law the shogunate does not deny the overlord's right to regular yearly dues but levies its own tax on the moneylenders. The law does deny special privileges, including tax exemptions and monopolies that the moneylenders had enjoyed as clients of Enryakuji. If enforced it would have eliminated a major advantage of having an overlord, diluting the "service" aspect of the moneylenders' guild and thus unwittingly forcing them to operate more autonomously.[105] The shogunate's assertion of the prerogative to tax, on the other hand, may have stifled any tendencies toward autonomy.[106] The law does not deny the original overlord's right to regular yearly dues, but simply levies its own additional tax on the moneylenders.

The second item details shogunal policy toward moneylenders who refuse to submit their taxes to the Bakufu. The shogun's tax agents, a group of powerful moneylenders—or if they fail, the shogunate itself—will confiscate their property or will charge them a penalty. This law also designates temples and shrines as beneficiaries, along with the shogunate, of confiscated property or penalty fees—perhaps a concession by the shogun to Enryakuji and its branch shrines.

Item three fixes the amount of the shogun's annual tax on the moneylenders and states its purpose—to pay for the operation of the Board of Administration. It also prohibits the levying of additional, incidental taxes on the moneylenders by temples, shrines, or Bakufu. The latter part of this law complemented Article One's denial of special privileges to the traditional overlords. If it had been strictly enforced, it would have brought welcome relief to the moneylenders who were taxed frequently. As we shall see, however, the moneylenders continued to be victims of capricious taxation, and the shogunate itself was a major culprit. In 1447, to take an extreme example, the moneylenders were taxed as often as eight and nine times a month.[107]

Item four is self-evident: the 6,000 *kanmon* yearly tax was not to be increased by sneaking in an extra tax during the intercalary month. In other words, the total annual amount was to be the same, regardless of the number of months in the year.

The final item protects the traditional right of the Distillery Office to tax the moneylenders, showing shogunal accommodation to this minor aristocratic sinecure. Collection of this tax became dependent on the shogunate, which first charged the prominent moneylender and brewer Jōsenbō with responsibility for collecting it, and in the fifteenth century shifted the process to another lender, Kawamura Shinjirō. Both were tax agents for the shogunate; control of the tax was thus firmly in the Bakufu's pocket until the early sixteenth century.[108] Rights to income from the office were then split between two aristocratic families, the Hirohashi family receiving the "court's portion" (chōyōbun) while the other half remained with the Nakahara.[109] Thus the traditional recipient, the Nakahara family, was eventually forced to share its income. Although the shogun preserved the Distillery Office tax on the brewer-lenders, he interfered quite substantially by dictating its method of collection and distribution.

These laws were once understood to mean that the shogunate effectively wrested the right to tax the moneylenders away from their overlord, Enryakuji. But this view has been displaced by the realization that the 1393 law established a shogunal tax on the moneylenders in addition to that of the overlord.[110] It was not in the shogun's interest to deprive other overlords of income completely, but only to garner some portion of it for itself. The Bakufu, a new—albeit powerful—member of the multisided ruling order in Kyoto, was dependent on the same techniques for the acquisition of commercial revenue as were other overlords. To usurp all such income would have required military and political resources the Muromachi shogunate did not have and, more important, a monolithic authority that did not exist in the medieval period. Accommodation and compromise would achieve the same ends without the risks inherent in a policy of confrontation. The authority of the other elites was limited but not usurped by this law.

The moneylenders for their part probably saw these laws as making permanent yet another tax. By encroaching on the moneylenders' relationship with Enryakuji, the shogunate arguably aided their self-sufficiency in the long run, but to the moneylenders in 1393 the Bakufu's denial of their special privileges was probably seen as a mixed blessing, at best. The shogun had become another overlord to them, nominally protecting them from such abuses as arbitrary taxation in return for monthly taxes. They were addressed by the shogunate collectively as the "association of moneylenders" (dosōkata isshū) or as the "brewer-lenders" (sakaya dosō), and the solidarity this implied could prove useful in dealings with the overlord.[111]

The mechanism for collecting the shogunal tax incorporated the most prominent of the moneylenders into the shogunate itself as tax agents. These agents already enjoyed prominence among the moneylenders, having had prior experience performing the same function for Enryakuji and other elites. It is, furthermore, quite probable that the shogunate was already in the habit of using these powerful moneylenders for its own ad hoc taxation efforts in Kyoto. In the eyes of the townspeople, the incorporation of these elite moneylenders into the shogunal structure further enhanced their prestige as members, however lowly, of the shogunate itself. A fundamental structural change in the status of the leading moneylenders occurred as they were absorbed into the Bakufu, in turn enhancing their standing as leading townspeople. In this sense the shogun was an important but unwitting agent of social change in the late medieval transformation of the moneylenders. This was significant to their medieval experience, both because of the increased prestige this affiliation gave them in the eyes of the townspeople and because their behavior within this mechanism is among the strongest evidence of their growing autonomy as townspeople.

The wealthier moneylenders had long experience as storehouse keepers (*mikura*) for aristocrats and the imperial court. During times of unrest and famine in the early medieval period, aristocrats entrusted valuables to merchants with storehouses, usually moneylenders, and to temples that also had storehouses. The Muromachi shogunate, as it did in other areas of urban administration, adapted an existing mechanism to its own purposes, employing leading moneylenders as its financial agents (*kubō mikura*, the shogun's storehouse keepers) probably about the same time that it began to collect urban taxes in the late fourteenth century.[112] In a process I shall describe later, these agents performed a variety of services for the shogun, and some of them became tax agents who collected from other merchants, including moneylenders. The shogunate also seems to have used the moneylenders as its agents to tie up loose ends in lawsuits involving collection of debts.[113] The Muromachi shogunate used another existing mechanism, the Enryakuji lenders' guild-like council (*dosō yoriaishū*), as the model for its own *dosōkata isshū*, or association of moneylenders.

The laws of 1393 stipulated that taxes in the aggregate annual amount of 6,000 *kanmon* be collected from the moneylenders. If evenly applied, each moneylender would have paid on average about 17 *kanmon* per year, collected on a monthly basis. In fact, however, they were assessed an amount based on the size of the individual establishment; in addition the available evidence indicates that the total amount collected annually varied over time. (The discussion below closely analyzes taxation.) In principle, brewers were charged 100 *mon* per cask, whereas moneylenders paid by the size of their storehouses, following the imperial court's practice.[114] In 1496, for instance, a moneylender in upper Kyoto was charged one *kan* as brewery tax and 200 *mon* as moneylender tax.[115] Yanagiya, the foremost brewer of Kyoto, alone submitted 60 *kanmon* to the Bakufu per month. In return for such high taxes, the Muromachi shogunate protected the Kyoto brewers' monopoly by forbidding the sale of non-Kyoto *sake* in the city.[116] Enryakuji, the original overlord, had guaranteed this very monopoly from the thirteenth century. The shogunate's additional guarantee reinforced the first, and the monopoly held until the early sixteenth century when the Muromachi Bakufu's authority eroded. At that point, the production and sale of *sake* began to take place at separate locations, and Kyoto retailers began to sell *sake* made in the provinces, threatening the monopolistic control of the local *sake* industry.[117] Neither Enryakuji nor the shogunate would be able to prevent this.

At any given time, a dozen or so of the wealthiest Kyoto moneylenders were employed as shogunal tax agents to collect from moneylenders and other commercial groups in Kyoto.[118] They served under the jurisdiction of the deputy head of the Board of Administration, that is to say, the Ninagawa family, for most of the Muromachi period. Appointees to their ranks were originally taken from the *kubō mikura*, the shogun's storehouse keepers. But in time, because the position of tax agent was so lucrative, in effect *kubō mikura* status became a sort of portal to the ranks of the tax agents as well. The functions of the two groups were generally distinct, though not without overlap. The storehouse keepers were financial agents in a comprehensive sense: they administered the shogun's property and handled receipts and disbursements.[119] Specifically, this included custody, storage, and disbursement of taxes from the Kyoto moneylenders, special levies on houses (*munabechisen*) in Kyoto to finance palace reconstruction, and storage of litigation documents and various items submitted to the shogun. The secular Momii family dominated this group until at least 1487, when their name disappears from sources. Others in the ranks of storehouse keepers included Shōjitsubō, who was also a tax agent, Jōsenbō, Jōkōbō, Zenjūbō, and, after the Ōnin War, Gyokusenbō. From the names of these lenders, it is clear that lenders with *santo* rank at Enryakuji dominated until the early sixteenth century.[120]

Shogunal tax agents, on the other hand, numbering from fewer than ten to as many as twenty at any given time, were responsible for the actual collection of taxes from townspeople who lent money, including storehouse keepers, *sake* brewers, bean paste merchants, and day lenders.[121] Collection took place monthly, with tax agents making their rounds on the second, fifteenth, and twenty-eighth days.[122] Their official commission was 10 percent of the total tax collected.[123] Confiscation of moneylender property, presumably in cases of nonpayment of taxes, was also the job of this group.[124] A shogunal law forbidding the use of violence in tax collection suggests indirectly that recalcitrant taxpayers could be roughed up by tax agents.[125] Another very important privilege enjoyed by tax agents was exemption from the taxes they themselves collected.[126]

Over time both secular and clerical names are found among the tax agents, although clerics dominated in the early decades: the Sawamura, Nakanishi, Yasui, and Kawamura were among the lay members, while Shōjitsubō, Jōsenbō, and Jōkōbō were among the clerics.[127] The ranks of the tax agents gradually included more laypeople, some of whom had not come up through the shogunal storehouse-keeper ranks. Since tax agents were only required to submit a designated amount of taxes to the shogunate, keeping a commission for themselves, appointment to their ranks was a coveted privilege, bringing with it a large increase in real income. The shogunate only intervened in tax collection matters to discipline moneylenders who refused to submit their tax or to protest imperial or religious incidental levies, the latter with limited success, as such levies were frequent and continued into the sixteenth century.

Although documentation of both the storehouse keepers and the tax agents is fragmentary, one is left with the impression that the scope of their functions was truly broad. Records of collection and disbursement contain brief items referring to amounts collected, names and addresses of Kyoto's moneylenders, disbursement of cash to an aristocrat in lieu of an item of clothing, an abandoned house (presumably regarding its disposal), a special impost for the shogun's palanquin, and so on.[128] Although sketchy, cumulatively they give the impression that the moneylenders who held tax agent or financial agent positions had a formidable grip on the day-to-day functioning of the shogun's financial affairs.

The attractiveness of a tax agent appointment should be obvious. Poised advantageously between shogunate and townspeople, basking in the shogun's aura of power, responsible to no one, and exempt from taxes themselves while claiming a portion of what they collected, shogunal tax agents were among the most privileged of townspeople.[129] Appointed from the ranks of the storehouse keepers, the tax agents as commercial collectors were an extension of that institution. In practice, duties and membership often overlapped. For example, the Momii family, head of the shogunal storehouse keepers from 1455 to 1482, tended to handle goods more than cash, including gifts to the shogun and also taxes submitted directly to the shogunate by the moneylenders. (Most taxes on money-lending were not directly submitted but went through the tax agents.) Shōjitsubō, a Kyoto moneylender and Enryakuji cleric who apparently moved from a *satobō* on the flanks of Mount Hiei into the city in the trend toward secularization among these rank-and-file monks, was in both the tax agent and storehouse-keeper ranks from the mid-fifteenth century, and although he was dropped as a shogunal tax agent in 1465, he was reinstated in 1535 and remained a tax agent until the fall of the Muromachi shogunate. Zenjūbō, likewise a secularized Enryakuji cleric, appears as a shogunal storehouse keeper in the 1430s collecting provincial taxes (*tansen*). Jōsenbō, another clerical moneylender and a storehouse keeper, was ordered by the shogunate in 1472 to collect the tax on money-lenders. In the following year he collected an emergency tax to cover the costs of a shogunal ceremony, an activity in which tax agents were nor-mally not involved. In 1475 he accepted appointment to the ranks of the tax agents, even offering to forgo the usual tax exemption. Jōkōbō, also a shogunal storehouse keeper and an Enryakuji priest, became a tax agent in 1486. Appointment to the ranks of the tax agents meant, of course, a great increase in income, tax exemption or not. Even as they continued to draw on Enryakuji's prestige, not to mention their own real power as wealthy moneylenders, these individuals through their shogunal connec-tion greatly enhanced their position among the townspeople.

The disadvantages, if any, of holding shogunal tax-agent status are unclear. There is no evidence, for example, that they had to make up tax arrears out of their own pockets; they could simply claim the money had not been there to collect. (Their cut gave them ample incentive to get the money, of course.) The only note of discord in their relationship with the shogunate is that they may have been bypassed on occasion, suggesting distrust on the part of the Bakufu.[130]

The Muromachi shogunate's dependence on wealthy townspeople as an income base and as revenue agents demonstrates not only its ability to adjust to and benefit from a monetized economy but also its medieval character in which established arrangements were adapted to fit local needs.[131] Yun In Bo, the interpreter for the Korean embassy to Japan in 1420, remarked on this situation: "There is no government storehouse in this country; rather, wealthy people support it."[132] This was a practical arrangement insofar as the moneylenders, with their extensive expertise in finance, were best suited to the collection of commercial taxes. In return, however, the shogunate had to settle for less than full control and was dependent on the moneylenders for a variety of services. Given the diffuse nature of medieval authority, such symbiotic arrangements were not unusual.[133] In this regard, one historian has wisely cautioned against bringing to any discussion of shogunal finances the assumption, even unconscious, that the Muromachi Bakufu in any way resembled a modern state.[134] He characterizes the relationship between the Kyoto moneylenders and the Muromachi shogunate both as inevitable, given the moneylenders' skills and wealth so needed by the shogun, and as ad hoc in character. The tax agent-moneylenders maintained a loose, autonomous relationship with the shogunate, and although nominally members of the Board of Administration, were in fact only peripherally so. It is more accurate to see them as townspeople who collected shogunal taxes among other activities than as busy bureaucrats in a honeycomb of government.

The moneylenders, then, were of some significance to the Muromachi shogunate. If the 1393 law was indeed enforced, then the annual income generated from them was considerable. The large portion of Bakufu laws concern moneylending is another strong indication of their importance to the shogun. There is also anecdotal evidence that the moneylenders were considered such treasures that they could expect velvet-glove treatment from the shogun, even in outrageous contexts. On the night of the thirteenth day of the eleventh month of 1476, for instance, the shogun's palace burned down.[135] The Bakufu ruled it to be not arson but an accident, and a moneylender named Baba Yoshirō living next door was found responsible, for the fire had spread from his premises. Accident or not, this would normally have been a very serious offense against the shogun himself, punishable by confiscation of property and banishment. (The latter included being prohibited from doing business in Kyoto.) The shogunate in fact handed this very punishment to Baba but at the same time suspended it, stating that if Baba, described as "a crucial source of income," would pay a substantial cash fine (300 kanmon—an amount approximating the annual taxes of the larger moneylenders), the shogun would let bygones be bygones and Baba could continue in business as a moneylender. Compared to what might have happened to him, Baba got away with a slap on the wrist.

Less outrageously, the shogunate would protect moneylenders faced with disastrous circumstances, presumably to enable them to stay in business as a source of tax income. The Bakufu's first debt amnesty of 1428 protected the moneylenders to the extent of stipulating that an amnesty did not mean that the debtors could attack moneylenders and seize collateral.[136] In the eighth month of 1494, a moneylender's (supposedly fireproof) storehouse was burned, possibly in connection with large-scale ongoing peasant uprisings demanding debt amnesties in the adjacent Yamashiro province. In response, the Muromachi shogunate issued an edict prohibiting the removal of collateral from lenders' premises.[137] (Looters would be looking for pawned items as well as receipt ledgers.)

As will be shown, even after the shogunate began to tax moneylenders regularly, Enryakuji continued to receive income from them.[138] There is some evidence that in claiming the right to tax the lenders the Muromachi shogunate weakened Enryakuji's power to tax, which never again approached that of its heyday, the thirteenth century. For instance, in 1394, the year after the promulgation of the Bakufu moneylending laws, Enryakuji appeared unable to tax its Kyoto moneylenders for the cost of Shogun Yoshimitsu's pilgrimage to Hie Shrine. Instead, it forced its Sakamoto moneylenders and other client groups like packhorse drivers to bear the brunt of the tax, while asking only for illustrated screens from twelve Enryakuji clerics living in Kyoto, at least two of whom were shogunal tax agents.[139] Although Enryakuji could not be counted out, its position in Kyoto had been undercut by the shogunate. The result was, if anything, a more intricate authority structure in Kyoto: from the commoners' viewpoint, *kenmon* rule by multiple elites was more evident than ever. The moneylenders devised ways to benefit from it.

Chapter Three

Transcending Subordination

AT THE END OF THE FOURTEENTH CENTURY the moneylenders occupied a position fraught with complexity as well as potential. At this point they were indeed victims of multiple taxation—Enryakuji, the imperial court, and the shogunate were each getting a piece of their profits. At the same time, however, they were merchants of great worth: not only did they provide credit, but their business acumen produced revenues for several overlords and their leading members' management skills were sought after as well. They parlayed their usefulness into a relationship of interdependence with the overlords that the latter could not upset without harming themselves. To put it more bluntly, exploitation characterized both sides of the relationship in the decades to come: multiple taxation was met with tax avoidance; incidental levies were imposed to fill the void but were offset by exemptions in return for bribes; monopolies were unenforced; and guild rules were flaunted. This state of affairs evolved gradually over the fifteenth and early sixteenth centuries, enhancing the moneylenders' prestige as leading townspeople who were indispensable to the elites.

SHOGUNAL PATTERNS OF TAXATION
AND THE DECLINING ABILITY TO COLLECT

The shogunal laws of 1393 made provision for the collection of 6,000 *kanmon* annually from the moneylenders to be used to cover the operating expenses of the shogun's Board of Administration. Some historians have concluded automatically from this decree that the shogunate added this amount from the moneylenders to its coffers each year, but this is no more than an assumption. It is more strictly correct to conclude only that in 1393, at least, it was the intention of the Muromachi Bakufu to extract this amount from the moneylenders. Beyond that, other sources must be analyzed to determine real levels of revenue received, and this can only be done imperfectly because of an imperfect record. Nevertheless, it is worth making an attempt, for the result may shed light on a number of issues: the relative importance of Kyoto to Bakufu finances; the actual level of shogunal control over the city; and, finally, from the point of view of the city's commoners, whether the moneylenders were indeed successfully coerced on an annual basis and over an extended period of time to pay a large, new tax. If the latter can be proven, then it would indicate that the shogunate made a successful intrusion into a still-thriving overlord system. If not, then shogunal control of commercial groups in Kyoto will be proven to have been more limited than is usually assumed.

The analysis that follows is heavily dependent on the records of the Ninagawa family. As vassal of the Ise family, the Ninagawa held the hereditary position of deputy head of the Board of Administration (*mandokorodai*), while the Ise was its actual head (*shitsuji*).[1] The deputy head tended to handle day-to-day affairs as the Ise's representative; thus the Ninagawa collection is useful as a record of the actual administration and execution of decrees rather than merely as statements of policy or intent. Furthermore, after the Ōnin War, the Board of Administration was the most vital Bakufu office—indeed, it was the only one that retained any real function and authority over time; hence the Ninagawa collection touches on a great range of shogunal matters.[2]

The Ninagawa records on the moneylender tax are a combination of amounts received and disbursements over a period of ninety-eight years, 1441–1539. (See Table 1 for a summary of the documents discussed here.) Amounts received are more relevant to this analysis, but disbursement records at least give an indication of minimal levels of tax income, if not necessarily of total amounts available to disburse.[3] Starting with the Muromachi shogunate's 1393 annual target of 6,000 *kanmon* from the moneylenders, the record yields nothing specific on collection of the tax for nearly fifty years.[4] Two factors may account for this gap: the haphazard survival rate of medieval documents and the uneven nature of shogunal record keeping. In the eleventh month of 1441, a tax on 327 brewers is recorded to have yielded 880 *kan*, 600 *mon*.[5] Because the latter half of this document lists the disbursement of these funds over a period of three months, the tax itself may be interpreted as being for a three-month period, or roughly one-fourth of the annual tax. If the annual tax were

TABLE 1. GROSS ESTIMATE OF MUROMACHI BAKUFU TAX REVENUES FROM THE KYOTO MONEYLENDERS

1393	Bakufu law decrees 6,000 *kanmon* as yearly target sum of moneylender tax
1441	327 moneylenders submit 880 *kan,* 600 *mon* as one-fourth of yearly brewery tax
	Estimated annual income: 3,532 *kanmon* + (unrecorded) storehouse tax = 6,000 *kanmon*
1475	41 *kanmon* collected in one month by one member of *nōsenkata* from commercial groups in Upper Kyoto
	Estimated annual income: maximum 2,000 *kanmon*
1495–1496?	78 *kan,* 300 *mon* to be collected from 57 moneylenders annually
	Estimated annual income *targeted* by Bakufu (assuming these were actually collected and that 57 people represent as much as one-half the moneylenders in post-Ōnin Kyoto), maximum 2,000–3,000 *kanmon;* minimum less than 1,000 *kanmon*
1505	30 *kan,* 200 *mon* of *nōsenkata* receipts disbursed in one month
	Estimated annual income: maximum 2,000 *kanmon*
1509	15 *kan,* 100 *mon* brewery tax collected in one month from Upper and Lower Kyoto
	Estimated annual income (assuming approximately equal amount of storehouse tax): minimum 360 *kanmon*
1539	20 individuals from Upper and Lower Kyoto pledge to submit 7 *kanmon* each month as brewery and storehouse tax
	Estimated annual income (if pledge was adhered to): maximum 1,680 *kanmon*

NOTE: The intercalary or thirteenth-month portion has not been included in any of these calculations because the 1393 Bakufu law regarding the tax on moneylenders states that such a portion will not be added to the total annual tax.

indeed about four times this amount (a hazardous assumption, perhaps), then that year's tax would have been about 3,532 *kanmon*. But this only takes into account part of the Bakufu's tax on the moneylenders that took two forms: a brewer tax (*sakaya yaku*) as well as a storehouse tax (*dosō yaku*). There is no record of the storehouse tax for 1441, and it is commonly assumed that the debt amnesty of that year brought ruin to many moneylenders.[6] The 327 brewers listed may have been the remaining active lenders when the tax was collected. Thus the storehouse tax for that year was probably lower than the brewer tax, and total shogunal income from the moneylenders was less than the original annual goal of 6,000 *kanmon*. The document also mentions that, of the 327 brewers, 25 are newly added to the list. New businesses were only required to pay half the tax for a period of six months, and this may have kept the collection for 1441 lower than normal.[7] Furthermore, 1441 was not only a year of great turmoil but came immediately after a major famine. Following this slender thread of logic dangling precariously from a sliver of evidence, then, it would appear that, in 1441 at least, the shogunate was collecting from the moneylenders a large amount in brewer taxes and somewhat less in storehouse taxes, totaling a considerable sum, but likely less than 6,000 *kanmon*. Even so, by this measure the Muromachi Bakufu was a powerful and effective overlord in matters of taxation.[8]

The next record of moneylender tax collection is dated the first month of 1475, toward the end of the Ōnin War.[9] This document records only the amount of 41 *kanmon* collected by a single tax agent, the power-ful moneylender Jōsenbō, and the balance of the document concerns dis-bursements. Supporting evidence is offered by a document with the same date recording the same amount collected by Jōsenbō.[10] It also includes a list of disbursements, proving that at least that amount was collected and submitted to the shogunate. Both documents note that Jōsenbō's area of collection for this amount included three neighborhoods in upper Kyoto (Kamigyō, including Tōgamae, Nishijin, and Shimojin). What fraction of the Kyoto moneylenders this comprised is not clear, but given their heavy concentration in lower Kyoto (Shimogyō), Jōsenbō's clientele were prob-ably well under half the total. Another problem with these sources is that the tax itself is only labeled "amount levied," without specifying if it was a storehouse tax, a brewer tax, or the two combined. It is also quite pos-sible, given the neighborhood notation on both, that this is simply what Jōsenbō as tax agent collected that month from merchants in that area. They would be moneylenders for the most part, but could also include some other commercial groups taxed by the shogunate.[11]

At the very least, these references indicate that the shogun was con-tinuing to derive some income from the moneylenders. But even assum-ing that Jōsenbō's collection represented one-fourth of the shogunate's total monthly income from them, the total annual revenues from all the city's moneylenders would have come to less than 2,000 *kanmon*. One therefore can hazard a guess that the Bakufu's income from the Kyoto moneylenders had declined significantly since 1441. An obvious reason would be that the year in question, 1475, was near the end of the Ōnin War during which large sections of Kyoto had burned, if mostly in the early years of the war, driving out all but the hardiest moneylenders and destroying the city's economy. (The neighborhoods under Jōsenbō's jurisdiction were likely to have been particularly hard-hit, being the loci of various warrior camps.) A drop in income in this period, therefore, is hardly surprising; the real question is whether it was temporary or part of a long-term trend. Income from the outskirts of the city listed at 26 *kanmon* for the first month of 1475, including nearly eight *kanmon* in special levies, partially offset loss of revenue from the Kyoto money-lenders.[12] During the Ōnin War the premises of many Kyoto moneylenders were destroyed; some fled to the city's outskirts. But if 26 *kanmon* was a representative monthly collection, even revenues collected outside the city would have been too small to offset the shogunate's losses from Kyoto's moneylenders.

Near the end of the fifteenth century, a detailed list of fifty-seven individuals who paid brewer and warehouse taxes was compiled by the shogunate.[13] Apparently used for verification during tax collection, it includes the names and addresses of these merchants, along with notations indicating which tax they were to pay and how much. Presumably the amounts listed are for monthly collections: they total 78 *kan*, 300 *mon*. Given the decline in the number of moneylenders in Kyoto after the Ōnin War, these fifty-seven may have represented a large portion of the total Kyoto moneylending community. Considering the prevalence of tax exemptions in the post-Ōnin era, they may even have comprised a large proportion of the moneylenders who actually paid taxes. It is also well to remember that payment amounts could vary by month. With all these caveats, then, annual moneylender income *targeted* by the Bakufu (this list does not, after all, represent amounts actually collected) totaled 2,000–3,000 *kanmon*, and possibly less.[14] Given the questions raised by this document, little more can be said, but this much is certain: the shogunate, through its tax collectors, had adjusted its tax revenue goal downward. How far downward is unknown, but in post-Ōnin Kyoto we can surmise that the shogunate was unable to achieve its original goal of 6,000 *kanmon* in annual income from the moneylenders.

In 1496 the prominent lay moneylenders Nakamura and Sawamura pledged to the shogunate that they would try to collect 80 *kanmon* in taxes per month, or 960 *kanmon* per year, even while allowing that some merchants were supposedly not paying their taxes.[15] This seems to allude to ineffective efforts by the shogun's long-time tax agents, *santo* of Enrya-kuji for the most part, and suggests an attempt to restart the collection process after many years of decline by turning to secular lenders. The post-Ōnin age was one in which an individual's abilities and know-how could be more effective than the backing of a traditional overlord, and thus an energetic secular lender might gather more taxes than one affiliated with Enryakuji.

The plan did not seem to work, however. In the first month of 1509, 15 *kan*, 100 *mon* of brewer tax was collected from upper and lower Kyoto (6 *kan*, 900 *mon* and 8 *kan*, 200 *mon* respectively).[16] This would suggest an annual figure of about 180 *kanmon* in brewer taxes, another precipitous drop in Bakufu income, if this sum included all the Kyoto moneylenders. It is quite possible that it did not, however, and it may be that this amount represents only one month's brewer tax collected by a single tax agent. Whether and how much storehouse tax was collected is unknown. Given the considerable limitations of this document and in the absence of others, one hesitates to make much of it. By even the most liberal estimate, however, one can only surmise that shogunal income from the Kyoto moneylenders continued to fall far short of its original target of 6,000 *kanmon* and was not recovering from the Ōnin War decline, even though the economy as a whole was. As oblique evidence of this, in the fourth month of 1505, 30 *kan*, 200 *mon* of tax agent receipts were disbursed by the shogunate, an indication that the Bakufu had this amount from Kyoto moneylenders to disburse that month.[17] The proportion of all moneylender tax for the year that this represented is open to speculation, but even if it were merely one-sixth of a month's receipts (assuming that at least six tax agents were active), it is another sign of dwindling income from the moneylenders. Collection remained anemic, even with lay agents in charge.

Other developments indirectly indicate that shogunal income from the moneylenders fell and remained low in the post-Ōnin decades. In 1490 Shogun Yoshitane, citing insufficient income from the moneylenders in the city, declared that a tax would be levied on brewer-lenders outside Kyoto proper, not only in Rakugai but also in the neighboring provinces of Yamashina and Ōmi.[18] Shogunal decrees decried tax evasion and the proliferation of exemptions, strongly suggesting falling income.[19] Demanding that all moneylenders, even those under another overlord, pay taxes, the Bakufu decreed in 1508 that collection would take place by a special shogunal envoy, not a member of the tax-agent corps.[20] (The suggestion that the tax agents were regarded by the shogunate as unreliable is significant—perhaps they tended to grant exemptions too freely.) This decree also implies that some moneylenders were claiming to be under the jurisdiction of other overlords and therefore not liable to the shogunal tax.

Though the shogunate dismissed this as an excuse, the very fact that it was put forth suggests that taxpayers regarded the shogunate as another overlord seeking a share of their income.

It is tempting to attribute any number of late medieval changes to the Ōnin War. The war was surely a major factor in the late-fifteenth-century decline in shogunal revenues from the moneylenders. Also partly as a result of the war, by the early sixteenth century new merchants were coming into the city, threatening the monopolies of the old. (The shogunate made some attempts to tax the new brewer-lenders among them.)[21] Declining shogunal ability to tax the provinces, another product of the war, may have led to a greater dependence on Kyoto.[22] The shogunate's commercial income, however, did not rebound and in fact continued to fall, if the 1509 record is representative. Thus even inside Kyoto, the seat of shogunal government, its taxing authority declined further in the early sixteenth century. To assign all blame for this to a war that had ended over thirty years before is to ignore other factors. After all, the figures above suggest that the Bakufu's income from the moneylenders started to decline before and continued to drop long after the Ōnin War. As early as 1445, for instance, the shogunate, exhorting moneylenders to pay their taxes, pointed out that their number had decreased after a debt amnesty was declared, with very adverse effects on Bakufu income, a point rather unlikely to arouse the lenders' sympathy.[23] (At least some of the "vanishing" moneylenders may have become day lenders to avoid shogunal taxes, according to the same source. Others may have "vanished" temporarily.) Similarly, from 1454 the shogunate imposed conditional debt amnesties as a policy to derive more income from either lenders or debtors yet at the same time a mechanism designed to address the problem of declining normal tax revenues.[24] Fundamental changes in the relationship of commoners to their overlords, to be explored later, were abetted but not initiated by the Ōnin War. With the changes came greater facility by commoners to avoid payment of taxes.

Moving abruptly ahead thirty years to the twelfth month of 1539 (the next period for which relevant documents survive), in acknowledgment of an order from above, twenty individuals, ten each from upper and lower Kyoto, pledged that, "concerning the brewer-moneylender tax in Kyoto," they will unfailingly submit 7 *kan* each to the shogunate every month.[25] Given the specific reference to the tax, the signatories were most likely shogunal tax agents, including some familiar names, whose position as prominent moneylenders allowed them to act as tax collectors for the Bakufu. They state further that both imposts will be submitted equally in the amount of 7 *kan*, except on those individuals with proper documentation proving that they have been granted tax exemptions. All others will duly submit the tax. This source is evidence of a common practice, the exemption, and will be discussed again later in that context. As an indication of the level of Bakufu income from the moneylenders, it supports the theory that moneylender tax income had fallen far below the original goal of 6,000 *kanmon*. Indeed, 1,680 *kanmon* at most was a more likely figure for the annual income, if the levels indicated in this document were attained every month. (As a sensible rule of thumb it is probably best to see Bakufu-imposed tax quotas as a maximum rather than minimum indication of actual income, given the potential for graft on the part of the tax agents themselves and for noncompliance by moneylenders in general.)

As in the mid-1490s, then, the shogunate once again scaled back its expectations of moneylender-derived tax income. (The timing of the 1539 document is also significant: after the destruction of the brief experiment in self-government by the Lotus leagues, discussed below, an overlord is reminding the townspeople that they are, as ever, expected to submit a traditional tax.) This source leaves uncertain the amount actually collected: the twenty signatories may have been required to pledge to raise this amount precisely because they had not been doing so, an attempt at coercion by a shogunate faced with a miserable level of compliance. The gross estimate above of 1,680 *kanmon* annually for 1539 is probably high even as the *goal* of annual shogunal revenue during this period.

Why, one might ask, take such pains to analyze these problem-ridden sources? Because it remains a truism, based on uncritical acceptance of the 1393 Muromachi Bakufu law and unwarranted assumptions about the extent of shogunal might, that the Kyoto moneylenders were a solid financial pillar on which the shogunate leaned until its demise.[26] Implicit in this assumption are two others: first, that the shogunate, in Kyoto at least, had the capacity to extract considerable sums from commercial groups on a regular, long-term basis; and second, that townspeople, like moneylenders, were passive victims of taxation. There are other views of the moneylenders' significance to the shogunate, but they also do not question the amount of the shogunal tax actually collected, weighing instead other forms of taxation and sources of income.[27] In fact, shogunal tax records show very mixed success in taxing the lenders—who were rarely passive.

The preceding analysis of tax records reveals how the 1393 shogunal law was executed. Over a ninety-eight-year period, shogunal income from

the moneylenders was not stable. It apparently continued high, if not necessarily as high as 6,000 *kanmon* annually, until the mid-fifteenth century, and probably was substantial if declining until the Ōnin War. Up to
that point, then, the Muromachi shogunate was a successful commercial
overlord, able to extract formal taxes regularly from the city's moneylenders. During and after the Ōnin War, shogunal tax income from the
moneylenders declined; and in the early sixteenth century it not only
remained low but declined much further, suggesting decreasing numbers
of moneylenders taxed by the shogunate and limited control over even
them. In this the shogunate did not differ much from other overlords.
There were, of course, other sources of shogunal income: land, provincial
taxes for a time, conditional debt amnesties (explained below in the context of peasant uprisings), trade with China, and appointment fees and
forced gifts from Zen monasteries. Also, as with other overlords, there
were individual arrangements for personal income by shogunal officials,
and these surely helped offset the decline in formal, institutional tax
income.

From the moneylenders' perspective, the shogunate was a considerable authority in the capital, whose ability to levy taxes could not be
taken lightly. The shogunate's use of leading moneylenders as a collection mechanism put this tax on the same basis, for the average taxpayer,
as the taxes of Enryakuji and the imperial court: a familiar duty payable
on a regular basis to a well-known moneylender-tax agent. Refusal to pay
would be difficult, as one's professional dealings with the collector extended to common membership in the moneylenders' guildlike organization, and on occasion to a credit relationship when the smaller lender
needed cash. At the same time, however, by his very familiarity the collector was perhaps approachable in ways that a warrior vassal-official of
the shogun would not have been. Some of the irregular adjustments that
collectors would accommodate will be described below; they derived from
the familiarity of the relationship more than from the collector's prestige as shogunal official. When the shogun decreed a debt amnesty, for
example, a fellow lender, however wealthy, could understand its dire consequences better than anyone and realize how burdensome a tax would
be. In addition to these professional concerns, the moneylenders knew the
shogun's tax agents as fellow townspeople whose activities embraced local
governance and protection, cultural pursuits, and business. The collector
therefore had to strike a balance between harsh insistence on payment
and flexibility in order to preserve a close tie of some standing.

This analysis illustrates some of the problems scholars face when

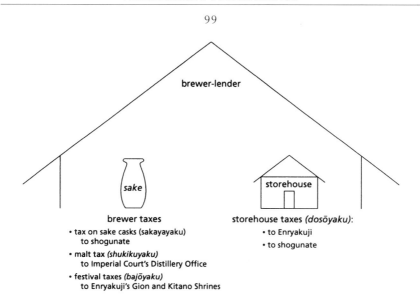

brewer-lender

sake

storehouse

brewer taxes
- tax on sake casks (sakayayaku)
  to shogunate
- malt tax (shukikuyaku)
  to Imperial Court's Distillery Office
- festival taxes (bajōyaku)
  to Enryakuji's Gion and Kitano Shrines

storehouse taxes (dosōyaku):
- to Enryakuji
- to shogunate

Figure 2: Multiple Taxation of the Moneylenders

piecing together the puzzle of medieval Japan, among them documents that raise more questions than they answer, and very few even of them. Nevertheless, although the exact figures of this calculus are questionable, a general trend of decline is clear. The moneylenders were indeed one of several financial pillars of the Muromachi shogunate, if a less reliable one after the Ōnin War. The shogunate's employment of wealthy money-lenders as tax agents may have proved a long-term weakness in this regard: while the use of agents probably facilitated collection of revenues from the moneylenders in the beginning, it also meant that the Bakufu lacked firsthand control of the moneylenders. For their part, the moneylenders were simultaneously serving as financial pillars of other overlords and, through the ingenious use of tax exemptions and bribes, perfecting the art of tax avoidance. Their behavior grew increasingly autonomous, as they became merchants and townspeople first and taxpayers second.

Multiple Overlords

Contrary to the way guild arrangements were intended by the overlord to work, lines of authority began to blur as taxation by multiple overlords increasingly collided in the late medieval period. The moneylenders' behavior in this situation reveals a consciousness of themselves as autonomous entities in a system rife with ambiguity. In other words, not only the shogunate but Enryakuji and its affiliated shrines, as well as the aristocratic recipients of the Distillery Office tax, laid claim to moneylender wealth in the fifteenth and sixteenth centuries. The documentary evidence of this trend is fragmentary, for it was not in the overlord's interest to create a written record celebrating the decline of his world. Taken in sum, however, the sources present persuasive evidence of multiple overlords making demands that the moneylenders often avoided or deflected. Less often are overlords seen providing patronage or protection to their clients, although the relationship did impart some prestige to the clients.

Enryakuji's Durability and Signs of Moneylender Resistance

Before the establishment of the Muromachi Bakufu, most of the Kyoto moneylenders had been under the control of Enryakuji and its subsidiary institutions. In 1393, the Muromachi Bakufu declared itself, in effect, the overlord of the Kyoto moneylenders.[28] But this is not to say that Enryakuji's authority was successfully undermined by the Bakufu either in whole or in part. Nor, indeed, was it in the shogunate's interest, as one of several *kenmon*, to deny Enryakuji its traditional share. On occasion the shogunate even offered its authority to support Enryakuji's claims over commerce. It is true that there are few sources for some time after 1393 attesting to Enryakuji's taxation of moneylenders, but for that matter, as was shown above, until 1441 neither are there any concretely demonstrating shogunal taxation of them. Nobunaga's destruction of Enryakuji in 1571 famously obliterated the monastery's documents, some of which might have shed light on these matters. At any rate, it is difficult to imagine Enryakuji's authority being destroyed at a stroke. Fragmentary evidence scattered here and there in the written record indicates unmistakably that Enryakuji continued on about its business not only in its dealings with the moneylenders but in its numerous other involvements as well.

Although its influence in Kyoto declined after the establishment of the Muromachi shogunate, Enryakuji continued to be a conspicuous force to contend with. Its ongoing squabbles with Kōfukuji (through the latter's Kyoto subsidiary, Kiyomizudera) were played out in the streets of the city throughout the medieval period, regardless of the shogun's presence there.[29] Also significant was Enryakuji's alliance with warriors in 1536 to crush the Lotus leagues, a mass religious movement of Kyoto townspeople, discussed in detail below. Again in 1536, in an armed dispute over doctrine with the Honganji, the headquarters of the True Pure Land movement of Buddhism, Enryakuji received troops as aid from the Rokkaku, *shugo* of Ōmi province, to do battle with Honganji forces in the Higashi-yama area of eastern Kyoto.[30] There were complicated reasons for odd alliances like this, but the lesson here is that Enryakuji remained an active player in the late medieval power structure and one of several active overlords of commerce in Kyoto.

Enryakuji's power could even insinuate itself into shogunal officialdom. There were, for example, shogunal administrators who, in order to supplement their official incomes, became stipended appointees of great religious establishments like Enryakuji responsible for representing their interests within the shogunate.[31] As a result of such conflicts of interest among officials of the shogun, there was a tendency for policy toward large traditional elites like Enryakuji to be rather conservative—that is, to favor them and the existing order. This is one example of how the plural ruling order operated in practice: because of their competing and overlapping interests, the elites tended toward preservation of their order and away from direct confrontation.

Direct confrontation was the stock-in-trade of Shogun Yoshinori, on the other hand, who ruled from 1429 to 1441 and tried to confiscate Enryakuji's lands wherever possible. In 1433 Enryakuji priests took a trip down the mountain bearing the portable shrine, a familiar form of protest, in this case over warrior incursions into the monastery's lands in Ōmi province. The shogunate reacted violently through its vassal, the Rokkaku, military governor of Ōmi, who in 1434 burned down the central hall of Enryakuji, the Konponchūdō, and left twenty-four people dead.[32] (Although he was the most despotic of the Ashikaga shoguns, Yoshinori was nonetheless an unlikely persecutor of Enryakuji: the fourth son of Yoshimitsu, he had taken the tonsure as a young man and risen to the position of head abbot of Enryakuji itself before being chosen shogun in a lottery in 1429.) During the Ōnin War there were some successful warrior incursions into the monastery's lands in Ōmi,[33] and after Ōnin the Rokkaku military governor once more intensified his campaign to dominate Enryakuji's rice bowl—its Ōmi lands.[34]

Even though it was increasingly beleaguered by local warriors, Enryakuji managed to guard its interests somewhat through a system of envoys (*Sanmon shisetsu*).[35] These were priests from the lowest level of the Enryakuji hierarchy, the *santo*, who, as explained earlier, possessed real power, economic and political, within the monastery, and among whom could be found some of the leading moneylenders in this study. Although the shogunate appointed them in order to better control Enryakuji—sending, for instance, all judicial decisions regarding Enryakuji through these envoys

—it can by the same token be argued that the envoy system extended Enryakuji's influence. For example, in a move designed to limit the power of the Rokkaku, military governor of neighboring Ōmi province, the shogunate assigned the envoys responsibility to settle property disputes in Ōmi in the latter half of the fourteenth century. Normally the governor himself would have had such a responsibility; by interposing Enryakuji's envoys into the matter, the shogun not only undercut the Rokkaku but also enhanced Enryakuji's status in a province that it already dominated as estate overlord.[36]

The clerical status of some of the powerful moneylenders appointed shogunal tax agents is another indirect sign that Enryakuji's influence continued to be strong. Some of them, for instance, served as religious attendants at Enryakuji, suggesting that their clerical status was not simply nominal.[37] The relative autonomy of the tax agents within the shogunate may itself be oblique evidence of the Bakufu's deference to their traditional link to Enryakuji.[38] The tax agents do not appear in lists of shogunal officials, suggesting a peripheral status, and it may have been not only their commoner status but also partly Enryakuji's continuing overlordship that distanced them from other shogunal officials. As further oblique evidence of Enryakuji's ongoing influence, the shogun's storehouse keepers, from whom the tax agents were chosen, were expected to finance certain shogunal ceremonies, but in fact did not always do so.[39] Enryakuji's support could have been what emboldened them to withhold their taxes on such occasions. Finally, shogunal denunciations of moneylender excesses in the fifteenth century suggest a certain audacity on the part of these merchants: their tie to Enryakuji may have emboldened them.

There are numerous indirect signs in shogunal sources throughout the Muromachi period that the close relationship between Enryakuji and the moneylenders endured. In 1425 and again in 1430, for example, the shogunate demanded that moneylenders who had been "donating" loans to temples and shrines or getting a third party to do their collecting first obtain permission from the shogun.[40] The reference to "temples and shrines" likely included Enryakuji and its subsidiary institutions, which, as a bloc, constituted the largest religious overlord of the moneylenders. Another indirect reference to Enryakuji is found in a 1433 law regarding moneylender responsibility for pawned items.[41] The shogunate required that any moneylender's overlord who pretended that the moneylender had fled but who was really shielding him would be responsible for paying the debt. The most obvious overlords in such a case would be Enryakuji and the Kyoto Zen monasteries. Similarly, in 1485 and again in 1498 the

Bakufu deplored the nonpayment of taxes by moneylenders, "either with the intention of using their connections or relying on the support of *kenmon seika* (houses of power and authority)," a term that could include Enryakuji.[42]

Again, in the early sixteenth century the shogunate prohibited the arbitrary use of coinage and promised punishment even if the violator was subordinate to a *kenmon*, a term that embraced institutions like Enryakuji.[43] In another significant example, in 1508 the shogunate sent a copy of a decree to Enryakuji envoys admonishing all those in the Kyoto area to obey orders regarding selection of coinage.[44] Also in 1508 the shogunate deplored nonpayment of taxes by brewer-lenders hiding behind great overlords as backing for exemptions.[45] In 1511 *kenmon* were accused of bringing outside *sake* into Kyoto, thus evading shogunal taxes. Enryakuji is not mentioned specifically, but through its subsidiaries it still exercised influence over many brewers; hence one is inclined to believe that the reference is at least in part to Enryakuji.[46] Indirect as they are, none of these references is convincing alone, but in the aggregate they suggest a strong continuing bond between Enryakuji and the moneylenders, a bond that the shogunate was helpless to break and therefore acquiesced in as inevitable.

In addition to these indirect hints at Enryakuji's continuing presence as a commercial overlord, there is also direct evidence of Enryakuji's taxation of the moneylenders, even in the sixteenth century. The first direct shogunal acknowledgment in documents of continuing Enryakuji authority over moneylenders after the 1393 law was in 1419, when the shogunate intervened to protect Kitano Shrine's malt guild.[47] Details of the malt controversy are related below; this shogunal intervention came sixteen years before the first documentary proof of Bakufu taxation of the moneylenders. The link between Kitano, a subsidiary of Enryakuji, and the brewer-lenders in its neighborhood was continuous; this only happens to be the first time the matter appears in extant documents.[48] After lengthy and complicated wrangling, under pressure from Kyoto's brewers supported by one faction at Enryakuji, the shogunate in 1444 abolished the Kitano malt monopoly.[49] Far from ignoring Enryakuji's prerogatives, then, the Bakufu protected them. Here is another instance of elites cooperating and reinforcing each other's interests.

Another indication of continued Enryakuji control of the moneylenders is the case of Kenkei, a moneylender and tax agent of Hie Shrine who came in for criticism by the shrine in 1482 for overdoing the granting of tax exemptions, thus causing shrine income to drop.[50] Hie's concern that exemptions would harm its income is a strong indication that the shrine was as dependent on urban revenues—specifically, from money-lenders—as ever. More direct Enryakuji involvement in commerce can be seen in a 1511 case in which the monastery confronted the shogunate to complain that a moneylender, Tateiri Munetsugu, was avoiding taxes. The Bakufu responded that as an imperial storehouse keeper Tateiri was entitled to an exemption from brewery and storehouse taxes as well as from incidental levies. Enryakuji countered that this case was different because the tax in question was expressly to cover the *kosatsukie* obser-vance at Hie Shrine, its affiliate. In response, the shogunate turned to the palace, which confirmed that indeed Tateiri should not be liable for such a tax.[51] Nothing else on this case survives, but it is probable that the shogunate defended the moneylender's exemption, having had confirma-tion of it from the palace. The exact origins of the Tateiri family are not clear; the name does not appear in earlier lists of Enryakuji-affiliated moneylenders and the scion, Muneyasu, who died in 1515, may have come to Kyoto after the Ōnin War.[52] Nevertheless, Enryakuji's attitude toward him is one of entitlement, suggesting that it was accustomed to ready submission of taxes. Not only that, but in taking this uncooperative case to the Bakufu, Enryakuji seemed to have expected shogunal support for its taxation of moneylenders. The shogunate's response confirms this: rather than a flat denial, the reason for the exemption was given, to which Enryakuji continued to object. The shogun then turned to the imperial palace to confirm Tateiri's status. The case suggests that, in the early six-teenth century, Enryakuji continued to levy both regular and incidental taxes on the moneylenders, with shogunal acquiescence. Even money-lenders with an airtight excuse—an imperial appointment—could find themselves persistently beset by Enryakuji for taxes. The Kenkei and Tateiri cases provide evidence that Enryakuji and its network endured as a commercial overlord in Kyoto.

Substantial taxes continued to be levied on moneylenders in the late medieval period to cover the cost of major annual festivals at both Gion and Hie Shrines, Enryakuji's subsidiaries.[53] In the case of the Hie tax espe-cially, sources reveal a moneylender penchant for resisting taxation on a variety of pretexts. In particular, the taxpayer learned to play to his ad-vantage the demands of multiple overlords, and Hie's income dwindled.

Kyoto moneylenders submitted brewer and storehouse taxes to Hie Shrine, Enryakuji's subsidiary on the opposite side of the mountain, to help defray the cost of the *kosatsukie*, the shrine's major annual spring fes-tival.[54] A group of about one hundred documents pertaining to aspects of this tax cover the period from 1389 until 1509, corresponding to much of the era of shogunal ascendancy in Kyoto.[55] Their content points unambiguously to ongoing Enryakuji taxation of the moneylenders, with shogunal support, for coverage of a major shrine ceremony.

Starting in the tenth century until it was discontinued in the late sixteenth, Hie Shrine held an elaborate annual observance on the third, fourth, and fifth days of the fifth month. The cost of the horses used in this festival was covered by a tax on brewer-lenders, bathhouses, day lenders, and bean-paste merchants in Kyoto and in Sakamoto, the town in which the shrine was located.[56] In addition, brewer-lenders also submitted swords and armor for the festival.[57] Familiar names of Kyoto lenders are found on the tax rosters, and the Enryakuji *santo* lenders Jōsenbō, Gyokusenbō, Shōjitsubō, and Jōkōbō were among the collectors. The names of major lay lenders like Yasui and Sawamura also appear. The method of collection was similar to that of other overlords: prominent lenders acted as tax agents, collecting from a specific group of merchants, and then turned the revenues over to *kunin* agents of Enryakuji, who disbursed them to the shrine.[58] (It will be recalled that Enryakuji and Hie were institutionally almost inseparable in the medieval period.) The tax was not a light one, but the size of the business was taken into account in levying it: lenders were classified as small, medium, or large, the former being the most numerous.[59] Brewer-lenders paid from 1 or 2 up to 10 *kanmon*, the higher figure being closer to the norm. Smaller brewers (*ukezakaya*) that were branches of main ones paid much less—from 500 *mon* to 2 *kanmon*.[60]

Throughout the period covered by these sources, tax avoidance appears to have been an issue. As early as 1389 the shogunate admonished lenders as Hie *jinin* to pay the tax, implying that they were not doing so.[61] Likewise, in 1416 ten clerical lenders under Shōjitsubō signed a pledge promising to adhere to precedent and pay the tax.[62] In 1445 a shogunal official confirmed that a merchant was affiliated with Ōyamazaki and therefore exempt from the Hie tax.[63] A full explication of tax avoidance tactics was provided in 1457 when the shogunate forbade withholding of the festival tax.[64] "Excuses" that would not be accepted included claiming to be *jinin* of other shrines and claiming to run a temporary or branch store of a larger business. (Kasuga Shrine in Nara and Ōyamazaki Shrine southwest of Kyoto were the two alternative overlords, probably because they charged lower taxes than Hie.) Merchants were advised that documentary proof was required of *jinin* status and that branch stores should pay as did main stores. This was an attempt to plug loopholes being exploited by merchants in order to avoid the tax. Numerous later sources are concerned with such claims and with attempts to prove or disprove *jinin* status at another shrine. If documentary evidence was sound, such claims were honored and the festival tax was not levied.[65] On the other hand, some claims were disallowed: Sawamura's claim no longer to be a Hie *jinin* but rather a Ōyamazaki *jinin*, having married into the Yanagi family of brewers, was rejected.[66] Marriage was not grounds for switching affiliation, according to Hie. Another case of a lender asserting affiliation with Ōyamazaki Shrine was examined by Hie Shrine, which took issue with his undocumented claim on the grounds that his father and older brother were both Hie affiliates; why, therefore, would he alone be a *jinin* of another shrine?[67] Moneylending and brewing were family operations, and younger sons sometimes established new businesses, but ties to the main business were usually maintained to the benefit of both sides.

Sometimes successful and sometimes not, claiming another overlord, specifically a non-Kyoto overlord, was a tactic for tax avoidance, according to these sources. This suggests that multiple overlordship extended only so far, and that merchants, like the lenders, could play overlords off against one another quite effectively. The shogun, the imperial court, and Enryakuji and its shrines could all levy taxes on the same merchants, but it was merchants claiming affiliation with Kasuga or Ōyamazaki, shrines outside of Kyoto, who successfully avoided taxation by the major Kyoto overlords. The sources include communications among the taxed merchants and tax agents, on the one hand, and officials of the shogunate, shrine personnel, and various parties at Enryakuji itself, on the other. They provide as good an illustration as there is of the phenomenon of the Kyoto "heavyweights" cooperating to coerce Kyoto merchants to pay them multiple taxes. Perhaps hoping to compensate for taxes not submitted, Hie Shrine attempted to tax merchants new to the city, and the shogunate supported this as well.[68] When merchants could prove an affiliation with major overlords outside of Kyoto, however, they acquiesced.

The Ōnin War provided another opportunity for avoidance of the Hie festival tax. Not only during the war years but for several decades thereafter, the tax proved difficult to collect, with many lenders out of business and in some cases even out of Kyoto altogether.[69] The system of collection itself seems to have broken down, moreover, with the Enryakuji *santo* agents seemingly rendered ineffective. On behalf of the overlord, shogunal officials in 1493 instead turned to prominent secular moneylenders, Sawamura and Nakamura, to accomplish Hie's collecting.[70] (Three years later the shogunate was to turn to these very lenders for the same service for its taxes, as described above. Perhaps the two had some success in the intervening years, enough to raise shogunal hopes about its own revenues.) As will be discussed in the context of the Ōnin War, an individual's own resourcefulness had come to mean more in some cases than the backing of a powerful traditional overlord.

Gion Shrine in Kyoto also levied a tax on the moneylenders for the costs of its summer festival.[71] Perhaps because Gion was in Kyoto itself, unlike Hie, and its summer festival had long been a major annual event for the residents, moneylender support for it does not seem to have declined as much. There is some evidence, however, that individuals tried to avoid the tax on the same pretext as that advanced for the Hie festival tax: by claiming an exemption on the basis of affiliation with another institution.[72] Shogunal acquiescence to Gion's taxation can be inferred from a 1500 reprimand from Bakufu officials to brewer-lenders who were delinquent in their payment of the Gion Shrine festival tax instructing them to pay the shrine immediately.[73] During the Muromachi period, the large sum of 300 *kanmon* was collected for this festival, if not necessarily every year, from a group called the *isshū*, the term used by the shogunate to refer to the group of Kyoto moneylenders it taxed, another indirect indication of shogunal support for this tax.[74] On the other hand, the shogunate may have been partially successful in blocking some taxation by Enryakuji's subordinate shrines: Gion Shrine apparently stopped collecting another tax, the *sechiryō*, originally to cover expenses for food and drink on days marking seasonal change. In 1352, for example, brewer-lenders and other merchants in Kyoto were charged 500 *mon* each per year; there is no record of such a tax again after the 1393 shogunal law claiming taxes from the same people.[75]

Although no longer as robust an institution as it had been in its early medieval heyday, Enryakuji in the late medieval period was still an authority of considerable note. On the one hand, its beleaguered position in Ōmi province gives an unmistakable impression of decline.[76] But in the realm of commerce Enryakuji and its snrines persisted along with the shogunate in taxing commerce. To the Bakufu, Enryakuji's continued taxation of the moneylenders was direct competition for revenue, yet Enryakuji no doubt felt at least as inconvenienced by the shogunate, which had intruded on its traditional domain. In spite of this the shogunate often supported Enryakuji's claims to revenues. By deriving taxes from the same merchants these overlords undermined each other, however, for medieval commoners faced with multiple demands proved adept at evasion, claiming war damage or affiliation with other overlords. From the late fourteenth century at least, Kyoto merchants showed a distinct lack of enthusiasm for the Hie festival tax, in particular, and devised creative ways to avoid it. Total avoidance was not possible, but noncompliance was widespread in spite of shogunal support of Enryakuji's taxing prerogative.

An Aristocratic Overlord

Another of the overlords taxing the moneylenders was the Nakahara family, aristocratic recipients of the Distillery Office tax on malt. The tax went uncollected during the Ōnin War, but otherwise the Muromachi shogunate controlled it through its tax agents, along with the regular tax on brewers, parceling it out to the Nakahara after it was collected.[77] Starting in the late fifteenth century the family, which had changed its name to the Oshikōji, made a bid to reacquire the right to the tax. They pleaded financial straits as a result of dwindling tax income in recent years, implying that they could do a better job of collecting it than the shogun's tax agents. The rationale behind this argument is not clear, and there is little corroborative material, these being years sparsely covered in diaries and chronicles. One of the main shogunal tax agents, the moneylender Sawamura, may have been knocked out of the picture at this point, having had his house in the center of the city occupied by Ōuchi Yoshioki, warrior boss of Kyoto for ten years starting in 1508; this may explain the decline in revenues collected. At any rate, the Oshikōji insisted on being allowed to keep any surplus beyond what the court actually used for entertainments, and on a complete separation of the Distillery Office tax from the shogunal tax on the brewers. Shogunal approval seems to have been obtained, and the Oshikōji began to collect the tax in 1511, hiring local brewers as tax agents, with one Hayata Kamematsu as overseer.[78] In 1513 modest taxes averaging 65 *mon* per brewer were collected from 122 enterprises; the number rose to 138 brewers taxed 55 *mon* on average in 1515, which suggests growing success in reaching the city's brewers.[79] The small amounts collected were offset by the large number of brewers taxed, most of whom were probably small enterprises. In attempting to tax many of the city's brewers lightly, the Oshikōji may have had a better chance of compliance and a smaller chance of clashing with the shogunate, which taxed larger brewers quite heavily.[80] It has also been suggested that payment to the court was regarded as a higher obligation than payment to the shogun, which was seen as merely a tax.[81]

Perhaps because of the family's penchant for living on credit, including borrowing from their own tax agent against future taxes, the Oshikōji botched the business after a few years. In 1529 the head of the family, Morokata, annulled his debts to his tax agent by paying a conditional debt amnesty to the shogunate and abruptly took the tonsure.[82] In 1538 the next family head, Moroyasu, was again appointed to lead the Distillery Office, and the Oshikōji continued in office, although income from the tax declined steadily until it was abolished altogether by Hideyoshi in 1585.

Overlord arrangements continued to function until at least the middle of the sixteenth century, but in an increasingly anemic way. Guilds no longer conformed to the neat design of early times, if indeed they ever had. For commoners this meant, among other things, that instead of having a single, powerful overlord, one could be importuned by several. By the same token, however, one could often successfully plead special treatment, for the overlords' grip was weakening. The next section relates the ways in which some commoners exploited this ambiguity, even playing overlords off against one another. From the moneylenders' perspective, their relations with Enryakuji and the shogunate were similar in nature, while minor overlords like the Nakahara could extract their portion as well. Overlord demands could be arbitrary and harsh, but the moneylenders found many ways around them.

IRREGULARITIES AND COMMONERS' LEVERAGE: INCIDENTAL LEVIES, TAX EXEMPTIONS, AND BRIBES

In principle, taxation even by multiple overlords was a predictable if burdensome aspect of life for moneylenders. But this was not the whole picture. Already in the fourteenth century overlords were imposing incidental levies (*rinji kayaku*) for extraordinary expenses like special construction projects, religious observances, and the like. In the fifteenth and sixteenth centuries references to such levies, especially prevalent on moneylenders, are so numerous as to suggest that they had become routine. Meanwhile the moneylenders were pressing their overlords for tax exemptions as extensive as they could get—from regular taxes or from incidental levies, or from both. That an overlord would agree at all to such demands would seem an unmistakable sign of weakness. Because bribes accompanied requests, however, the granting and periodic renewal of tax exemptions could itself bring the overlord some income, even while negating other income. Although overlord income was declining, then, it had by no means disappeared.

The prevalence of tax exemptions and bribes suggests that, for their part, the late medieval moneylenders were as mindful of the overlords as ever but were now negotiating conditions with them from a position of strength not evident earlier. Not only that, but after the Ōnin War in particular it appears that in at least some cases individual moneylenders rather than guilds negotiated directly with the overlord. In other words, there are few signs that the guild was functioning effectively to protect its members from overlord abuse. If anything, individual moneylenders with their real power—money—were successfully making demands of the overlord.

The practices to be discussed here fall into a category that the modern mind neatly labels abnormal or even illegal. It is quite true that they could be regarded as lying outside the norm of the early overlord system at least; at the same time, however, they were routine occurrences in the late medieval period, openly or tacitly accepted. Another way of characterizing them, again in a way that accommodates the modern mind, is to posit a dichotomy between official and personal practices. The former were characterized by adherence to laws, decrees, or at least documents establishing or upholding precedent. The latter were marked on the one hand by enhancement of the personal income of individuals within a larger entity (like the shogunate, a temple, or a shrine) by processes like bribes, and on the other hand by dogged attempts, clandestine as well as open, by commoners to avoid all forms of taxation. Bakufu laws rarely acknowledge these practices, which were quite outside official or intended policy.[83] But especially after the Ōnin War, records of transactions and disputes in the shogunate and other institutions increasingly contain references, direct or indirect, to such behavior, suggesting that it was tacitly accepted as part of everyday procedure. However one labels such practices, they are symptomatic of a declining overlord system. Particularly relevant to this study is the degree to which commoners who paid taxes were exploiting to the fullest the cracks in the system.

Not surprisingly, as the Muromachi shogunate's ability to tax the moneylenders declined as described earlier, its preoccupation with doing so increased. All Bakufu laws dealing with the moneylenders after 1485, except for an occasional debt amnesty, concern the payment of taxes. Commercial income was more important than ever to the shogunate, but the very frequency of tax-related decrees suggests strongly that the moneylenders did their best to evade payment whenever possible. The Bakufu was not alone in its dwindling control, however: the moneylenders proved to be skillful evaders of taxation by all overlords. As a result, the shogun and other overlords relied ever more on incidental levies, and a vicious cycle developed.

The third article of the landmark shogunal decree of 1393 concerning taxation of the moneylenders pledged to exempt them from religious or shogunal incidental levies in return for yearly taxes.[84] There is, however, fairly copious evidence, at least by medieval standards, that the Bakufu did not live up to this promise: not only shrines like Hie and Gion but even the shogun himself imposed special taxes on the moneylenders aside from the regular brewer and storehouse levies. Particularly after the Ōnin War, with the political weakening of the shogunate and the impoverishment of many Kyoto moneylenders, the shogun increasingly broke his own promise not to impose incidental levies.[85] Indeed, the matter-of-fact nature of this practice casts the whole problem of overlord rule in a very different light. Regular, yearly taxation by an overlord implies a system characterized by consistency and adherence to precedent. Levying an impost whenever an incidental expense arose, on the other hand, suggests that in practice overlord rule was arbitrary, unpredictable, and financially painful for commoners. Undeniably prosperous, the moneylenders were recognized by several overlords as an unlimited source of income. The idea that an overlord could impose a tax whenever he needed income is fundamentally at odds with any image of medieval institutions as orderly or respectful of precedent. At the same time, however, frequent incidental levies may suggest not harshness on the part of the overlord so much as ineffectiveness. That is, regular taxation was so unsuccessful, commoners having become adept at avoiding it, that incidental levies became necessary to overlord survival. The frequency of incidental levies, especially after the Ōnin War, signified that the system was no longer bringing great benefits to the overlord.

Shogunal incidental levies could take several forms: *tansen* was a tax on cultivable land to be used for special ceremonial expenses; *yakubu takumai* was estimated on the basis of land area and was originally imposed for the reconstruction of Ise Shrine; and *munabechisen* was a tax on residential structures. The latter hit Kyoto residents the hardest, although moneylenders, to the extent that many had acquired land through usury, could find themselves subjected to the other two as well. This is not to say that taxpayers complied cheerfully: in 1422 the shogunate threatened to confiscate the land of those who failed to pay *tansen* and *yakubu takumai*, suggesting some noncompliance.[86]

Shogunal incidental levies occurred for a variety of reasons, a common one being the cost of ceremonies. In 1494 a tax on Kyoto merchants was levied to cover the expenses of Shogun Yoshizumi's coming-of-age ceremony.[87] Particularly notable in this case is that enterprises normally exempted from the *sake* and moneylender tax were not permitted exemption from this one. In the post-Ōnin period, this type of stipulation was not particularly unusual, as shogunal resources were dwindling. The Bakufu's stern admonition that "punishment will be imposed on disorderly fellows" (*rōzeki no yakara*, here meaning those who fail to pay up) suggests that there were many such culprits—in other words, that the moneylenders did not meekly submit to such demands. Whether resistance to them was effective or not, the incidental levies were frequent enough to be a substantial irritant to those already bound to pay regular taxes. On the other hand, it is likely that incidental levies became necessary precisely because regular taxes were not coming in.

Incidental levies on moneylenders, in particular, intensified over the course of the fifteenth century. The *Ōninki,* an account of the Ōnin War, cites an extreme example of a regular tax, that on the moneylenders' storehouses, being abused by the shogun: it was imposed so frequently from the mid-fifteenth century that its repeated collection became, in effect, a form of frequent incidental levy.

> In Shogun Yoshimitsu's time [late fourteenth–early fifteenth centuries], taxes on [moneylenders'] storehouses were levied. In Shogun Yoshinori's time [1430s], this became twelve [levies] per year. Under the present shogun [Yoshimasa, ruled 1443–1473], storehouse taxes for the imperial succession ceremony [Daijōe] numbered nine in the eleventh month and eight in the twelfth month.[88]

Indeed, from 1442 the 1393 shogunal pledge to the moneylenders not to impose incidental levies was broken repeatedly: in the second month of that year a special levy was imposed on brewers, followed in 1446 by a structural tax (*munabechisen*) of 30 *hiki* on each brewery. In 1447 a large special levy totaling 400 *kanmon* was collected from the city's moneylenders. Similarly, in 1463 the city's brewer-lenders and bean-paste merchants had to come up collectively with a whopping 500 *kanmon* to cover the costs of the funeral of an aristocrat.[89] The amounts exacted from the moneylenders in incidental levies were considerable, whether necessitated by regular tax avoidance by the moneylenders or by an insatiable overlord appetite, or a combination of both.

Special levies may have been necessitated in part by the fact that commoners devised ingenious ways to circumvent or reduce regular taxes. One way to avoid taxes was to blur the distinction between different categories of taxes and pay as a group in a lump sum less than what was actually owed. This made it difficult for the overlord to pinpoint responsibility. Hence the right to pay any tax en bloc was an important measure of a group's autonomy from the overlord. It is quite likely that paying less through the lump-sum method required the complicity of the tax agent and therefore that the practice entailed a bribe. In 1511, for example, the bean-paste merchants were suspected of combining the bean-paste tax with the moneylender and *sake* taxes, causing shogunal revenues to fall. The shogunate in its decree responding to this problem emphasized that these were three separate taxes and should be collected separately each month, by the same people, and not by the tax agents.[90] Instead, the Bakufu declared that other officials, perhaps meaning Board of Administration functionaries, were to collect it and reallocate it. The last item, eliminating the tax agents, represents a change in procedure, suggesting a strong appetite for bribes on the part of the moneylender-tax agents.

Another widespread "irregularity" of medieval taxation was the exemption. In moderation this could be, for the overlord, a means of maintaining at least some income from guild members, even while losing formal tax income. Because the exemption was not granted gratis but usually involved a bribe, often payable on an annual basis, the loss of income by the overlord was not total but merely reduced.[91] But if tax exemptions became too common, the damage to the overlord—and by extension to the overlord system—could be extensive. The latter occurred with some frequency in the sixteenth century as that system began to totter. Usually a low-ranking member of the overlord institution, like a tax agent, granted an exemption in return for a fee paid to him personally. Thus the individual income of functionaries in the overlord establishment was assured even as its formal income diminished.

The tax exemption was a common practice even before the Ōnin War, utilized by the shogun and other overlords in certain types of cases. For example, moneylenders whose premises were destroyed by fire were routinely allowed exemptions of several years by the Bakufu.[92] Another example involved a religious overlord: in 1434, Hie Shrine and an affiliated moneylender formed a contract part of which was designed to allow them to recover from financial difficulties. To that end, they were exempted from the *bajōyaku*, a major annual shrine tax that moneylenders and some other commercial groups were liable to pay.[93] In 1453, the shogunate informed Hie Shrine that its tax agent, the very prominent moneylender Shōjitsubō, and those under him were to be exempt from this tax.[94] The Bakufu suggested that the shrine get others to pay the tax, and if difficulties arose, promised to back the shrine up. This is a good example of commoners under multiple overlordship avoiding taxes by getting one overlord to pressure another to grant or honor an exemption. It also illustrates the relative strength of the shogunate vis-à-vis Hie Shrine (and by extension Enryakuji), and the importance of the tax agents within the Bakufu. It is particularly revealing of the way overlords sometimes cooperated even while competing, in this case by offering their authority to pressure taxpayers. But it is most striking for its matter-of-fact treatment of the tax exemption.

Another indication that exemptions were commonplace is a 1467 claim by a Hie Shrine tax agent that his exemption from the large annual festival tax (bajōyaku), as granted in imperial edicts of the 1260s, 1290s, and 1330s, would continue, including both the original exemptees and those exempted since the list was drawn up.[95] This document was apparently posted publicly in Kyoto, implying shogunal sanction. (Previously the emperor had granted exemptions from other institutions' taxes; the shogunate may have absorbed this state function.) At any rate, this source implies that the tax agent took his exemption for granted and went to some length to see that his overlord did, too.

A routine form of the exemption was that bestowed by the shogunate's Board of Administration on its own tax agents. In return for their tax collection service to the Bakufu, these individuals were exempted from the storehouse and brewer taxes, a major perquisite of the office. In the sixth month of 1474, for example, a moneylender with the religious name of Sen'un was added to the ranks of the tax agents as his generation's Jōsenbō.[96] It was normal practice for the shogun to grant a tax exemption to these officials, but Sen'un requested specifically that the tax exemption be waived in his case. Instead, he asked for a promise of shogunal support in cases of moneylender resistance to taxation. (His rationale may have been that he could collect more with warrior backing than an exemption was worth.) His request for special treatment—waiving the usual exemption—demonstrates indirectly the routine nature of this type of tax exemption.

The tax agents themselves frequently granted tax exemptions to other moneylenders. To aid them in their collection of taxes, they were armed with lists of exemptees, including the names of the moneylenders, their addresses, pertinent information such as the individual's line of work, and the amount of tax he had submitted prior to being exempted. Presumably the tax agents had the authority to demand taxes of any individual not on such a list. The lists, though not comprehensive, indicate that tax exemption was a very widespread phenomenon. One from the end of the fifteenth century, for example, contains twenty-seven such individuals.[97] From the late fifteenth century exemptee lists increase in number, suggesting a further decline in the traditional overlord system, though not necessarily the demise of any particular overlord.[98] Another bit of indirect evidence of the prevalence of exemptions is found in the 1539 example of shogunal income from Kyoto moneylenders cited earlier.[99] It specifies that moneylenders with exemptions will not be held to this regular, yearly (brewer and storehouse) tax, though it does not indicate what percentage of the total moneylending community they might represent. The tax agents, and even higher shogunal officials who sometimes received a cut,[100] were not only acquiescing in the face of widespread bribery but directly participating in it as recipients. Although the accompanying fee or bribe rarely gets a direct mention in sources, the entire procedure was thoroughly routinized in post-Ōnin Kyoto.

A parallel situation of exemptions in return for bribes can be found between the moneylenders and the institutions of Enryakuji, especially after the Ōnin War. One example that is particularly striking for its candid discussion of both exemptions and bribes is an altercation in 1482 between Hie Shrine and one of its functionaries (*zasshō*) with the religious name Kenkei. (His name and title suggest that he was one of Enryakuji's larger Kyoto moneylenders.) Higher-ups in the shrine were apparently disturbed that the tax (*bajōyaku*) for the fifth-month festival had declined drastically, Kenkei having overdone the granting of tax exemptions to moneylenders. (As if to emphasize the economic bind that the shrine was in, the following month thirteen clerics of Enryakuji and Hie Shrine signed a pledge to return a loan of three *kanmon*, quite possibly borrowed from Kenkei for the festival.)[101] While it is true that granting tax exemptions was Kenkei's privilege as tax agent, his exercising it to excess had resulted in financial difficulties for the overlord. But, according to Kenkei in a communication (*ukebumi*) with the shrine, the moneylenders he collected from had argued that times were bad and they could not raise the money to pay the tax.[102] Accordingly, Kenkei had granted them tax exemptions, although he promised in this document to the shrine to lift them if economic conditions improved. He also promised not to give everyone an exemption, then added, "while saying this, however, the times make it impossible . . . [to collect properly]." Whether the excuse of hard times was valid is hard to say: in 1482 only five years had passed since the end of the Ōnin War and its great destruction. On the other hand, the war could have been a very convenient excuse. Kenkei, for his part, submitted sixty *kanmon* annually to the shrine—a substantial "bribe" allowing him to take a cut of the tax he collected. He then offered to give the shrine a loan if needed, but warned that he would charge interest.

If all had been right in the overlord world, Kenkei would have been doing his job as tax collector and such a loan would have been unnecessary. His modus operandi is extraordinary from the overlord's perspective: he prospered individually as shrine functionary by granting tax exemptions in return for bribes or fees even as his overlord languished in straitened circumstances, brought on in part as a result of Kenkei's leniency toward the moneylenders. The moneylenders, for their part, claimed that hard times prevented them from paying their shrine taxes, although they had enough money to pay the bribe for their exemptions. The exemptions, in turn, enriched Kenkei enough to allow him to offer the shrine a loan! This communication from Kenkei, while very correct in form, is in substance remarkably frank: Kenkei is telling the shrine, his overlord, the limits of what he is willing to do, including the terms under which he will lend the shrine money. (It is possible that the shrine had coerced him into "lending" it an interest-free loan in the past and he was eager to discourage a recurrence.)

Also remarkable is a confirmation by four Hie Shrine officials of Kenkei's position as tax agent, specifying that moneylenders like Kenkei who have exemptions will not be required to pay taxes even if the shrine interferes or makes a special request that they do so.[103] This amounts to a promise by the overlord to uphold the tax exemption system, regardless of the economic straits in which he finds himself. Coming the very same month as Kenkei's defiant *ukebumi*, the confirmation suggests that Kenkei had successfully applied pressure to the shrine—not to say that it was at his mercy. In the seventh month, a Hie Shrine official writing to Kenkei on his collection of the festival tax confirmed that the contents of a 1434 contract with an earlier tax agent were still a firm precedent, and that Kenkei could decide who would be exempted from taxes.[104] It is stipulated, however, that the exemptees must pay half the gratuity (*goreimotsu hanbun*) to the shrine itself, and they were not exempted from various other Kyoto taxes. Thus the shrine quite openly acknowledged the system of bribery, promised to preserve it, and attempted to derive at least a portion of the bribe for its own coffers.

This exchange between Kenkei and Hie Shrine, unusually well documented for an "irregular" practice, illustrates how the medieval economic structure was breaking down, with those in the middle using the situation to their advantage. Kenkei, a shrine functionary and a moneylender living in Kyoto, had moved beyond the official position of tax agent in the shrine organization to one of personal power exercised by dint of his own economic standing. The overlords seemed to be losing some of their clout, to say the least.

Commoner records are few, but those which exist offer evidence of how treasured tax exemptions were. The Kyoto moneylender and imperial financier Tateiri Munetsugu and his descendants through the sixteenth century kept imperial and shogunal confirmations of exemptions from the regular tax on moneylenders and from incidental levies as well.[105] Clearly this was a coveted right, and one not to lose upon the passing of a generation.

By means of the tax exemption, the overlord's income decreased somewhat while the taxpayer's burden was also diminished. If exemptions increased in number to overwhelming levels, however, the overlord's rule was impaired as the autonomy of the taxpayers was bolstered. Post-Ōnin Kyoto had evolved to just such a juncture, with overlord arrangements continuing but weakened from within by widespread if irregular practices like the tax exemption. This is not to say that commoners in general reaped the benefits of the overlords' slow demise: if anything, it was those poised advantageously at the top of the commoner class, especially the most prominent moneylenders, who garnered monetary gain and social advancement for themselves from the topsy-turvy conditions.

As the previous discussion of tax exemptions suggests, bribery was endemic to the overlord system of the late medieval period.[106] As the overlord system declined after the Ōnin War, "real power" (*jitsuryoku*) more than connections or patronage became the determining factor for success throughout the society. To warriors, "real power" meant prowess in battle and skill in forging new alliances; to urban commoners like the moneylenders, it meant money and its skillful application in the form of bribery. The very term "bribery" may be a misnomer, with its modern, distinctly illegal ring, when applied to a widely accepted if not often openly admitted (in documents) late medieval practice. Indeed, it is probably less than accurate to characterize this practice as specifically illegal, as it did not necessarily carry the negative, dishonest nuances associated with the word today. "Gratuity" or "fee" might be closer to the medieval spirit of the practice, which is in fact found in many societies, medieval or otherwise, and which becomes particularly acute when an institution has broken down or fails to perform adequately for the parties involved.[107] In order to keep the institution functioning, even if not as originally intended, by individually enriching its officials while aiding others in accomplishing an "irregular" goal, bribes are a useful lubricant.

In late medieval Japan, bribery seems to have worked as follows. An overlord was not about to grant special favors, such as tax exemptions, for nothing. Instead, the overlord, or a functionary of the overlord, received a payment in return for bestowing a favor. If the favor was to be ongoing, like a permanent tax exemption, payment was required every year, or even every month. (Obviously this worked only if the payment was perceived to be less than the benefit accruing from it.) As a result, the official income of the institution might decline even as its income was supplemented privately, through bribes. In the long term, such a practice was not healthy for the overlord and indeed could lead to his ruin if carried to excess by terminating tax revenues altogether. But it did allow *members* of the overlord institution to survive in the short run under a somewhat mutilated version of the old arrangements. Those who tendered the bribes realized a benefit as well, without having to confront the system head-on. Mutual manipulation and accommodation characterized the relationship between overlord and client, and the resulting arrangement was adequate if not fully satisfactory for everyone involved.

Some outright tax resistance or noncompliance can also be detected on the part of clients, but usually indirectly, through overlord complaints or proliferating incidental levies. It might have been one factor in the case of Sen'un, the moneylender cited earlier who was appointed to the ranks of the tax agents in 1474. Sen'un eschewed the usual tax exemption that accompanied such an appointment on the condition that the shogunate, in return, back him up should other moneylenders complain that he took too large a cut of the tax for himself. Sen'un was bold to make such a demand of the shogunate; his request for shogunal support is indirect evidence of widespread moneylender resistance to taxation.

Because they were usually involved in another line of work, moneylenders could avoid storehouse taxes by claiming the other line as their only business. For instance, a brewer could claim to be only a brewer, and a bean-paste merchant only that. A moneylender could also claim to be a day lender, taxed at lower rates because their loans were much smaller. The shogunate's use of moneylenders knowledgeable about the city's merchants as tax agents would seem to have helped guard against such fraud, but bribes may have been useful here as well, and the Bakufu decried such tax evasion.[108]

All the traditional Kyoto overlords, Enryakuji and shogun included, faced declining incomes by the late fifteenth century. Symptomatic of their predicament was the frequency of tax exemptions, bribes, incidental levies, and outright tax avoidance, devices by which the moneylenders manipulated the overlord arrangement to their benefit by depriving the system of some of its harshness. But the same irregularities lent flexibility to the system, extending its existence, if in altered form, far into the six-

teenth century in the Kyoto area. Even in decline overlords proved remarkably resilient, and the moneylenders might even be characterized as a conservative influence, delaying the demise of the Kyoto overlords with their
taxes and bribes. To the extent that political and social disorder was not
to the moneylenders' benefit as merchants, stable if declining overlord rule
worked to their best advantage, as these wily participants squeezed every
advantage out of it for themselves.[109]

Widespread irregularities like bribery and exemptions may be symptomatic of a system in decline, but the sources in their self-interested way
reveal such practices only very grudgingly. Precisely because they were
undesirable to the overlord, who kept the records, these practices were
seldom recorded, except in some individual disputes. The case of Kenkei
and Hie Shrine is exceptional: usually references to bribery or tax exemptions are indirect. Given the elite bias of the record keepers, that such
practices are documented at all suggests that they were common by that
time. Although bribery was widespread, sources rarely address it directly.
Medieval record keepers enjoyed a remarkable degree of control over the
portrayal of their age.

The Kitano Malt Disturbance

In theory guild arrangements allowed the overlord to prosper even as subordinate tradespeople did likewise. In actual practice, however, and especially in late medieval times, they functioned less smoothly because of
the complex of overlapping interests that impinged upon them. We have
seen how multiple overlords competed for income from moneylenders,
and how the moneylenders learned to avoid taxation by a variety of
strategies. In a fifteenth-century controversy over guild prerogatives, the
moneylenders successfully resisted overlord demands that defied economic reality and common sense. This long-running dispute involving
brewer-lenders in and out of Kitano Shrine's malt guild also illustrates
the complicated relationship between overlords and their dealings with
moneylenders.[110]

The very year after the third shogun, Yoshimitsu, began formal, regular
taxation of the brewer-lenders, he passed the office on to his son, Yoshimochi who, ironically, would establish policies temporarily harmful to
the brewing industry. Yoshimochi remained in his father's shadow for
some years, but after Yoshimitsu's death in 1408 he began to go his own
way. For about two years from 1419 to 1421, he issued a series of edicts
banning liquor in certain situations.[111] To the brewers, the most damag-

ing of these was in 1420, when liquor was not to be consumed "throughout Saga," a western suburb of Kyoto that had the highest concentration of brewers outside of Kyoto proper. The prohibition was to be in force during the dedication period of a large new Zen temple in the neighborhood, the Hōdōji. Yoshimochi had a strong interest in Chinese Zen culture and was deeply knowledgeable about Zen thought and ritual. Hardly an ascetic in his personal life, as shogun he nevertheless sought in various ways to reform the *gozan* monasteries, whose regulations for monks were somewhat lax, at least by ideal Zen standards This included enforcing the ban on liquor in monasteries and, on this single occasion, even among non-clerical residents of the area near a Zen temple.

The Saga prohibition passed quickly, but Yoshimochi took other actions affecting brewers that were of longer duration. Residing in northwestern Kyoto were the brewers who had been subordinates (*jinin*) of Kitano Shrine since early medieval times.[112] In 1379 the Muromachi Bakufu, probably in response to a bribe from Kitano Shrine, exempted members of the malt guild from the imperial court's Distillery Office tax, a sinecure of the aristocratic Nakahara family.[113] In 1387 the shogunate, perhaps again nudged by a bribe from the shrine, "reminded" the malt guild members that they had been exempted from the Distillery Office tax a few years before, but that the equivalent amount should now be submitted to the main overlord, Kitano Shrine, instead.[114] In the same communication, the shogunate confirmed that the Kitano guild's brewers were specialized producers of malt, which all brewers, not only those under Kitano, should buy rather than make themselves. The monopoly implied here would be unpopular because the guild's price exceeded the cost of making malt privately. (Building one's own malt chamber was part of the brewing operation and was actually cheaper than buying malt from a guild.)[115] Hence the difficulty of enforcing the monopoly, and there is no sign for some years of shogunal interest in doing so.

The fact that Kitano was a branch temple of Enryakuji may partly explain the shogun's actions supporting Kitano in 1387, and again in a 1419 shogunal decree ordering the Kitano guild members to refrain from extra-guild activities and to pay their dues to the shrine.[116] Such elite support of the guild system, which supposedly worked to the mutual benefit of overlord and members, was not always matched by enthusiasm on the part of guild members, however. Indeed, the fact that members of the Kitano guild themselves sometimes bolted suggests that they saw the relationship as one-sided, working mostly as a convenient mechanism for taxation to the overlord's benefit. At the same time, the Kitano guild's monopoly on

malt and the shogun's and Enryakuji's support of it would of course enrich guild members by protecting them from outside competition.

But it was Yoshimochi himself, not Enryakuji, who decided to enforce
the Kitano monopoly. A shogunal order of 1419 forbade brewers from
building malt chambers outside the Kitano guild and exhorted the guild
members to pay their dues to Kitano. Two days later a decree from the
shogun's deputy to the military governor of Yamashiro province south of
Kyoto directed that the shogun's order be carried out.[117] Some fifty-two
offending malt chambers were then destroyed in the presence of a representative of the shogun, and their owners signed pledges promising to
refrain from such activities in the future.[118] Twenty-five of the signatories
were Kitano guild members, showing that the problem was not only one
of Kyoto brewers refusing to buy Kitano malt, but that a significant number of the malt guild members themselves were doing business outside
guild auspices—namely, selling the malt at lower prices. In its decree the
shogunate extended the Kitano guild's monopoly rights to a broader area
—all of Kyoto. In 1420, 116 non-Kitano brewers signed pledges not to
make malt.[119] The policy was apparently successful for a time, or at least
attempts were made to enforce it: a roster of 347 Kyoto brewers compiled
by Kitano Shrine seven years later for that purpose is so comprehensive
that it is the best available documentation of the size of the medieval
brewer-lender establishment in Kyoto.[120]

With shogunal enforcement, Kitano's malt monopoly could have grave
effects on the Kyoto economy. The Sakamoto packhorse drivers' riot of
1426 was directly related to Kitano's control of the malt market, which had
damaged not only the brewing industry, by in effect limiting the amount
of malt available but, by extension, rice consumption as well, causing a
drastic drop in the price of rice in Sakamoto.[121] The packhorse drivers
understood exactly the cause of their problems, for their goal in invading
Kyoto was to attack the residence of a high-ranking cleric at Kitano Shrine
who was a close advisor to Yoshimochi.[122] Their actions demonstrate how
closely Kyoto *sake* production was tied to the economy of the region.

These shogunal actions were atypically drastic, and the malt monopoly,
alluded to by the shogun in 1387, was now a reality. On the rare occasions
in Japanese history when liquor has been prohibited, famine or morality,
and sometimes both, have been the causes.[123] A major famine occurred in
1420–1421, but the malt monopoly enforcement was too early to be a
reaction to it. It is possible that Yoshimochi, who at the same time was
issuing several decrees banning consumption of liquor in certain quarters,
enforced the malt monopoly in order to depress *sake* consumption overall.

Not one of the more despotic Ashikaga shoguns, Yoshimochi was nevertheless a religious idealist and may have yearned for a wider observance of Zen-style asceticism. As part of the observance of the thirteenth anniversary of Yoshimitsu's death, for instance, he banned temporarily the killing of living beings.[124] At any rate, a shogunal policy inimical to the brewing industry was quite at odds with simultaneous dependence on brewer-lenders for revenue.

Unresolved tensions over the Kitano malt monopoly erupted in the so-called Bun'an Disturbance of 1444, named after the reign period. Yoshimochi had died in 1428, and prohibition ceased to be a shogunal concern. Non-Kitano brewers of Kyoto, unwilling to tolerate any longer the inconvenience and expense of Kitano's malt monopoly, first secured the support of Saitō, Enryakuji's western branch, and then refused to buy Kitano malt, demanding the right to produce their own instead. Their exasperation over the economically stultifying effects of the monopoly was strong enough to seek an outright end to it rather than simply to avoid it. Their strategy, however, was not to rebel on their own but to enlist the aid of an overlord and, as a result, play several authorities off against one another. Displaying their usual flair for the dramatic, the group of Enryakuji priests championing the non-Kitano brewers locked themselves inside a hall at Saitō and threatened to keep the portable shrine and other sacred objects on Mount Hiei until the shogun recognized the brewers' right to produce their own malt. (One might think this was a welcome alternative to the usual tactic of carrying the portable shrine into the city, but in fact there were times when it was customary to move it. Thus threatening *not* to move it could also cause unease.) The irony of the situation is that both sides were ultimately under Enryakuji's "protection"—the brewers under Saitō and the malt guild members indirectly through Kitano Shrine. The multifaceted nature of the Enryakuji organization easily accounts for this state of affairs. The shogunate found itself in a quandary—having to rule in favor of one Enryakuji faction over another. While shogunal officials were mulling over the problem, a rumor that they had ruled in favor of the non-Kitano brewers reached the malt guild members, who in protest locked themselves in a hall of Kitano Shrine. (Locking oneself in a sacred place was another common form of protest in medieval times, not unlike the dumping of the portable shrine in the streets of the city, insofar as it constituted an irregular use of a sacred place or object, thus arousing unease and consternation among the populace. Burning a sacred place had even greater shock value.) Finally Hatakeyama Mochikuni, the shogunal deputy, sent troops to drive out the guild members who, as they fled, set fire to the shrine. The conflict ended with forty dead, and the fire spread, heavily damaging parts of western Kyoto.

Shogun Yoshimochi had been eager to enforce the Kitano monopoly, but the high price of malt, which had aroused the other brewers boldly to defy the monopoly with the support of one faction at Enryakuji, brought matters to the breaking point. In the end, the shogunate was not willing to support a guild that was impeding commerce and had incurred the wrath of a powerful faction in the Enryakuji organization. The guild members' blasphemous act of burning the shrine was the last straw for the Bakufu, which ruled against them. They had gone too far in the eyes of the overlords, both shogun and Enryakuji—and perhaps Kitano Shrine as well, which had been put to the torch, after all! Enryakuj's Saitō, in return for support given at a crucial time, procured the right to annual taxes from the eastern brewers. Not insignificant as well is the seriousness with which shogunal judicial decisions were regarded by all parties in this conflict and the ability of the shogun to take drastic action when he made up his mind to do so—strong indications of the Bakufu's authority in the city in the early fifteenth century.[125]

For about a century the record is silent on malt guild activities. Outside of *sake* brewing there was no demand for malt, and once the Kitano guild lost its monopoly it had presumably gone back to its special status as a group of brewer-lenders exempted from the Distillery Office tax. From 1545, however, suddenly a spate of documents appear giving the impression that the clock had been turned back to the early fifteenth century.[126] This time, the Enryakuji faction at Saitō instructed the Kitano guild members to refrain from extra-guild malt production, and the shogunate ordered them to pay malt dues to Kitano Shrine.[127] Furthermore, the Bakufu ordered all brewer-lenders of the Kyoto area to submit a malt tax to Kitano Shrine, charging that they had been "selling selfishly" in recent years.[128] This may be an accusation of noncompliance with the Kitano malt monopoly, followed by an order that, in return for making their own malt, the Kyoto brewers were all to be taxed as Kitano Shrine guild members. The Kyoto brewers expressed their indignation and opposition in a rebuttal that recounted both the events of a century before and the subsequent decades of prosperity in which the malt guild was absent from Kyoto.[129] This time, the shogun's Board of Administration ruled in favor of the shrine's guild as the party with monopoly rights to malt, refusing to recognize the claims of the other brewers.[130] The matter then disappeared as abruptly as it had surfaced. In 1561 the shogunate once again ordered the malt producers to pay their dues to Kitano,[131] and in the Edo period they were enfeoffed to the shrine, to which they rendered service.[132]

Several explanations are possible for this series of events in the sixteenth century. The shogunate's order to Kitano guild members to submit taxes to the shrine may be a reference to the old Distillery Office tax on malt, uncollected during the Ōnin War but revived by the Oshikōji family early in the sixteenth century.[133] Perhaps their efforts to collect it had been so successful that Kitano lost income from its guild members. Or it may have been that the shogunate was attempting to revive the monopoly in order to gain income itself from the malt producers—that is, in return for a bribe. The role of Enryakuji in the matter is not clear, but it would appear that the Saitō faction was now in control of Kitano, and the Bakufu's actions could have been in response to pressure from that quarter.[134] In a broader sense, these events may represent a desperate attempt by the now crumbling Kyoto power structure, including both the shogunate and Enryakuji, to retain some control over its sources of income. (It is likely that the shogunate—that is, some officials therein—received a cut of the guild's taxes from Kitano in return for this favorable judgment. As the discussion of bribery above suggests, money commonly greased the wheels of the late medieval order.) The events of 1545 could also reflect the increasingly complicated politics of the city at a time when control of the shogunate itself was up for grabs and the townspeople's Lotus leagues had been crushed by an Enryakuji-warrior coalition a decade earlier.

As in other sixteenth-century instances of overlord activity, however, these events betray a surprising resilience in overlord arrangements, particularly if one has been inclined to write them off as overwhelmed by local warriors by the late fifteenth century. The old guard stubbornly continued to crop up alive and, if not terribly well, at least surviving to the end of the medieval period. As before, the shogunate's designs on the moneylenders paralleled those of Enryakuji: to control them as a source of income in return for protection and special privileges. Yet in the case of the Kitano malt producers, a subgroup of brewer-lenders, the shogunate was willing to defend the rights of the overlord (Kitano) until the smooth operation of commerce seemed threatened. The guild was a convenient control mechanism into which the Bakufu could intrude without excluding other elites already entrenched there. But shogunal dependence on existing institutions would eventually lead to declining income. Even at the point when their monopoly was destroyed, the malt producers remained subordinate to Kitano Shrine. Overlord control continued, though in mutilated form, and the benefits of the guild system were still great enough to give sustenance to the elites. The Muromachi shogunate's support of and participation in this system only reinforced and prolonged it.

As important as the attitudes and roles of the elites in the 1444 controversy is the fact that it would not have taken place at all had the exasperation of the non-Kitano brewers not risen to intolerable levels, provoking a response. Insensitive to the brewers' economic threshold of tolerance, the overlords insisted that a narrow guild monopoly be enforced, even if it made little economic sense and caused discontent among moneylenders in their capacity as brewers. As in the case of widespread tax exemptions, the brewer-lenders manipulated an imperfect system rather than passively accepting it. Instead of attempting open rebellion on their own, however, they cagily took advantage of factionalism within the overlord institution to gain the support of one group at Enryakuji. Without this key element, it is not at all certain that they would have been victorious against the Kitano guild. After many years, the desire of Kyoto's brewer-lenders to do business in an economically rational way was finally recognized.

The Kitano Malt Disturbance raises questions about monopolies, supposedly one of the major advantages of a guild for the clients and one justification for characterizing the overlord as a patron, with the beneficial nuances of that term. In this controversy, we see some merchants defying a monopoly and others opting out of a guild that lacked economic viability. The Malt Disturbance suggests that when prices on a product were kept artifically high, the monopoly became ineffective and was disregarded, with even the members abandoning the guild. Only with shogunal determination was the monopoly enforced, and at that only for a time. Rarely in late medieval sources are monopolies even mentioned. Furthermore, it is commonly understood that during the post-Ōnin economic recovery of the late fifteenth century some merchants in Kyoto thrived without any guild ties. Without effective monopolies, the benefits of the overlord arrangement tilted even further away from the clients. To them the overlord was an intruder, not a patron, who cut into profits and gave little in return. In this light, then, the widespread avoidance of taxes documented above is hardly surprising.

In the decades following the shogun's announcement of a policy to tax the moneylenders, these merchants actively took measures to realize the potential of their new situation. Rather than acquiescing to crushing and multiple taxation, they found mechanisms of avoidance, including exemptions, bribes, playing overlords off against each other, and disregarding guild rules like monopolies. By the late fifteenth century new merchants tended to avoid guild membership, but those who remained transcended mere subordination. The most successful moneylenders made the overlords dependent on their skills, while the others were keenly aware of their value as a source of revenue. The overlord tie continued to hold, suggesting that some intangible benefits accrued to the clients. Among these was the prestige factor, of special value to them as townspeople.

Chapter Four

Responding to Siege

THE LAST TWO CENTURIES of the medieval period in Japan differed from the preceding ones in several ways. For this study, the most important of these was the ascendancy of an urban culture and monetized economy centered on Kyoto, in which not only traditional overlords but also commoners participated fully. At the same time, peasant resentment over mounting debt began to find a voice at the village level in large and well-organized leagues demanding debt amnesties. Initially successful, for about a century attacks by these forces repeatedly inflicted damage on moneylenders' premises and invited regulation of their lending practices by the shogunate. Also endemic in late medieval times were shifting warrior alliances. The most intense of their upheavals was the Ōnin War of 1467–1477 in which Kyoto was the central battleground. Along with the townspeople in general, the moneylenders endured the chaos and then adjusted to new realities, some of which were to their benefit. Not coincidentally, simultaneous with these outbreaks of violence were the general symptoms of overlord decline described earlier; in the process the townspeople began to shape an identity separate from both peasants and overlords. In some cases prodded into defensive action and in others seizing opportunities to advance collectively or individually, the moneylenders emerged from the chaos smaller in number but with well-honed traits of leadership.

Ikki: The Moneylenders under Attack

Conflicts involving moneylenders were not limited to matters of guild monopolies and taxation. Perhaps the most startling medieval development, from the viewpoint of both moneylenders and overlords, was the growing tendency from the late thirteenth century for peasants to form leagues (*ikki*), initially in conflicts with estate overlords over the amount and method of tax collection. Later they focused on the capital itself, and from 1428 for about a century Kyoto was periodically beseiged by peasant invasions called *tokusei ikki*.[1] These rural leagues would descend en masse upon the city, burning, looting, and demanding debt amnesties. Although other medieval cities also experienced these attacks, Kyoto, where the moneylenders and the most prominent overlords were concentrated, was the hardest hit.

Tokusei is a Confucian term meaning virtuous government, but it was used in ancient Japan on special occasions such as the accession of a new emperor as a euphemism for amnesties, including debt amnesties, in the broad sense of rectifying matters or returning them to their proper state.[2] The Kamakura Bakufu, as noted earlier, issued debt amnesties for its own vassals, and although this was a narrow application, it can be seen in retrospect as the precedent for the broader debt amnesties granted by the Muromachi shogunate.

The word *"ikki"* means "of one mind" and by extension referred to rural leagues made up of peasants and local warriors. The development of these leagues can be traced from village communal organizations known as *sō*, which joined together in common cause against estate overlords.[3] These leagues resorted to armed struggle in campaigns that transcended estate barriers and therefore caused great alarm to the overlords. In the past, the scattered nature of estate holdings had worked to the overlords' advantage by dividing the peasantry geographically. With the formation of leagues, peasants of a certain area were able to oppose one or more overlords collectively, achieving some degree of solidarity among villages.

The vertical composition of the leagues was as important as the horizontal bond they represented among villages. Well-to-do peasants (*dogō*) and local warriors (*jizamurai*) as well as cultivators joined in, and it was this inclusiveness that made the leagues so strong. (In some locales like Ōmi province, packhorse drivers also held positions of leadership in the leagues.) The general anti-overlord tone of such movements remained very strong: they demanded remission of estate taxes as well as debt amnesties. Indeed, because their target was not only moneylenders but overlords including the shogun, the *tokusei ikki* can be seen as the climax of a long peasant struggle against the overlord class dating from the late thirteenth century.[4]

To a peasant, land was livelihood and survival. Opposition to overlord rule in general coupled with rage against moneylenders who deprived them of their land was the driving force behind peasant uprisings demanding debt amnesties. A specific target of the uprisings, not surprisingly, were the moneylenders' receipts and ledgers, without which debts were uncollectable. Moneylending, to peasants, was a one-sided affair: putting up their cultivation rights to individual plots of land as collateral, they might typically procure enough cash to get them through a hard winter and buy new seed for the spring. Interest rates were onerous, ranging from 60 percent to over 300 percent annually.[5] If a poor harvest followed the next year, a peasant could find himself unable either to pay annual taxes to the overlord or to fulfill the terms of the loan. As a result, he would be forced to default on the debt and end up a tenant on what had been his own land, with the moneylender in effect his landlord holding the cultivation right. And very probably he would also have to take out a new loan, perhaps on another piece of land, to pay his taxes and make it through until harvest time. Thus, although a new class of rich peasants enjoying the benefits of the burgeoning economy emerged in the fourteenth and fifteenth centuries, this was only part of the story. Among the cultivator class, even in central Japan, indebtedness was a chronic state leading to permanent tenantry for many. The appeal of a debt amnesty is not hard to understand.

Distribution of the harvest, including its taxation, became a matter of great concern to moneylenders who accepted land as collateral in loans to peasants. The lenders themselves began to intrude into the agricultural calendar by tying the terms of debt repayment to the harvest schedule. The understanding between lender and debtor was that the harvest would be used to resolve the debt. Even members of the overlord class would seek credit when they were unable to come up with cash, and might specifically contract to repay the debt from their estate tax receipts. One example concerns a large loan (430 *kanmon*) taken out by the aristocratic Kujō family in 1433 from the Zen temple Shōkokuji. Repayments included modest monthly amounts plus substantial sums scheduled for the tenth month—harvesttime—of each year. After eight years, the Kujō family still owed 24 *kanmon* but had paid back 800 *kanmon* in total, nearly twice the principal.[6]

Moneylenders, including laypeople as well as clerics from various Kyoto temples, sometimes served as tax agents on Kyoto area estates.[7] Thus peasants on these estates had direct contact with the high-handed ways of these Kyoto lenders. They could, for example, demand taxes in kind instead of in cash, commute them to cash at favorable rates, and then submit them to the overlord. Furthermore, although it was customary for peasants themselves to transport taxes to the overlord if the distance was a day or less, a moneylender hired by the overlord as tax agent might insist on handling the transport of the taxes and charge the peasants for it. Not only that, but such moneylender-tax agents commonly treated late taxes as loans, for which they charged interest. Still another role of Kyoto lenders in estate tax collection was that of money exchanger.[8] By the fifteenth century, taxes from even remote estates were often commuted to cash, but the risk of robbery when carrying it as far as Kyoto was great. Instead, an exchange note issued at the estate was taken to Kyoto, where it was commuted to cash by a moneylender. In various ways, then, Kyoto moneylenders intruded into the lives of peasants on estates.

Not all peasant uprisings of the fifteenth century sought debt amnesties. Some demanded the dismantling of toll stations, and some opposed taxes, including those imposed by the overlord as well as provincial taxes called *tansen* exacted by the military governor. But the majority wanted debts erased. This suggests several things about the economy and society of late medieval Japan. First and most obviously, indebtedness had become pervasive with monetization. Second, through their smaller-scale struggles with the overlords at the estate level in the previous century peasants had developed a consciousness of themselves and their common needs and a growing awareness of the effectiveness of solidarity. Finally, the first half of the fifteenth century in particular was an optimal time for mass action by all peasants under the strong leadership of wealthy peasants and local warriors. Later, local warriors would be coopted by provincial lords.

Although the motives behind peasant uprisings were apparently tied to moneylending, it is probably not correct to assume that peasants in these uprisings necessarily targeted the individual Kyoto moneylenders to whom they were personally indebted. Zen temples, along with individual lenders, were often targets of attack because of their moneylending activities, and also for their close ties to the shogunate.[9] It would be quite difficult, however, to carry out personal vengeance in a mass attack. Indeed, a stated goal of the leagues was to force the moneylenders to return *all* collateral, not just that of league members.[10] Moreover, peasants, even those near Kyoto, tended to borrow from local village moneylenders, be they merchants or rich peasants, more than from city moneylenders.[11] Thus participation in an uprising was not necessarily tied to personal indebtedness to a particular Kyoto moneylender.

Then why did the leagues attack Kyoto moneylenders in particular? At least some league members were probably indebted to Kyoto lenders.

In addition, by making debt amnesty their main demand, the leagues, well coordinated and informed by strategy, may have been extending earlier estate-centered uprisings to Kyoto, the home of most overlords, including the shogun. In this sense, attacking moneylenders, an important source of shogunal income, was a very effective way of hurting the shogunate itself.[12] (The other effective tactic for forcing the Bakufu to sit up and take notice of the uprisings was to occupy the city entrances, thereby stifling commerce and even cutting off food supply to the city.) More likely, indebtedness was so widespread that the prospect of a general attack on moneylenders may have been a foolproof way to rally league members. Furthermore, there is evidence that the leagues were seeking support throughout the levels of society: they may have calculated that demanding debt amnesties would draw both debt-ridden aristocrats and townspeople to their cause.[13] But the force and persistence of the debt amnesty movement also suggest that something beyond strategy was behind the attacks on moneylenders: namely, the genuine rage and frustration of the indebted. A debt amnesty would erase debt, rural and urban, and that, after all, was the goal of the uprisings.[14]

Inevitably, Kyoto as a whole suffered from these attacks. Commerce could come to a halt when well-organized peasant leagues blockaded the city entrances and invaded the city. The Muromachi shogunate was not eager to harm the moneylenders, a steady source of income, but the threat posed by the uprisings to the peace and stability of Kyoto was so serious that over and over the shogun issued debt amnesty decrees. For a time, then, peasant uprisings dominated and even dictated shogunal policy toward the moneylending establishment. Although their long-term effectiveness may have been limited, these uprisings were immediately successful insofar as they forced the shogunate repeatedly to regulate the activities of the moneylenders. Thus their effects on the moneylenders were dramatic: fire and looting could wipe out a business, and with shogunal military response often inadequate or nonexistent, the moneylenders and their neighbors had to learn to defend themselves. And if fire had not already done the job, a debt amnesty decree could ruin a moneylender, or at least deal him a temporary setback. Thus the history of these uprisings throws into sharp relief the economic vicissitudes of moneylending and at the same time illuminates the growing self-sufficiency of the townspeople.

In 1428 Kyoto was invaded by leagues of peasants demanding debt amnesties, including the destruction of receipts and contracts. Called the Shōchō Ikki after the reign period, it began in the eighth month in Ōmi province to the east of Kyoto at the instigation of packhorse drivers blaming their poor business on, among other things, the high interest rates charged by the moneylenders. In the ninth month, leagues in Yamashina province immediately south of Kyoto staged an uprising demanding debt amnesties and the destruction of debt contracts. The scale of the uprising can be estimated by the fact that the shogun sent several hundred warriors on horseback to protect the temple Daigoji.[15] Late in the ninth month the leagues struck again, this time in Kyoto. Then, in the eleventh month, a full-scale attack was launched, starting at the southern edge of Kyoto, besieging the temple Tōji on the fourth day, and from there spreading out over the city, which they terrorized for nearly three weeks.[16] On the twenty-second day of the eleventh month, Akamatsu Mitsusuke, head of the shogun's Board of Retainers, posted a ban on leagues and at last the invaders left the city. But this was only after the peasants had burned and pillaged the moneylenders' storehouses and adjacent areas of the city, seizing pawned items and destroying receipts, thus effecting an amnesty on their own, if only temporarily. (Such an action was called a private debt amnesty—*shitokusei*.)[17] This scene was to recur in Kyoto repeatedly for over a century, with variations in size, organization, and success.

The Shōchō Ikki, the first to shake the establishment in Kyoto, was so alarming that the shogunate, fearing it might spread to include warriors, demanded written promises from provincial military governors that their warrior vassals would not join the marauding peasants.[18] As a measure of its size and shock value, the Shōchō uprising is referred to in a cleric's journal as "the first peasant revolt since the dawn of Japan."[19] Though the shogunate never issued a debt amnesty during this uprising and managed to rid the city of the invaders after several weeks, the uprising spread to other areas and amnesties were issued in a number of locales. Three simultaneous uprisings in the Nara region (Yamato province) were not easily put down. Continuing throughout most of the eleventh month, their persistence and boldness finally persuaded Kōfukuji to issue a debt amnesty for Nara city, making it the first uprising to achieve its goal of an official debt amnesty. (That a religious overlord and not the shogun issued this debt amnesty indicates the widely recognized authority of Kōfukuji as the major overlord in the Nara area.)

The terms of the Nara amnesty, although limited to that area, in general resemble those of later amnesties. Debts were forgiven if one-third was repaid. Estate taxes in arrears were completely forgiven. Debts over five years old were canceled on the assumption that the lender had already been sufficiently compensated by interest payments. The amnesty,

TABLE 2. TOKUSEI IKKI IN KYOTO

1428	After bad harvest and coinciding with shogunal succession controversy, large *ikki* invades Kyoto, demanding a debt amnesty; amnesty not issued in Kyoto
1441	Large *ikki* occupies city entrances, surrounds and invades Kyoto; shogunate issues first debt amnesty. Coincides with political crisis in shogunate
1447	*Ikki* pillages Ōmiya Shichijō area of southern Kyoto
1454	*Ikki* invades Kyoto; first conditional debt amnesty issued by shogunate
1457	*Ikki* invades Kyoto; conditional debt amnesty issued; moneylender-led townspeople participate in defense of Kyoto
1459	Famine year; Kyoto invaded by peasant leagues from the west
1462	End of severe famine, large *ikki* under warrior leadership invades Kyoto
1463	*Ikki* invades Kyoto
1465	Ōmi packhorse drivers invade Gion Shrine and Ōtani Hongan'in; routed by *inujinin* of Gionsha under orders from Enryakuji
1466	*Ikki* invades Kyoto under warrior leadership; conditional debt amnesty issued by Board of Retainers to apply to area of city south of Sanjō (i.e., Shimogyō)
1467–1477	Ōnin War; no *ikki* in Kyoto
1480	Largest post-Ōnin *ikki*; leagues demanding debt amnesty and abolition of new toll stations destroy stations at seven city entrances; conditional debt amnesty issued after *ikki* was quelled
1485	*Ikki*, led by Miyoshi and other vassals of the Hosokawa, attacks Kyoto moneylenders
1486	Area peasants joined by some Kyoto residents demand debt amnesty, attack Kyoto four times. Leagues occupying Tōji compound are driven out by townspeople
1488	*Ikki* demands debt amnesty; invades and burns Shimogyō
1490	Leagues occupy, invade, and burn Kitano Shrine
1491	Ōmi's packhorse drivers demand amnesty, occupy Kitano Shrine
1493	Shimogyō invaded by leagues from the south and southwest; ringleader is warrior vassal of the Akamatsu
1495	*Ikki* invaders battle townspeople, led by moneylenders. League ringleader decapitated
1499	*Ikki* invades Kyoto, driven out by troops of Akazawa Munemasu
1508	*Ikki* invades Kyoto, attacks moneylenders in Shimogyō
1511	Yamashiro leagues block city entrances
1520	*Ikki* of Kyoto area attack the city; shogunate issues debt amnesty in first and second months
1526	*Ikki* attacks Kyoto; shogunate issues debt amnesty
1532	Townspeople under moneylenders attack *ikki* strongholds in north and western outskirts of Kyoto

however, was limited in some important ways: it was only to be in effect for four months, and furthermore it did not apply to any debt outstanding more than three months beyond the originally contracted term. Debt amnesties were also issued in other locales in the central provinces of Yamato, Harima, Settsu, and Kawachi.[20]

The Shōchō Ikki was an epochal event: it was the first major uprising of its kind, setting the pattern for future invasions of Kyoto. Furthermore, its timing was crucial: it occurred while the Bakufu was preoccupied with a succession dispute following the death of Shogun Yoshimochi. (Less significantly, a candidate in the long-defeated southern court briefly fought to succeed to the throne on the death of the Emperor Shōkō in the seventh month of 1428, distracting the shogunate for a while.) Concurrent famine, epidemic, and a poor harvest in the previous year may have been contributing factors to the timing of this uprising. It is also noteworthy that from this point on there was a large increase in the number of shogunal laws pertaining to moneylending.[21] To some extent these were in the nature of damage control—to placate aggrieved peasants and protect the moneylenders at the same time—but another effect they had was to regulate some lending practices, however briefly.

Uprisings demanding debt amnesties occurred in central Japan almost yearly thereafter, but the next one to invade Kyoto was the Kakitsu Ikki of 1441, the largest and most successful of all. It was launched soon after the Kakitsu incident in the sixth month, in which the despotic Shogun Yoshinori was assassinated by a resentful vassal, Akamatsu Mitsusuke, military governor of Harima province. As a consequence of the assassination, the shogunate was thrown into confusion over the twin problems of avenging the dead shogun and settling on a successor. Bakufu troops were dispatched to Harima, where they finally forced the assassin to commit suicide on the tenth day of the ninth month.

In Kyoto, meanwhile, bereft of most shogunal troops, a huge army of peasants descended on the city at the end of the eighth month. The invaders demanded a debt amnesty, claiming that it was justified on the grounds that this was the start of a new shogun's reign.[22] Even more than the uprising of 1428, the timing of the Kakitsu Ikki strongly suggests the ability of the peasant leagues to turn government turmoil to their own advantage. Fourteen forty-one also corresponded to the year of the bitter chicken in the East Asian calendar, the third from the end of the sixty-year cycle and considered a year of revolution. It may have been mere coincidence, but the timing of the uprising suggests a consciousness that this was an auspicious moment to seize, a year of renewal and restoration of things to their proper state.

The course of this uprising likewise indicates careful planning: instead of indiscriminate looting and burning, starting on the twenty-eighth day of the eighth month the seven entrances to the city were blockaded for one week, during which the leagues' members conducted periodic forays upon the moneylenders. On the third day of the ninth month, league members overran shogunal troops and occupied Tōfukuji. The shogunate, unable to do more than protect Kyoto proper (Rakuchū), ordered money-lenders in outlying areas (Rakugai) to come into the city with their valu-ables, including items entrusted to them for safekeeping and those held as collateral. The leagues got wind of this and brazenly threatened to burn Tenryūji, the Zen temple on the city's western edge closely associated with the Ashikaga shoguns. On the following day, the Shirakawa league from north of the city attacked. On the fifth day of the ninth month, the inva-sion was at its height: its encirclement of Kyoto was complete, the be-siegers encamped at sixteen points on the city's periphery.[23] Contemporary accounts, although probably guilty of exaggerating the number of partici-pants, suggest that they formed distinct leagues from particular areas: two or three thousand from the south besieged Tōji; one thousand people from the area near the Tanba entrance to Kyoto attacked the shrine Ima Nishinomiya; one thousand from "five estates" and two to three thousand from the west invaded temples in the city proper.[24]

With no food coming into the city and the invaders standing fast, the possibility of famine loomed. Shogunal officials met to discuss policy. When the Bakufu still refused to issue an amnesty, the invaders encircled one moneylending establishment after another, demanding the return of pawned items and debt contracts. Moneylenders who did not comply had their premises destroyed. Shogunal forces provided negligible defense. Attacking league members were masked to ensure anonymity—perhaps to preserve their future credit rating, perhaps to avoid being hunted down.[25] In desperation, the moneylenders collectively bribed the deputy shogun, Hosokawa Mochiyuki, 1,000 *kanmon* for protection. The bribe was re-turned, however, when Mochiyuki's archrival, Hatakeyama Mitsuie, and other major warriors threatened to ignore future orders if ordered to fight the uprising.[26]

Under attack in Kyoto, the site of its headquarters, the shogunate pro-posed an amnesty for peasants in which all debts incurred to date would be canceled. It was promptly rejected by the leagues as inadequate, how-ever; they demanded instead a general cancellation of the debts of all classes, not only peasants. The motivation of the league in making such a demand is open to speculation: it may have been part of an understand-ing with elites with whom they already enjoyed links,[27] or perhaps league leaders sensed the danger of fighting from an isolated position and hoped that the demand for a general debt amnesty would bring large numbers of aristocrats and warriors as well as non-moneylender townspeople into their camp, at least in spirit.[28] Having paralyzed and occupied the capital, the peasant leagues may have decided that now was the time to press their demands to the limit. At last, on the twelfth day of the ninth month, the Muromachi shogunate granted its first debt amnesty and posted it at the city entrances.[29] Still the leagues refused to give in. This time they demanded an amnesty that specifically included land sold in perpetuity. (See "The Business of Lending Money" for a discussion of different types of land transactions.) About a month later, the shogunate caved in to league demands, and an amnesty was extended to such lands if twenty years had not yet elapsed, and in the case of commoners regardless of the time elapsed.[30]

This debt amnesty, which was acceptable to the leagues, was similar to those issued subsequently: unpaid estate taxes were canceled, as were debts in the form of cash, goods, and land. Included in the amnesty were items pawned for less than a month, houses and land "sold" on a short-term basis (i.e., land put up as collateral for a loan), and commoners' land sold in perpetuity. Exempted entirely from the debt amnesty were loans made by Zen temples and "offerings" (i.e., collateral) in the form of both land and money to Zen temples.[31] The shogunate's decision to exempt temple loans was an expression of its preferential treatment of the *gozan* establishment, while individual moneylenders under Enryakuji's patronage had to bear the full brunt of the amnesty.

Enryakuji then stepped into the picture, protesting that it would be ruined by the amnesty on land sold in perpetuity, as would its client moneylenders and temples and shrines in Kyoto in general.[32] In response, the shogun again revised the amnesty to apply to such land only in cases where the debt was not yet delinquent.[33] This softened the blow the amnesty dealt the moneylenders, thanks to Enryakuji's intervention—and made the amnesty less generous to peasant debtors. In spite of this, however, there was no recurrence of the uprising, its momentum perhaps having been broken by the long negotiations.

It is thought that many moneylenders were ruined by the debt amnesty of 1441 and for a time had to fall back on brewing alone to make a living. In addition, their claim to land held in perpetuity was to be unstable for decades to come, in spite of the eventual terms of this amnesty, because of the recurring, persistent demands for amnesty for this type of transaction. To the average peasant, of course, the cancellation of debts provided considerable relief. Furthermore, the persistence of the leagues in pressing their demands was remarkable and suggests that they were informed, to some extent, by strategy. Intensive negotiating between shogunal officials and league representatives preceded the various amnesty decrees to the extent that the leagues actually dictated the terms—an extraordinary turn of events in Kyoto, the site of shogunal and imperial government. One also is struck by the sense that these persistent peasants felt they were entitled to an amnesty, not that it would be an act of official benevolence.[34]

Not all uprisings were as organizationally unified as those of 1428 and 1441, but they tended to follow a similar pattern. A very large uprising in the sixth month of 1454, for example, began with the destruction of a toll station erected to raise money for the reconstruction of Tōfukuji's pagoda and expanded in the ninth month to a debt amnesty invasion of lower Kyoto. Moneylenders there closed up shop only to be destroyed anyway.[35] The leagues continued on to the northern part of the city, where lenders in the area of Ichijō, good brewers all, brought peace offerings of *sake* to the invaders on the eleventh day and promised to return all pawned items.[36] Thereupon the *ikki* moved on, and on the fifteenth day invaded Shōkokuji, the Zen monastery, stealing its debt receipts. This time the shogunate took action, raising troops from its vassals—some of whom were apparently reluctant to participate—and eventually pursuing the invaders back to their villages. On the sixteenth of the month the last invaders were driven out of the city, two weeks after the invasion began. On the twenty-sixth of the tenth month the Bakufu issued a debt amnesty cancellation decree prohibiting further uprisings.[37] Although this uprising resulted in a conditional debt amnesty, whose terms are discussed below, the shogunate showed some determination to pursue its ringleaders, demanding that overlords in the area find them. Insofar as the northern and southern portions of the city were attacked separately, this uprising, although highly destructive, seemed to lack the organizational cohesiveness of the 1441 attacks.

The uprising of 1457 was also characterized by uncoordinated attacks on various parts of Kyoto by many small leagues over a one-month period. Rioters from the countryside looted moneylenders of all their pawned items, while those from the Kyoto area more systematically took one-tenth.[38] This lack of a unified strategy diminished the overall effectiveness of the attack on the city, which might otherwise have been successful, given the lackluster warrior defense. As it was, this invasion is known for the unprecedented fire damage it inflicted on the city, the area from

Shijō to Shichijō having been put to the torch.[39] No amnesty was forth-coming from the shogunate during this *ikki*, however, so it cannot be counted a success for the debtors.

The great disruption of the Ōnin War (1467–1477) was an inhospi-table climate for *ikki*, and their attacks on Kyoto ceased during those years. Leading peasants in areas southwest of Kyoto, among the major organizers of peasant leagues, were absorbed into the warriors' forces and were thus too distracted to organize leagues. In the eighth month of 1468 intensive fighting moved to the southwest of the city, where peasants loyal to the eastern camp held out against the forces of the western camp until 1480, when all of Yamashiro province was finally overtaken by the western forces. Many peasants who had fought against the victors had their pad-dies destroyed; clearly, there was no opportunity to stage a league upris-ing during these years of warrior-instigated turmoil.

After the Ōnin War large-scale *ikki* comparable to those of 1428 and 1441 once again plagued the city for a time, but several developments were to limit their success. In a general sense, friction within the peasant class undermined league solidarity as cultivators became increasingly in-debted to wealthy peasant moneylenders in the same village. In addition, in reaction against repeated invasions, the moneylenders and other towns-people began to organize effectively in self-defense against the invaders, whose ability to inflict damage on the city was thus curtailed. Finally and most specifically, the shogun began to issue conditional debt amnesties (*buichi tokusei*), which sharply limited the application of an amnesty. These developments occurred more or less simultaneously, especially over the last half of the fifteenth century.

The first factor in the decline of the *ikki*, the indebtedness of culti-vators to wealthy peasant moneylenders in villages, opened a rift in rural society that is often blamed for growing disorganization within the leagues themselves. During the fifteenth century the accumulation of land by well-to-do peasants accelerated noticeably. Such peasants levied their own tax (called *kajishi myōshushiki*) on cultivators, the effect of which was to ab-sorb any agricultural surplus not claimed by the overlord. The cultivators as a consequence frequently found themselves not only sinking into debt but losing their land to wealthy peasants in their own villages.[40] The resulting split in village society made a continuing strong rural alliance of all peasants against the urban moneylenders increasingly unlikely.

The problem with linking the emergence of a wealthy peasant class directly to the decline of *tokusei ikki*, however, is that the former cannot be assigned even an approximate date, as some moneylending took place in villages as early as the Kamakura period while taxation of the agricultural surplus by wealthy peasants occurred from about the fourteenth century. While it is true that land accumulation by means of moneylending (i.e., defaulted debts) accelerated in the fifteenth century, it began well before that. Thus positing a causal relationship between the late-fifteenth-century decline of *tokusei ikki* and the earlier appearance of wealthy peasants may be an excessively determinist approach to the chronology of actual events. Wealthy peasants occupied an ambiguous position in society, sometimes casting their lot with village interests and other times working for elite overlords. Thus it is not contradictory to assume some wealthy peasant leadership of leagues even in the early sixteenth century, and active military service for leading warriors by the same group in the Ōnin War.

It is true, nonetheless, that a lack of organization among leagues participating in uprisings can be detected from the 1450s, and this may be an indication of waning peasant leadership resulting from village disunity. This rural stratification is expressed overtly in sworn statements by peasants from Kyoto area estates, in which they are divided into two separate groups, *samurai* and *hyakushō*, the former essentially wealthy peasants and the latter cultivators.[41] Even so, the authorities for their part continued to fear the effectiveness of wealthy peasant leadership of the leagues: the shogunate ordered peasant vassals southwest of Kyoto to report for guard duty in the city in 1465.[42] The motive behind bringing them into the capital was probably to keep them out of an uprising then rumored to be on the rise in the Nishigaoka area. The uprising subsided and the order was withdrawn, but, to the authorities at least, village society did not appear to be as disunified as it does with hindsight.

Another factor contributing to the eventual demise of *tokusei ikki* was the defense of the city by townspeople. The ineffectual shogunal defense of Kyoto during the 1441 attacks must have been a stunning blow to the moneylenders and other townspeople, as well as to temples that suffered damage. Subsequent attacks on the city in 1454, 1457, 1466, and 1480 were met with similarly ineffective warrior defense. Diary entries note that any rumor of attack by peasant leagues led townspeople and clerics alike to block their doors and windows with dirt and cover themselves with straw matting, cowering in anticipation.[43] During an invasion of 1457, the head of the shogun's Board of Administration as good as acknowledged the shogunate's weakness by ordering the moneylenders to come to the defense of the city.[44] On the ninth day of the tenth month, a large *ikki* from Yamashiro province blockaded the city's eastern entrances and occupied Hōjōji. Three days later "moneylender troops" (*dosōgun* in sources, probably referring to a force of townspeople under moneylender leadership) gathered at Inabadō, a temple in the commercial district of southern Kyoto. When the morning temple bell sounded at 6 A.M. this army of townspeople attacked the leagues encamped at Hōjōji, killing seven or eight people and taking two captive. The moneylender troops then set fire to houses in front of Inari Shrine, whose head official had been captured as a league ringleader. To the extent that the city entrance near Hōjōji was reopened, this skirmish could be counted a triumph for the moneylender defenders.

This was only the first of several league attacks on the city in the fall of 1457, however. Moneylender troops alongside shogunal forces were beaten back in the area of Shichijō Horikawa and Shijō Ōmiya on about the twenty-fifth day of the tenth month by a league from Nishigaoka, a southwest suburb, which then overran the city as far north as Sanjō. On the twenty-seventh day, however, "storehouse priests" (*kurahōshi*—possibly a reference to Enryakuji-affiliated moneylenders), led by one Umegaki, struck back, outnumbering and beating off the invading peasants 1,000 to 230.[45] Umegaki was a casualty of the conflict, however, so the shogunate called for reinforcements from its major vassals. The next day a large warrior force sent to pursue the leagues took flight in the event, in ignominious contrast to the moneylender troops.

Some of the contemporary accounts of *ikki* portray the moneylenders in a flattering light, commenting on their considerable military prowess. One moneylender, Yasui, was so successful in leading the urban forces against the leagues in a 1490 attack on the city that he was exempted from shogunal taxes for a generation.[46] Sawamura, another moneylender who led the townspeople against invading leagues, apparently acquired a macho arrogance from his fighting experience, for he skirmished with vassals of leading warrior houses in the streets of Kyoto on occasion in the 1490s.[47]

Even taking into account the chroniclers' penchant for exaggeration, the number of "moneylender troops" in the 1457 defense suggests that not only moneylenders, who in Kyoto numbered only in the hundreds, but also ordinary townspeople made up this force. That they were led by moneylenders, however, can be inferred from the terms "moneylender troops" and "storehouse priests." The extent to which non-moneylender townspeople participated voluntarily in defensive actions against the *ikki* is a thorny issue. Indebtedness to moneylenders by urban commoners was as widespread as that of peasants, and the moneylender was a singularly disliked figure in medieval society.[48] Thus it may be hard to imagine city

debtors jumping with alacrity at the chance to vanquish their rural counterparts. Advocates of a class-based interpretation of medieval society,
therefore, tend to reject the notion that all urban commoners, moneylenders and others, could have allied against the *ikki* invaders.[49] Indeed,
city people are recorded to have joined the leagues in some cases. A
league attack in Kyoto's south on the twenty-sixth day of the tenth month
of 1457, for example, included "Kyoto people" (*Kyōjū no mono*) as well
as peasants, as clear an indication as any of support of the leagues by
townspeople.[50]

But the threat of imminent invasion may have overridden any feelings
of solidarity with *ikki* members as fellow debtors. Although the moneylenders' premises were a main target of the invasions, damage, especially
by fire, was widespread in commoner neighborhoods. Thus joining moneylenders in defensive action may have been a practical bid for survival
by townspeople, regardless of their feelings as debtors toward moneylenders. Most likely of all, the medieval reality was inconsistent but quite
understandable: many townspeople, as debtors, disliked moneylenders
and sometimes lent their support to league invasions, but at other times
as city residents defended their neighborhoods, alongside moneylenders,
against *ikki* destruction.

The Kanshō Ikki of 1462, in the wake of a severe famine, marked another turning point in the defense of the city against peasant invasions.
As before, the seven entrances to Kyoto were occupied by the leagues,
and a full-scale siege began. Four days later, on the eleventh day of the
ninth month, thirty *machi* neighborhoods were burned in the downtown
area of great moneylender concentration.[51] Warrior troops immediately
drove them out, but they were back the next month: leagues from Matsugasaki in the north, Nishigaoka to the southwest, Uji and Yamashina to
the south invaded the city. Some participants hailed from the fringes of
Kyoto itself, namely, Tōji's precincts and the community at Tōfukuji's gate.
According to one account, city streets became impassable and commerce
was disrupted, but there are no specific reports of attacks on moneylenders
this time, suggesting that the leagues did not penetrate that far into the
city.[52] The same source offers a vivid description of the invasion: "A great
commotion: ringing of bells, beating of drums, and blowing of horns."[53]
Instead of issuing a debt amnesty, however, the shogunate, aided by townspeople, routed the leagues and pursued them back to their villages, where
houses were burned and ringleaders arrested.

In addition to repelling peasant leagues in unified attacks, the townspeople of Kyoto defended their individual neighborhoods, the *machi* dis-

cussed in Part 1.[54] During the early large-scale *ikki* invasions, the *machi* was in a state of transition between a community whose members lined one side of a street and one whose members faced each other across a street. (These were called *katagawamachi* and *ryōgawamachi*, respectively; see Part 1 and Fig. 1, *c* and *d*.) The peasant attacks hastened the emergence of the latter stage to the extent that they forced the townspeople to take matters of defense into their own hands when faced with the reality of an unwilling or ineffective Bakufu. (As will be pointed out, the Ōnin War erased any delusions that the shogunate could defend the citizens of Kyoto, and this form of the *machi* became the norm throughout Kyoto.) The main advantage of the *machi* community facing itself across a street, besides easier communication, was that both ends of the street could be closed off by gates to keep out invaders. The effectiveness of such gates, made of flammable bamboo and wood, was quite limited, but since each *machi* had them, they could, in the aggregate, retard the invaders' progress through the city. Wooden towers also dotted the city, from which lookouts warned the residents of fire or invasion. These structures were erected on an ad hoc basis during the early invasions and became a regular feature of the city only when the Ōnin War and later *ikki* attacks made them essential.[55]

Defense measures by townspeople against the *ikki* were not active efforts to empower themselves so much as a necessary reaction against a present danger to which the ineffectual shogunate and unwilling warriors left them exposed. In an *ikki* attack in the tenth month of 1495, for example, townspeople led by moneylenders provided the *only* defense of the city.[56] Commoner defense of city neighborhoods was a significant step in the emerging autonomy of the townspeople because they were not organized from above but, by default, had to take matters of self-defense into their own hands.

The final factor in the decline of league attacks on Kyoto was the shogunate's use of the conditional debt amnesty (*buichi tokusei*), first imposed in 1454.[57] The debt amnesty of 1441 had had the immediate effect of cutting off the shogun's storehouse tax on the moneylenders for about six months, so seriously did it damage the moneylenders.[58] To prevent this from happening again, after a 1454 *ikki* invasion the shogunate issued a debt amnesty with a twist—namely, a debt would be canceled on the condition that one-tenth, later increased to one-fifth, be paid by the debtor to the shogunate.[59] There were hardly any takers, however, so in 1455 the shogunate ruled that if the debtor did not pay this new debt tax, then the creditor could do so in return for the right to pursue the debt.[60]

Thereafter conditional debt amnesties became standard shogunal policy and were included in amnesty decrees. In 1457, the shogunate even addressed the moneylenders as debtors in conditional terms: their own debts would be canceled if they paid one-tenth their value to the shogunate.[61] An amnesty decree containing a conditional clause, as those after 1454 did, was thus either a debt amnesty or a shogunal confirmation of an existing debt, depending on whether the debtor or creditor came up with payment to the Bakufu first.[62]

For indebted peasants, the conditional amnesty was a particularly heavy wet blanket thrown on their hopes for debt cancellation. Most, indebted already, probably could not hope to come up with 10 or 20 percent of their debt. Furthermore, applying for an amnesty with payment to the shogunate was procedurally complex and intimidating to illiterate peasants, whereas a simple amnesty was not.[63] Even worse, while one could escape current debts through this procedure, in doing so one's future standing with the lender might be harmed.[64] To the moneylenders, on the other hand, the conditional debt amnesty blunted the full effect of an amnesty on debts: if they acted quickly enough they could prevent the cancellation of their loans. At the same time, however, the conditional debt amnesty constituted a new, de facto tax on them by the shogunate whenever Kyoto was invaded.[65] A shogunal decree of 1457 threatening to punish debtors and creditors who conspired in fulfilling the terms of the conditional debt amnesty suggests that both debtor and lender disliked the new procedure.[66]

One historian has pointed out that the conditional debt amnesty of 1457 in one sense protected moneylenders.[67] To the extent that they borrowed some capital to finance loans, moneylenders could benefit from debt amnesties as debtors themselves.[68] If they paid one-tenth of their own loans to the shogunate within fifteen days, they were freed of the duty to repay the debts. Having lost collateral, receipts, and the right to collect on loans in an *ikki*, the moneylenders at least were excused from their own debts. This was a minor effect of the amnesties, however.

Although the shogunate was still unable to make Kyoto safe from invading peasant leagues, it had cynically discovered how to derive some benefit from them for itself. A deliberate measure to generate more income from moneylenders, the conditional debt amnesty became part of shogunal tax policy. Following the 1480 amnesty stipulating a 20 percent payment to the shogunate for an amnesty, over a period of six years the Bakufu collected from lenders 1,120 *kan*, 500 *mon* and from debtors 981 *kan*, 500 *mon* for a hefty total of 2,012 *kan*.[69] (It is interesting that although more lenders than debtors ponied up to prevent amnesties, the difference was not great, especially considering the relative wealth of the lenders.) If regular shogunal tax income from the moneylenders was indeed on the decline in the years following the Ōnin War, as posited earlier, then the occasional conditional debt amnesty, like bribes and incidental levies, helped make up the difference.

A debt amnesty decree was an immediate victory for the peasants to the extent that it officially recognized and sanctioned their demands and even extended them to a broader geographical area in the case of general amnesties. In the long run, however, as the shogunate became more adept at fashioning terms to suit itself, amnesties actually served to curtail uprisings. Debt amnesties were usually only briefly in effect to assuage the grievances of those who invaded the city. Once placated, they departed, and it was in both the moneylenders' and the shogun's interests to revert to the status quo. To the shogunate, the more prosperous the moneylenders, the more stable its income base. In the long term, debt amnesty decrees brought peasant uprisings under control, first by establishing a procedure for dealing with their demands (and thus stopping the chaos), and then by imposing precise conditions, which at first regulated lending practices but increasingly served to limit the effectiveness of the amnesties. The conditional debt amnesty in particular curtailed the financial benefits of debt amnesties to peasants.[70]

For the moneylenders battered by the Ōnin War, the end of that conflict only brought a resurgence of *ikki* attacks on Kyoto, although their effectiveness waned for the reasons discussed above. Still, for a few years there was enough vitality left in the *ikki* movement for them to disrupt lending in Kyoto frequently, and occasionally on a large scale. The largest post-Ōnin *ikki* occurred in 1480 and consisted of two sustained, lengthy attacks on Kyoto, in the ninth and tenth months.[71] (It was a year of widespread unrest, with similar uprisings in Tanba, Yamashiro, Yamato, and Harima provinces.) The first attack on Kyoto was accompanied by demands for a debt amnesty and the abolition of new toll stations. The second focused on the toll stations, demanding their destruction at all seven entrances to Kyoto. A new station had been established by the shogunate at the Tōji entrance (and perhaps at the other six entrances as well), purportedly to cover the cost of rebuilding the imperial palace, but a priestly chronicler recorded the widely held suspicion that they were really for the private enrichment of Hino Tomiko, the unpopular wife of former Shogun Yoshimasa.[72] Thus the moneylenders were vilified together with Tomiko and her toll stations. The toll stations were so unpopular and the leagues' demand that they be dismantled enjoyed such widespread support that most shogunal vassals ignored the shogun's order to rout the *ikki* at its height, in the middle of the ninth month. Tōji itself had demanded that the toll stations be dismantled as soon as they went up, and they were in fact destroyed by the leagues in their second attack on Kyoto in the tenth month. The chronicler, no doubt conveying the true feelings of many, commented approvingly: "How laudable, how laudable!"[73]

It is significant, however, that while the leagues won on the toll stations, no debt amnesty was forthcoming this time; on the contrary, the shogunate in the twelfth month, after all had died down, issued a decree forbidding debt amnesties with a conditional amnesty clause—a tax on the moneylenders—gratuitously tacked on, just to be sure that it obtained some income for itself.[74] Thus the leagues had united with enough force to kill the toll stations, but their effectiveness regarding debt amnesties had waned. Thereafter small-scale uprisings demanding debt amnesties plagued the city frequently but with little lasting effect, marking the end of this phase of peasant uprisings. Such *ikki* as did occur, and about a dozen more did until 1532, sometimes featured leadership by renegade warriors.

Tokusei ikki have been characterized as primarily peasant uprisings against overlords, a continuation of the estate-based uprisings that took place earlier in the medieval period.[75] The leagues' focus on Kyoto and the demand for debt amnesties are seen primarily as signs of strategic refinement and sophistication of organization: an attack on the moneylenders would be an attack on the shogunate itself. According to this view, in spite of all the damage the uprisings caused to moneylenders, their target was primarily the overlords. This class-based interpretation relegates the moneylenders to the periphery, when in fact they were at the center of the action.

If the proportion of documentation devoted to it is any indication, attempts to regulate moneylending practices consumed much of the energy of the Muromachi shogunate, particularly from the mid-fifteenth century. Often these were debt amnesty decrees responding to invasions of the city by peasant leagues. Although the formation and development of these leagues was undeniably tied to the dynamics of village life, egregious lending practices also offered the peasants strong inducement to act. Thus the Muromachi Bakufu donned its official city administrator hat in trying to keep lending practices within reasonable bounds in order to prevent peasant invasions of Kyoto. The shogunate was also protecting a major source of income: violent attacks on the moneylenders, if not checked in some way, were a sure way to drive them out of business. Thus shogunal policy attempted to placate the *ikki* and get them out of the city, but it also limited the applicability of debt amnesties.

Warriors sometimes refused to defend the city against peasant invaders. One would expect them, as vassals of the shogunate, to have dutifully routed the invading leagues, but in fact they were frequently recalcitrant. Indeed, their dilatoriness was the main reason the moneylenders had to learn to defend themselves, starting with the 1441 stand-off between Hosokawa Mochiyuki and Hatakeyama Mitsuie. The reason for warrior inaction in this particular case might be interpreted narrowly: warrior rivalries impaired the shogunate's police functions, which extended over the city of Kyoto. (Unlike the old Bureau of Capital Police that it replaced, the shogun's Board of Retainers was made up of fractious vassals.) But warriors refused to fight the leagues on other occasions as well, and a strong dislike of moneylenders may have aroused their sympathy for the leagues. The latter interpretation is given credence by the shogunate's order of 1428 that provincial military governors extract from their vassals written pledges not to participate in *ikki*.[76] In a 1454 invasion of Kyoto, shogunal vassals were reluctant to participate. Their forces took flight from a skirmish in 1457, leaving the townspeople to fend for themselves. Although warrior defense of Kyoto was decisive in the 1462 invasion, the opposite was the case in 1466, when forces of the Yamana and Asakura military governors, demanding a debt amnesty themselves, attacked moneylenders' shops around Kyoto, looting them and setting them on fire.[77] (The previous night warrior vassals of Shiba Yoshikane had raided *machi* neighborhoods, confiscating swords and daggers, thus rendering residents incapable of self-defense.)[78] In 1480 and 1495 warriors refused to take part in the defense of the city against the *ikki*, and warrior leadership—albeit by renegades, for the most part—can be detected in some of the post-Ōnin uprisings. Latent sympathy for the goals of the uprisings may have been quite widespread: moneylenders, after all, had enemies throughout society. Although general resentment against overlords was among the motivations for attacking Kyoto, specific rage focused on moneylenders was the driving force of the uprisings.

The shogunate, as we have seen, learned how to take care of its own income during uprisings through the ingenious device of the conditional debt amnesty. Elite debtors, however, who had come to accept credit as a way of life, often suffered the indirect ill effects of amnesties. The middle-level aristocrat Nakahara Yasutomi, mentioned previously, found himself in the awkward position of being unable to get his ceremonial robe out of hock because his moneylender had temporarily closed up shop in the wake of the 1454 *ikki*. Another aristocrat, Madenokōji Tokifusa, in need of an infusion of cash in the midst of the 1441 uprising, got a priest to lend him a robe, which he then took to a moneylender to pawn. But the lender refused to give him a loan, fearing—correctly—a debt amnesty to be imminent. Also in 1441, a moneylender returned three debt contracts to Tōji in accordance with the terms of the general amnesty, but appended a note that the large loan of 83 *kan*, 853 *mon*, which Tōji had borrowed the year before for preparations for a shogunal visit, should be repaid. If repaid, the moneylender added, business would be transacted as usual in the future. This, of course, was a backhanded way of saying that refusal to pay up would result in credit being cut off. Tōji promptly drew up a new debt contract, promising to pay off the debt in three years, amnesty or not. The need for cash, in other words, could render debt amnesties meaningless in individual cases. And, finally, even the shogun himself was not exempt from the ill effects of a debt amnesty. In 1480, Shogun Yoshihisa, who had just issued a debt amnesty, called in vain for his own pawned items. "These peasant leagues! Such a state of affairs!" grumped an aristocratic diarist in dismay.[79]

To the elites, the *ikki* drama presented the disconcerting spectacle of the lower orders taking matters into their own hands and getting their way, at least for a while. When the uprisings petered out, it was only partly due to the efforts of the authorities, partly to developments in village society, and partly to the organizational skills and defensive actions of the townspeople led by the moneylenders. In hindsight, all of these factors help to account for the decline of *tokusei ikki*; they do not, however, provide a completely satisfying explanation of the gradual disappearance of the leagues. Instead one looks at a new development: peasants were enlisted in province-wide uprisings by their local warrior leaders, a trend exemplified by the Yamashiro provincial uprising of 1485. There local warrior-peasants boldly demanded the disencampment of major warriors and their armies still pursuing their lofty tribal aims of mutual destruction —the sporadic continuation of the Ōnin War.[80] The remarkable success and cohesion of these "samurai of the land" is another story, and another stage of indigenous activity eclipsing the more truly peasant-based *tokusei ikki*. In other locales peasant discontent was channeled into the religious uprisings (*ikkō ikki*) of the sixteenth century.

During most of the fifteenth century the shogun's administration of Kyoto was dominated by matters related to moneylending, and nearly all its regulation of the moneylenders was in response to peasant uprisings.

Generally, shogunal policy in this area was to issue debt amnesties when severely pressured by an uprising, but to balance this with some support for the moneylenders. This included tax exemptions for moneylenders in the event of fire or burglary, generally harsh treatment for recalcitrant or absconding debtors, and the setting of generous (to lenders) limits on interest rates. The shogunate also exploited the moneylenders, however, with conditional debt amnesties as a way to benefit economically from the *ikki* problem. Although eventually peasant uprisings ceased to plague Kyoto, for a century they were an ongoing problem for which expensive solutions had to be fashioned. These developments occurred as the Muromachi shogunate's ability to tax its vassals in Japan as a whole was on the wane. Increasingly dependent on Kyoto commerce for its own survival, the Bakufu not surprisingly strove to protect its local sources of income.

For the townspeople, *ikki* could range from nuisance to disaster, repeatedly inflicting destruction and financial losses on the moneylenders.[81] In the absence of a decisive military response by the shogunate, the townspeople defended themselves, led by the moneylenders. Indeed, their response to *ikki* shows the extent to which the townspeople, at least in part, determined their own fate and made their mark on medieval Japanese society. Having attained a degree of internal autonomy as guild members, led by the moneylenders they defended their neighborhoods against attack. But the continuing ability of peasant leagues to invade Kyoto seemingly at will and to destroy the moneylenders' premises long after they had lost the ability to extract official debt amnesties from the shogunate put the moneylenders in an ongoing, if sporadic, position of precariousness. As with other aspects of the disorderly medieval "order," many elements, elite and otherwise, sometimes in concert and sometimes at cross-purposes, were responsible for this state of affairs. In the case of the moneylenders, ultimately demand for credit outlasted the violent attacks on them.

THE ŌNIN WAR AND ITS EFFECTS

For a ten-year period from 1467 a power struggle raged among leading warrior houses, starting in Kyoto and eventually spreading throughout Japan to the warrior class as a whole.[82] Usually called the Ōnin War (or Wars) in English, it was an ongoing realignment of warriors through skirmishes and battles that resulted in a changed political landscape, especially in the provinces. Incursions by local warriors onto lands held by traditional overlords like Enryakuji intensified, seriously and permanently

damaging their interests.[83] The damage to Kyoto was particularly extensive: although the warfare was not constant and unrelieved for the entire
decade, Kyoto was a major battlefield especially in the first two years of
the conflict, and over half the city was devastated, damaging commerce
and wiping out many moneylenders.

The Ōnin War is traditionally seen as a watershed marking the end
of Muromachi shogunal rule and heralding the beginning of the Sengoku
or Warring States era. The war put into motion an irrevocable decline
among the ruling elites, starting with the emasculation of the Ashikaga
house, a sharp contraction in the amount of land controlled by traditional
overlords, and the eventual dominance of a new type of warrior with
stronger local roots than elite connections. In Kyoto as elsewhere, some
changes resulted directly from the conflict, while others were an intensification of earlier trends furthered by the decline of the old elites. Some
trends, like efforts to separate from the overlords and the proliferation of
incidental levies and briberies for exemptions, began well before the Ōnin
War, but the conflict was catalytic in making effective counteraction by
traditional overlords, now irreparably weakened, very difficult. The war
dealt traditional overlord arrangements with commoners by far the most
severe blow yet, and although they continued in the Kyoto area until Nobunaga's destruction of Enryakuji in 1571, they were in such an advanced
state of deterioration that the room for maneuver by subordinates like
the moneylenders was considerable.

During the last third of the fifteenth century political instability in
Kyoto, if not necessarily constant violence or unrelieved warfare, was the
order of the day. For commoners in particular, it was a period fraught
with possibility as well as danger. For commercial groups or, increasingly,
individual entrepreneurs, the new disorder meant relying on one's wits
and abilities rather than depending on a traditional overlord's patronage.
The war brought on, in succession, destruction of the city, especially its
northern sector, depopulation and contraction of its boundaries; a stronger
and more vigilant neighborhood organization; independent entrepreneurs
happy to flaunt guild conventions; the survival of some hardy and influential moneylenders amid many new small-scale operations; and overlords debilitated yet still garnering income, however limited, from the city.
These Ōnin-induced developments impinged on the moneylenders both
for better and for worse: the social and commercial landscape of Kyoto
was permanently altered in ways that could reward or punish. Individual response rather than guild solidarity became the key to survival and
prosperity.

The War in Kyoto

Although the third shogun, Yoshimitsu, had succeeded in consolidating Bakufu control of the provincial military governors in the early fifteenth century, in a few decades leading warriors became restless and began to pose a threat to shogunal power.[84] Resentment over the arbitrary reassignment of some provincial governors' lands by the despotic shogun Yoshinori led to his assassination in 1441 by Akamatsu Mitsusuke. This, the Kakitsu Incident, can be seen in retrospect as the beginning of long-term trouble for the Muromachi shogunate. Made vulnerable by two child shoguns in the 1440s, the Bakufu became increasingly dependent on the support of a few powerful warrior families, the Hosokawa, Hatakeyama, and Shiba, who together monopolized the office of deputy shogun, and the rising Yamana Sōzen, who had vanquished the assassin in 1441. The four began to seek allies and followers to strengthen their respective positions, and slowly the factions aligned, the leaders throwing support to local warriors in minor power struggles throughout the land. The Hatakeyama became embroiled in a family succession dispute when its head, Mochikuni, died in 1455. During the confusion, Hosokawa Katsumoto stepped in to monopolize the shogunal deputyship for twelve years. The Shiba likewise descended into fratricidal conflict over succession.

Another factor in the growing disarray was the question of shogunal succession: the ineffectual Yoshimasa, without a male heir, had intended for his younger brother, Yoshimi, to succeed him and had busied himself with palace building and cultural pursuits. The birth of a son, Yoshihisa, in 1465, sparked a fierce determination by Yoshimasa's wife, Hino Tomiko, to see her child succeed his father, and thus a need was born to eliminate Yoshimi as a candidate for shogun. Deadly personal rivalries led to further alliances, as Tomiko sided with Yamana Sōzen while Ashikaga Yoshimi, her brother-in-law, not eager to lose the shogunacy promised him, allied with Hosokawa Katsumoto, the powerful deputy shogun.

But it was a dispute within the Shiba family over succession to the headship of the Board of Administration that set the sabers rattling in the seventh month of 1466. Shogun Yoshimasa appointed one family member to the position, passing over another who then cried foul, whereupon Yoshimasa dismissed and banished his first choice. The Yamana and one branch of the Shiba gathered their forces and brought them to Kyoto; in the twelfth month the Hosokawa, now allied with one branch of the Hatakeyama, followed suit. In the first month of 1467, at Yamana Sōzen's urging, the shogun thickened the plot again by ordering Hatakeyama Masanaga to relinquish both his residence and the office of shogunal deputy, which he had recently assumed. On the seventeenth day of the first month, Masanaga responded by burning his own house and fleeing to Kamigo-ryōsha, a shrine in northeastern Kyoto where he set up camp. On the next day his kinsman, the new deputy shogun, Hatakeyama Yoshinari, routed him and he fled from Kyoto.

Yamana Sōzen and Hosokawa Katsumoto, ally of the defeated Masa-naga, emerged in an uneasy standoff as the dominant warriors in Kyoto. General fighting subsided for a time, but the Hatakeyama continued to fight out their family problems. Prior to the initial fighting of the first month, the undisciplined (and probably hungry) followers of Masanaga looted and burned many moneylenders' shops in upper Kyoto. In the eyes of the warriors there may have been ample reason for resort to arms; to the townspeople they were uninvited guests whose behavior tended toward wanton destructiveness.

Hosokawa Katsumoto soon became dissatisfied with the inconclusive standoff and summoned more forces to Kyoto. Tensions rose as the warriors set up camp in city temples early in the fifth month. Katsumoto gathered his troops on the twentieth and began to organize an attack. At this point the warriors were lined up in two camps, east and west, as follows: Hosokawa Katsumoto, occupying the shogun's Palace of Flowers in the eastern side of upper Kyoto, was joined by Hatakeyama Masanaga, Shiba Yoshitoshi, and members of the Kyōgoku, Akamatsu, Takeda, and Togashi houses, while Yamana Sōzen in his residence on the western side of upper Kyoto was allied with Hatakeyama Yoshinari and Yoshimune, Shiba Yoshikado, and the Rokkaku, Isshiki, and Toki families. Hostilities began in a scattered way: unluckily located between the shogun's palace and Yamana Sōzen's residence, the prominent moneylender Shōjitsubō first had his residence occupied by the western Isshiki troops and then sacked by eastern forces, between the twentieth and twenty-fifth. On the twenty-sixth, all-out fighting commenced. The eastern forces were victorious the next day and for a time held the upper hand.

The short duration of this battle, not to say skirmish, was typical of limited medieval warfare; the fires of battle, however, had the capacity to destroy large areas. Northern Kyoto had suffered damage with many temples and residences burned. Commerce stopped and food was unavailable. Troops of the eastern camp looted moneylenders' shops, adding to the chaos.[85] Townspeople of both upper and lower Kyoto began to leave the city, heading south. One aristocrat started to have a moat dug around his residence for protection, but then changed his mind, realizing that he would be trapped in the event of a fire.[86] A sense of mortal danger was widespread. As if to make this official, it was announced on the seventh day of the sixth month that the popular Gion festival was canceled. On the very next day the smoldering fires of war were fanned by a great wind; it was recorded that thirty thousand houses of high and low alike were obliterated in upper Kyoto in the vicinity of Nijō and Muromachi.[87] As a functioning city, Kyoto was starting to shut down.

At this point the Hosokawa held the military advantage with their centrally located lands and vassals, including wealthy peasant-warrior vassals in Yamashiro province to the south. But in the sixth month the redoubtable Yamana Sōzen gathered thirty thousand troops in Tanba province to the west and reentered Kyoto in the eighth month, where he was joined by several thousand troops of two important allies, the Ōuchi and Kōno. The Ōuchi made a particularly strong impression with their large force entering the city on the twenty-eighth day, encamping at Tōji in the south. Commerce came to a halt and traffic through the city entrances in the area ceased. The Ōuchi then marched to the far northwestern corner where they set up camp at Funaokayama. But the Rokkaku and Yamana forces had camps in lower Kyoto by now; they burned nearby neighborhoods in the eighth month.

A chronicle of the war reports that wealthy townpeople, including brewer-lenders, fled to Ōtsu in Ōmi province.[88] Perhaps the Enryakuji connection paid off at last, for Hie Shrine's authority in Ōtsu was sufficient to shelter these refugees. They must have left in great numbers, for in 1470 the need for credit in Kyoto was described by a diarist as acute.[89] Many townspeople who were adherents of the Lotus school of Buddhism fled to Nara where they had temple connections, only to be persecuted by Kōfukuji. On the other hand, the renowned outcaste gardener Zen'ami was invited to Nara by Kōfukuji in 1471 and created a garden there as he waited out the war. High-ranking aristocrats began to leave for their provincial estates, where they would sit out the war; clerics had similar options.[90] Low-ranking aristocrats were perhaps worse off than rich commoners like moneylenders: they had to try to survive in Kyoto, moving their residences occasionally.

The two camps' strengths were still lopsided: the eastern forces numbered perhaps 160,000, while Yamana Sōzen from his westside residence was said to command between 90,000 and 110,000. (Historians agree that the forces were immense, though probably fewer than the figures given.) Nevertheless, from early in the ninth month the western forces began to accrue victories in battles and skirmishes bearing familiar Kyoto names

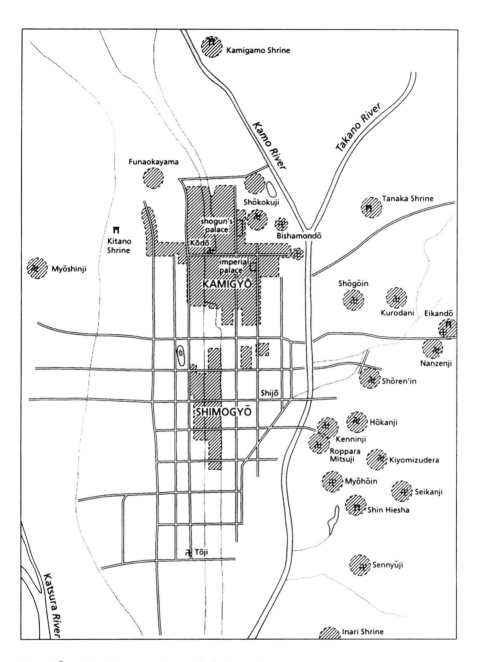

Map 5: Ōnin War Damage to Kyoto (shaded areas)

(Map 5). Sanbōin, part of the Daigoji temple southeast of Kyoto, was attacked by the western troops on the third day of the ninth month because eastern forces were encamped there. Eastern Iwakura Mountain was the site of a large battle on the eighteenth; much of the area east of the Kamo River, including Nanzenji and Shōren'in, was destroyed as fires spread. Shōkokuji, adjacent to the former shogunal palace where the eastern forces were encamped, was leveled in a bizarre series of events in the tenth month. Some Shōkokuji priests, supporters of the eastern warriors, in a provocative action set fire to a western encampment nearby. Eastern troops in the vicinity, seeing the flames, believed that Shōkokuji had been attacked by the western forces and rushed to its rescue. A battle ensued, with Shōkokuji fiercely attacked by the western side and heavily damaged by fire. The victors quickly established themselves in the ashes, placing themselves directly adjacent to the shogun's palace, held by the now cornered eastern troops. Hatakeyama Masanaga sent reinforcements, however, and Shōkokuji was attacked again. The eastern troops held the shogun's palace, but both sides suffered losses.

Temples were hit especially hard in the fighting because warriors encamped in them. A fundamental breakdown in the existing order is suggested in this disregard for the temples' sacredness by the warriors who chose them for camps, by their attackers, by thieves, and, occasionally, by their own monks eager for battle. The descent into chaos was complete when gold statues and ritual implements began to disappear from temples and shrines. Gion Shrine's golden oxhead, one of its main images, was taken and sold by a shrine employee to cover living expenses.[91] Ten priests who set fire to their temple in 1467, hoping to provoke the western troops, were beheaded.[92] Chinkōji was destroyed in 1470 by a squatter's cooking fire.[93] A priest at Kōfukuji noted the presence of 170–180 Kyoto priest-beggars on the streets of Nara in 1471.[94] In the second month of 1473 some gold objects at Tōji were stolen; when the thief returned in broad daylight and killed a nun, Tōji took action, hunting down a suspect and burning his house.[95]

After nearly a year of fighting the war bogged down, with little progress for either side. Subsequent to the Shōkokuji battle no more attacks were made on the main east and west encampments because, even though they were little more than a stone's throw from each other, they had become impregnable, fortified with large walls and moats. A massive moat separating the two sides was dug in the area of Ichijō; each side built huge watchtowers in the fourth month. North-central Kyoto had taken on the appearance of an armed camp. Most fighting for the next several years took the form of skirmishes or guerrilla-style attacks by warriors of each side, repeatedly cutting off supplies to the opposing side, setting fire to each others' camps, attacking assembled troops from the rear, and causing great destructon to the city in the process. Many of these warriors were recruited from peasants in the area and even from the ranks of the townspeople; they roamed the city in small bands, and their casualty rate was probably high. Renegades also disrupted city life. With frequent switching of sides and inconclusive fighting, some warriors withdrew from their camps and lived off the townspeople. Lodging them was forbidden, but they offered armed protection, like bodyguards, in return for a room. This could be dangerous, for they became well acquainted with the commoners' areas of the city and were responsible for looting unrelated to warrior campaigns. Homeless townspeople, some of them joining bands of thieves, also roamed the streets, occasionally causing fires as they squatted in deserted temples and houses.

The next major battle was in the ninth month of 1468 at Funaoka-yama, the camp of the western Ōuchi, who had left only a nominal force there as they departed for Tanba province for another battle. The Funaoka battle forced the Ōuchi out of the area, mostly a psychological victory more than anything—the area was too far north and the eastern forces had burned it as they invaded, rendering it useless. Such gratuitous, useless destruction characterized much of the war, and its only traces in Kyoto are the place-names Nishijin (western camp) and Yamana-chō in the northwest. The Yamana neighborhood scrupulously observed the annual Jizō festival in subsequent centuries, for legend had it that the ruthless Yamana Sōzen would return on a white horse seeking vengeance if services were neglected.

From 1469 the fighting spread to the provinces, a signal for many provincial governors to depart Kyoto for good to defend or expand their provincial bases. A lull ensued, but in the summer months of 1471, a deadly measles epidemic swept the city, striking commoners, aristocrats, and warriors alike. Townspeople, behind their now walled neighborhoods, held entertainments to drive the illness out of the city; in the eighth month this emerged into the open in a festive celebration featuring a parade of floats—a sort of impromptu festival—which even brought some warriors out to gawk.[96]

The heavy damage of the war was initially to neighborhoods of upper Kyoto, but in 1473 the Ōuchi, now a dominant force in the western camp, set fire to houses in a merchant neighborhood at Nijō between Ōmiya and Horikawa and then dug in at Rokujō to the south. The eastern forces of the Hatakeyama meanwhile established themselves between Nijō and Sanjō. The area in the middle—that of greatest moneylender concentration—between Shijō and Gojō became the battlefield. In the same year Yamana Sōzen and Hosokawa Katsumoto, chief instigators of the war, both died. A makeshift bridge was built over the moat dividing the city at Ichijō to allow townspeople to visit temples and merchants to carry on business, the beginnings of recovery in a wasted landscape. One diarist, pathetically delighted at even this small return to normalcy, exclaimed that people high and low were coming and going across the bridge, visiting acquaintances.[97] East of the Kamo River, an area previously thick with temples and retirement villas, only the Yasaka pagoda of Hōkanji remained intact.

In the seventh month of 1475, fighting in Kyoto flared up again, with a Nara chronicler noting "burning and dying in Kyoto" once more.[98] Fires spread through upper and western Kyoto, but on the thirtieth the same source noted that locals drove the warriors out—if true, a sign that the townspeople had had enough. In the ninth and tenth months, "normal" events occurred like leaf viewing in northern Kyoto and the installation of a bronze bell at Seiganji, a popular Pure Land temple in the northwestern corner of the city.[99] But the danger was not over yet: a group of aristocrats on a pilgrimage to a site north of the city in the seventh month of 1476 were attacked by a band of western forces.[100] The wife of one was assaulted and wounded, and a servant was killed. This attack on noncombatants, including a woman, shows the vicious, unpredictable nature of the violence. The long presence of encamped warriors in the city had made it a dangerous place. Fire remained a threat: the shogun's palace was burned and totally destroyed in the eleventh month of 1476; spreading north it destroyed scores of neighborhoods.[101]

In the first month of 1477 the Akamatsu and Takeda forces sparred in the city; in the sixth month Yamana forces burned villages to the west of Kyoto; in the ninth month Hatakeyama Yoshinari and company mercifully left Kyoto. Finally, in the eleventh month, the Toki and, most important, Ōuchi Masahiro pulled out of Kyoto, torching their own residences in a final blaze of violence. A few days later a group of aristocrats went to view the warrior ruins, then headed to a popular temple where they held a drinking party with singing and dancing.[102] Their actions reveal the enduring strength and success of Kyoto as a capital, which dismissed the warriors' decade-long barbarism and destruction, and looked to the future joyfully.

With the 1477 exodus of leading warriors from Kyoto the war sput-

tered to an end, a nominal victory for the eastern forces, now led by Hosokawa Masamoto. The original principals were dead, and several parties
had switched sides before it was over, leaving the Ashikaga effectively out
of politics, the Shiba and both Hatakeyama families defeated, the Yamana
reduced to insignificance, and the Hosokawa alone surviving to control
once again the office of deputy shogun, now bereft of any national significance. Upon Masamoto's death, however, that house too split in dispute,
leaving the Ōuchi the sole intact survivors. The Hatakeyama family standoff continued after the war, with Masanaga serving as deputy shogun until
1484. His attempt to move into Yamashiro province to the south was re-
buffed by the Hosokawa, long based there. The Hatakeyama were ousted
from the province by its warrior-peasants in an extraordinary assertion of
local strength, the Yamashiro provincial *ikki*. The shogun, Yoshimasa, had
retired during the conflict, retreating into his villa, while his wife, Hino
Tomiko, continued for a time to prey on moneylenders and rice dealers
for income and to dominate the lucrative toll stations at the city entrances.
Yoshimasa's son, Yoshihisa, as the next shogun strove to revive the authority of the shogunate and the lands of the religious establishment,
with but limited success. The long-term political significance of the Ōnin
War can only be understood by looking beyond Kyoto. Warrior disputes
continued to smolder but the political configuration of Japan was permanently altered. For its part, Kyoto in 1477 turned to the task of recovery.

The War's Effects on City Life

The course of the Ōnin War in Kyoto conjures up the image of a city as
battlefield, reduced to ashes, depopulated, and rife with conflict and crime.
These are not incorrect impressions, but the modern tendency to conceive
of war as total must be resisted when treating a medieval context. This
particular war lasted for ten years and destroyed probably half the city,
but most destruction occurred in the first two years of the war and thereafter was only sporadic. Thus a warped version of normalcy could prevail,
and indeed many residents had no choice but to remain in the city. This
is not to deny the war's destructiveness, however, which was multifaceted.
Fire, more than battle itself, was the most deadly threat. As a result of
the fighting most neighborhood blocks in Kyoto burned at least once, as
did major temples and shrines including Shōkokuji, Kitano, Tenryūji, Ninnaji, Tōji, and many aristocratic mansions as well. Looting by warriors
seems to have been chronic and perhaps necessary for daily sustenance;
the leading warriors, after all, lacked the means to support large forces

over time. But most damaging to the cultural essence of the capital was the breakdown of civility and respect that brutalized its residents: the wanton attack on a group of aristocrats and the sacking of temples were events on a scale that, even including recent peasant invasions of the city, had not been seen since the late twelfth century. Finally, in the short run commoners had to concentrate on survival; opportunity knocked after hostilities ceased.

The population began to return to the city from about 1476, but solid economic recovery and rebuilding took at least twenty years.[103] Two more huge fires wiped out much of the reconstruction: in 1494, between fifty-four and sixty-four *machi* burned in the central downtown area, another direct blow to the merchant community concentrated there. And in 1500 between twenty and forty thousand buildings burned in a fire that swept through upper Kyoto. The psychological blow to all Kyoto's residents must have been intense, for this fire occurred immediately after the Gion festival, revived for the first time since the Ōnin War, had temporarily lifted the spirits of the citizenry. The large number of *machi* neighborhoods and structures obliterated by these fires does suggest that the city had already gone a long way toward rebuilding itself when the fires occurred.

Post-Ōnin Kyoto gradually took on a long, narrow shape roughly like an hourglass whose upper and lower portions were joined by the north–south Muromachi street and surrounded by empty space that had hitherto been a solidly populated urban area (Map 6). Although the population fell as a result of the war, its density increased as the city's parameters contracted; this was the beginning, in Kyoto at least, of the densely packed urban lifestyle so characteristic of early modern Japanese cities.[104] The new living pattern is curious given the availability of much space nearby. Cramped circumstances may have provided a sense of security to the war-weary townspeople; fear, defined or otherwise, could induce a preference for high density in the post-Ōnin decades. For over a century, culminating in Hideyoshi's earthen wall built in 1591, which physically hemmed the city into its long, narrow parameters, Rakuchū—Kyoto proper—was a lively but crowded urban space more clearly separated than ever from Rakugai, the now lonely suburbs.

One of the changes in part attributable to the Ōnin War was already emerging earlier as a result of peasant invasions of the city: the neighborhood block (*machi*) was gradually transformed into a community facing itself across a street with gates at either end of the street (Fig. 1d). Accompanying this were architectural details for self-defense incorporated into the structures of individual homes. A 1467 list of twenty brewers

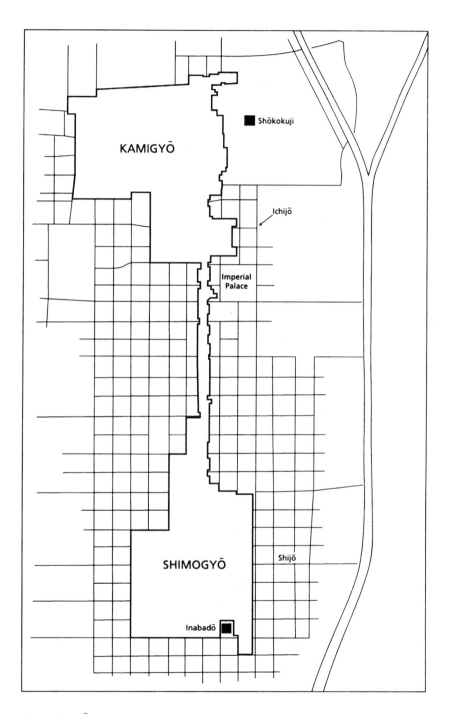

Map 6: Post-Ōnin Kyoto

compiled for tax purposes enumerates several defense features.[105] Some were previously found only in elite residences, suggesting that they had recently been incorporated into the homes of at least well-to-do townspeople like moneylenders. Among them were tall earthen-faced walls and fortified gates. Communal defense features also appeared in some late-fifteenth-century neighborhoods, including moats, gates at the ends of streets, some topped with small forts, walls enclosing entire blocks, and the use of temple bells to warn of impending danger.[106] These became routine neighborhood features in the sixteenth century, as militant Lotus temples, discussed below, extended their influence.

The recovery of the city was also expressed in the revival of festivals in the post-Ōnin decades. The most common type was the festival that originated as a religious ceremony to appease vengeful spirits (goryōe), like those of Gion, Inari, and Kitano shrines, which had been popular observances in Kyoto for centuries. The Gion festival, the most lavish of these and the one most closely tied to the lives of the townspeople, was canceled in 1467 because of the war and not revived for thirty-three years.[107] Then it once more became an opportunity for the ostentatious display of beauty and elegance by prosperous townspeople, including moneylenders. Only ten floats participated in the main procession in 1500, and twenty-six in the pre-festival religious activities, a sharp drop from fifty-eight before the war, but impressive nonetheless given the expense of mounting a float.[108] It is thought that the organization of the procession, moreover, was increasingly determined by the townspeople from about this time.

Postwar Commerce and the Shogunate

The long-term effects of the Ōnin War on the Muromachi shogunate were grave: weakened permanently, its national authority all but extinguished, even in Kyoto its presence was fainter than before. The office of shogun went into permanent eclipse, and the Bakufu's governing powers were severely curtailed.[109] The Board of Administration took over some functions of the Board of Retainers as the ranks of reliable vassals shrank.[110] To supplement their paltry incomes, shogunal administrators sometimes became lobbyists for religious institutions, diluting their loyalty.[111] At the same time, however, the shogunate's revenues from outside of Kyoto had declined, and so it was important to squeeze what it could out of commerce: incidental levies and conditional debt amnesties were more frequent than ever.

In the early sixteenth century the shogunate attempted to prescribe currency types that could be used in commercial transactions. Although not necessarily enforced successfully, this move resulted from a chaotic post-Ōnin monetary situation in which the value of currencies in use varied so widely that real prices in any financial transaction could also vary greatly. This allowed merchants, including of course moneylenders, to manipulate real amounts of income and of tax submitted. Presumably the same did not apply to their customers: the lenders were experts in setting currency conditions to suit themselves in loan transactions.

Currency had not been officially minted in Japan since the Heian period; hence the quality and value of coins in use in late medieval times covered a wide range. In addition to Chinese copper coins of recent vintage, copper coins dating from as far back as the Tang, Sung, and Yuan dynasties were also in use in Japan as well as a few privately minted domestic coins. Thus currency chaos reigned in the post-Ōnin decades, with nothing close to a standard existing. Long use meant that the older coins were often worn or broken, and privately minted coins were not universally accepted.

After the Ōnin War standardization of currency was desirable both for commercial stability and for the Bakufu's financial well-being. This concern is reflected in a spate of shogunal laws specifying which types of currency were acceptable and in what combinations. Called "money-choosing decrees" (erizenirei),[112] their purpose was to maintain a standard in the use of currency and thus ensure uniformity in financial transactions. Arbitrary currency selection by merchants—that is, refusing base currency and accepting only sound—was forbidden by the shogunate in 1500.[113] In order to get base currency out of circulation, special exchangers (akuzeniya) were designated to replace it with sound. Rules issued five years later disallowed very inferior quality coins (called kinsen, originally meaning copper coins from Nanking) and counterfeit coins (uchihirame, coins that had been hammered flat to appear larger and therefore worth more).[114] Otherwise, according to this decree, even flawed coins from China were acceptable. In 1506, Kyoto moneylenders specifically were chastised for disregarding repeated shogunal currency decrees, were forbidden to engage in arbitrary currency selection, and were commanded to accept all coins.[115] This is definitive proof that moneylenders in particular were guilty of currency manipulation. Four months later the same decree was reissued.[116] At about the same time, the shogunate declared that counterfeit and inferior coins were no longer to be used in transactions, but that all other Chinese coins, unless completely broken, must be accepted at the rate of one-third in transactions.[117] These instructions were reiterated in 1508 and posted on placards through-out the capital.[118] Significantly, Enryakuji's envoys were supplied with a copy of these decrees, with an appended note decrying widespread noncompliance.[119]

In 1509 the same currency rules were issued again with the added observation that arbitrary coin selection caused prices to rise.[120] The fol-lowing year brewer-lenders were once more singled out in a shogunal command that arbitrary currency selection was to cease and that severe punishment would be meted out to offenders. This stopped short of con-fiscation, however: "the next generation will be allowed to continue the business."[121] In the same year the shogunate vowed to arrest those who personally punished merchants engaging in arbitrary currency selection, a hint of a fair degree of rage on the part of customers who got the short end of the currency stick.[122] Also in 1510, the shogunate railed against arbitrary currency selection causing the price of goods to rise.[123] In 1512, shogunal currency rules became very specific regarding the exact mixture of coinage types to be allowed in transactions: 10 percent could be old coins; 2 percent each Hung-wu (Kōbu) or Hsuan-te (Sentoku) (types of Chinese coins); 6 percent Yung-lo (Eiraku); up to 20 percent good coins in mixed transactions; and another 5 percent coins minted in Japan as copies of Chinese and Korean coins, but only if they had characters visi-ble on the back, indicating better quality and less wear.[124] Japanese coins were to be accepted unless broken.[125]

Given the inconvenience of the cumbersome new currency system, it is hardly surprising that it was disregarded. Indeed, the decrees are marked by a tone of frustration urgently decrying widespread noncompliance. It has been suggested that these regulations represent a deliberate shogunal attempt to increase or maintain its own income without actually raising taxes but by tinkering with the value and supply of the currency instead.[126] In fact, however, no medieval authority had the comprehensive grasp nec-essary even to mint currency, let alone adjust its value. In addition, indirect, elaborate, and unenforceable measures like currency regulation were not necessary for the shogunate or any other overlord to increase income when an incidental levy would do the job quite well. Medieval authority by its very nature was simultaneously arbitrary and limited. Thus over-lords, including the shogunate, could impose and at least partially collect frequent incidental levies, but they could not micromanage individual commercial transactions.

Twenty of twenty-five shogunal decrees on currency regulation are narrowly concentrated in the period 1500 to 1512. This does not suggest deliberate, long-term policy. Rather, all signs point to a currency situation that was out of control in the post-Ōnin decades: by demanding only high-quality currency as payment, moneylenders and other merchants were raising the real price of goods and services and enriching themselves. As the closest thing to a government in Kyoto, the shogunate was reacting, through currency regulations, to a situation which harmed not only its own tax income but also the economic well-being of many in Kyoto. The main lesson of currency regulations is not that the shogunate manipulated the currency to enhance its own income but that merchants were doing so quite freely.

A further measure of the gravity of the situation and the shogunate's desire to gain control of it is that two out of only four times the death penalty is mentioned in Muromachi Bakufu laws are for violation of currency regulations. In one instance, it is stated that violators of currency regulations will be executed and their homes confiscated, while in another punishments for violators include decapitation for males and cutting off fingers for females.[127] (The other times the death penalty was invoked were in 1336, for large-scale bribery of officials, and in 1516 for "offensive warfare.")[128] These are the harshest punishments in all Bakufu law. The shogunate also threatened violators of currency laws, even those with elite connections, with corporal punishment and confiscation of residence.[129] In the absence of any evidence of enforcement however, one concludes mainly that these decrees indicate a strong shogunal desire to impose order in currency use, whether realized or not. Indeed, shogunal edicts on currency regulation strongly suggest a lack of control rather than the opposite. A number of factors—tax exemptions, vassals' defections, war—had taken their toll, permanently weakening the shogunate. Merchants, including moneylenders, were setting the rules in business transactions.

Currency regulations are seen only once more in Muromachi Bakufu law. In 1542 the shogunate issued five decrees prohibiting the use of base currency, specifying the exact ratio of coins and warning offenders of corporal punishment and confiscation of residence.[130] In one of these, moneylenders of upper Kyoto were singled out for a warning to adhere to laws on currency regulation, suggesting that they were again setting currency terms to favor themselves in transactions.[131] In the latter half of the sixteenth century, various local lords, as well as Oda Nobunaga and Toyotomi Hideyoshi, also issued some currency regulations. Effective control of the currency would be imposed by the Tokugawa shogunate, a more comprehensive authority than had existed in medieval times.

Another aspect of commerce, the toll stations at Kyoto's seven entrances, were for a time after the Ōnin War an especially lucrative source
of income to the shogunate, as income from other sources shrank. Hino
Tomiko, the wife of Shogun Yoshimasa, dominated them from the late
1450s until her death in 1496. At the age of nineteen she orchestrated
the dismantling of existing toll stations and the installation of new ones,
the proceeds from which were nominally designated for the reconstruction of Ise Shrine.[132] This was a form of control she already enjoyed elsewhere. A toll station of hers in Ōmi province, for instance, brought in
600 *kanmon* per month in the 1450s, and Kyoto's toll stations would
have been even more lucrative.[133] Indeed, tolls were the scourge of travelers: a Kōfukuji envoy mentioned paying a total of 1 *kan*, 500 *mon* in
tolls as he traveled from Nara through Kyoto to Mino province on a single
journey in 1479.[134] Packhorse drivers were especially vulnerable on their
frequent trips in and out of the city carrying taxable goods.[135] For over
thirty years the shogunate under Tomiko's influence generally deprived
traditional recipients of their toll income, claiming it instead for itself.
The individual, self-aggrandizing nature of this policy was in contrast to
the more general aims of shogunal currency regulations.

Tomiko's interest in the toll stations became intense after the Ōnin
War. Of nearly forty shogunal decrees pertaining to toll stations, only eight
predate the Ōnin War, while the majority fall into the four decades after
the war. By this time most shogunal revenues from outside Kyoto had
ceased, hence a heightened interest in the toll stations is understandable. Some sources even refer to the stations as *goryōsho*, directly administered shogunal sites.[136] During the war the toll stations had suffered
damage; in 1478 a temple diarist commented on this and speculated that
the shogun would order them rebuilt.[137] And so in 1480 new toll stations
were established at the seven city entrances, ostensibly for rebuilding the
palace.[138] But at this point the shogunate was allotting to the court only
the miserly sum of 10 *kanmon* per month, so the lion's share was likely
going into Tomiko's coffers.[139] In the same year marauding peasants
demanding a debt amnesty destroyed all of the new stations, but they were
in place again by 1485, their revenues designated for the shogun and
their management under the deputy head of the Board of Retainers.[140]
Each traveler was to be charged 16 *mon*, in addition to a "reasonable"
amount on baggage. In 1487, more toll stations were erected at the seven
official entrances, supposedly to cover palace costs. A priest at Kōfukuji,
however, noted in his diary that they really served Tomiko's interests.[141]

Her expropriation of toll revenue—in this case even building multiple stations at single entrance points—was an intrusion into a domain traditionally belonging to the court and aristocracy.

Once Tomiko was gone in 1496, the shogunate administered the toll stations more responsibly, allowing tolls to go to their traditional recipients but endeavoring to keep them at reasonable levels in order not to impede trade. During a famine in 1499 the shogunal deputy Hosokawa Masamoto ordered toll stations to keep vital supplies like salt and rice from leaving Kyoto.[142] In 1516, the Bakufu forbade an imperial officer to collect firewood in the area of a northern entrance, presumably because firewood collection was a ruse to interfere with the tolls.[143] The shogunate routinely ordered toll stations abolished or reprimanded the aristocratic recipients of their income for improper conduct like obstructing traffic and confiscating goods. These are all indications, after Tomiko's long but anomalous years, of a generally constructive shogunal policy toward commerce as the economy revived. The only caveat is that there is no evidence that any of the decrees was obeyed or enforced. Indeed, the frequency of shogunal decrees about Kyoto's toll stations suggests, as in the case of currency regulations, if anything a lack of control over temples, aristocrats, warriors, and even merchants erecting their own stations. Shogunal decrees decrying this practice have the hollow sound of an ignored scolding.

Even in post-Ōnin Kyoto, however, the shogunate continued to be the court of main resort for other elites trying to extract taxes from merchants. As has already been demonstrated in the context of Hie Shrine's tax for its spring festival, the Bakufu intervened both before and long after the Ōnin War to admonish moneylenders to pay up. A similar case is that of Minami Gosho, a sobriquet for a daughter of the emperor who was living at Hōkyōji, an imperial retirement convent. In 1498 the shogunate supported her traditional claim to taxes from the white cloth guild.[144] Later the same year she appointed a shogunal functionary as her tax agent, her best hope for successful collection.

In rare cases an enterprising aristocrat could reassert commercial overlordship independently of the shogunate, with at least modest success. A good example of this is the Oshikōji family, traditional recipient of the Distillery Office tax, whose post-Ōnin fortunes were related earlier. By persistence, and perhaps also because their tax was quite modest, the family was able to revive the tax on brewers and live on it for at least half of the sixteenth century. After that it became more difficult to collect, as commoners disregarded the traditional overlords with impunity.

The War's Effects on Moneylenders

The lengthy Ōnin War reduced the ranks of the moneylenders already hurt by *ikki* attacks and conditional debt amnesties. During the war the moneylenders were a frequent target of looters, and many took refuge in warrior encampments, even for extended periods.[145] Some left the city altogether, heading for Ōtsu where an overlord, Hie Shrine, was located. Others withdrew to Kyoto's periphery where they set up businesses.[146] Their absence may have created a credit vacuum in the city at a crucial time when loans were needed to help finance and survive the war in Kyoto. More than individual lenders, Zen temples in the city would have been a likely wartime source of such credit, given their size and warrior contacts, but they too were under attack and suffered extensive damage. The Ōnin War was of such scale and duration as to effectively preclude business as usual, including moneylending.

After the conflict ended, some moneylenders returned to Kyoto and new lenders from the provinces set up in business there as well, such was the demand for credit. Some hardy and powerful lenders, like Kenkei, the tax agent discussed earlier, had survived the war in Kyoto. Their relationship to their overlords became even more autonomous, and tax evasion through exemptions and outright refusal to pay was on the increase. The city had to be rebuilt, and a high demand for credit no doubt encouraged such boldness. Fewer moneylenders meant a drop in overlord tax revenues, although incidental levies and conditional debt amnesties helped take up the slack. Many newcomers were unaffiliated with any overlord, avoiding guild membership altogether.

An anecdote from 1479 illustrates the social prominence of some post-Ōnin moneylenders. Vassals of two warrior houses, the Yamana and the Akamatsu, were in a standoff over an incident of adultery between a warrior of the Akamatsu camp and the wife of a brewer-lender at Gojō and Karasuma, in the heart of the commercial district. It seems that the jealous lender had encountered his wife's lover on the street and killed him, an act that would have been quite acceptable had it been done in a house. But because the murder took place on the street, the Akamatsu sent a retainer to attack the lender in revenge. At this point the Yamana entered the picture, because the lender's son was a retainer of the Itakura, a relative of whom was a Yamana retainer.[147]

This squabble shows the relative prominence of one brewer-lender whose "honor" had been sullied and who could, apparently, kill a warrior with impunity and then count on support from other warriors. Vassalage between the lender's son and a warrior house is reflective of an Ōnin War practice, quite new to Kyoto civil society, allowing for ties of fealty between townspeople and warriors. A realignment of commercial ties may also explain the warrior involvement in this matter: anticipating the early modern period, some individual merchants already may have become, in effect, enfeoffed to warriors, as new merchants avoided guilds in the post-Ōnin years.

A shift occurred in the moneylender ranks over the fifteenth century from clerical to lay status and became pronounced after the Ōnin War. A comparison of names on pre- and post-Ōnin tax rolls and other sources reveals a declining number of lenders with priestly names (see Appendix). In the earliest and most exhaustive list, Kitano Shrine's roster of 1425, 256 or over two-thirds of all the lenders are listed with clerical names.[148] Ten used Ji sect names, suggesting lay status, and sixty-one others are lay names. Of the latter, twenty are youth-names, indicating that they may later have become priests. If so, then over 70 percent of the total can be considered clerics and only about 15 percent lay. The eight province names may refer to laymen or be incomplete entries, while two of the three women are nuns, a status indicative of widowhood.

The next list of Kyoto brewer-lender names is dated 1467/4 and contains forty-nine individuals.[149] The date follows the opening salvos of the Ōnin War but precedes the main fighting, which began in the fifth month of 1467. Thus it is appropriate to see this group, although not comprehensive, as representative of the Kyoto moneylending establishment on the eve of the Ōnin War. This list, unlike the others, conveniently applies a specific status label to each individual. This may reflect different treatment accorded clerical and lay lenders, or the detailed labeling may have been done for easy identification by the tax agent. Thirty-one, or over 60 percent are lay, including one woman and one child or outcaste. Four are nuns (widows). Of the fourteen clerics on the list three are labeled *shami* and eleven *sō*. Although the exact meaning of these terms had become vague by the late medieval period, *sō* were probably individuals with monastic training who may have worn priestly robes but were currently leading a secular life. *Shami*, on the other hand, were either novices or laymen with only rudimentary training as priests without progressing beyond the novice stage.[150]

In addition to the fact that only about 35 percent of the lenders on these lists are clerical, it is striking that the documents are at pains to distinguish between the two priestly ranks, suggesting faintly that the eleven *sō* priests were of higher status among the brewer-lenders than the three *shami*. If representative, this list of status divisions among lenders and the need to note them indicate a tendency toward a secular lifestyle already under way as the Ōnin War began. The ratio of lay to clerical lenders (60–28 percent) found in these lists is nearly an exact inversion of that found in the 1425 list.

Another source of moneylender names in this period is the shogunate. As will be recalled, by the middle of the fifteenth century the Bakufu learned to turn debt amnesties to its benefit by demanding a percentage of the loan in return for an amnesty. Such conditional debt amnesties, issued frequently from 1454, required that the lender or debtor submit a request to the shogunate to have the loan confirmed or annulled, as the case might be. Some of these requests survive in shogunal document collections.[151]

While these sources do not document the entire moneylending community, they are still helpful as indicators of its general makeup. Of one hundred thirty-three requests dated 1480–1485 by lenders for shogunal confirmation of loans following a conditional debt amnesty, seventy-eight or nearly 60 percent are from nonclerics, among them a member of the Hino family, a couple of individuals in the imperial palace, and the giant brewer Yanagi who loaned 28 *kanmon* to an imperial villa in the west of Kyoto.[152] Fifty-four or 40 percent of the requests are from clerics or temples. Among these are Zen temples such as Nanzenji, Tenryūji, and Shōkokuji, well known for moneylending. But also among the fifty-four religious names are those of nine individual priests, two of whom definitely had an Enryakuji connection.[153] Thus, only 7 percent of the names in this group at most appear to be Enryakuji-affiliated monks. If this particular group of moneylenders is representative of lenders in general, the decrease in Enryakuji lenders seems to have intensified after the Ōnin War. Unlike other lists of moneylenders, this source also indicates the broad range of sources of credit in the city. Although this study focusses on individual lenders, it is apparent that Buddhist temples of all types were routinely involved in moneylending as well.

The tax rosters of 1495 in the Ninagawa collection contain a large number of secular names.[154] In fact, of a total of 144 entries, only one, Gyokusenbō, is obviously clerical. These documents are admittedly problem-ridden, as discussed earlier, with many entries lacking any name at all and some probable duplication. Nonetheless, it is quite striking that clerical names have all but vanished. There is, moreover, a tendency, not seen before, for lay lenders to use both surnames and given names. This suggests wealth and individualism among lenders, a primary identification with the city, and therefore a detachment from Enryakuji, the religious overlord.

A different sort of tax roll is a list of Kyoto brewers used by the Oshikōji family in connection with their collection of the Distillery Office tax in the first month of 1511.[155] Fifty-two different brewers appear on this list, some paying the tax and some apparently exempted. As in the Ninagawa list of 1495, one brewer, Gyokusenbō, is clearly an Enryakuji monk, while another uses the surname Yasu as well as his Enryakuji clerical name, Zenshōbō. Many names appear on both the Ninagawa and Oshikōji lists, but neither list necessarily gives a complete accounting of the Kyoto brewer-lender establishment. They are all we have to go on, however, and the fact is that the 1511 list confirms the earlier impression that the Enryakuji connection was increasingly rare among brewer-lenders in the post-Ōnin years. In the case of shogunal and Enryakuji tax agents discussed previously, moreover, the trend in the post-Ōnin years was toward employment of lenders with lay names.

Although these moneylender tax rolls indicate a strong tendency toward secularization, they do not prove that clerical lenders had disappeared. For one thing, the lists analyzed above are not necessarily complete. Furthermore, the taxing authorities differ in each, and this could account for some differences in the names: that of 1425 is Kitano Shrine; that of 1467 is Hie Shrine; that of 1480–1485 and 1495 is the shogunate; and that of 1511 is an aristocrat collecting an imperial court tax. The low number of clerics on the 1495 and 1511 lists may indicate that the Bakufu was not taxing many of them but was instead focusing on new lenders or on new ways, like conditional debt amnesties, to extract revenues from them. If so, these lists confirm that much extra-guild activity occurred after the Ōnin War as new merchants entered the city, but they are not proof that Kyoto moneylenders with an Enryakuji tie had vanished or broken that tie. (The copious evidence from Hie Shrine's festival records, analyzed earlier, demonstrate quite the opposite.) They do, however, encourage the interpretation that most Kyoto moneylenders were nonclerical by the end of the fifteenth century. This seems to have been true of the most prominent moneylenders as well: previously dominated by clerics, the ranks of the shogunal tax agents in the post-Ōnin years were increasingly dominated by lenders with lay names, suggesting at least a flagging ability to collect on the part of the remaining clerical lenders and at most a failure to survive. Also, there may have been among the townspeople a new preference for using secular names, which suggests an emerging individual identity.

Finally, it must be emphasized that none of these lists is necessarily comprehensive, though that of 1425 is usually considered to be. That judgment is probably sound, given the relatively robust state of overlord arrangements at that time. The lists of 1467 and 1495, however, appear to be fragmentary and may include some merchants who were not lenders. By the end of the fifteenth century, with multiple overlords taxing multiple merchants to get what they could amid much tax evasion, no list is completely reliable. The exact size and makeup of the post-Ōnin moneylending establishment remains obscure, but all signs point to a more secular character than before the war.

The post-Ōnin decades witnessed an influx into Kyoto of a new type of entrepreneur who flaunted guild conventions by operating entirely outside them. Such behavior harmed the traditional overlords, including the shogunate, who were dependent on commercial groups for income. But significant to the moneylenders of this study is the damage such individuals could do to their monopoly on *sake* in Kyoto. If their volume of sales decreased as a result of the new competition, then their capital available for credit also decreased; hence the predominance of small lending operations in the post-Ōnin decades. Guild members and traditional overlords found themselves on the same side in this struggle against independent newcomers.

Some attempts were made to tax the newcomers. In 1500 the shogunate promised a five-month tax reprieve to new lenders but emphasized that they must pay taxes and inform the shogunate that they were in business, an indirect indication that they were not doing so.[156] In 1508, newcomers claiming to be only brewers or bean-paste merchants were in fact lending money but evading taxes on that activity, according to the shogunate.[157] *Sake* retailers who evaded taxes were again denounced by the shogunate in 1511.[158] It was noted that "original" brewers were paying their taxes, but evasion by others was causing shogunal revenues to drop. A post-Ōnin development, the retailing of *sake* at a site separate from the brewery was done by newcomers as well as by older breweries, which established shops in other neighborhoods for that purpose.[159] This decree could be referring to both types of retailers. In addition, the decree's concern over falling revenues suggests that retail shops constituted a significant portion of the brewing establishment in post-Ōnin Kyoto. At the same time, the shogunate forbade the practice of bringing *sake* into the city from the outside for sale, as this hurt "original" brewers.[160] This conjures up an image of many small breweries on Kyoto's outskirts selling in the city. But the same decree also accused "houses of authority" (*kenmon*) of involvement in this matter, claiming that the *sake* brought in was for their personal use when they were in fact selling it. Perhaps enterprising aristocrats or warriors had found that brewing was a way to make money. Thus the original guild's Kyoto monopoly on *sake* appears to have been seriously undercut by newcomers by the early sixteenth century. Roughly simultaneous with these shogunal decrees on brewing were some attempts to enforce other commercial monopolies.[161] In the early sixteenth century, independent merchants were threatening prior arrangements.

The post-Ōnin period, then, was one in which entrepreneurial skill more than elite connections increasingly determined success or failure. For the townspeople, this meant the growing importance of individual wealth and the dwindling influence of overlords. As the overlords weakened and became less effective in their traditional role as guarantors of monopolies, their commercial subordinates began to pull away. The increasing aloofness of moneylenders from their religious overlords after the Ōnin War was part of a larger trend in which the townspeople asserted a separate identity. This had begun long before the war, which then intensified the trend as merchants learned to survive by their own wits. It occurred in the self-governing neighborhood unit, in the organization and financing of the Gion festival, in the proliferation of secular names, and in cultural pursuits like the tea ceremony, on which wealthy townspeople, especially moneylenders, spent their money.

The Ōnin War clinched the functional transformation of Kyoto that had started in the thirteenth century from a political and administrative city to a commercial center.[162] Kyoto before the war had been both the country's political capital, as home of the Muromachi shogunate and the imperial court, and a consumer center where the elites absorbed and spent tax revenues. During the war most provincial governors stopped maintaining residences in Kyoto and returned to their provinces for good, some put out of power and others hanging on and even expanding their local base. There remained in Kyoto the shogun, aristocrats, and temples, all weaker than before, possessing little landed income beyond the capital area. As the city recovered, its vitality was concentrated increasingly in its merchants and craftsmen, who were less bound by and dependent on their overlords. The earlier consumer orientation of the city was gradually balanced by an export aspect; the provinces now were prosperous enough to provide a steady demand for Kyoto products like textiles. The nature of the relationship between Kyoto, center of manufacture, and the provinces changed in another aspect as well: raw materials used in the textile industry, for example, were as before imported into Kyoto, but now mostly as products for purchase, not as estate taxes. This commodity economy thrived more than ever on credit, the preserve of the moneylenders.

Chapter Five

Urban Affairs

By NO MEANS WERE the last two centuries of the medieval age in Kyoto merely a time of unrelieved chaos. Even as they endured periodic attacks by peasant leagues and the strife of warriors, many moneylenders thrived in the late medieval city. With their wealth and status they were at the forefront of neighborhood self-governing efforts, advancing collective aims in the face of weak overlords and often nonexistent city administration. As financiers and participants, the wealthiest of them played a prominent role in the urban cultural efflorescence of the late medieval period, mingling easily with elites and other townspeople alike. Indeed, the pleasing eclectic blend known as Muromachi culture was the product of a commitment to culture at all levels of Kyoto society, and moneylender glue helped set the bond. Defying overlords in matters of taxation and internal neighborhood affairs, the moneylenders nevertheless kept the old links in good repair, recognizing the value of elite connections for financial and cultural prosperity. As leading urban commoners, they buttressed the autonomous stance of the townspeople and simultaneously enabled cultural synthesis in late medieval Kyoto.

Self-Governance

The moneylenders were merchants operating individual businesses in Kyoto, but along with other townspeople they also behaved collectively in several capacities. One was through occupational guilds, in varying degrees of distance from the overlord. Another was as residents of neighborhoods (*machi*) that increasingly assumed responsibility for security and internal governance. Finally, the late medieval proliferation of religious movements affected moneylenders along with most townspeople, and in the early sixteenth century some were swept into the Lotus movement, a popular Buddhist organization exhibiting paramilitary characteristics. These three collectives overlapped temporally but were functionally distinct. Each was a means through which townspeople learned self-reliance and autonomy. Adversity like peasant invasions and warrior battles in Kyoto further promoted these qualities. Considered by some a sixteenth-century phenomenon, self-governance by townspeople, defined broadly, can be detected in various forms throughout the late medieval period.

Precise definition of the moneylenders' role in urban self-governance is problematic. A position of leadership is often assumed from their wealth and status and from their prowess in self-defense efforts against peasant invasions of Kyoto. On the other hand, we have seen signs in the record of resentment by townspeople toward these creditors and their harsh practices. Identified with the elites, especially as tax agents, the moneylenders nevertheless were, by the sixteenth century, secular townspeople whose interests generally corresponded with those of their neighbors. Moreover, lenders came in all sizes, some probably leaders and others followers. At any rate, the historical record is mostly silent on the matter of individuals' participation in neighborhood governance and in religious movements, but implicitly the range of known activities by moneylenders connotes their full participation in city life.

In some Japanese scholarship the investigation of moneylenders as townspeople has been dominated by an ideological tendency to invoke a class-based analytical model. According to such a mode of analysis, the moneylenders are usually defined in one of two ways: (1) as natural enemies of the townspeople because of their credit function and wealth, and in this sense as an extension of the rulers into local affairs; or (2) as the leaders of the townspeople, aided by their great wealth and status in elite organizations like Enryakuji and the shogunate. The two views have been combined into the assertion that the moneylenders, initially at odds with other townspeople, were successfully absorbed into the emerging bourgeoisie in the late medieval period, thereby enabling the townspeople as a whole to wield considerable economic power.[1] Another result of this class-based approach has been a determination to find instances of popular self-governance in the sixteenth century, specifically the "free city" model of early modern Europe. This prize is usually awarded to midsixteenth-century Sakai and, to a lesser degree, Kyoto, especially in the 1520s and 1530s when the Lotus movement was at its height.[2] This is by no means an insignificant historical observation: in Sakai, with its relative absence of traditional overlords and a strong merchant community tied to the port's flourishing trade, a comparison to early modern Europe is particularly apt. In sixteenth-century Kyoto, too, home of the declining elites, issues of commoner rule can be fruitfully addressed.

A rigid class-based analysis, however, to some extent predetermines the historical agenda and can render obscure other realities. The money-lenders were prominent and widely recognized merchants, but this is not to say that they successfully bundled the townspeople into an effective self-governing union. It might be argued, on the contrary, that their tie to the declining elites, while helpful to them, actually hindered the emer-gence of self-governance among the townspeople by dividing the loyalty of their most prominent element, the moneylenders. This is not to say, however, that the moneylenders were aloof, absorbed only in their own enrichment. Nor were they a shunned or marginalized, if wealthy, group. They were prominent townspeople whose ties to leading overlords bene-fited them in business and in social status; they conducted business ener-getically and looked out for their own interests, which often coincided with those of other townspeople. Even after the Ōnin War the lenders were still a large and successful group of merchants. It is logical, therefore, to assume some moneylender participation in the two major experiments in autonomy in late medieval Kyoto, the neighborhood and the Lotus move-ment. Some Japanese scholarship of urban history, it should be noted, has eschewed a class-based analysis in favor of a careful investigation of the details of city structure and daily life.[3] This approach can help to pro-duce a more nuanced understanding of the moneylenders' existence, in-cluding its uncommon richness alongside its very common concerns for safety and protection.

Patterns of self-governance evolved slowly among the townspeople, responding to both internal needs and external pressures. Prominent moneylenders had led groups of townspeople in self-defense against fifteenth-century *ikki*. During the Ōnin War the neighborhood unit called the *machi* turned inward in self-defense, facing itself across a street and gated at either end (the *ryōgawamachi*, Fig. 1d). In the instability of the early sixteenth century defensive *machi* features remained intact, and a collective approach governed aspects of daily life in the neighborhood. Even in early medieval times, *machi* residents probably had had an orga-nized approach to some internal matters, but as a unit of self-governance it seems to have come into its own in the wake of the Ōnin War. The political outcome of the war in Kyoto had left a faction of the Hosokawa family in power, but this is hardly to say that anyone was in control, even by medieval standards.[4] As the shogunate continued to perform some of its functions and the economy revived, a succession of warlords alternately neglected and placed severe stress on city life. Political turmoil above meant that at the neighborhood level there was nothing for it but to handle one's own affairs. *Machi* members served on a monthly basis as the neighborhood representatives (*gachigyōji*), organizing internal affairs like garbage disposal and guard duty and mediating disputes with other neighborhoods. Moneylenders may have been natural candidates for this role because of their privileged status and economic dominance. By no means were they the only leaders, however, for they tended to be concentrated in certain neighborhoods. Especially in upper Kyoto, even aristocratic residents participated in the *machi* organization as communal effort became the norm. This socially mixed character of some *machi* may well have contributed to the cultural syncretism of the time.

Not all of post-Ōnin Kyoto conformed to the *machi* pattern of communal self-government. There were also self-contained communities in the neighborhoods of major temples and shrines, like Kitano and Gion. Even within *machi*, some were but a facade of shops along the street, with vacant land or agricultural plots dominating the interior.[5] Nevertheless, the *machi* was the most common urban form. According to an aristocratic diary there were 120 organized *machi* in upper Kyoto in 1550.[6] Lower Kyoto, densely populated by merchants, also had a large number: sixty-six neighborhoods of lower Kyoto had the wealth to contribute floats to the Gion Festival in 1533, suggesting that at least that many were active there.

From about the 1530s the *machi* began to expand into a citywide network. *Machi* clusters, called *machigumi* and consisting of fourteen or fifteen neighborhoods each, coordinated self-defense and interneighborhood affairs. Each neighborhood chose a member to represent it in the larger cluster. Documentation is sketchy at best, but as an indication of the size of this network, by the late 1530s in upper Kyoto there were five or six clusters, each with ten to fifteen neighborhoods as members, while lower Kyoto had at least five such clusters.[7] Clusters of upper and lower Kyoto neighborhoods worked together in a council of elders as a limited city government: internal policing and patrolling, mediation of disputes among neighborhoods, the collection of incidental shogunal taxes, and some litigation were seen to by the council, with official acquiescence. The extent of this body's powers and even an approximate date of its ascent are unclear. Furthermore, the arrangement was neither democratic nor comprehensive: powerful and wealthy individuals tended to dominate neighborhoods, and powerful neighborhoods dominated clusters, while the shogunate did not relinquish its authority to adjudicate. In court cases, neighborhood clusters could petition the shogunate on behalf of a member facing lawsuit.

Simultaneous with these manifestations of self-governance in sixteenth-century Kyoto was the militarization of Kyoto's civil society. In the aftermath of the Ōnin War aspects of city life that were abnormal versions of a peacetime existence took on a permanent character. Even before the Ōnin War, the townspeople of Kyoto, in fighting off peasant invasions, had become experienced fighters and experts in self-defense tactics. To the extent that some were drafted to fight by warriors in the Ōnin conflict as well, their military skills were further honed. In the eleventh month of 1527, as warriors fought out their latest differences in the streets of Kyoto, an aristocrat had a wooden fence built on the street around his property. When marauding warriors attacked a mat maker's house, the entire neighborhood raised its own enclosure collectively.[8] Fortified fences and gates at the end of neighborhood streets, first seen in the Ōnin War, were still found in Kyoto in the 1530s.[9] In ledgers of neighborhood expenses for 1573–1592, the Reisen neighborhood made regular notations on the maintenance and rebuilding of such street gates, suggesting that they had become a regular part of the urban landscape over the course of the sixteenth century.[10] The European missionary Joao Rodrigues observed that every neighborhood street had them in the early seventeenth century; they numbered several thousand throughout the city.[11] Kyoto itself took on a long, narrow shape, which it maintained even as its population began to rise again. The very use of space, therefore, was itself a sign of awareness of danger. An incident of 1535 is suggestive, but only that: the prominent clerical moneylender Shōjitsubō was granted permission by the shogunate to build a small house on an empty lot adjacent to his own, "as a precaution" (yōjin no tame).[12] This seems a routine matter except for the last phrase: Shōjitsubō was not building a house for his children or a storehouse, but wanted to put to rest a feeling of unease at having an empty space beside his house. In other words, in the urban perception of space, emptiness implied danger. Fire, perhaps during the Lotus Sect uprising, may have destroyed an earlier structure on Shōjitsubō's land. If the fire caused death, a fear of contamination may have prompted his unease. Security, the moneylender's perpetual concern, may have been the main issue. Moneylenders were no more well-liked than they had ever been, and a vacant lot on one side made them quite vulnerable to attack. The case suggests that being closely surrounded by buildings imparted a sense of security to Kyoto's inhabitants; lack of structures caused the opposite. Even as the economy recovered, governance was up for grabs and the citizenry remained on the lookout.

In such an atmosphere it is not surprising that an organization which developed paramilitary traits, the Buddhist Lotus movement, became for a short time the most conspicuous way in which the townspeople asserted their autonomy from the established elites. It is thought that by the early sixteenth century nearly all Kyoto townspeople were part of an organization, the Lotus leagues (*Hokke ikki*), whose religious roots gave it an appeal and strength that far surpassed, at least for a few years, those of the older guilds and neighborhood blocks. Ultimately this organization was crushed by the combined forces of Enryakuji and leading warriors, but its brief efflorescence marked the culmination of social trends seen from the time of the Ōnin War. At their height the Lotus leagues achieved self-governing powers autonomous of the traditional overlords, an impressive and unique, if brief, achievement in Kyoto.

However peculiar it may have been to its unsettled times, the Lotus movement should be seen as one—albeit the most popular one in Kyoto —of a medieval proliferation of Buddhist forms with universal appeal. This occurred, not coincidentally, at the same time as secularization took hold: as we have seen, fewer moneylenders used clerical names, the authority of the traditional religious establishment was eroding, and cultural forms, although they had religious roots, were increasingly appropriated by townspeople. The townspeople were eclectic in their piety and interested in doing well in this world, and they participated eagerly in various religious movements. The Ji or Time Sect of Pure Land Buddhism was one of the most visible of these, with its trademark street dancing and proselytizing in medieval Kyoto. The widely popular True Pure Land movement never counted Kyoto as its major stronghold, although the Bukkōji, one of its main temples, was located there.[13] There was also something of a revival of "old Buddhism" in the medieval period, as older temples opened their doors to commoners in the hope of attracting a mass following. Not to be overlooked is the Rokkakudō, popular since Heian times as a center of the Kannon bodhisattva cult. Never a Lotus temple, in the medieval period it was a focal point of citizens' lives in lower Kyoto; the sound of its bell was the signal for defensive action in that part of the city.

The movement that was to pack the most political force in the post-Ōnin years was the Lotus, with its zealous townspeople followers.[14]

Brought into Kyoto at the end of the thirteenth century by Nichiren's disciple Nichizō, and called the Lotus sect after its primary text, over the fourteenth and fifteenth centuries it built a rock-solid base, especially in lower Kyoto where thirteen of its twenty-one Kyoto temples were concentrated. Particularly in the late fourteenth century, Lotus priests from eastern Japan came to Kyoto to proselytize. Their success was especially disturbing to Enryakuji, with which they clashed occasionally.[15] One particularly famous Lotus priest, Nisshin, became legendary for his many conversions not only in Kyoto, but throughout Japan. In 1439, he attempted to convert the shogun, Yoshinori, who responded with characteristic vehemence: Nisshin was jailed in a crowded cell, and was said to have had a glowing hot pot placed over his head and the tip of his tongue cut off.[16] The latter measure was intended to make future proselytization difficult. Yoshinori was assassinated two years later, and Nisshin was released in a general amnesty. His speech seriously impaired, he nonetheless continued to spread the Lotus message, with strong backing from prominent adherents in eastern Japan. Jailed once again by the shogunate in 1460, he was again released, thanks, ironically, to the intervention of the mother of Shogun Yoshimasa. He died at the ripe old age of eighty-eight. Such charismatic leadership was part of the reason for the Lotus movement's dramatic growth.

At the time of the Ōnin conflict, about half the city dwellers were said to have Lotus affiliation, but thereafter Lotus influence over the population of Kyoto increased as more townspeople joined the leagues. The religious and social atmosphere of the city was fluid, allowing some sectarian and class intermingling as individuals changed religious affiliation.[17] Some aristocrats and warriors, like the Miyoshi, became Lotus members, but in Kyoto it was predominantly a sect of commoners. Lotus encouragement of worldly success made it especially attractive to merchants.[18] Nichiren taught that one becomes a buddha in one's present body and makes this world the Buddhist paradise. Furthermore, Enryakuji had long emphasized the Lotus Sutra as its foundational text; hence adherence to the Lotus sect would be an easy step, doctrinally, for moneylenders with Enryakuji connections. For many of them, moreover, the link with Enryakuji was either nonexistent, in the case of newer enterprises, or had weakened so that affiliation with another religious group was not unthinkable. The giant brewer-lender Yanagi was a Lotus adherent from the late fourteenth century and one of its leading patrons.[19] In the early Muromachi period he donated one thousand *kanmon* for the rebuilding of the Lotus temple Honmyōji, and later contributed to the rebuilding of the Myōhōrenji as well. That some moneylenders chose to affiliate with the Lotus sect was another indication of their identity as townspeople whose link to the overlord was substantially weakened. Membership in a Lotus temple did not indicate subordination to another overlord but was rather a sign of independence from the traditional elites. As a relatively new form of Japanese Buddhism, the Lotus movement lacked the institutional solidity of older schools with their long-standing control of land and commerce. Instead, its support came directly from its followers, many of them wealthy commoners like moneylenders.

In addition to doctrines friendly to merchants the Lotus movement also had a militant aspect, which may have imparted to its members a sense of security in unsettled times. The Kyoto Lotus temples, each called a *honzan* or main temple, seem to have been quite independent of one another, and some rivalry existed among them. Typically a massive, fortresslike structure encompassing up to eight city blocks (*machi*) and surrounded by a wall and moat, these temples conveyed a certain exclusivity and belligerent isolation. Each Lotus temple had a "parish" of followers and an individual character somewhat dependent on its priest and its lay leaders. The temple leadership's ability to mobilize its followers was probably facilitated by this lay element. When mobilized, they were referred to as *Hokke ikki*, or Lotus leagues, whose paramilitary character was intensified by their religious fervor. This tended to encourage exclusivism and even armed conflict.

As early as 1413 harshly exclusive sectarian policies began to emerge, with one Lotus temple forbidding contributions to or participation in the activities of other temples.[20] Other Lotus temples followed suit, and eventually even bathing with non-Lotus people was outlawed. Lotus temples tended not to participate in shogunal and other public events normally attended by a range of Kyoto temple representatives, and in this way set themselves apart from the established order. On the thirty-third anniversary of the death of Shogun Yoshimitsu in 1440, for example, only eight of the twenty-one Kyoto Lotus temples sent representatives to the commemorative ceremony.[21] Exclusiveness applied within the Lotus movement as well: in the sixth month of 1496, followers of two Lotus temples fought a battle over doctrine that was quelled only by shogunal intervention.[22] On other occasions in 1504, 1511, and 1520 they supported various Hosokawa warriors in conflicts in return for concessions such as a half-tax and rent exemptions.[23] Their prowess was acknowledged at the highest levels: in 1527 Shogun Yoshiharu briefly moved into a Lotus temple fortress to escape a warrior, Miyoshi Motonaga, himself a Lotus adherent![24]

The Lotus cells utilized "forcible conversion by persistent argument" (*kyōgi shakubuku*), a coerciveness perhaps not surprising in a mass religion with charismatic leadership. It was said that on Nichiren's death date each month the streets of Kyoto rang with the Lotus chant.[25] The Lotus combination of military might and religious zeal created a powerful chemistry.

In the years of political confusion from 1527 to 1533 when the Muromachi Bakufu ceased to be a viable government, the Lotus leagues were coming into their own as a limited form of self-government alongside but not replacing the neighborhood unit.[26] The shogun, Yoshiharu, fled to Sakamoto in Ōmi province in 1527, while the real Ashikaga power holder, Yoshitsuna, backed by the strongman Hosokawa Harumoto, controlled central Japan from his base in Sakai. (Yoshitsuna, son of eleventh shogun Yoshizumi, never held the position of shogun, but his authority was recognized for a time by the Kyoto elites.) With a power vacuum at the top in Kyoto, the Lotus leagues and neighborhood units (*machi*) assumed defense and internal policing duties, including the disposition of criminal cases, although the exact allocation of duties and other organizational details are not clear.

In the eighth month of 1532, peasant leagues (*ikkō ikki*) made up of followers of True Pure Land Buddhism (Jōdo Shinshū) invaded Kyoto to attack the Lotus leagues there. Unlike similar forays into Sakai and Nara, however, they found themselves outnumbered and were driven off. The Kyoto Lotus leagues were then called upon for assistance by Hosokawa Harumoto and Rokkaku Sadayori, Ōmi military governor, in destroying the Honganji in nearby Yamashina, headquarters of the True Pure Land leagues.[27] Sadayori was a main player in a crowded field of power contenders, and was probably eager to rid the adjacent province of the powerful Honganji organization.[28] The assistance of the Lotus leagues proved crucial in the defeat of the Honganji in 1532, and for a time Harumoto was to treat them well. The leagues' credentials as defenders of the city were now widely acknowledged, and they succeeded in garnering exemptions from taxes and land rent in Kyoto, in addition to charging a half-tax of their own.[29] Their self-governance was thus complete, having earlier achieved control over policing and criminal investigations.

The years 1532–1536 were the height of Lotus strength in Kyoto, and self-governance occurred on many fronts. The shogun was in Ōmi and Hosokawa Harumoto in Sakai most of the time, so the townspeople had to take responsibility for security and the resolution of disputes. In 1533, for example, the aristocrat Yamashina Tokitsugu witnessed a neighborhood council led by Lotus adherents to decide what course of action to take against three arsonists.[30] The scope of Lotus activities can also be inferred by accusations, however exaggerated, leveled against it by Enryakuji in 1536: committing violence against other sects; digging up land belonging to overlords throughout the city, including agricultural land, in order to lay temple moats; arbitrarily sentencing and executing people; expropriating taxes at Lotus priests' orders—in short, threatening others and exercising aspects of governance in Kyoto.[31]

Particularly insofar as rent was successfully withheld from overlords by Kyoto residents, the townspeople's ability to mobilize both by neighborhood and by temple combined for a time to create a force sufficiently threatening that overlords could not fight back easily. Their ability to do so was also impaired by the absence of both the shogun and Hosokawa Harumoto during most of the years of Lotus dominance. Since the shogunate was the ultimate guarantor of the overlords' right to exact land rent, its absence created a vacuum in which rent could be withheld with relative impunity.[32] This is not to say that the townspeople as Lotus adherents had an absolute ability to withhold rent. By the late Muromachi period lands held by overlords in Kyoto were typically scattered, precluding control of a large area by a single overlord. Conversely, however, this also meant that because within single neighborhoods residential plots were often held by a number of different overlords, residents could not necessarily negotiate their rent en bloc.[33] Opposition by townspeople to overlord control was thus fragmented, and even at the height of Lotus power, the townspeople were not always able to deny the traditional overlords rent from urban land. Many rent disputes continued to be resolved on an individual basis between overlord and tenant.[34] In the tenth month of 1534, the shogunate ordered one neighborhood in lower Kyoto, Rokkakuchō, to pay land rent, suggesting that warrior tolerance of the withholding of rent was wearing thin.[35]

The success of the Lotus leagues in Kyoto was galling to the traditional elites, who were losing income because of widespread nonpayment of taxes and rent by Lotus adherents. The situation had come to seem permanent in the stiffening posture of the neighborhoods, which by 1536 were collectively refusing to pay any land rent in protest over what they perceived to be diminishing special treatment by the shogunate.[36] Moreover, traditional schools of Buddhism were discomfited over the success of Nichiren's unorthodox movement. Matters came to a head in the second month of 1536, when an Enryakuji monk lost a religious debate to a Lotus priest at a temple in Kyoto. Little remarked at the time—the debate went unmentioned in the detailed diary of Yamashina Tokitsugu[37]—the humiliating loss nevertheless festered at Enryakuji, and eventually become the excuse for a full-scale attack on the Lotus leagues. In the following month Enryakuji successfully pressured Shogun Yoshiharu into stripping the official "Lotus Sect" designation from the movement and switching it to Enryakuji, a symbolic assault on the movement's religious legitimacy.[38] In the sixth month, the Enryakuji monks agreed that the time had come to attack the Lotus leagues and sent out a call to battle to such bastions of traditional Buddhism as Tōji, Kōyasan, Negoroji, Onjōji, Tōdaiji, and even Enryakuji's old nemesis in Nara, Kōfukuji. The Honganji, now at Ishiyama, also received an invitation to battle, apparently on the assumption that it would delight in vanquishing its adversaries, the Kyoto Lotus leagues. Of these temples, Onjōji, Enryakuji's longtime rival in the hills east of the city, elected to participate. Rokkaku Sadayori, governor of Ōmi, at first tried to mediate the matter, but failed, declared himself on Enryakuji's side, and set up camp in preparation for battle.

Tensions mounted as monk and warrior forces, swollen with peasant recruits, surrounded the city in daunting numbers: Enryakuji's forces impossibly high at between 30,000 and 150,000, Onjōji's at 3,000, and Sadayori's at 30,000. The Lotus leagues' combined strength of twenty to thirty thousand, even allowing for numerical exaggeration on all sides, was to prove insufficient. On the twenty-second day of the seventh month, Enryakuji's forces attacked and burned the Lotus fortress at Matsugasaki on the city's northeastern periphery. The turning point came in the early morning of the twenty-seventh, when the Rokkaku forces invaded Kyoto and began to set fires. In the next two days all of lower Kyoto and one-third of upper Kyoto burned, inflicting more damage in thirty-six hours than the Ōnin War had in ten years. All twenty-one great Lotus temples were targeted and destroyed; many adherents died in battle (estimates range from three to ten thousand dead), and a Lotus priest committed suicide by disembowelment. Thousands of townspeople adherents took refuge in the imperial palace compound, which had been spared, but the invaders pursued and killed many there, including women and children. The survivors grabbed sacred images and texts and escaped, mostly to Sakai, home to many branch temples of the Kyoto Lotus establishments.

In the ninth month of 1536, the Lotus leagues now obliterated by other forces, Shogun Yoshiharu entered Kyoto under the protection of Harumoto. His was to continue to be a turbulent reign, however: he was forced repeatedly to come and go over the next fourteen years, and eventually died in exile in Ōmi province in 1550. Harumoto was de facto head of the shogunate until 1549, and Bakufu laws reflect his fierce treatment of Lotus adherents, his former allies. In the tenth month of 1536, the shogunate ordered action to be taken against Lotus priests and followers in the Kyoto area.³⁹ Unspecified punishment was also to be doled out to Lotus priests who returned to lay life or pretended to belong to other sects, presumably to avoid suppression. Anyone tolerating these "gangs" would also be punished. Furthermore, the three houses adjoining one displaying a Nichiren amulet to ward off evil were to be confiscated.⁴⁰ So common was Lotus adherence among the townspeople, apparently, that residents of houses adjacent to that of an adherent were construed to be so as well. Finally, the reconstruction of Lotus temples and the revival of Lotus leagues were prohibited.⁴¹

In other words, the shogunate forbade adherence to the Lotus movement. In these shogunal decrees the sect is identified by its founder's name, Nichiren, as the Lotus appellation had been removed by the shogunate during the spring before the suppression. These decrees were rescinded by imperial consent in 1542 following aristocratic lobbying for permission to reconstruct the Lotus temples, but only fifteen were eventually rebuilt, and the leagues did not reappear. This is not to say that the Lotus Sect itself withered into obscurity, even in Kyoto. In the 1560s the European missionary Gaspar Vilela visited the Honkokuji, reported on the dazzling appearance of its interior, and noted that it was surrounded by a moat and supported 370 monks. In 1569 Oda Nobunaga tried to dismantle the Honkokuji and reuse its huge beams for the new shogunal palace, but 1,500 of the temple's wealthy adherents implored him to spare "this temple known throughout Japan" and even offered to supply building costs in gold and silver.⁴² Nevertheless, the brief age of Lotus governance in Kyoto had come to a dramatic end in 1536.

The decisive suppression of the Lotus movement in 1536 by a combination of traditional religious overlords and warriors was arguably the single greatest blaze of violence and destruction in Kyoto's history. Its long-range effects were also grave for the townspeople, for self-governance and autonomy were curtailed as warriors resumed policing and adjudication in the city. The overlords, seemingly on their last legs in the Ōnin War, had successfully reasserted their control.⁴³ The resilience of the traditional hierarchy of control and the determination of the overlords to maintain their hold are unmistakable in this series of events. Enryakuji, traditionally the greatest Kyoto overlord with a monastic tie to many of the city's moneylenders, led the charge against the townspeople. Its ferocity and determination to crush the Lotus leagues at any cost graphically demonstrates how brutal religious conflict in late medieval times could be. Also a key though unrecorded factor in the defeat of the Lotus leagues was the assistance given the victors by rural peasant recruits, perhaps involuntarily but certainly without loyalty to the townspeople. Finally, the speed with which urban autonomy was wiped out is striking. In all of Kyoto's history, the preceding four years had been the apex of commoner autonomy; once the traditional authorities were galvanized to form a coalition, however, only two days of fighting resulted in the reinstitution of their authority.[44] Hierarchical prerogatives successfully had reasserted themselves.

But the hierarchy was to be peopled by a new cast of characters. In 1536 Hosokawa Harumoto typified the new power holder: although he relied on the office of shogunal deputy for prestige and legitimacy, his rise to power had been outside the shogunate. Dependent at first on the Lotus leagues for control of Kyoto and the surrounding area, once he had gathered enough allies and followers among regional warriors, Harumoto turned on the leagues and their pesky demands for a rent-free existence.[45] A succession of such warlords rose and fell, culminating in Oda Nobunaga, who began the dismantling of the old order. Such strongmen, far from offering the townspeople breathing room, reimposed control from above as arbitrary and confining as that of the traditional overlords.

This bleak interpretation of the suppression of the Lotus leagues, though accurate as far as it goes, need not be the only way of viewing these events. The very ferocity with which the leagues were destroyed is testimony to the extent that commoners, propelled by religious militancy however briefly, had taken matters into their own hands and defied traditional authority. And although it was not allowed to escape the control of the authorities again, the neighborhood continued to manage internal affairs autonomously and to function as the local unit of city administration. For example, New Year's greetings in the form of monetary offerings were brought to the shogun by representatives of five chastened lower Kyoto neighborhood clusters in 1537.[46] Judicial authority over internal disputes may have been maintained by individual neighborhoods for as long as fifteen years after the Lotus leagues' suppression.[47] As a measure of commoner accomplishment, the Lotus leagues' four-year control of Kyoto was a giant step beyond neighborhood defense by townspeople during fifteenth-century invasions of peasant leagues. Along with the material and cultural accomplishments of prominent townspeople like moneylenders, their political achievements as Lotus adherents, albeit temporary, were one facet of a great flowering of commoner life in the sixteenth-century city.

There is fragmentary evidence that townspeople continued to withhold rent collectively even after suppression of the Lotus leagues in 1536. In a 1547 altercation between two temples, Rokuōin and Seikōin, over control of a piece of land in Kyoto, for example, the townspeople residents were withholding land rent.[48] When the shogunate tried to determine which party's claim to the land was valid on the basis of receipt of rental income, Seikōin responded that it had not been paid rent in Kyoto generally during the Lotus leagues' period of dominance; Rokuōin said the same, adding that nonpayment of rent during those years was the norm in Kyoto and thus immaterial to the case at hand.[49] However, Rokuōin insisted that payment of land rent had been resumed again in Kyoto in 1537, so Seikōin's failure to receive rent in recent years could not be blamed on the Lotus leagues but on the fact that Seikōin's claim to the land was invalid. Rokuōin's position was that, once the Lotus leagues had been crushed, the overlord system returned to the status quo. Nevertheless, it is clear from the documentation of the case itself that even as of 1547 rent was not being paid on the land.

There is also evidence that the emboldened attitude of commoners to press for rent reduction persisted beyond the period of Lotus dominance. In 1544, for example, residents of a neighborhood in downtown Kyoto struck an agreement with the overlord, Rokuōin, by which they would each pay rent of 100 *mon* per month minus a 15 percent discount.[50] This was after refusing to pay rent for an unstated period—probably since the Lotus years. The overlord agreed to the arrangement on the condition that they divulge the discount to no one outside the neighborhood or the agreement would be nullified. This case is significant for revealing that urban rent could be collectively negotiated with the overlord even after the suppression of the Lotus leagues. Rokuōin's insistence on confidentiality regarding the discount hints that other neighborhoods might demand —and receive—similar treatment. Even eight years after the Lotus leagues were crushed, then, the townspeople could still find success in collective dealings with an overlord.

Such, then, was the short-lived experiment in urban autonomy called the Lotus leagues. A sign of their times, they stood outside the traditional religious and overlord world but were spiritually satisfying and physically protective to their adherents. Probably because its expansion into a larger network coincided with that of the Lotus movement, the *machi* is sometimes linked directly to the Lotus league—namely, it is asserted that the leagues were built on the neighborhood clusters and citywide council.[51] Given the strong lay character of Lotus leadership, overlapping leadership seems plausible, although sources to support this notion are lacking. Nevertheless, it was hardly a coincidence that the *machi* and the Lotus leagues became successful urban organizations in the same period, for the communal character of the neighborhood accelerated in the early decades of the sixteenth century in tandem with the consolidation of the Lotus leagues. The first evidence of neighborhood clustering was in 1534, as noted, and again in 1537, just before and after the suppression of the Lotus leagues.[52] On the other hand, the two were physically distinct institutions. The large Lotus temples stood somewhat aloof from their surroundings. Those of lower Kyoto were not located within any known neighborhood clusters even as late as the mid-1550s, casting doubt on the notion that the neighborhood and the leagues were directly linked.[53] Lotus temples were vertical religious organizations of a paramilitary nature led by priests and lay leaders with the religious authority to mobilize adherents. Parallel to these religious organizations were neighborhoods, also led by prominent residents, acting individually or in clusters as self-defense and self-governing units. Membership in the two organizations, one religious and one geographic, overlapped to a great extent. The *machi* was a neighborhood unit of collective rule that expanded into a city council. The Lotus leagues were based on temple membership and the religious devotion of their adherents. They were two expressions of urban autonomy, one geographic and one religious, whose success reinforced and emboldened one other.

Townspeople took action through the temple or the neighborhood, as appropriate. The specifically Lotus-based nature of military action was clear when Honganji forces attacked Kyoto in 1532 and townspeople responded in groups displaying banners with the Lotus inscription.[54] It was also clear in 1536 when the Lotus leagues were destroyed. But, even in the same period, military action by townspeople was not always based on the Lotus leagues. In 1532, for example, "moneylender forces" (*dosōshū*) purportedly numbering 20,000 eradicated suspected hotbeds of peasant leagues directly west of Kyoto.[55] There is no indication that this was specifically a Lotus league action. It may have been a continuation of neighborhood vigilance against attacks by peasants seeking a debt amnesty. In skirmishes with invading Honganji adherents in 1532 and the forces of Enryakuji in 1536, the townspeople of Kyoto were called to action by the bells of Kōdō in northern Kyoto and Rokkakudō in the south, neither of them Lotus temples but nonetheless central rallying points for mobilization.[56] *Machi* solidarity lay behind a bold gesture by neighborhood leaders in 1533, when the shogun canceled the parade of floats for the Gion Festival.[57] His stated reason for doing so was that Hie Shrine in Ōtsu had canceled its festival, but the real reason was probably uneasiness about the capacity of the Lotus leagues in Kyoto to cause unrest. In response, officials of sixty-six neighborhoods collectively issued a statement demanding that the parade of floats be reinstated, even if the religious portion of the festival was canceled. Admittedly only a single incident, it was contemporary with the powerful Lotus movement at its height and suggests that the two organizations' successes reinforced one another.

It is logical to assume that some of the leadership of both *machi* and the Lotus leagues was supplied by moneylenders, given their already prominent role in Kyoto. In the decades following the Ōnin War, Kyoto had gradually recovered and the moneylenders had made a comeback. More prosperous than ever, they nonetheless differed markedly from those of a century before. Their numbers reduced by war and debt amnesties, some ran large, older establishments, some still with enduring ties to Enryakuji, while others were small businesses, some only retail shops, which for the most part lacked any clerical character. The link to the shogunate as taxpayers continued, although noncompliance was common. By the sixteenth century, in other words, moneylenders were prominent lay townspeople. A leadership role followed naturally from their wealth and prestige, from their commercial dominance of credit and brewing, and from their direction of neighborhood defense during fifteenth-century peasant invasions of the city. Disliked particularly as creditors, in other respects they enjoyed high status and respect. Especially in lower Kyoto, moneylenders were numerous, and it is most likely that they played a leading role in many neighborhood organizations there. As noted above, some are known positively to have been Lotus adherents and patrons. Building on their individual leadership of city self-defense efforts during peasant invasions and the Ōnin War, they could offer military expertise to the Lotus leagues, extending what had been an occasional seizing of the initiative. Furthermore, as tax agents for overlords and as experts in finance, moneylenders could assume tax collection duties as neighborhoods garnered that privilege. As past masters in tax evasion through exemptions, they could offer their talents to the *machi* effort to withhold rent. And insofar as prominent moneylenders who were shogunal tax agents had performed confiscation and other duties following shogunal judicial decisions, it can even be assumed that they were skilled in disposing of criminal cases. Indeed, given their wide experience in finance, self-defense, and administration, the moneylenders' leadership may have been a crucial factor in the rapid success of the townspeople at self-governance in the 1530s.

Logically, then, we can assume some moneylender participation in the Lotus leagues. The historical record, however, does not provide specific evidence of moneylender civic leadership in the 1530s. Nor does it reveal much of anything else very specific about either Lotus league or neighborhood leadership. The elite authors of medieval sources had no incentive to record details of commoner life unless their own income or safety was affected. The source of most material on the moneylenders, the Muromachi shogunate, was for all intents and purposes absent from Kyoto during much of the period of Lotus dominance. Not expert record keepers themselves, the townspeople of Kyoto conducted a short experiment in autonomy in the 1530s that went all but unrecorded. It is likely that many moneylenders participated in that experiment.

To the extent that some moneylenders were Lotus adherents, the destruction of the leagues meant the termination of one organization in which they were active. On the other hand, just as in the aftermath of the Ōnin War, rebuilding and economic recovery required credit; moneylenders who survived were thus in a position to profit, and sources indicate that a good number did so. Although the size of the moneylending establishment after 1536 is unclear, its makeup can be discerned from lenders' requests for shogunal confirmation of their loans following a conditional debt amnesty.[58] Of seventy-nine such cases dated 1546–1547, fifty-six, or more than two-thirds, were from nonclerical moneylenders. They were a rather diverse lot, including two lay credit circles, a woman in the imperial palace, and Yoshida Munetada of the very large Suminokura establishment, with a long list of loans. Fewer than one-third of the requests were submitted by temples or individual clerics, and no more than six, or 10 percent of the total requests, could have been from Enryakuji priests.[59] This source, while not a comprehensive list of the Kyoto moneylenders, proves that ten years after the destruction of the Lotus leagues, the city was once more, as throughout the medieval period, supporting a large number of lenders, most of whom were nonclerical townspeople.

The shogunate's taxation of the moneylenders also continued after the Lotus leagues' suppression. It is not clear that it had ever stopped, but notations in the diary of Ninagawa Chikatoshi, deputy head of the Board of Administration, indicate that in 1539, at least, it was occurring as before. Twenty lenders of upper and lower Kyoto submitted a jointly signed letter to the shogunate in the twelfth month regarding collection of brewer and lender taxes.[60] The shogun's financier and an Enryakuji lender of long standing, Shōjitsubō is listed as the main lender in charge of the monthly collection of the two taxes. Three lay lenders, Sano, Nakayama, and Yasui, are also named in connection with the monthly collections. Another isolated example, this source nevertheless suggests that long-standing arrangements with overlords endured to some extent. The shogun himself commanded little authority by this time, but the Muromachi shogunate was a resilient institution in Kyoto, continuing to derive some revenues from the moneylenders. The suppression of the Lotus leagues may have been a blow to moneylenders as townspeople, but their business lives do not appear to have been significantly altered.

Self-governance, broadly defined, was achieved by the townspeople of late medieval Kyoto partly by default and partly by their own insistence. Although the Lotus leagues are the most spectacular example of their efforts, commercial guilds and neighborhood self-rule were also instances for asserting autonomy. Hence self-governance, although most comprehensively attained in the sixteenth century, was a medieval achievement of several centuries' duration. The brewer-lenders, numerically and financially the most dominant element in Kyoto commerce, could apply their many skills to aspects of self-governance in Kyoto. But their unique and leading place in city life cannot be fully appreciated without an examination of their cultural activities.

CULTURAL PURSUITS

With their social prominence and disposable wealth moneylenders were in a position to lead active cultural lives. Fragments in the record suggest a range of activities. As townspeople concentrated in Kyoto's commercial district, moneylenders were full participants in the city's culture. In the Gion festival, Mibu Kyōgen and other dramatic forms, and as an audience for companion stories and epic narrations, they had much in common with other townspeople. Their talent for poetry brought them into linked verse gatherings with aristocrats, while a love of tea was shared with both elites and commoners. Such cultural hobnobbing probably served a business purpose as well, smoothing relations with clients. The moneylenders' cultural significance was not that their interests necessarily differed from those of the other townspeople, but that they fully participated in and patronized a range of cultural forms reflecting their unique economic and social status in the middle—between commoners and elites.

If not generally steeped in comprehensive knowledge of the classical canon, all moneylenders had functional literacy and numeracy at least, and many pursued cultural pastimes of some sophistication. Those with an Enryakuji connection possessed some religious erudition as well. The term most closely applied to the moneylenders, "the well-to-do" (*utoku-nin*), connoted an elegant way of life. To the extent that they had employees, they also had leisure time to fill with expensive and prestigious pursuits. If they chose, they could take time for recreation, constructively and self-consciously developing an aesthetic sphere of life beyond that of most commoners. There is evidence that some moneylenders did so, as in the case of Magojirō, below. But moneylenders were also busy, typically involved in both lending and brewing. They most likely imbibed culture as part of their business and social lives.

Well before the sixteenth century moneylenders acquired extensive exposure to cultural riches. They may have provided financial backing for Yoshimasa's glittering pursuits, the Higashiyama culture.[61] Art works, including imported Chinese objects of a quality surpassing anything made in Japan, passed through their hands as collateral, and moneylenders were not only aware of but helped determine their value in loan transactions. Some lenders were themselves possessed of art objects of high quality: for example, the lender Hōsen in 1431 loaned the imperial prince Fushimi Sadafusa two pairs of illustrated screens.[62] At a more basic level, it has been pointed out that the utility and practicality of many art objects of the late medieval period—illustrated screens used as room dividers, vases, tea bowls—suggest the influence of commoners like moneylenders.[63] Such practical utility of cultural forms and the profit therefrom were an important part of late medieval culture.[64] Through loans, purchase, and patronage, moneylenders were the commoners best poised to contribute to this development.

The aristocrat Yamashina Tokitsugu left intriguing references in his diary to his friendship with a moneylender named Takaya Magojirō.[65] A member of the Takaya family of lenders, Magojirō had his own shop on Mushakōji Street. This was on Tokitsugu's way to Seiganji, a popular Pure Land temple in northwest Kyoto at which he often prayed. In the second month of 1534, Tokitsugu dropped by the shop. Magojirō greeted him warmly, tugging him by the sleeve and begging him to enter. He served *sake* to his aristocratic visitor, played music, showed him various books in his collection, and the two became fast friends. On his third visit Tokitsugu played the flute and discussed poetry with Magojirō, under the moon. The moneylender thereupon prepared ceremonial tea for Tokitsugu. Later Tokitsugu received a branch of cherry blossoms from the moneylender to commemorate their party; Tokitsugu responded with a poem.

Socially, the relationship between these two men is striking: as related in the diary it appears to be a true friendship and not a commercial arrangement. One cannot discount the possibility, however, that Tokitsugu was also Magojirō's debtor-client. It is also possible that Magojirō saw such an acquaintance as an opportunity for another type of gain: surely it would enhance his prestige among other wealthy townspeople if he could drop the name of a cultured aristocrat as someone who sought his company on occasion.[66] After all, their friendship is a remarkable example of social mingling, even in the relatively fluid medieval society.

Most striking about the relationship, given their social differences, is their cultural commonality. Magojirō's accomplishments are both advanced and varied: he is conversant with poetry, he is a connoisseur of books, he enjoys music, and he can perform tea ceremony. Moreover, he loves all of this and is eager to share it with an aristocrat, by definition a man of culture. Although a member of a prominent moneylending establishment, Magojirō himself seems to have been a fairly typical neighborhood moneylender. We can assume, therefore, that his cultural achievements were common to many of the city's lenders.

Another intriguing relationship cutting across status lines was that of the lender Hōsen with the imperial prince Fushimi Sadafusa, father of Emperor Gohanazono. From about 1417 until his death in 1437 Hōsen served as Sadafusa's storehouser and financier. But there are enough entries in Sadafusa's diary over this period to indicate that a deeper cultural bond existed between the two.[67] In 1417 they attended a linked-verse party on a boat, at which Sadafusa composed the initial stanza (*hokku*), which Hōsen, in a subordinate position, followed with his own. In 1420 Sadafusa graciously presented Hōsen with a *sake* cup on the occasion of the latter's son's appearance in a *sarugaku* theatrical performance. In 1422 Hōsen played host to Sadafusa and numerous aristocrats at an oral narration of the medieval epic *Tale of the Heike*. Three years later Sadafusa recorded giving Hōsen a gift of tea, presumably in connection with tea ceremony. Sadafusa may have even felt a twinge of envy at the extent of Hōsen's material resources: he notes the receipt of a loan of illustrated screens from Hōsen in 1431, and in 1418 remarks that Hōsen had seven or eight priests from Ninnaji in attendance at a service in honor of his deceased mother. In 1437 Hōsen died; his passing was much lamented by Sadafusa in his diary.

This relationship of many years was a professional one in the beginning but soon blossomed into a friendship in which cultural forms were celebrated and enjoyed. At the same time, each cultural occasion was also one on which Hōsen reinforced his business tie with this imperial prince, further enhancing his own status. In other words, culture became a vehicle for social advancement by this moneylender. What did Sadafusa, on the other hand, derive from the relationship? Presumably the loyalty of a creditor, but something more personally satisfying as well: the companionship of a moneyed individual who had cultured tastes sufficiently in tune with his own to merit repeated renewal. In the company of one another, these two individuals of such different backgrounds enjoyed a wide range of cultural activities.

Other sources corroborate such cultural achievements by moneylenders, especially in linked verse and tea ceremony. The diary *Kanmon gyoki* notes the participation of commoners, a possible reference to moneylenders and low-ranking warriors, in tea gatherings in 1417 at the Fushimi palace, residence of imperial prince Sadafusa.[68] (Hōsen, Sadafusa's financier friend, may have been in attendance.) Ninagawa Chikatoshi, deputy head of the shogunal Board of Administration, attended a tea ceremony at the home of the moneylender Yasui in 1538.[69] He noted a tea bowl worth 350 *kanmon*, an enormous sum. On another occasion in 1539 he spied a bamboo tea scoop that Yasui had purchased for the lordly price of 5 *kanmon*.[70] Yasui was a shogunal tax agent—Chikatoshi was his boss, in effect—and one of the wealthiest people in Kyoto. (Chikatoshi's interest in the exact monetary value of these items might be explained by the fact that he oversaw the financial affairs of the shogunate.) The Kyōgen play *The Little Thief* (*Konusutto*) features the burglary of a house of a rich man —likely a moneylender. Upon entering, the thief is stopped in his tracks, stunned to see a collection of valuable tea implements, including a choice tea bowl from Korea.[71] These examples, along with those of Hōsen and Magojirō, suggest that in the late medieval period the more prominent moneylenders had attained a level of wealth and culture sufficient to host aristocrats and warriors and even befriend them on occasion. Such contacts helped to produce the rich hybrid culture characteristic of the late Muromachi period—Japan's earliest version of a common culture.[72]

A noteworthy aspect of late medieval Japanese culture is its social character, which particularly encouraged the development of art forms featuring interpersonal contact.[73] When people of different statuses participated together in such cultural forms, the result was the pleasing blend of aristocratic and commoner elements typical of late medieval Japanese culture. Among these interpersonal cultural forms was linked verse, which required at least two participants to compose a cohesive series of short, thematically unified poems. Both raucous and sedate versions existed, and moneylenders probably participated in both. The townspeople had enjoyed linked verse for some time: in 1336, for example, the Muromachi shogu-nate's legal formulary called for the suppression of public drinking and carousing, and particularly deplored gambling at tea parties and linked verse gatherings, in which incalculable sums of money were lost.[74] From the sound of it, in their own rowdy way, commoners with money to spend were enjoying some culture along with their liquid refreshment. It is not hard to imagine moneylenders, with their ready cash, among these revelers. On a more sedate level, they could also be found among the participants in "serious" poetry gatherings, such as the previously mentioned nautical affair with Sadafusa and Hōsen in 1417. (As a reflection of his status, Sadafusa composed the initial stanza.) In 1435 a linked-verse mania of sorts seems to have taken hold, for a total of thirty-four linked-verse gath-erings were held by a group consisting of members of the imperial family, aristocrats, clerics, and others.[75] One was hosted by Hōsen at his home in Fushimi. This is an outstanding example of the Kyoto pattern of social-izing in late medieval times in which superiors visited subordinates for hours or even days of entertainment. The host, of course, was required to provide adequate facilities, namely a banquet room for his illustrious guests.[76] Hōsen, it will be recalled, had also played host in 1422 to a nar-rative performance of the epic *Tale of the Heike*, so presumably his resi-dence was suitably lavish.

Especially in the latter half of the medieval period, commoner partic-ipation in linked verse became widespread, with such gatherings often being held on temple grounds rather than in court or aristocratic resi-dences.[77] Commoner poets participated in what was known as the *hana no moto* tradition—"under the blossoms."[78] The social origins of some of the foremost fifteenth- and sixteenth-century linked-verse masters like Sōgi and Sōchō are obscure, and there was considerable commoner accom-plishment in this cultural form.[79] The conventionalization of linked verse in the late medieval period also suggests simplification of a poetic form for commoner adherents.[80] More positively, the commoner influence on linked verse imparted to it a this-worldliness that set it distinctly apart from *waka*, the traditional poetry that remained the preserve of the aristocracy.[81]

Medieval linked verse has been characterized as a separate phenom-enon from its classical courtly forebear: it was primarily a medium of social and cultural discourse among various classes.[82] Thus linked-verse gatherings provided an occasion for the dissemination of a classical courtly tradition among commoners who lacked classical erudition. Concordances or handbooks containing verbal correlations compiled by linked-verse teachers were the tools enabling commoners to participate in this cultural form. These correlations in many cases were drawn from classical allusions, with which most commoners would have had no firsthand acquaintance. When one's turn approached in a linked-verse gathering, one could consult such a source under the key word in the last line of the previous couplet or triplet and find a handy entry of correlative words or phrases that might evoke a similar mood by their meaning or by their close association in a classical work, like *The Tale of Genji*, with the term in question. Thus the thorough classical knowledge of the compiler could stand in for the minimal literary background of the commoner participant. This sort of literary gathering might seem rather less authentic than the elite gatherings of aristocrats drawing on years of exposure to a whole body of literature to create poetry spontaneously. On the other hand, such handbooks made accessible to commoners elements of the classical tradition, and they probably had a high old time using them. Writing one's poem down was usually not necessary, for these oral events had a scribe in attendance. Most linked-verse gatherings of commoners were so informal that no transcription even occurred, especially in those that were drinking parties as much as poetry gatherings. As with other forms of medieval documentation, those specifically commissioned by a powerful patron like the emperor were the ones that survived in written form. But commoner participation in medieval linked verse is understood to have been widespread and frequent, if perhaps limited to the wealthier among them, such as moneylenders.

Not all wealthy commoners had to rely on written sources like handbooks for the composition of poetry. Renowned linked-verse poets were also employed as tutors by amateur poets, including merchants. In 1463 the poet Shinkei mourned the decline of the art of linked verse as a result of the proliferation of such amateurs.[83] The popularity of linked verse spread further as a result of the Ōnin chaos in Kyoto: poet-teachers, no longer able to make a living there, fled to the provinces in search of patrons.[84] The poet Shōhaku, for example, moved to Settsu province during the Ōnin War and then on to Sakai, where he became the teacher of amateur poets in the commercial sector.[85] If merchants in Sakai were doing this, it is reasonable to assume that members of Kyoto's commercial sector, dominated by moneylenders, patronized poets as tutors even before the Ōnin War. Such formal study of poetry gave its practitioners a sophistication that allowed them to participate with aristocrats in the production of poetry.

A simpler form of oral verse making, the round of poems (*tsugiuta*) was even more accessible to commoners like moneylenders than the linked-verse gathering.[86] A popular communal event, the round elicited spontaneous poems on topics assigned on the spot; but unlike linked verse, each poem stood on its own merit and was unrelated in any way to those around it. Less sedate and formal than linked-verse gatherings, the poetic round provided moneylenders and other commoners an opportunity to enjoy the company of friends through such poetry.

Another medieval cultural form marked by interpersonal qualities was tea ceremony. In both simple and elaborate versions tea was the perfect form of cultural and social discourse for moneylenders. As tea connoisseurs and as creditors, moneylenders had close dealings with other commoners as well as with elite members of society. A medieval pastime cultivated by aristocrats and warriors alike, tea reached its apotheosis as a synthesis of elite and popular elements in the mid-sixteenth century. Subsequently, tea ceremony at elite levels calcified into a form of political discourse manipulated by politicians like Nobunaga and especially Hideyoshi, in which tea masters even acted as political go-betweens. But long before, there had been the commoner's cult of tea, epitomizing the cultural niche of the moneylenders. Described as "downtown tea" (*Shimogyō no chayu*), the tea ceremony rage was widespread among Kyoto merchants as early as the fifteenth century.[87] Tea did not require a detailed knowledge of the classics or a lengthy investment of time; it did entail monetary expenditure for the implements and the tearoom; and finally, it constituted a truly aesthetic pastime that could nevertheless be pursued in small pockets of calm in the heart of the city. Its two opposing tendencies were both appealing to moneylenders, for different reasons: ostentation on the one hand, including the vulgar impulse to collect and display, especially noticeable in the acquisition of expensive Chinese imports; and, on the other, austere elegance and an appreciation of simplicity and serenity. Both aspects were present in "downtown tea": tranquillity in the midst of urban bustle with nothing required beyond a small house or room, and the display and admiration of tea implements satisfying materialistic urges. The acquisition of tea implements by moneylenders could have been through purchase or through defaults on debts, for they were a common form of collateral. It was not uncommon for tea masters like Murata Sōju to maintain teahouses in the bustling commercial sector of Kyoto—"mountain dwellings in the city."[88] This form of tea ceremony, therefore, was emblematic of the urban culture patronized by the moneylenders: a pleasing and sociable cultural form, fully accessible to commoners.

In the evolution of tea ceremony there was an important shift from "tea as an event to tea as a practice."[89] This occurred when the host of a tea gathering prepared the tea himself rather than having attendants do so. Merchant tea connoisseurs, although amateurs, made this a regular practice, either on a simple level, presumably in a room in or adjacent to their shops, or in a more zealous way, constructing teahouses, acquiring choice tea implements, studying with tea masters, traveling to visit like-minded adherents, and hosting elaborate tea gatherings. Some of these gatherings were recorded in tea diaries, most of which date from the middle of the sixteenth century and were kept by tea adherents in Sakai, Nara, and Hakata.[90] The entry for each tea gathering contains basic information: the date, the location, the host's name, the names of guests, the (named) implements used, the art objects on display, and the menu of the meal following the tea ceremony itself. All in all, the diaries convey a strong sense of tea having become a secular cult. Tea diaries are quite late as sources for this study and do not apparently include the Kyoto moneylenders as hosts, though occupations are not specified in the entries. The prevalence of major Sakai merchants among the diarists reflects fundamental economic changes of the mid- to late sixteenth century, when warehouser-wholesalers, especially of port cities, rose to dominate trade in Japan. Although some Kyoto moneylenders may have been pursuing tea at this level of passion and attending such gatherings, none left tea diaries as proof. Nonetheless, the full-blown tea ceremony hosted by the rich merchant of the late sixteenth century had a simpler and more accessible "downtown tea" antecedent, equally but more modestly "tea as a practice." Popular from before the Ōnin War among moneylenders and other merchants, it provided a friendly and elegant oasis in a workaday world.

Some cultural pursuits favored by medieval townspeople were an extension of religious practice. Gion Shrine's festival, arguably the central cultural event of the summer, had a religious ceremonial core that in the medieval period was all but smothered in lavish display by townspeople participants. Originating in the widespread belief that deadly epidemics like smallpox were inflicted on the city by vengeful spirits, some festivals began first as ceremonies held at the imperial palace and later at certain shrines, to appease the spirits and stave off disease.[91] Gion's festival is the main example of this genre. First held in 863, it became an annual event in 970, and from 1157 took to the streets with a parade of floats. The role of the townspeople centered on the parade, and preparation of the floats was carried out on an organized, neighborhood basis. Many of these neighborhoods were packed with moneylenders; hence their direct participation in this aspect of the festival can be assumed. The floats grew ever larger and more ornate, until by the late fourteenth century the festival had evolved into what it is today: a procession of elaborately decorated floats and carts, stunning visual evidence of the townpeople's cultural sophisti-cation.[92] Another aspect of festival participation by moneylenders and other wealthy merchants was their lavish display of screens, kimono, and tea implements at the entrance to their homes in the neighborhood of the shrine on the eve of the festival. The religious aspect of the festival, meanwhile, had become less conspicuous. In the late fourteenth century, the term goryōe (ceremony to placate vengeful spirits) was dropped from the festival name in favor of simply "Gion'e" or "Gion sairei," terms simply connoting a shrine celebration, and perhaps to be taken also as a signifier of greater participation by townspeople.[93] These events have been called a sign of Kyoto's transformation into a medieval city: sacred and ceremonial observances that had previously been the monopoly of the elites now in-cluded prominent participation by commoners.[94]

For the moneylenders, participation in the festival also entailed busi-ness obligations to the shrine as overlord. From about the late twelfth cen-tury Gion Shrine had a system in place for financing the festival, which, as in the case of Hie Shrine's spring festival, involved taxing some of Kyoto's merchants, including the brewer-lenders, for the horses used in the religious segment of the festival in which the portable shrine was moved.[95] During the late medieval period moneylenders contributed even more substantially by giving the shrine, in addition to the tax, the proceeds from their collective annual sale of confiscated items (acquired in their duties as shogunal tax agents) and collateral from defaulted loans.[96] To its moneylender supporters, however, the festival was more than an occasion to be taxed: their highly visible support and participation made it finan-cially possible, and this in turn enhanced their prestige as townspeople.[97]

Communal concern over the organization of the festival was keen. The order in which participating floats would appear in the parade was an important issue for the commoner participants. From 1500, the year the festival was revived after a long hiatus in the wake of the Ōnin War, the order of participating floats was determined by a lottery, overseen at the Rokkakudō temple by an official of the shogunate.[98] The financing of indi-vidual floats may have fallen to each neighborhood communally from about this time.[99] Similarly, the theme and decor of each float was a com-munal decision within each neighborhood. The Kyōgen play, Kujizainin, presents a group of townspeople racking their brains to come up with a catchy theme for their neighborhood's float.[100] Ideas are rejected one after another as being too similar to existing floats, a repetition of one of the pre-vious year's that was widely ridiculed, and so on. When a theme is finally agreed upon, the respective roles on the float are immediately assigned by lottery, to the delight of those who win prominent ones and the chagrin of those who do not. Although a work of fiction, the play conveys well the townspeople's deep involvement in the festival.

Another annual cultural event with religious roots and popular among the townspeople was Mibu Kyōgen, performed each spring at Mibudera, a temple just northwest of the Shijō-Karasuma intersection, which was a neighborhood thick with moneylenders.[101] Already popular as a cultic center to the bodhissatva Jizō, from 1257 Mibudera enhanced its fame further through its encouragement of a religious practice known as the *yūzū nenbutsu*, a melodic, emotional chanting of the name of the Buddha by large numbers of people. Uttering the Buddha's name was a mainstay practice of many Pure Land groups in the medieval period, but this particular form was especially appealing to merchants not only for its simplicity but because it taught that all living creatures would benefit whenever the name of the Buddha was uttered by anyone, and that merit would thereby be accrued by all. To the townspeople in general, merit was commonly understood to include profit in this world. To the extent that many moneylenders in Kyoto in the early medieval period had had some training at Enryakuji, the Tendai Buddhist concept of enlightenment extending to all sentient beings (*hongaku shisō*) that underlay the *yūzū nenbutsu* was already familiar to them.

The monk Enkaku, who had earlier introduced the *yūzū nenbutsu* at Mibudera, is credited with initiating in about 1300 the Yūzū Dainenbutsu Kyōgen, a spring event consisting of dances, songs, an especially popular act featuring people dressed like monkeys performing acrobatic stunts on a net, and short skits on all manner of topics. The last were eventually expanded into a repertoire of Kyōgen—short, comical plays. In keeping with the setting, some of the Kyōgen plays were religious in character, including skits depicting Jizō saving people and the king of hell interrogating criminals about to be cast into the depths. Such vivid presentations of aspects of popular religion were surely appealing to all the townspeople, but at least one Kyōgen play, called "*Sake* Storehouse, Gold Storehouse" (*Sakakura, kanekura*), suggests a strong awareness of the business lives of brewer-lenders. Today Mibu Kyōgen is a ten-day theatrical marathon that takes place every spring, but in the medieval period it was a participatory event for *yūzū nenbutsu* adherents, who likely made up the cast of the Kyōgen skits.[102] It is not known if moneylenders were among the performers, but to the extent that they lived in the immediate vicinity in large numbers, they were surely in the audience. As we have seen, the son of the lender Hōsen appeared in a *sarugaku* performance in 1420 attended by his father and the imperial prince, Fushimi Sadafusa. Moneylender patronage of such popular dramatic forms is also likely, but cannot be documented.

Storytelling was a particularly accessible form of oral entertainment in the medieval period that anyone could enjoy as audience member. The chanting by blind minstrels of the *Tale of the Heike*, the monumental medieval epic, was a perennial favorite throughout the country.[103] Kyoto was no exception, and we have seen that the moneylender Hōsen sponsored such a performance at his residence, with aristocratic guests in the audience. As literacy became more common in the late medieval period, people turned to written stories as well, and companion stories (*otogi zōshi*) emerged as a widely popular genre.[104] Indeed, late medieval cultural forms like this are properly understood as the ancestors of the bourgeois culture of the Edo period. Judging from their wide-ranging content, companion stories appealed to a broad audience, and conceivably among their authors were some merchants.[105] The characters in companion stories included all sorts of individuals, anthropomorphized animals being especially popular. Unlike classical literature, the setting could be places beyond Kyoto, and the clergy and other elites could as easily be gently ridiculed as honored.

To posit a moneylender audience for companion stories requires little more than common sense: many lenders were sufficiently literate and had the leisure time to read these short prose works. We know for a fact that Magojirō, the lender friend of Tokitsugu, collected storybooks. To prove moneylender authorship of this or any other literary form, however, is problematic. There is virtually no proof that any townspeople actually authored works of literature in the medieval period.[106] Nor does an entrepreneurial impulse characterize medieval stories. In the area of prose literature, then, it is most likely that the moneylenders' place was in the audience.

Finally, ink painting can be counted among the cultural pursuits of some moneylenders. An accomplishment requiring a large investment of time and training, some lenders nonetheless pursued it professionally. On the twenty-fifth day of the fifth month of 1440, some moneylenders of Kyoto were asked to paint folding fans as a test of their ability.[107] The purpose of the test was for the Zen temple Shōkokuji to select and appoint a "painter of Kyoto" (*Rakuchū eshi*), presumably to paint for the temple. After the test, one moneylender was granted the appointment. There is also an ink painting on paper from the temple Gyokuryūin depicting Sakyamuni on a rock undergoing self-mortification of the body.[108] The artist's signature reads "Moneylender (*dosō*) Eishū 73," an unambiguous indication of his occupation. (It is not clear what "73" means: there may have

been a numbering system for this artist's works.) The painting was com-
pleted in or before 1577, for an inscription on the painting is signed by a
person who died in that year. The moneylender's name, Eishū, is a clerical
one; his temple affiliation is not known. Thus two sources over a century
apart offer evidence of moneylender accomplishment in the area of ink
painting. It is possible that these artists started out as moneylenders and
then became professional painters. There may have been some wealthy
lenders who trained as painters or whose children did so. In any case, the
individuals in these sources are clearly identified as moneylenders, and
not as professional temple artists.

The moneylenders pursued a full range of cultural forms including
some appealing to commoners, others favored by elites, and a few enjoyed
by both. Social interaction marked these pursuits, further enriching the
lenders' status. Combining the ostentation of wealth with some erudition,
the most prominent moneylenders were admitted to cultural gatherings
with aristocrats and leading warriors, and in this way used culture as a
vehicle for social advancement. Ink painting, pursued by a few, was a
serious individual interest that also gave the lenders valuable ties to elite
circles. Achieving relative proximity to the aristocracy in a cultural sense,
the lenders remained grounded among the townspeople, as their participation in the Gion festival demonstrates. From their unique position in
the middle, moneylenders enjoyed elements of both worlds and thus epito-
mized the hybrid culture of their day.

Of all the aspects of the moneylenders' lives their cultural pursuits
have left only the faintest and most fragmentary traces in the historical
record. Nevertheless, we can assume that in their hobbies and entertainments moneylenders expressed their values and what they saw as their
place in the world. They approached culture with a sense of practicality:
in tea and linked-verse gatherings aesthetic enjoyment was one goal; another was the enhancement of their social and business position. Religion
provided an entree to some forms of culture like Kyōgen drama, while
prestige and ostentation was the attraction of others, like festivals. Linked
verse was a more elevated participatory pastime; companion stories enter-
tained the literate townspeople. Cultural forms like ink painting were
beyond most commoners, but some moneylenders tried their hand at it,
with a modicum of success. Love of beauty and ostentation, and the
means to pay a high price for it, placed moneylenders in the ranks of
the cultural connoisseurs of the day. Their patronage was vital to late
medieval culture, a pleasing synthesis of mass entertainments and aristocratic interests.

Chapter Six

The Fate of the Moneylenders in the Early Modern Period

THE FORTUNES OF TWO successful moneylenders, Shōjitsubō, originally of Enryakuji, and the lay family Suminokura, provide contrasting examples of long-term survivors in the business. The experience of each in his own way illuminates the hazards and survival strategies of successful merchants. Undeniably, luck played some role in the success of the two, but business acumen and shrewdness in dealings with overlords were also essential to their longevity. Shōjitsubō served various overlords while the Suminokura were by contrast nearly independent businessmen. The Suminokura survived beyond the medieval period and Shōjitsubō flourished at least through Nobunaga's time.

Shōjitsubō was an anomaly among the Enryakuji lenders, for he weathered changes in the political world like no one else in his cohort—or at least like no one else is recorded to have done.[1] Like the other clerical lenders of Enryakuji, he was taxed by the Muromachi shogunate. In 1433 the shogunate appointed him its agent (*daikan*) in the port of Hyōgo, near present-day Kobe and quite a distance from his Kyoto base. At least by 1436, if not before, he was appointed to the ranks of the shogunal tax agents and until 1465 served generally as head of both the tax agents and the shogunal financial agents. As such, he was quite active in various areas of shogunal finances, including being ordered in 1464 with Jōkōbō, another clerical lender, to manage the reconstruction of one of the two piers in Hyōgo used in the continental trade. This entailed covering the expenses of the operation, and both he and Jōkōbō refused, saying they lacked the funds to do so. His refusal can be interpreted as a measure of his autonomy from the shogunate; on the other hand, the very fact that the shogunate importuned him to perform an expensive task is an indication of his subordinate status. At any rate, the following year he was dropped from the ranks of the tax agents, possibly in retaliation for his uncooperative behavior. This was more than a minor snub, for he did not regain that appointment until 1538. The lay lenders Yasui, Sawamura, and Nakamura began to dominate the shogunal tax agents from the time of Shōjitsubō's departure.

Expulsion from the ranks of the shogunal tax agents would seem a serious blow, but Shōjitsubō, successful merchant that he was, continued to pursue a prolific career as a brewer and lender. His business success can be ascertained indirectly from the fact that his house was deemed sufficiently grand for warriors establishing themselves in the city to expropriate it at least twice—the Akamatsu in 1455 and the Hosokawa during the Ōnin War. His prime location in northern Kyoto near shogunal headquarters made him vulnerable to attack by peasants and warriors alike, but this too was a measure of his prominence. Shōjitsubō also cultivated ties with other elites, even as his standing with the shogunate fell. As financial agent he served the aristocratic Yamashina house, collecting their estate taxes, and may have done the same at times for the imperial palace. The shogunate reinstated him to the ranks of the tax agents in 1538, but the following year added twenty others to the list, thus cheapening the significance of the appointment. The snub seems to have made Shōjitsubō even more determined to associate with other overlords, and in 1552 he received the rank of imperial financial agent (ōkurakyō), a significant accomplishment for a commoner. Shōjitsubō was to outlast the shogunate, for in 1573 Oda Nobunaga, now well established in Kyoto, confirmed him as tax agent with compensation of 10 percent and rights to land.[2] Thus Shōjitsubō regained a position of prominence with the current ruler quite as impressive as that he had held with the Muromachi shogunate. After this point he does not resurface in documents, suggesting that he failed, along with the other moneylenders, to make a successful transition to the early modern period, possibly continuing as a small-scale lender but no longer in the brewing business.

The factors contributing to Shōjitsubō's success included entrepreneurial skill, reflected in the size of his operation and its longevity, and his skill in affiliating with multiple power holders on terms that were to his benefit. Although he was expelled from the Muromachi shogunate for over seventy years, he compensated for this by affiliating with other elites. One is left with an impression of a leading merchant who could weather misfortune quite successfully, maneuvering among elites.

In contrast to Shōjitsubō, the Suminokura of Saga in western Kyoto was a lay moneylender who survived the Ōnin War and the sixteenth-century decline of the overlord system by existing outside of it from the beginning. The family's Kyoto connection began when a son of an Ōmi sorcerer-doctor named Yoshida came to the city in the early years of the fifteenth century in service of an unspecified nature to the Muromachi shogunate.[3] He had settled in the Saga area by 1428, and there the family started a brewery and lending business in the next generation. Soon the Suminokura was recognized as the leading member of that profession in the Saga area. (Their trade name, Suminokura, means "the corner store-house.") Flourishing conditions continued throughout the fifteenth and sixteenth centuries, in spite of the unrest of the Ōnin War, peasant invasions, and the suppression of the Lotus leagues. Here luck may have been the key: a relatively remote location, yet still in the Kyoto area, protected the Suminokura from the worst of the fire and looting. Late in the sixteenth century the family provided medical and financial services to Toyotomi Hideyoshi, and later to officials of the Tokugawa shogunate. It was one of the financial backers of Hideyoshi's "vermillion seal" trading ships to Vietnam and continued to thrive in the early modern era.

The ability to maneuver skillfully through treacherous political waters was essential to the family's success, but it is also significant that the Suminokura were never subordinates in the Enryakuji network. Also, shogunal affiliation probably aided their initial establishment of business in Kyoto, yet the family was independent enough, amassing land through moneylending and maintaining a large brewery with both wholesale and retail functions, that the decline of the Muromachi shogunate did not harm its fortunes. By remaining outside of any guildlike arrangement, the Suminokura was not pulled down with the traditional overlords in the sixteenth century. In the late sixteenth century the Suminokura may have become subordinate to Daikakuji, the dominant temple in the Saga neighborhood.[4] The so-called *monzenmachi* neighborhood form, in which merchants were concentrated in neighborhoods around major temples, became prevalent in this unsettled time; proximity to Daikakuji may well have imparted some security to the residents. Such relationships were early modern in nature, characterized by individual ties of fealty unlike the occupational guild arrangements of medieval times. At any rate, while most other prominent moneylenders of medieval Kyoto disappear from sources in the late sixteenth century, the Suminokura, operating successfully in a new political and economic order, continued to prosper and figure prominently in Kyoto commercial life.[5] As an outstanding exception to the general pattern of Enryakuji moneylenders examined in this study, the case of the Suminokura is especially instructive as we turn to the fate of the moneylenders in the twilight of the medieval age.

During the middle decades of the sixteenth century, medieval commercial relationships seem to have continued somewhat as before. In 1539 twenty representatives of upper and lower Kyoto communicated with the shogunate about the dates of collection of the brewer and lender taxes, implying business as usual. The taxes were either being resumed after the Lotus years or had never stopped. Similarly, large numbers of moneylenders' requests for exemption of their loans from a conditional debt amnesty were processed with the shogunate in 1546–1547, also suggesting continuity with past practice. In 1545 there was even a brief recurrence of the Kitano malt-tax controversy discussed above, in which Kitano Shrine, with shogunal support, demanded that the city's brewers observe its malt monopoly. The shogunate and the shrine may have been attempting to revive the monopoly in order to increase sagging tax revenues. It is not known if the attempt was successful, but the mere fact that an attempt was made indicates overlord desire to maintain the medieval status quo.

There were signs, however, that all was not well in the world of the overlord. In addition to the examples of tax evasion and exemption cited earlier, the Distillery Office, a sinecure of the Oshikōji family, was gradually squeezed out of the commercial overlord business from the 1550s.[6] Significantly, collection of its tax was hindered not by more powerful overlords like Enryakuji's network of shrines or by the shogunate, but by organized efforts to resist the tax on the part of retail brewers, new brewers, and small and medium brewers in their own groups. Large brewers like Yoshida Munetada of the Suminokura ignored the traditional overlords, organizing and managing smaller brewers on a neighborhood or family basis. This included administration of taxes, a development that could only have been regarded as deeply threatening by the traditional overlords. Yet sources enlighten us no further regarding this mid-sixteenth-century state of affairs. Indigenous brewer-lender organizations may have been able to shut out the small Distillery Office; taking on the shogunate or shrine overlords would have constituted a real sea change. From the point of view of the moneylenders, at least, it would seem that their position was precarious, as the Hosokawa, Miyoshi, and Matsunaga warlords followed one upon the other in their marches to power in Kyoto, each grasping power for a few years. If a merchant was protected by one warrior, he ran the risk of having his business confiscated by the next. The overlord system was less able to offer real protection than ever before. In such an atmosphere one would think that imperial overlordship was, in its innocuousness, as safe as anything. But the fate of the Distillery Office would suggest that even this was shunned, as brewer-lenders banded together, turning their backs on ineffectual overlords.

With the coming of Oda Nobunaga to Kyoto in 1568, after decades of warlords jostling for power, a consolidation of national authority was set in motion that eventually could not be ignored by anyone, including the moneylenders. Enryakuji was burned in 1571 by Nobunaga and rendered impotent as an economic and political force in the capital. By then most of the city's lenders lacked real ties to Enryakuji, and dealing with Nobunaga himself was a more pressing concern. In 1573, the missionary Luis Frois noted that Nobunaga destroyed upper Kyoto, burning or pillaging the moneylenders' storehouses there, perhaps as a warning to anyone disinclined to accept his regime.[7] It is hard to believe that Nobunaga's attack included Shōjitsubō, the long-term survivor among the Enryakuji lenders. He was located in the middle of the northern half of the city and in this very year was confirmed as tax agent on favorable terms by Nobunaga, who clearly saw him as useful.

Oda Nobunaga is directly associated with the decline of the medieval overlord and guild systems not only because he had the audacity to burn Enryakuji but because he abolished guilds and monopoly markets. The latter policy, however, was directed primarily at castle towns, whose economy he hoped to stimulate by freeing trade. Nobunaga's policy toward Kyoto, already a thriving market economy, was to allow the continuation of the existing order and even reconfirm existing commercial monopolies, like that of the oil merchants.[8] Nobunaga inevitably had a profound effect on the moneylenders, however, in the sense that he dealt a mortal blow not only to Enryakuji but to the Muromachi shogunate as well, which came to an abrupt end when Nobunaga drove the last shogun, Yoshiaki, out of Kyoto in 1573.

It was Toyotomi Hideyoshi who eventually abolished the guilds of Kyoto. For a time, Hideyoshi too had tolerated commercial guilds, perhaps for their stability in a time of turmoil. But after assuming the title of imperial regent in 1585, he abolished them along with tolls and commercial taxes in general.[9] The Tokugawa shogunate continued this policy as part of its early efforts to encourage free trade. The formation of guilds or their reconstituted early modern form, the monopolistic commercial groups called *nakama*, were explicitly forbidden by the shogunate through most of the seventeenth century. Apparently some continued to function secretly, however, for they were banned again in 1659. Thus the guild system, within which the rise and establishment of the moneylenders had occurred and against whose constraints they had chafed, went out of existence after a long period of decline.

This is not to say that either credit or brewing ceased to be lucrative professions. Both endured, but through institutions different from the medieval brewer-lenders of this study. A new order, both political and economic, made survival difficult for Enryakuji's moneylenders and split the functions of the medieval creditor into different professions. In the countryside especially, brewing and lending continued to be joint occupations, with some brewers eventually specializing only in moneylending.[10] In the cities, however, credit was not necessarily associated with brewing but tended to be divided between large- and small-scale lenders. Significantly, the term *dosō* (earthen storehouse), synonymous with moneylending in the medieval period, disappears from sources in the early modern period. Instead, two other institutions, the pawnbroker (*shichiya*) and money exchanger (*ryōgaeya*), offered credit. Sources do not indicate that former Enryakuji moneylenders were found in either group. Some may have been, but collectively the moneylenders of medieval times did not make a smooth transition to the new age, for reasons now to be discussed.

The term "pawnbroker" (*shichiya*), in both English and Japanese, refers to the practitioner of a small-scale operation that offers petty loans to individuals down on their luck. This had been but one function of the medieval lenders. It is only partially correct, therefore, to characterize pawnbrokers as their descendants. More numerous than the medieval brewer-lenders, pawnbrokers also differed from their predecessors in that they did not occupy a position of prestige and influence among the townspeople. The textile manufacturers of Nishijin, discussed below, were among the merchants who took over the leadership role among the townspeople of early modern Kyoto.

In the area of regulation, however, the treatment of pawnbrokers did resemble that of the earlier moneylenders. Itakura Shigemune, the Tokugawa shogunate's Kyoto deputy from 1619 to 1654, issued edicts regulating commerce in the city, including pawnbroking.[11] These included measures like those taken by the Muromachi shogunate designed to curb abuses: pawnbrokers must write their receipts legibly; they must not take stolen goods as collateral; two-thirds of the price of the item pawned must be returned to the owner upon redemption, while one-third would go to the pawnbroker as profit. Severe punishment was threatened to violaters, but the very necessity of issuing such edicts, as ever, suggests widespread abuse by creditors. Regulations of 1629 even suggest that Kyoto residents in financial distress were taking their possessions to pawn-brokers in order to come up with enough money for the day's food, and during famines the capacity for brokers to abuse their clients would have been high. The need for police oversight of pawnbrokers was recognized, and in 1692 the shogun's Kyoto deputy directed them, for easier control from above, to form *kabu nakama*, commercial monopoly groups in which membership took the form of stock shares. In 1699, there were 628 pawn-brokers in Kyoto organized into such groups paying monthly dues. These could be considered reconstituted guilds, in a sense, with the important difference that they lacked a medieval-style overlord whose taxation had sometimes been arbitrary as well as widely evaded. Instead, the *nakama* was more like a business license granted by the shogunate or domainal lord, acquired and renewed through payment of fees, in return for which the member acquired a business placard and membership in a protected monopoly.[12]

Loans on a larger scale were granted by a new institution, the money exchanger (*ryōgaeya*).[13] Originally these were actual moneychangers deal-ing in gold, silver, and copper coins, and found only in Edo, Osaka, and Kyoto. Eventually they were established by the shogunate and domainal lords in cities and towns throughout Japan. They exchanged rural currency for that of the shogunate as part of the process of currency standardization. During the seventeenth and eighteenth centuries their functions grad-ually expanded and they became prototypical banks. They granted loans, functioned as depositories for valuables and cash, issued promissory notes, and managed the exchange into cash of taxes in kind for the shogunate and domainal lords. In function they can be compared to the most powerful medieval moneylenders who served as tax agents to overlords. Another early modern institution, the wholesaler (*toiya*), may have also usurped the medieval moneylenders' role as protectors of valuables. Comprehensive or sometimes specialized warehousers and transporters, wholesalers of Sakai and Osaka began to dominate commerce in Japan during the sixteenth century.

Money exchangers in Kyoto by the eighteenth century were organized into guilds (*nakama*). The main guild was divided into five groups—east, west, south, north, center—whose functions included exchange of old and new gold and silver, and serving as financial agents for the Tokugawa shogunate, the Kyoto deputy, and the neighborhood administrators. They took deposit of goods and cash, lent money, and issued promissory notes. In addition, some local merchants, not necessarily brewers, received ap-pointments as smaller exchangers. It is of course possible that some of these money exchangers were descendants of the medieval lenders, but sources do not offer any evidence of this. At the very least, we can say that as a group the medieval lenders were not transformed into early modern money exchangers.

One factor in the failure of medieval lenders to continue into the early modern age may have been changes in the brewing industry. *Sake* brewing, the major capital-generating activity of the medieval money-lenders, underwent significant changes in the early modern period, becoming very large-scale operations in the process.[14] Large regional breweries, such as those of Itami and Ikeda in Settsu province and later in Nada to the west, eventually dominated the national market, making survival difficult for smaller operations. Brewing on this scale was beyond the capacity of the older Kyoto brewers, and their disappearance from sources probably indicates that they were overwhelmed by the successful bigger brewers. Large-scale brewers thrived in Fushimi, south of Kyoto and near a good water supply from early modern times, and probably lent money as a sideline, but these were not descendants of the medieval brewers. The dominance of Osaka in brewing arose from the availability of large amounts of capital among merchants there, who acquired official appointments to confirm their commercial position. The relatively small Kyoto brewers, bereft of an overlord or official sponsor, were driven out of business by superior forces.

The decline of the medieval moneylender must be explained in political as well as economic terms. As part of the demise of the medieval commercial institution, the guild, many moneylenders were bypassed by the new system and may have become small-time pawnbrokers. The decline of the tax-absorbing overlords was a blow to the moneylenders in the sense that their prestige as merchants and townspeople had partially derived from their overlord connections. The monopoly privileges the guild arrangement provided had initially protected the lenders and allowed them to solidify their urban position. In spite of sometimes heavy taxation, the moneylenders continued to thrive in that system even as it declined. Had a strong overlord system continued to protect them, perhaps they could have enlarged their operations to compete successfully with the new brewers. For the most part lacking ties to the new ruling warriors, however, the old moneylenders failed to receive the "designated merchant" (*goyō shōnin*) appointments so essential to long-term success in Edo period Japan. Nonparticipants in the new political order, they were swept into obscurity. For all their medieval vitality the moneylenders were unable to thrive after the death of the overlord system. The new political order bypassed them, although they possessed valuable skills, and for the most part they were probably relegated to the petty status of pawnbroker. For that matter, Kyoto itself was eventually bypassed: over the course of the late sixteenth and early seventeenth centuries, Sakai and then Osaka gradually usurped Kyoto's dominant position in commerce, while Edo consolidated its position as ultimate national center in the eighteenth century. The brewer-lenders' continued prosperity through the long medieval period had owed much to Kyoto's centrality in the national economy; that, too, vanished in the early modern period.

The early modern experience of another Kyoto commercial group, the textile manufacturers of Nishijin, offers a successful contrast to that of the brewer-lenders. Originally weaver-craftsmen to the imperial government in the Heian period, they reorganized themselves as a guild when the ancient order declined. Known as the *ōtoneri* guild in the medieval period, they were clients mostly of aristocratic houses like the Madenokōji and of shrines like Gion and Kasuga.[15] They fled to Sakai during the Ōnin War and then reestablished themselves in Kyoto from the 1490s quite independently of any overlord. They did receive a shogunal appointment in the mid-1500s, but this was of no long-term significance. In the late sixteenth century they suffered some competition from the textile industry of Sakai, which, as Japan's central port city, had the advantage of new technology in the form of looms from the West as well as exotic foreign fabric and thread.[16] Eventually, however, the Nishijin merchants recovered their position as the center of textile production in Japan, their reputation intact as producers of the highest-quality luxury fabric. In spite of a devastating fire in 1730 and some competition from the provinces, Nishijin prospered through most of the early modern age, generally astute about when to mechanize and expand.

A significant difference between the Nishijin merchants and the brewer-lenders, both of whom offered products and services with perennial demand, was the degree of attachment to an overlord in the crucial sixteenth-century era of transition. The Nishijin merchants were more independent, adapting well to new conditions and not clinging to an overlord. They displayed the entrepreneurial flexibility to turn negative events to their advantage. Their exile in Sakai is a good example: it actually helped the Nishijin merchants in the long run, because it gave them exposure to new technology. There is a sense, in the case of this group, of independent, dextrous, and purposeful movement through changing political and economic conditions. The moneylenders, though increasingly identifiable as townspeople, instead of building a new system, remained tied to a dying one that offered only immediate benefits.

Ultimately, the factors discussed above are merely aspects of the general context within which the moneylenders declined. The decline itself remains invisible to us, for it was unrecorded—they simply disappear from the sources. The institutions of brewing, credit, finance, and currency exchange had altered, their various functions apportioned differently. Overlord arrangements, within which they had prospered, vanished. The multiskilled moneylenders, lacking key political ties, were excluded from the new order. With the exception of a handful of independent brewer-lenders like the Suminokura, their long and prosperous run in the medieval overlord system had come to an end. Instead, money exchangers, wholesalers, and, in Kyoto, textile manufacturers now dominated the commercial sector.

Conclusion

The Moneylenders in the Sources

In an essay on the culture of medieval commoners in Japan, Barbara Ruch makes a strong case for the representation of ordinary people in history.[1] Toward this worthy goal the sources by no means yield information readily. Nearly all medieval sources, whether official documents, diaries, literature, or works of art, are elite in focus and origin. Thus they tend to ignore commoners altogether or to treat them in a fragmentary manner, depreciating their role. To pursue the history of commoners requires wresting from the sources a perspective of the medieval age that their authors never intended and probably lacked themselves. The moneylenders are no exception. As objects of research they could be likened to a fragile endangered species, flitting in and out of sight. They are portrayed most regularly in sources as taxpayers or abusive creditors needing regulation. Otherwise they crop up anecdotally, when the clerical or aristocratic diarist notes something striking or amusing. The modern historian's challenge is to employ the sources in a balanced manner to arrive at a comprehensive portrait. Sometimes the broader context of the age must fill in for lack of extensive evidence about moneylenders, who are then inserted, through assumption and inference, where they seem to fit best, incurring the risk that the context itself will become the main story, into which the lenders vanish. In the face of dominant institutions like the shogunate or the greater events of which they were a part, such as the peasant invasions of Kyoto, the specific role of the moneylenders, never well documented, can quickly be overwhelmed. Even a major event like the rise and fall of the Lotus leagues in the early sixteenth century is itself recorded only sketchily, yet its influence on the lives of all townspeople was immense. In the end the sources furnish only a blurry outline of the lives of the moneylenders.

This study is based on a variety of sources: official documents and chronicles of temples, shrines, shogunates, and aristocratic houses; diaries of clerics, aristocrats, and warriors; illustrated screens of Kyoto; an ink painting; a Kyōgen play. But aside from the painting and a few documents of litigation and petition, not a single source emanates directly from a moneylender. Their writings were limited to contracts, receipts, and appeals to overlords for special treatment. Their own reflections on business, taxes, commerce in general, the city, their neighbors, and cultural interests do not exist. Their portrayal in sources therefore is secondhand, one-dimensional, fragmentary, and often casual and incidental, primarily reflecting overlord interests. The result is undue emphasis on overlord concerns, on taxation, and on the regulation of harsh lending practices. While these were important aspects of moneylender existence, they were only part of the whole. The fragmentary, anecdotal nature of sources on moneylenders is in contrast to the more systematic record available for, say, the shogunate or warrior houses, which chronicled their affairs regularly. If the record yields the experience of the relatively literate, well-to-do moneylenders so grudgingly, how much more obscure are the lives of lesser commoners. To portray their lives comprehensively demands a judicious use of fragmentary evidence, which is true to some extent of all historical research but becomes a central concern in a study of commoners.

The credibility of sources on commoners likewise requires careful consideration by the historian. Their authors had their own motivations, and their purpose was not to convey some impartial truth to future generations of historians. In official records, in particular, the authors wrote formulaically and rhetorically in order to make themselves appear authoritative, dominant, and always in the right. For example, the overlords of the late medieval period presumably did not want to convey the impression that they were being successfully manipulated by their commoner tax agents. Likewise, enforcement is rarely addressed in such sources but should nonetheless be a consideration of the historian: simply because an overlord, including even the shogunate, issued an order is hardly evidence that compliance with that order ensued. Official decrees should be taken primarily as an indication of intended overlord policy. Causal assumptions based on a single biased source make for brittle history, yet corroborating evidence is often nonexistent. Given the diffuse and limited nature of authority in the medieval period, the historian must tread a thin line between overskepticism of sources on the one hand and exaggeration of their significance on the other.

The major single source for this study is the collection of laws of the Muromachi Bakufu. Among the most conventionally acceptable sources to historians, their use is nonetheless fraught with more problems than are usually acknowledged. Indeed, they are a prime example of sources whose credibility must be constantly questioned. Aspects of Muromachi law exemplify two problems posed by medieval sources generally: their elite bias obscures the activities of commoners; and the degree to which they were enforced is unknown. "Decrees" might be a more appropriate term than "laws," for these sources may have been widely disregarded by those they were intended to regulate.

Taking as a model the original military legal code, the *Goseibai shikimoku* of the Kamakura Bakufu, and its supplementary laws, as well as customary estate law, Muromachi shogunal administrators devised a legal system based on precedent.[2] Like its predecessor, it placed great emphasis on observing established procedure and due process in petitions to the shogunate and in litigation.[3] Overlord rights to estate lands were carefully protected, and the duties of shogunal officials were outlined in some detail. But the new legal code broke ground in some important ways, reflecting the changed conditions of the times. These included the widespread use of roadside placards to inform the public of shogunal decrees, a custom that was to continue through the early modern period and that was primarily for the benefit of commoners. Application of the law also expanded significantly: one scholar maintains that, under Muromachi law, for the first time commoners were treated as beneficiaries and not just targets of the law.[4] Debt amnesties, for instance, applied to all classes of debtors. In the many laws regulating commerce, especially moneylending, an intent to make them universally applicable can be detected, for they were applied to all parties except temples and shrines. Muromachi law also encompassed regulation of the Zen *gozan* network of monasteries, a new intrusion by warriors dictated by the close relationship between the shogunate and the major *gozan* temples. (No other temples' internal matters were affected.) In the name of order and security, Muromachi law attempted to control the unruliness of Enryakuji's monks in Kyoto, a problem that had been beyond the reach of the Kamakura shogunate in the first half of the medieval period. Finally, the number and scope of Muromachi laws pertaining to commerce provide a sharp contrast to the Kamakura legal code and attest to the significance of commerce in the fifteenth and sixteenth centuries.

The *Kenmu shikimoku*, the original legal formulary of the Muro-machi shogunate that prefaces the later decrees, is more a list of injunctions than a legal code per se. Addressed to warriors, it limits their rights, especially to property, vis-à-vis those of the aristocrats. It stresses good government and excludes aristocrats therefrom. It reserves the right to judge lawsuits of religious institutions. Most significantly for the moneylenders, it reveals the importance the shogunate placed on civil order and commerce in Kyoto. Heavy emphasis on Kyoto and commerce carries through the 542 supplementary laws (*tsuikahō*) that follow the *Kenmu shikimoku* and are dated from 1337 to 1570. Of the 268 laws dated before the Ōnin War, 15 are concerned with disorder and 72 with commerce, especially moneylending. Local administration of Japan by warrior vassals of the shogun, in contrast, is the concern of only 39 decrees, suggesting his rather limited national scope even before the Ōnin War. Twenty-four laws focus on penal matters and litigation. Regulation of the Zen monastic system is the greatest single pre-Ōnin distraction of the shogunate, with 78 laws on that issue. After the Ōnin War, the centrality of Kyoto and its commercial prosperity for the shogunate is manifest in the large number (144) of decrees in that area. Zen regulation is negligible—one law—while local administration and litigation account for about as many laws as in the pre-Ōnin period. When analyzing the proportion of laws in certain areas, it is important to remember that there are many gaps in the record due to loss, and the body of Muromachi law as it remains today is not the same as that of five centuries ago. Supplemental sources like diaries and chronicles make reference to laws no longer extant; this is the only way to appreciate how much we do not know.[5]

Fully 40 percent of the extant 542 shogunal laws deal with aspects of moneylending, a compelling indication of the important role of credit in the economy of the period. The shogunate's twin concerns in the area of moneylending were the smooth functioning of commerce and the maintenance of regular tax revenues. Therefore Bakufu laws deal mostly with regulating moneylenders' excesses and with accommodating or suppressing peasant uprisings. The business practices of the moneylenders are only indirectly revealed by these sources.

Penal aspects of Muromachi law have been discussed above in the context of early-sixteenth-century shogunal attempts to regulate the use of currency; the official rarity of capital punishment has been particularly noted. Muromachi law has been characterized as less severe than Tokugawa or Ming law, being not without reasonableness and equity, and the shoguns as tolerant, by default, of itinerancy, insubordination, and diversity.[6] Because of its vagueness in specifying punishments and in the arbitrary nature of enforcement, however, it is hard to characterize Muromachi law as benign or lenient. (The laws are more exact regarding punishment of warriors, which is perhaps indicative of a relatively uncontested sphere of shogunal control, at least in the early Muromachi period.[7] At the same time, recorded instances of harsh punishments actually carried out against warriors are hard to find.)[8] Thus Muromachi law in practice —that is, when it was enforced—could just as well have been arbitrary and harsh as responsible and equitable, depending on the enforcing officials.

Punishments either specified or alluded to indirectly in Muromachi law include: arrest and imprisonment, banishment from office (including warriors, shrine officials, and Zen priests), exile and banishment (including expulsion from the Zen *gozan* network and prohibition from carrying on a business), confiscation of property (including land, crops, shops, residence, or a percentage thereof), eviction from one's home and destruction of same, corporal punishment, monetary fines or fines in kind (crops), imprisonment in cages, cutting off of hands, death (in four cases), and torture.[9] But most laws contain only a vague warning: "Violators will be punished." Considering that commoners were among the recipients of these punishments, one becomes reluctant to characterize Muromachi law as reasonable or equitable, regardless of its severity relative to Ming or Tokugawa law. It is likely, for example, that corporal punishment was meted out to commoners more often than to other offenders. Other punishments, moreover, had a harsher effect on commoners than on elites: confiscation of property, for example, would have been more devastating to a merchant than to a warrior, who could probably use force or allies to rebuild resources. High levels of violence and vigilantism, especially against commoners, were tolerated in some situations: for example, anyone who brought the shogun the head of a ringleader of a peasant league was promised a special reward.[10] At the same time, however, the Bakufu's lack of comprehensive authority most likely hampered its ability to enforce and to punish. The characterization of so-called shogunal tolerance as being by default is well taken. "Muromachi law" is really a conglomeration of decrees that, although they reveal some long-term policies, are more notable for their reactive nature: decisions were handed down in an ad hoc manner, responding to crises as they arose. By comparison to the Tokugawa period, then, Muromachi Japan was an unregulated society, but this was primarily thanks to the limitations, not the largesse, of this governing authority.

The documents of the Ninagawa family, deputy head of the Board of

Administration and responsible for its day-to-day functioning, are useful supplements to shogunal laws to the extent that they are a record of the actual collection and disbursement of tax revenues. This collection contains a wide variety of source material: diaries kept by various heads of the family; documentation of relations with its lord, the Ise, which held the headship (*shitsuji*) of the Board of Administration; documents exchanged with the Board of Adjudicants (*hikitsukekata*), including matters related to lawsuits and requests for land confirmation by the shogun (called *kubari hikitsuke*) and matters concerning Board of Administration decisions (*gohan hikitsuke*, the most numerous category); and some documents on the house governance of the Ninagawa and Ise families. The limitations of this source are also serious, however: in addition to being rather few in number, tax records do not always distinguish moneylender taxes from commercial taxes generally. The Ninagawa records are also revealing as a record of what the Bakufu spent money on, another topic of research altogether. There are other important shogunal sources, including the proceedings of the Board of Adjudicants, the *Muromachi Bakufu hikitsuke shiryō shūsei*, and a collection of administrative directives, the *Muromachi Bakufu monjo shūsei: bugyōnin hōsho*.

The uneven nature of shogunal record keeping is traceable to several factors. First, it was common for various offices within the shogunate to keep official records while at the same time the officials kept individual records, such as diaries. Neither was comprehensive, or at least neither survives in comprehensive form. In the case of the Ninagawa family, three of its scions, Chikamoto, his son Chikataka, and, skipping a generation, Chikatoshi, kept relatively thorough records, including both public and private types. The record is not complete, however: no diary survives for Chikayori, Chikataka's son, for example. The second factor in the uneven nature of shogunal record keeping is more complex: the Muromachi Bakufu is, to historians, a confusingly protean institution, constantly evolving and changing. Relevant to this study is the concurrent rise to power in the middle decades of the fifteenth century of the corps of administrators (*bugyōshū*), a group of hereditarily appointed legal experts, and the Board of Administration, which by the late fifteenth century dominated the shogunate like no other organ.[11] As a result, even as its leadership fell into disarray with the approach of the Ōnin War, the shogunate functioned in a notably more legalistic manner from the middle of the fifteenth century: the issuance and preservation of documents improved and became routinized. Thus it comes as no surprise that matters like collection of the moneylender tax, which fell under the jurisdiction of the dominant

Board of Administration, make an appearance in documents for the first time during that period. In other words, it is quite possible that the Bakufu's collection of taxes from the moneylenders functioned regularly from 1393, even though no documents survive to prove it.

Aristocratic and clerical diaries are useful sources for reconstructing aspects of city life, but they too have limitations. Although full of vivid observations, diaries and chronicles by their nature tend to convey an anecdotal and impressionistic image of the age, and sometimes have a pessimistic, alarmist bent. This bias is reflective not necessarily of the realities of city life, however disruptive the times were, but of the (accurate) perception that the lot of aristocrats was worsening. These are the same people, after all, who had collectively been lamenting hard times in literary and other works since the eleventh century. During the Ōnin War things only grew worse for them, with the regular imposition by warriors of a commisariat tax amounting to half their estate taxes, not to mention outright takeover of their lands by local warriors. (Great temples like Enryakuji had the clout to demand and eventually obtain a partial rollback of such taxes.) Their increasingly threadbare existence produced pessimistic and poignant narratives that demand critical evaluation as much as any other source. The Ōnin War, precisely in turning things topsy-turvy, created opportunities for many townspeople like the moneylenders, but this is not reflected in the aristocratic sources.

New historiographical problems also loom from the time of the Ōnin War. With decline and periodic disarray in the shogunate, its official sources diminish in number, and coverage by diaries and chronicles can be uneven. Instead, one turns to sources such as the illustrated screens of Kyoto, stunning in their detail and vitality. Most were produced in the sixteenth and seventeenth centuries, so care needs to be taken about attributing to the late medieval period the contents of these later works. Also to be considered are the purposes for which the screens were produced.[12] Commissioned by aristocrats and warriors, their depiction of palaces, temples, and aristocratic homes leaves little space for commoners' quarters. Some screens may have been intended as actual guides to Kyoto for, perhaps, a warrior new to the city. Or they may be a reconstruction or recollection of the city in earlier times, reliable for the most part. On the other hand, given their fundamental nature as art, it is also possible that they reflect fantasy on the part of the author. The most useful screen for this study was that of the Machida family, probably painted between 1510 and 1525, but not representing the city at that time.[13] Most likely it is a mental image of the city in an early, Ōnin-era incarnation, and therefore useful as a reflection of contemporary architectural and defense features. The screen's most curious omission, from the perspective of this study, is that it does not contain a single moneylender's storehouse, even though there were hundreds in the city. Perhaps artists judged that storehouses took up precious space on a surface that had to encompass all of Kyoto. Or it may have been that artists, like others, were frequently in debt to moneylenders and thus not keen on showcasing them in their art. To some extent artists depict what they like, including pleasant vignettes of everyday life, but probably not usury![14]

The records of religious institutions like Kitano and Yasaka Shrines are helpful in illuminating guild affairs. Like shogunal records, however, the overlord's concerns governed the record keeping, and the moneylenders' lives are only partially revealed as a result. Occasionally there is a flash of moneylender will, as in the case of Kenkei bargaining for better treatment. Sometimes after many centuries documents of religious institutions surface through unusual channels. A case in point is the *Yase dōjikai monjo* collection, a portion of which pertains to the moneylenders.[15] Held by the self-governing village of Yase, apparently for centuries, the documents were only made public in the year 2000. Those pertaining to commerce are unrelated to the bulk of the collection, which concerns village affairs. They number nearly one hundred in all, and came from a variety of sources—shogunate, moneylenders, Hie Shrine, and various parts of Enryakuji itself. All of the documents relate to the period before Nobunaga destroyed Enryakuji. They may have been entrusted by someone at Enryakuji to the group of imperial palanquin bearers who lived in Yase. (Located in the northeast of Kyoto, in medieval times Yase was an entrepôt to Enryakuji at the western base of the mountain.) There are similar cases of aristocratic documents reappearing after centuries in obscurity. For the retrieval of lives from the past, such events are felicitous indeed.

All historians must be judicious in their use of sources, given that their purposes may differ from those of the original authors. When searching for commoners in an age of diffuse authority the problem becomes especially acute. A conservative approach to sources risks limiting scholarship to narrow studies that may miss the larger significance of the age. Looser interpretation of data, on the other hand, produces unnuanced, gross generalizations. Sources will dictate the outcome of research when interpreted on their own terms in accordance with the specific reasons for their creation—to establish legally the right of inheritance of property or title, to record the payment or receipt of taxes, to challenge claims to property or income. This is not to say that such matters are unimportant. But another stage should follow this initial scrutiny, entailing more critical interpretation, if a comprehensive picture of the medieval age is to emerge. Sources must be analyzed for information that they may not focus on directly and that they may provide only stingily. The historian must question the sources assiduously as to the authors' perspectives and motives, and speculate broadly as to what they omit. Such a critical approach is necessary, vexing, and ultimately rewarding.

Over several decades, historians in Japan have determinedly sought tiny needles in the haystack of medieval source materials in an effort to piece together a portrait of commoner life. They have combined conventional methodologies with freer approaches in order to mine sources thoroughly of all their layers of meaning. Speculation based on slivers of evidence; broad assumptions and generalizations applied to several centuries or to a variety of geographical regions; the application of the general to the specific and vice versa, with little corroborating evidence; the citation of literary sources to bolster an argument; supposition and inference that may stretch the original intent of the sources radically—such are the unorthodox tools used when working a source-poor landscape. A willingness to mine every source and occasionally to tolerate evidential fragility allows the history of commoners to be retrieved. The result is well worth the effort. As in the example of the moneylenders, a sketch of medieval commoners brings new depth to that age. Without them, medieval Kyoto appears less vital economically and culturally, less diverse socially, and less intricate politically.

THE MONEYLENDERS IN MEDIEVAL SOCIETY

During the late medieval period Kyoto's moneylenders prospered as wealthy merchants and leading townspeople. From early medieval times their guild tie to a powerful overlord, Enryakuji, had endowed them with privileged status to flourish in brewing and lending, the former as a protected monopoly. The Muromachi shogunate, a curse in its capacity as a taxing overlord, at the same time further enhanced the lenders' status by using their skills as storehouse keepers and tax agents, and by granting them considerable autonomy in fulfilling those duties. From the late fourteenth century, even while maintaining overlord ties, the moneylenders' character as autonomous townspeople and merchants became conspicuous. Their leadership of neighborhood self-defense against invading peasant leagues was forced upon them in the absence of shogunal military protection but was at the same time a natural response, given that their storehouses and receipts were the prime targets of the invaders. The Ōnin War also threatened moneylenders, this time not as creditors but as townspeople caught in the line of fire. Their identification with collective goals of self-defense at the neighborhood level was reinforced during this conflict, and the tendency to distance themselves from weakened overlords, now bereft of many of their landed holdings in the provinces, became marked. New arrangements, such as new guilds or extraguild activity, accompanied the intensification of old irregularities like incidental levies and bribes for exemptions. Prominent moneylenders, more essential than ever as tax agents and bolder in defying overlord demands, took full advantage of their position in the middle of the hierarchy to enhance their material and social standing. After the war as before, the moneylenders were central participants in a culture of festivals, tea, linked verse, and other recreations, whether leading, financing, or simply enjoying. Along with other townspeople, their participation in neighborhood self-governance and Lotus league activities can be assumed. Portrayal of their prosperity, autonomy, and cultural efflorescence is fragmentary, however, as the record keepers noted their lives only in passing.

The moneylenders' prosperity and longevity were predicated on a strong and steady demand for credit in medieval Kyoto. The extension of credit had begun in the Heian period, when it was usually in kind, especially by monasteries like Enryakuji. It was not until currency came into wide use in the medieval period that it became an everyday occurrence, and from that point on credit was widely sought after by people in all sectors of society. But was it sought by necessity or by custom? Was the size of Kyoto's moneylending establishment a reflection of the desperate economic circumstances of people living on the edge, or was credit perceived primarily as a convenient service? Obviously there were debtors of both kinds, and premodern life was precarious enough that credit was a tool for survival in many cases. But the widespread willingness, even by the well-to-do, to seek credit for immediate needs in spite of punishing interest rates suggests an acceptance of it as manageable and appropriate. That is, medieval people had a sophisticated grasp of the function of money. For instance, an aristocrat who chose to put up a favorite tea bowl as collateral for a loan rather than for outright sale was implicitly ranking an immediate and mundane need for cash below love of the tea bowl, and was willing to pay interest for some months rather than give up the bowl. He was, in other words, making a choice in favor of the bowl and the pleasure he derived from it over short-term solvency. Nor was this sense of money's function and worth limited to aesthetic pleasures. Peasants who needed cash for basic necessities like seed rice, food, or taxes, rightly saw credit as a better solution to an immediate problem than the sale of precious rights to land, loss of which would create severe long-term problems. They took a gamble that the coming harvest would be good enough to allow them to pay off the debt, and if not, they might organize to demand a debt amnesty. This is hardly to deny that many lost the gamble, sinking into poverty and becoming tenants on their own land. But debtors high and low generally adopted the same strategy: to meet daily needs as well as possible while always seeking the best long-term situation. Sometimes this backfired and default resulted, leading to unfavorable long-term results anyway. The prevalence of credit, however, suggests that many debtors were choosing it for its convenience, and these customary debtors probably sought credit regularly—hence the size and prosperity of the Kyoto moneylending establishment.

On the other hand, many of those seeking credit were cash poor. Peasants and elites both had resources in the form of rights to land, and credit was a way to translate this into cash, if for a price. Townspeople likewise might have the tools of their trade, items used in daily life, and some luxury items that could be put up for a loan of cash. Others were cash poor in the most basic sense: they became debtors not as a choice but for lack of any alternative. To them the ruthless practices of moneylenders, suggested by the Muromachi shogunate's regulations, were especially painful. They might resort to organized protest to demand a debt amnesty, but with limited chances of success. The urgency of the cash-poor debtor as well as the calculation of the customary debtor can both be detected in *ikki* when those uprisings are considered as a manifestation of a credit problem rather than as a political or social problem.

As in many societies, status, even if not yet legally formulated, determined the nature of many relationships in medieval Japan. In this respect, the most prominent of the moneylenders occupied a unique social niche: in their merchant capacity as lenders and as brewers they functioned as creditors to people from all walks of life, while as guild members they were taxpayers to overlords, and as tax agents they were tax collectors. The last connection, in particular, endowed them with a privileged aura among the townspeople. In cultural matters their status cut both ways, and they interacted with aristocrats, warriors, and other townspeople in a variety of pursuits. Indeed, their cultural sophistication may have approached that of low-ranking aristocrats. Taxed frequently, moneylenders also benefited from the overlord tie as brewers whose prosperity was aided by guild monopolies, as tax collectors with monastic and shogunal appointments, and as wealthy residents whose ties to major temples and shrines garnered them the respect of their peers. Thus one aspect of the moneylenders' lives, the overlord tie, was a useful arrangement of many centuries' duration, offering benefits to both sides. While essentially a vertical relationship, its exploitative aspects were tempered by a degree of autonomy exerted by the moneylenders and acquiesced in by the overlord. The lenders acted in self-interest, distancing themselves from the overlord when beneficial to do so but exploiting the connection when helpful. Remaining in the relationship had a high cost, however, for they went down with the overlords at the end of the medieval period.

In this study the Muromachi shogunate's policies toward moneylenders are characterized as those of an overlord, very nearly parallel to the guild system. Given its rather limited national scope, the shogunate made a shrewd choice in taxing some commercial groups as a way to maintain itself firmly in the capital. Also shrewd in the short run was following the example of traditional overlords in appointing prominent lenders as its tax agents. Experienced in performing this task for Enryakuji, these moneylenders would bring income to the shogun quickly. In the long run, however, the shogun was making his income dependent on the skills of commoners whose loyalty to any overlord was not complete. The benefits of taxation of commerce were great, however, and with its military power, in Kyoto the shogunate was accommodated by the traditional elites even as they all competed for income from the same sources. The long-term risk, eventually played out, was that the shogunate would become no more than the greatest among equals, one *kenmon* in a city of *kenmon*. Bereft of national authority by the sixteenth century, it was in the dangerous position of dependency on a faltering order. Having neglected to carve out an entirely separate niche for itself, the Muromachi Bakufu was to collapse with the other overlords.

There was also, however, a comprehensive quality to Bakufu authority in Kyoto that prevents classifying it as simply another overlord. Because the shogunate had absorbed most of the administrative functions of the imperial court, it was universally recognized as the primary authority for adjudication in the city. Disputes over rights to land, for example, were routinely brought before it by various overlords, not only warriors. Overlords likewise sought shogunal confirmation of their landholdings in order to thwart legal challenges to their right to rent income. (Even with shogunal confirmation, however, a single land dispute could rage for decades, suggesting that the Bakufu's ability to enforce its legal decisions was lim-

ited.) Official dealings with elites and commoners were generally conducted through shogunal administrators (*bugyōnin*).[16] Their rise was originally part of Yoshinori's drive to increase the shogun's power within the
Bakufu, but the long-term effect was quite different: under their influence
the shogunate became a legalistic institution, somewhat comparable to
the imperial government in ancient times. With the decline of the office
of shogun after the Ōnin War, this administrative system became the only
constant in shogunal governance. Thus, even as it weakened and the
shogun himself became powerless, the shogunate remained a functioning
institution in Kyoto, the governing authority of the city for much of the
late medieval period.

Acting through decrees and legal process in accordance with precedent, the Muromachi shogunate through its administrators dealt with the
moneylenders in litigation and regulatory matters as a government. At
the same time, through its moneylender tax agents, its stance toward most
lenders was indistinguishable from that of other taxing overlords like
Enryakuji. Thus the lenders used the same tax evasion tactics against the
shogunate as they did against other overlords. Yet the shogunate also issued
comprehensive laws of a public, regulatory nature, like debt amnesties and
decrees prohibiting punitive activities by moneylenders, indicating a concern not only with its own income but with public order in the city as
well. This was the unique character of the Muromachi shogunate; it was
simultaneously commercial overlord and heir to the ancient imperial government in Kyoto as city administrator.

The influence of religion in the moneylenders' lives was pervasive.
Most conspicuous in the record is the resilient institutional power of Enryakuji and its network of shrines. The dominant overlord of Kyoto commerce from the thirteenth century, the monastery acknowledged the Muromachi shogunate's authority in Kyoto but continued to assert its own
interests there. Its ability to influence adjudication is evident in the
Kitano Malt Disturbance, while its authority to tax continued even with
competition from the shogunate. The awe in which it was held as a
sacred entity is clear from the universal agitation aroused by the movement of Hie's portable shrine. It was Enryakuji's rage at the Lotus movement in Kyoto that precipitated the latter's violent suppression—and the
destruction of much of the city—in 1536. Some moneylenders continued
to have a clerical tie to Enryakuji, even serving in a liturgical capacity in
the late medieval age, and efforts to tax the lenders continued as well. The
resiliency of Enryakuji as a comprehensive religious presence to the very
end of the medieval period belies any insistence that warrior dominance

had become complete. Although imperial and aristocratic authority languished in the shadow of the shogunate, the religious estate had the adaptability and dominance to survive and even prosper in the late medieval order.

Other aspects of medieval religion discernible in the moneylenders' lives are its diversity, detectable in the multiple affiliations of the townspeople, and its spiritual appeal and daily pervasiveness, seen in simple, accessible rituals and pious practices. As an extension of this, the access to culture that religion provided to all members of society was multifaceted. Noh and Kyōgen drama were informed in content by Buddhism and provided a stage by temples. Street dancing, perhaps the most basic cultural form of the townspeople, had its origins in the collective chanting of the name of the Buddha. Festivals like that of Gion Shrine were a vibrant aspect of city life deriving from religious roots. The tea ceremony, though quite secular in the form practiced by moneylenders, owed its presence in Japan to Zen, as did ink painting. The Lotus movement provided spiritual and physical security to its followers in the unsettled early decades of the sixteenth century. In no other age was the force of religion felt so powerfully and inclusively by all members of the society.

Opportunity and limitations marked the last two centuries of the medieval age. The limitations placed on the multiple elites in the *kenmon* balance of late medieval Kyoto are apparent in their dealings with subordinates like moneylenders and with one another. The shogunate supported the tax claims of Enryakuji and the imperial court even as it taxed the same individuals for its own income. For their part, the lenders' behavior became less collective as guild arrangements weakened and autonomy from the overlord grew from the late fourteenth century. Their business success varied widely according to individual, as did their cultural lives. The most prominent ones found opportunities everywhere: they were in close proximity to the elites, at work and in cultural matters. Most of the lenders, however, were small fry, townspeople struggling to survive in business and fending off taxation whenever possible—in other words, as hemmed in as other commoners. Although the sources tend to obscure it, the lenders were individuals, not a homogenous group, who brewed *sake* and lent money for a living. As time passed they did many other things as well, and in the late medieval era their lives embraced Kyoto in all its complexity.

Appendix
Lists of Kyoto Moneylenders

No. 1. *Sake* Brewers/Moneylenders of Medieval Kyoto
according to Kitano Shrine's Roster of 1425–1426

Kitano Monjo no. 62 ("Sakaya kōmyō," list of *sake* brewers), includes 324 names for 1425/11/10 (pp. 34–46), and twenty-three appended in 1426/2/16 (p. 46). These rosters are thought to have been compiled by Kitano Shrine as a way to enforce its malt monopoly on Kyoto brewers. The list is considered the most complete available of the Kyoto moneylenders. Each entry contains a name, sometimes a nickname such as a province or youth name, and a location. The names only are transcribed below and categorized according to the presence or absence of an obvious nonclerical name, youth name, or province name. "X" indicates unclear character.

Clerics

Enkyū	Gen'yū	Sōken
Chōritsu	Jōkō	Yūon
Tsūshun (two shops)	Jūkaku	Enshu
Jōkei	Jōyū	Shōkan
Yūken	Sōzen	Jōkaku
Enkei	Sōga	Enken
Yūsō	Kōshu	Ryūshun
Jūken	Eikaku	Jūken
Sōen	Jūchū	Enkei
Chōkō	Yūga	Kōkyū
Daijō	Myōken	Shōken
Jōzen (two shops)	Jitsuyū	Eishun
Sōei	Yūshun	Ryōen
Yūkei	Jittsū	Jūen
Ryōken	En'yū	Jōken
Zōsei	Ryōshō	Jōzen
Zonchū	En	Sōkei
Jōyū	Kenson	Yūken
Ryōshō	Enshun	Jūzen
Myōjū (two shops)	Yūen	Yūken
Rokō	Zechō	Myōken
Shōchi	Kensen	Ryōsei
Kanshō	Ryōkaku	Kōyū
Yūkō	Yūsei	Jūshū

Clerics (cont.)

Shōen	Shūkō	Ryōken
Shinsei	Senzen	Kōkaku
Yūzen	Kenjō	Shunkei
Enkai	Sōyū	Keishun
Chōun	Engei	Tayu
Enkaku	Senshun	Kyōen
Keishun	Dōkon	Yūshun
Sentsū	Shōen	Kense
Kaku X	Kenkō	Shūbai
Jōyū	Chōsen	Shinchin
Sōyu	Shin'yū	Jōyū
Ken'ei	Jōsei	Shōken
Yūshun	En'un (three shops)	Sōen
Shishū	Kohōshi	Shin'ei
Enta	Sōgen	Jōshun
Shōyū	Shōsen	Shōyū
Ken'yū	Ryōkaku	Jōgen
Eisen	Jitsuyū	Senshun
Ryōyū	Shinkaku	Shin'yū
Nanrin	Eiyū	Genkaku
Teikei	Sōkei	Ken'ei
Kenryū	Sōen	Ryōshin
Eishō	Ryōsan	Soyū
Tōke	Mokuchō (two shops)	Chōen
Kenkei	Gyōtsū	Enkon
Shinshū	Jūjun	Yūsen
Sōchi	Shōei	Sōsei
Eishō	Kōkon	Myōsei
Kankaku	Ryūhan	Eiryū
Shōki	Yūjitsu	Seikyū
Jikkei	Jitsuyū	Eisei
Shun'i	Kenjitsu	Jōken
Shōchō	Enkei	Yūkyū
Shōkei	Yūson	Keijū
Yūkei	Jūken	Shinbō
Ken'ei	Kakuen	Jōsan
Eishū	Jōkei	Jōshun
Sōen	Shinshō	Ran
Keison	Jōchō	Chōyū
Chōei	Sōgen	Shōkei
Ryōyū	Jissen	Kenjō
Enkei	Ensō	Chōen
Jōgen	Kenjitsu	Chōgen
Jōkei	Kensei	Sōsen
Yūhan	Jōsei	Kendō

Clerics (cont.)

Ryōkyū	Yūken	Yūen
Jūken	Kagen	Myōsan
Ryōsan	Gyōgen	Jōyū
Zen'ei	Gyōkei	Kenbō
Shūyū	Yūgen	Myōyū
Zenchin	Yūkei	Chōchō
Eien	Mokushun	Kenchō
Eikō	Jison	Ninki
Xshun	Jōjitsu	Chōsui
Jōshun	Sōkō	Shōsen
Sōgen	Dōchin	Hōju
Eishun	Jūken	Ryūshō
Shinkaku	Keiyū	Jōchō
Jisshū	Kyōkan	Sōzon
Sōjun		
Yūken		

Ji Sect Adherents

Kichia	On'ami	Kōa
Hon'a	Dōami	Yūami
Kakua	Shūa	
Hon'a	Chōa	

Laymen

Kunitsugu (Eimon)	Saemonshichirō	Saeimonkurō
Nobumitsu	Tomohisa	Sanehisa
Takashige	Magosaburō	Hikokurō
Nagatoshi	Saburō	Matsukuma
Munemori	Tsugumitsu	Shirōgorō
Munetoshi	Tomoyuki	Saeimonjirō
Shirōgorō	Nagamitsu	Hebi (Snake)
Akishige (two shops)	Norimori	Yoshifusa
Xshige	Suzume (Sparrow)	Magosaburō
Sadayoshi	Kunihisa	Takashige
Masahiro	Hisashige	Nobuhisa
Ujisada	Rokurō	Kogorō
Tameuji	Yaya	Hikoshirō
Noritomo	Norizane	Jirōsaburō
Kunitsugu (Yajirō)	Shingorō	Yajirō
Ujikatsu	Kiyoda	Kurōtarō
Yoshishige (two shops)	Yoshihisa	Emonjirō
Yoshinaka	Tomohisa	Shigehiro
Morishige	Munehisa	Saburōzaemon
Shirōgorō		
Hyōbu		

Province Names

Echizen	Echizen (incomplete entry)
Kōzuke	Hōki
Hōki	Harima
Izumi	Owari

Laywoman

Memeko

Nuns (widows)

Shōani
Hosshōni

Chinese

Rai

Korean

Goun

No. 2. Kyoto Brewer-Moneylenders on the Eve of the Ōnin War

The following lists were drawn from three documents in the *Shinjōin monjo* collection dated 1467/4 and include brewers taxed by Hie Shrine. They may refer only to those with exemptions from the tax. They may be new businesses. Each entry includes a status label (cleric [either *sō* or *shami*], layman, nun), an individual's name, a location, and a description of the building, including some architectural features that were defensive in nature. The latter suggest self-defense measures against *ikki* attacks. Also significant about these lists is that the status label gives some sense of the extent to which the moneylenders were becoming a secular group, even before the Ōnin War. By the fourth month of 1467 the opening salvos of the Ōnin War had already been fired, but the major fighting between the eastern and western camps, which laid waste the city of Kyoto, started late in the fifth month of 1467.

Clerics

Enkei (*sō*)	Enshun (*sō*)
Dōgo (*shami*)	Jōshun (*sō*)
Jōgon (*sō*)	Yūgen (*sō*)
Chōyū (*sō*)	Chōshun (*sō*)
Shun'yu (*sō*)	Jōyū (*sō*)
Ishibe Nyūdō (*shami*)	Jōshun (*sō*)
Minbu Nyūdō Daishukujiki (*shami*)	Shunjō (*sō*)
Munega (*sō*)	

Laymen

Yūkichi	Magogorō
Fukuichimaru (child or outcaste; not an adult's name)	Matsuwakamaru (child)
	Ozaki
Shikibushō	Yubuka
Nobumasa	Yoshisada
Yūhide	Moriyū
Shigekichi	Munetsugi
Jirōsaburō	Yūmune
Muneshige	Yūken
Chikashige	Yukichi
Sadamaru	Kaneshige
Hidekichi	Sadayū
Yūmitsu	Gorōjirō
Hidesada	Yoshitaka
Masushige	Chigikumaru
Yūsada	Masu

Nuns (widows)

Yūsha	Hōshun
Chiyū	Shōnin

Laywoman

Uujo (?)

No. 3. Moneylenders in 1480–1485

The following is a summary of moneylenders by status in requests to the shogunate for confirmation of loans following conditional debt amnesties in 1480 and 1546. The first group includes 133 requests dated from 1480 to 1485; the second, 79 requests dated 1546 and 1547. Source: *Muromachi Bakufu hikitsuke shiryō shūsei*, vol. 2, pp. 51–82 (1480–1485 requests), pp. 235–288 (1546–1547 requests).

1480–1485 Requests

78 lay people
54 clerics and temples, including at most 9 individual monks who could be affiliated with Enryakuji.

1546–1547 Requests

56 lay people
23 clerics and temples, including at most 6 individual monks who could be affiliated with Enryakuji.

No. 4. Kyoto Moneylenders in 1495

These lists are transcribed from documents in the *Ninagawake monjo*, a record of day-to-day transactions of the shogunal Board of Administration. As discussed in Chapter 3, the interpretation of these documents is problematic: exactly what the names represent and what they were used for is unclear. The titles of some documents suggest that these were rosters used by the shogunal tax farmers to collect commercial (*sake*, storehouse, and bean-paste) taxes, but it is uncertain how complete they are: some seem to record new businesses, while others list those granted exemptions. Some names occur on more than one document. Nevertheless, they are useful in two respects: as records of shogunal income, they give a rough idea of the amount of moneylender taxes actually being collected, and the mostly secular names of the moneylenders, combined with a large number of exemptions, suggest a strong lay identity and influx of new businesses in the post-Ōnin decades. Notations referring to new businesses and new establishments at old premises suggest great movement and influx of new merchants in the post-Ōnin decades. SOURCE: *Ninagawake monjo*, vol. 2, pp. 71–86.

No. 302: Sakaya shinka chūmon (List of Newly Added Brewers) 1495/12/23

(Addresses are of Upper Kyoto)

Shimada Yoichi	Shinoda (new, from twelfth month)
Tsuda (remains)	Sano
Tani Yajirō	Ohara (widow, paid recent tax)
Horiike Sukejirō	(Ko)yama
Okuno	Ohara (remains)
Kamogawa	Kobuya
Yasu Kōichi	Sawamura Shōkan
Fuji Jirō	No name
Katayama	No name, located in Jissōin

No. 303: Sakaya dosōra shinka kenchi zaisho chūmon (List of Newly Added Survey of Locations of Brewer-Lenders)

(Mixed Upper and Lower Kyoto Addresses)
Fujō/Gamaiki(?)
Ishibe
Horiike Sukejirō
Shimada Yoichi
No name – in Jissōin
No name – said to be at Sawamura Heijirō's premises, but not so observed
No name – pawned items, said to be at Sawamura Yagorō's premises
No name – of 49 casks, 21 in use
No name – of 60 *sake* casks, 30 in use
No name – of 60 *sake* casks, 39 in use
Sono – of 120 casks, 13 observed, but *sake* said to have been consumed

Zenyō – pawned items
Nakamura Yosaburō – bean paste, 2 tubs, a few pawned items
Teragi – bean paste, 5 tubs

No. 304: Sakakura misoyaku menjo (Exemptions from *Sake*, Moneylending, and Bean-Paste Taxes)

(Mixed Upper and Lower Kyoto Addresses)

Shimada – *sake* tax: 1 *kan*, 400 *mon* already paid, 2 *kan*, 500 *mon* due now; storehouse tax: 1 *kan*, 500 *mon*

Tsuda – same as before; 2 *kan* already paid, but no funds at present

Yasui – 3 *kanmon* as before

Sano – bean-paste tax: 3 *kanmon* as before

Yasu – *sake* tax: 1 *kanmon* as before

Same, Yagorō – new business, exempted, no funds

Imae Yajirō's place, remains of grandmother Yanagi – 1 *kan*, 400 *mon* submitted

Uno – *sake* tax: 1 *kanmon* submitted

Mori – same as before, *sake* tax: 1 *kanmon* submitted

Nakanishi – Formerly run by a person named Oka, paid 2 *kan*, 800 *mon*

Nakamura – *sake* tax: 1 *kan*, 400 *mon* as before

Sawamura Heijirō – same as before, 1 *kan*, 400 *mon*; storehouse tax: 400 *mon*

Ohara – exempted, pays imperial tax, changed proprietors

Uno Magotarō – same as before, *sake* tax: 1 *kanmon*; bean-paste tax: 3 *kanmon*

Mokake – *sake* tax: 1 *kanmon*

Ohashi – same as before, 2 *kan*, 800 *mon* submitted

Gyokusen – same as before, *sake* tax: 1 *kan*, 400 *mon* submitted

Nakanishi – same, *sake* tax: 1 *kanmon*

Nakamura Yazaburō – when this was Aomo Xri, previously paid 700 *mon*

Sawamura Yagorō – when this was Nakaoki Shirō Ueimon's shop, paid 1 *kan*, 400 *mon*, exempted since the survey

Nakaoki Matashirō – *sake* tax, when called Takekura, paid 1 *kan*, 400 *mon* of *sake* tax; since then has submitted 700 *mon*

Imae – same, 1 *kan*, 400 *mon* submitted; storehouse tax: 300 *mon*

Mori – previously submitted, bean-paste tax: 500 *mon*; now no funds

Kawasaki – same, both brewer and lender; until this year submitted 3 *kan*, 500 *mon*

Shimogasa – exempted, but liable for *jōyaku* (?), same as Shimada

Nakaoki – same as before, no funds

Mano – details same as before

No. 305: Dosō sakaya chūmon (List of Brewer-Lenders)

NŌSENKATA

Baba – 1 *kan*, 500 *mon*	Tanaka Shōkan – 1 *kanmon*
Fukui – 2 *kan*, 500 *mon*	Ozaki – 900 *mon*
Nakamura – 3 *kanmon*	Yanagi – 500 *mon*
Kamoashi – 3 *kanmon*	Uno – 500 *mon*

Shino – 3 *kanmon*
Shimada Yoichi – 2 *kanmon*
Shinoda – 1 *kan*, 500 *mon*
Baba – 400 *mon*
Baba Yozō – 1 *kanmon*
Tsukamoto – 500 *mon*
Tanaka – 2 *kanmon*

Etō – 500 *mon*
Sakurō – 400 *mon*
Takaya – 1 *kan*, 500 *mon*
Zenyō – 1 *kan*, 500 *mon*
Endō – 300 *mon*
Endō (widow) – 400 *mon*

MONEYLENDERS (MOSTLY UPPER KYOTO ADDRESSES)

Nakamura – 1 *kan*, 500 *mon*
Matsui – 2 *kanmon*
Baba – 1 *kanmon*
Edo – 1 *kan*, 500 *mon*
Katō – 300 *kanmon*
Takaya Magosaburō – 1 *kanmon*

Takaya Magojirō – 1 *kanmon*
Baba Yozō – 300 *mon*, temporary exemption
Sakurō – 1 *kan*, 800 *mon*, temporary exemption
Tanaka Shōkan – 200 *mon*, temporary exemption
Nakai – bean paste, 1 *kan*, 500 *mon*
Tomita – bean paste, 600 *mon*

LOWER KYOTO BREWERS

Sawamura Hikojirō – 1 *kanmon*

Maruga – 1 *kan*, 500 *mon*

Kichi'a – 2 *kan*, 500 *mon*

Sono – 3 *kan*, 500 *mon*

Nakanishi – 3 *kan*, 500 *mon*

Miyajima – 2 *kanmon*

Kawashima – 3 *kan*, 500 *mon*

Tsuda – 2 *kanmon*

Okuno – 900 *mon*, temporary exemption,
   no funds
Mizutani – 400 *mon*, temporary exemption,
   no funds
Nakaoki – 2 *kan*, 800 *mon*, temporary exemption,
   no funds
Katayama – 500 *mon*, temporary exemption,
   no funds
Otomi – 500 *mon*, temporary exemption,
   no funds
Kosodeya –1 *kanmon*, temporary exemption,
   no funds
Hasegawa – 400 *mon*, temporary exemption,
   no funds
No name – 300 *mon*, temporary exemption,
   no funds

Sawamura Matajirō – 1 *kan*, 500 *mon*

Teragi – 1 *kan*, 500 *mon*

Kitamura – 1 *kanmon*

Okuno Shōkan – 300 *mon*, temporary exemption,
   no funds
Tsuda – 900 *mon*, temporary exemption,
   no funds
No name – 300 *mon*
No name – 800 *mon*

MONEYLENDERS (LOWER KYOTO ADDRESSES)

Nakaoki (Yanagi) – 300 *mon*, temporary exemption
Katayama – 200 *mon*, no funds, temporarily not submitted
Kumagi – 1 *kan*, 500 *mon*
Uno – 400 *mon*, no funds, temporarily not submitted
Katayama – bean-paste tax, 1 *kan*, 500 *mon*

No. 306: Dosō sakaya kozaisho narabini shinkazaisho chūmon (List of Old and Newly Added Premises of Moneylenders and Brewers)

(Names with addresses, mixed Upper and Lower Kyoto. No comments.)

Sano Fujigorō	Kojima Hikojirō
Ōhashi Matahachi	Nakanishi
Yoshida	Noda
Yasu Yagorō	Nakamura Okitsugu
Ishi X	Kimura
Tomita	Wakamatsu (?)

No. 307: Sakaya hizeniya kasōbun chūmon (List of Additional Brewers and Day Lenders)

(Upper Kyoto addresses. Amounts suggest partial exemptions. No names; addresses and amounts only.)

Brewer: 1 *kan*, 400 *mon*, 500 *mon* submitted at present
Brewer: 400 *mon*, 200 *mon* submitted at present
Brewer: 300 *mon*, 100 *mon* submitted at present
Brewer: 300 *mon*, 100 *mon* submitted at present
No name: currently out of business
Day lender: 300 *mon*
Brewer located in Jissōin: 300 *mon*
Day lender: 300 *mon*

No. 308: Dosō sakaya chūmon (List of Lender-Brewers)

(Upper Kyoto addresses)

Eastern sector:
Brewer: 1 *kan*, 400 *mon*; 700 *mon* submitted at present
Lender: 2 *kan*, 500 *mon*; 1 *kan* submitted at present
Lender: 1 *kan*, 500 *mon* submitted at present

Southern sector:
Brewer: 1 *kan*, 400 *mon*; 300 *mon* submitted at present
Lender: 2 *kan*; 300 *mon* submitted at present
(The brewer and lender above have the same address, suggesting one establishment.)

Western sector:
Brewer: 2 *kan*, 800 *mon*; 1 *kan*, 400 *mon* submitted at present
Brewer: 700 *mon*; 400 *mon* submitted at present

NO. 5. MONEYLENDERS IN 1511

The following list of Kyoto brewers may have been compiled by the Muromachi shogunate for the reference of its tax farmers; it is also possible that it was compiled by the

Distillery Office for the purpose of tax collection. It is not clear whether it is an exhaustive list. SOURCE: "Sakachūmon" (1511/4/17), list of moneylender-brewers in *Konishi Yasuoshi shozō monjo* X, II, 3, index, reproduced in Kurushima, "Sengokuki no shukikuyaku," pp. 75–77.

Takaya Hyōeishirō
Baba Kageyu
Nakaoki Shinhyōei
Fukui Shirōzaemon
Shino Yazaburō
Yasu Zenshō
Uno Kageyu
Uno Chūmushō
Yamamoto Magogorō
Imae Hyōkō
Uno Shirōuemon
Sawamura Shirōjirō

Mizutani Taiken
Tsuda Yoshichi
Takebe Jirōgorō
Oharaishi Chiyo

Shimizu
Takaya Magotarō
Endō Fujijirō
Endō Yagorō
Katayama

Tanaka Shichirō Saemon
Tanaka Yozō
Nakamura Kozaburō
Nakamura Yoshirō
Tanaka Shōgen
Ishibe
Nakamura Yazaburō

New houses (extended families):
  Hagiwara
  Tamanosakaya
  Nōtoya
  Baba Hikogorō

Nakaoki Shinhyōei (Yanagi)
Baba Kageyu
Katayama
Shimada Yoichi
Gyokusen
Takaya Hyōeishirō
Uno Kageyu
Echigoya

Lower Kyoto

Nakanishi
Teragi
Hasegawa
Nakanishi Fujitsugu
Shino (new house, extended family)
Uwashi (retailer only)
Katayama (new house, extended family)
Tsuteya
Oi
Shimada Yoichi
Takaya Heiuemon
Sawamura Yagorō
Kojima Jirōzaemon
Hasegawa Otōto (younger brother, new house)

Lower Kyoto (cont.)

Umeno Sakaya
Murota (fire last year)
Ohashi Matashichi
Tanaka Shinzaemon (child, new house)
Echigoya

Notes

ABBREVIATIONS

MBL   Muromachi Bakufu Law(s) (*Muromachi Bakufu tsuikahō*, in *Chūsei hōsei shiryōshū*)
CHJ   Cambridge History of Japan
CHS   Chūsei hōsei shiryōshū
KR   Kyōto no rekishi
KDJ   Kokushi daijiten
NRD   Nihon rekishi daijiten
SKR   Shiryō Kyōto no rekishi
KM   Kitano tenmangū shiryō-komonjo

INTRODUCTION

1. Japanese scholars have studied this group of lenders extensively. See, for example, Wakita, "Ryōshu keizai," especially pp. 276–290, "Shōkōgyōsha no seichō" pp. 457–462, and "Dosō to bōeki," pp. 231–244; Kuwayama, "Muromachi Bakufu keizai kikō"; Noda, "Chūsei Kyōto ni okeru kōrigashigyō no hatten"; Suma, "Dosō ni yoru nengu shūnō no ukeoi ni tsuite," and "Dosō no tochi shūseki to tokusei," on the activities of moneylenders on estates; Okuno, "Muromachi jidai ni'okeru dosō no kenkyū"; Ono, "Muromachi Bakufu no sakaya tōsei" and "Chūsei shuzōgyō no hattatsu"; Shimosaka, "Chūsei dosōron," on moneylending in Kyoto, especially before the Ōnin War; Kurushima, "Sengokuki no shukikuyaku," on the money-lenders after the Ōnin War; Hashimoto, "Dosō no sonzai keitai"; Shimosaka, "Machishū no seikatsu"; Murayama, *Nihon toshi seikatsu no genryū*, pp. 102–133; and Hayashiya, *Chūsei bunka no kichō*, pp. 192–316, the last on their cultural activities in particular.

2. A typical example is that of the Tōji monk Meisai who, returning to Kyoto in 1396 with considerable personal wealth after serving as an estate official, joined with neighborhood merchants in a moneylending business even as he pursued an illustrious career as temple administrator. Itō Toshiichi, "Kin'yūgyō wo fukugyō ni suru jisō," p. 30.

3. See Collcutt, *Five Mountains*, pp. 241–242, 253–254, 262. As in the case of Meisai at Tōji, *gozan* monks, too, sometimes returned to Kyoto after fulfilling assignments as estate officials in the provinces with sufficient personal wealth to engage in moneylending (Collcutt, p. 277). Shogunal debt amnesties did not apply to loans from Zen monasteries.

4. See Nakajima, "Chūsei Kyōto ni okeru shidōsen kin'yū no tenkai," pp. 10–18. This study was undertaken to determine the reason for the *gozan*'s low interest rates, which were somewhat comparable to a modern prime rate available only to certain clients.

5. The term "medieval" (*chūsei*) was applied to Japanese history by Meiji period scholars using periodization common for European history. Hara Katsurō, in his *Nihon chūseishi* (1906), was the first to apply this periodization extensively to the

centuries in question. Placing the emperor at the center of his analysis of Japanese history, he defined the late Heian rise of the warriors up to the founding of the Kamakura Bakufu as the beginning of the medieval period in which a new culture, comparable to that of the Germanic tribes of early medieval Europe, emerged as the old court culture, parallel to that of the late Roman imperial court, declined. Among Japanese scholars there was also a tendency to carry over the "dark ages" stereotype from medieval European historiography. For a discussion of the early-twentieth-century development of Japanese historiography along Western lines, see Kuroda, "Chūseishi josetsu," pp. 3–5.

6. Among the main postwar proponents of a warrior-centered view of the medieval period have been Nagahara Keiji, *Nihon no chūsei shakai kōzō no kenkyū*, Satō Shin'ichi, *Nihon no chūsei kokka*, and Ishii Susumu, *Nihon chūsei kokkashi no kenkyū*.

7. Kuroda Toshio's theory, called the *kenmon taiseiron* in Japanese, was first put forth in his "Nihon chūsei no kokka to tennō." See Gay, "Muromachi Bakufu Rule in Kyoto," pp. 50–52, for a summary in English of the salient points of this theory. Among works in English on Japanese history, it has been utilized by Varley, *Imperial Restoration in Medieval Japan*, Tonomura, *Community and Commerce in Late Medieval Japan*, Adolphson, *The Gates of Power*, and has been cited by Keirstead, *The Geography of Power in Medieval Japan*, p. 15.

8. A standard definition of the term *"kenmon"*: "A pedigreed family with high official rank and power. Influential family. A person from such a family." *Nihon kokugo daijiten*, vol. 7, p. 364. The entry includes a 1054 citation from the *Heian ibun* containing the term *kenmon shōen* (*kenmon* estates). The term is a contemporary medieval one, usually found in the compound *kenmon seika*—houses of authority and power.

9. Kuroda, "Chūsei no kokka to tennō," p. 299.

10. The *kenmon* theory was most effectively attacked by Satō Shin'ichi, who rejected the idea of a single medieval state and instead proposed for the Kamakura period a dual governing scheme, with the imperial court in Kyoto and the shogunate in Kamakura, each pursuing a policy of noninterference with the other. See Satō, *Nihon no chūsei kokka*.

11. In a very useful review in English of Japanese historiography on the fourteenth century, Ōyama Kyōhei discusses the pervasive influence of Kuroda's theory. He also notes that Kuroda considered the emphasis on the warrior class by prewar medieval historians as ideologically motivated and thus a product of its times. Ōyama, "The Fourteenth Century in Twentieth Century Perspective," pp. 358–361. In addition, by insisting on the continuing significance of the emperor in Japanese history, Kuroda effectively "rehabilitated" the emperor, a taboo topic of academic research among historians since the end of the war. Kuroda's influence can be seen in the works of younger scholars, notably Taira Masayuki, who has further explored the social role of religion in the medieval period. See Taira, *Nihon chūsei no shakai to Bukkyō*. Even Nagahara Keiji came to acknowledge the central role the emperor played in the medieval political order. See Nagahara, "Nihon zenkindai shakai no tenkai to tennō," pp. 1–18.

12. In 1441, for example, the Muromachi Bakufu ordered the imperial court's *mizushidokoro*, a small shrine within the palace, to hand over its toll income to the Madeno-

kōji family, suggesting that court and aristocrats benefited from toll stations. No. 42 (*Kennaiki*, 1441/intercalary 9/16), *SKR*, vol. 3, pp. 288–289. The temple Tōji also seems to have been able to tap into the tolls collected at the station nearby, with Bakufu acquiescence: in 1404 Tōji received toll income from it for building repairs. See no. 39 (*Tōji hyakugō monjo, chi* section, 1404/3/14), *SKR*, vol. 3, pp. 287–288.

Part One: The Setting

1. Citing the work of Japanese scholars, Ronald Toby has characterized the move of the capital as part of a decades-long struggle between the Temmu and Tenji lines of the imperial lineage. He further argues that Nara was but one of many early "courts," and that it was only with the establishment of Kyoto that Japan at last had a true "capital." See Toby, "Why Leave Nara?" p. 343. Friction between clerics and officials rather than rivalries within the lineage is the reason commonly given for the transfer of the capital from Nara. See Inoue and Nakayama, "Nagaoka sento," pp. 193–218, and Murai, "Heiankyō no keisei," pp. 219–323. These works contain a description of the city's founding and physical appearance, as do Abe Takeshi, "Heiankyō," *Encyclopedia of Japan*, vol. 3, pp. 121–122, and Hall, "Kyoto as Historical Background," pp. 3–38.

2. Medieval Japanese cities differed from those of China and medieval Europe in that they were relatively unfortified. An island country, premodern Japan was not threatened by foreign invasion except for two unsuccessful attempts made by the Mongols in the late thirteenth century. Thus Kyoto's protected setting was a point in favor of, but not the main reason for, adoption of the site as capital.

3. Ponsonby-Fane, "The Capital and Palace of Heian," p. 131. On Heian period flooding of the Kamo River and flood control measures, see Katsuyama, "Heian jidai ni okeru Kamogawa," pp. 17–27. For an analysis of the development of Kyoto during the Heian period using literary sources, see Kuroda, "Konjaku monogatari' ni arawareta toshi," pp. 1–48.

4. In addition to Hosshōji, five more temples were built in the area by retired emperors by the mid-twelfth century. With Hosshōji, they are collectively called the Rokushōji or Rikushōji and included retired emperor Horikawa's Sonshōji, Toba's Saishōji, Sutoku's Jōshōji, Konoe's Enshōji, and an imperial consort's Enshōji. Murai, "Rokushōji to Toba-dono," *KR*, vol. 2, p. 119.

5. Hayashiya Tatsusaburō, "Kyōto," *KDJ*, vol. 4, pp. 325–326.

6. Hayashiya, Mutō, and Moriya, "Sōron," in *Kyōtoshi no chimei*, p. 19.

7. Hayashiya, "Kyōto," *KDJ*, vol. 4, p. 325.

8. Sasayama Akio, "Kebiishi," *KDJ*, vol. 5, pp. 116–117.

9. On the Kamakura period court and *kebiishichō* administration of Kyoto, see Amino, "Chūsei ni okeru tennō shihaiken," and, in English, Kiley, "The Imperial Court as a Legal Authority in the Kamakura Age," pp. 29–44.

10. Inoue and Kawashima, "Rokuhara tandai," in *KR*, vol. 2, pp. 414–417. For more on the policing of Kyoto from the tenth to thirteenth centuries, see Kuroda, "Chūsei Kyōto no keisatsu seido," pp. 124–159. For a summary of shogunal politics in Kyoto from the founding of the Kamakura Bakufu to the Ōnin War, see Varley, *The Ōnin War*, pp. 6–135.

11. Moriya, "Rakuchū Rakugai," p. 45. Amino Yoshihiko has credited these security

measures by the Kamakura Bakufu with transforming Kyoto into a true medieval city. Amino, "Chūsei toshiron," p. 274.

12. Weber, *The City*, p. 55. Weber's medieval urban community is typified by European trade cities whose burghers or guilds demanded and received a measure of autonomy from the ruling nobles.

13. Yamamura, "The Growth of Commerce," p. 368.

14. Toyoda, *Chūsei Nihon no shōgyō*, pp. 102–108. For economic advances, see Koizumi, "Nairanki no shakai hendō," pp. 123–126.

15. Toyoda, *Nihon no hōken toshi*, p. 9; Wakita, "Nihon chūsei toshi no kōzō," pp. 15–17.

16. Wakita, "Nihon chūsei toshi no kōzō," pp. 15–17.

17. Kuroda, "Kyōto no seiritsu," pp. 24–25.

18. Murai, "Heiankyō," p. 43.

19. Kenneth Grossberg characterizes Muromachi Bakufu law as in part derivative of that of Kamakura, with some important innovations. One was its application to members of all classes. See Grossberg, *The Laws of the Muromachi Bakufu*, pp. 9–10, citing Ishii Ryōsuke's analysis.

20. A late-fifteenth-century dispute between the Honnōji and the Nishibōjō family over a parcel of land in Kyoto is one example of the shogun settling a dispute not involving warriors. The shogun reconfirmed Honnōji's right to the land. See *Honnōji monjo*, confirmation edict (*andojō*) dated 1488/10/23. See Part 2 for more on this case.

21. For a discussion of the fourteenth-century power shift from *kebiishichō* to the shogunate's Board of Retainers (*samuraidokoro*), see Gay, "Muromachi Bakufu Rule in Kyoto," pp. 54–55.

22. *Kemmu shikimoku*, Article 5 (1336/11/7), *CHS*, vol. 2, pp. 4–5.

23. Details in Tanuma, "Muromachi Bakufu zaisei," pp. 1–26. The term *"daijōe"* was used in the medieval period for the imperial accession ceremony. The final character, *e*, means a Buddhist ritual. The modern ceremony is called the *daijōsai*, with the final character, *sai*, indicating a Shinto ceremony.

24. Yoshimitsu, the third shogun, not only patronized the arts but sought the prestige that went with aristocratic status in other ways as well: becoming a member of the imperial family by having his wife named mother of the emperor, taking the highest aristocratic rank of *dajō daijin*, building a palatial residence, housing the emperor at his own "palace" after the *dairi* burned, affecting the lifestyle of a retired emperor, taking the title "King of Japan," etc. For a study of Yoshimitsu's expropriation of various imperial symbols and manipulation of the emperor, see Imatani, *Muromachi no ōken*.

25. MBL no. 48 (1346–1349), *CHS*, vol. 2, p. 26.

26. Varley, "Ashikaga Yoshimitsu and the World of Kitayama," p. 184.

27. See Kuroda, "Shinto in the History of Japanese Religion," pp. 1–21.

28. Collcutt, *Five Mountains*, pp. 98–129, includes aspects of the *gozan's* close relationship with the Muromachi shogunate.

29. Kuroda, "Chūsei jisha seiryokuron," p. 247.

30. Collcutt, *Five Mountains*, p. 105. Collcutt interprets this incident as a victory for the shogunate and the *gozan* over Enryakuji.

31. Atsuta, "Basara no bunka," p. 529, citing *Sanmon gōsoki* and *Gukanki*, entries for 1345/8.

32. Atsuta, "Basara no bunka," p. 529, citing *Zokushōbōron*.
33. On Nobunaga's destruction of Enryakuji, in English see McMullin, *Buddhism and the State in Sixteenth Century Japan*, pp. 145–151. For a detailed study of Nobunaga in Japanese, see the works of Wakita Osamu, especially *Oda seiken no kisō kōzō*, vol. 1. In English, see Wakita, "The Emergence of the State in Sixteenth Century Japan," pp. 347–349.
34. See, for example, MBL nos. 66–77 (1354/9/22), in *CHS*, vol. 2, pp. 33–37; and MBL nos. 91–96 (1368/2/13), in *CHS*, vol. 2, pp. 41–42.
35. For example, MBL no. 123 (1372/11/18), in *CHS*, vol. 2, p. 53, asserts the shogunate's right to bring to trial those who kill or wound shrine personnel in litigation-related disputes. But it goes on to explain that in fact much fighting, especially over property and debts, is occurring before litigation is even brought; in such cases, shrine personnel, whose "wicked scheming" caused the problems in the first place, will not be protected by the shogunate, but will be punished and dismissed from office.
36. Takao, "Sekai no naka no Kyōto," pp. 37–39, contends that commoners comprised half the population of medieval Kyoto, though this could be quite off the mark and probably varied over time.
37. Ishii Ryōsuke considers the inclusion of commoners within the purview of its law code to be an innovation of the Muromachi shogunate. See Ishii, *Nihon hōseishi gaisetsu*, p. 92. Of 542 Muromachi Bakufu laws, 210, or about 40 percent, concern moneylending. Still others concern other aspects of commerce. Thus about half the Bakufu laws pertain to commerce in Kyoto.
38. On the development of the *machi* during the medieval period, see Akiyama, "Jōbōsei no 'machi' no hen'yō katei," in *Kyōto 'machi' no kenkyū*, pp. 88–169. *Chō* and *machi* are two readings of the same character. Some historians, like Hayashiya Tatsusaburō and Wakita Haruko, favor *machi* as the more common reading in the medieval period; hence, *machishū*, not *chōshū*. Others claim the reading of *machi* changed to *chō* during the medieval period. See Akiyama and Nakamura, "Shūshō," in *Kyōto 'machi' no kenkyū*, pp. 366–367. Hayashiya, in *Chūsei bunka no kichō*, p. 196, points out a case in which nearly half the pledges by *sake* brewers to destroy their malt facilities in 1419 have signatories referred to as *chō* or *chōnin*, written in some cases in phonetic script, leaving no doubt as to the contemporary pronunciation. In the English literature, *machi* is the more common reading. See, for example, Yamamura, "The Growth of Commerce," p. 377, and Hayashiya, "Kyoto in the Muromachi Age," pp. 27–30.
39. The four stages are outlined by Akiyama, "Jōbōsei no 'machi' no hen'yō katei," in *Kyōto 'machi' no kenkyū*, pp. 88–169. In English, see Hayashiya, "Kyoto in the Muromachi Age," pp. 27–30.
40. Takahashi, *Chūsei Kyōto no tenkai katei*, p. 11.
41. On nightsoil removal and public toilets, see Takahashi, *Rakuchū Rakugai*, 84. The Jesuit missionary Joao Rodrigues marveled at the cleanliness of late medieval Kyoto, whose streets were swept and watered twice daily. Cooper, *They Came to Japan*, p. 277.
42. Hayashiya Tatsusaburō characterized medieval Kyoto townspeople according to these two types, with the *machishū* the later of the two. See Hayashiya, "Machishū no seiritsu," pp. 189–214; *Chūsei bunka no kichō*, p. 197, and *Kyōwarabe kara machishū e*, pp. 66–95.

43. Moriya, "Rakuchū Rakugai," pp. 45–46. Machikōji's distinction of being the first *machi* may explain the origin of the term.
44. Yamamura, "The Growth of Commerce," p. 377.
45. Moriya, "Rakuchū Rakugai," p. 46.
46. See Map 4, derived from one entitled "Shūkyō to shōgyō no toshi—Kyōto," insert in KR, vol. 3, depicting the location of shops by product. A more vivid though less literal depiction of the same can be found in illustrated screens of Kyoto, *Rakuchū Rakugai zu byōbu*, to the extent that they include commercial portions of the city. The early-sixteenth-century Machidabon screen of Kyoto, reproduced in *Rakuchū Rakugaizu taikan*, is especially helpful for details of city life and material culture, for it lacks the heavy use of obstructive gold leaf found on later screens. But even the Machidabon screen depicts only the four major north–south-running streets and gives only a glimpse of the assortment of shops on the equally busy east–west avenues.
47. Noguchi, *Chūsei Kyōto no machiya*, p. 3.
48. See *Rakuchū Rakugaizu taikan*, Machidabon screen of Kyoto, commercial district sections. Also see Takahashi, *Rakuchū Rakugai*, p. 69, illustration 13.
49. See Wakita, "Dimensions of Development," pp. 302–309, for a discussion of taxation in English. On continued overlord control of land and their dealings with residents, even as late as the 1540s, see Nishio, " 'Machishūron' saikentō." Umata Ayako points out that the overlords' urban holdings were scattered in the late medieval period to the point that a single *machi* normally encompassed holdings of several overlords. See Umata, "Chūsei toshi to shotōsō," p. 146.
50. Also pronounced *munebetsusen, munebechisen*, and *munabetsusen*.
51. This is the conclusion reached by Nishio Kazumi, contradicting the theory that the townspeople enjoyed considerable local control in the late medieval period. Nishio, " 'Machishūron' saikentō," pp. 56–75.
52. See Umata, "Tōjiryō kōsho," pp. 62–86.
53. Takahashi, *Rakuchū Rakugai*, pp. 110–116.
54. This can be deduced indirectly from MBL no. 103 (1369/2/27), *CHS*, vol. 2, p. 45, which specifically proscribes such garb for commoners—a dead giveaway that commoners were indulging in such apparel.
55. *Rakuchū Rakugai zu taikan*, pp. 144–148, includes a detailed analysis of clothing and hairstyles depicted in the screens.
56. Shimosaka, "Machishū no seikatsu," p. 104. The word *"furo"* in the medieval period referred to steam baths, while *"yuya"*—hot-water shops—was the term for regular baths.
57. In the Machidabon screen of Kyoto, a Kanze Noh performance on a stage near Tōfukuji is portrayed in the extreme upper-right corner of the left screen. Some members of the audience could be commoners judging from their dress, as are some passersby peeking curiously through the fence. See *Rakuchū Rakugai zu taikan*, p. 12.
58. MBL no. 100 (1369/2/27, *CHS*, vol. 2, p. 44) and no. 186 (1428/10/23, *CHS*, vol. 2, p. 68) prohibit gambling. Shogunal decrees against these and other activities were posted on roadside placards. Grossberg, *The Laws of the Muromachi Bakufu*, p. 9. This custom, which continued in the Edo period, fostered at the very

least a general awareness of law among commoners, whether or not they actually obeyed.

59. For a detailed discussion of the depiction of animals in the screen, see *Rakuchū Rakugai zu taikan*, pp. 148–149. These include dogs, oxen, horses, fish, monkeys, hawks, birds, and chickens.

60. On monkeys in medieval Japan, see *Rakuchū Rakugaizu taikan*, p. 149.

61. Shimosaka, "Machishū no seikatsu," p. 79.

62. The extreme lower-left corner of the right screen of the Machidabon contains such a scene. *Rakuchū Rakugai zu taikan*, p. 82. The Muromachi shogunate banned congregating in the streets in 1480 and dancing, specifically, in 1506. MBL nos. 279–282 (1480/4/28), *CHS*, vol. 2, p. 86, and MBL nos. 336–343 (1506/7/11), *CHS*, vol. 2, pp. 110–111. The aristocrat Sanjōnishi Sanetaka disapprovingly notes the disruptiveness of the street dancing, in *Sanetaka kōki*, vol. 4, p. 433, entry for 1505/7/18.

63. Shimosaka, "Machishū no seikatsu," pp. 79–81; Ruch, "The Other Side of Culture," p. 519.

64. On the worship of money, see Shimosaka, "Machishū no seikatsu," p. 80, and *Tsurezuregusa*, no. 217: "Money should be feared and respected like a master or like a deity, not used like a slave." *Hōjōki/Tsurezuregusa*, p. 264.

65. This and the following two anecdotes are taken from Shimosaka, "Machishū no seikatsu," pp. 80–81.

66. Niunoya Tetsuichi, for example, has pointed out that lepers, cripples, and beggars, all found among medieval outcastes, were not subjected to discrimination in the ancient legal codes, but received land allotments like regular peasants. Koyama, "Chūsei senminron," p. 164, citing Niunoya, "Chūsei zenki ni okeru hinin." Nagahara Keiji makes a distinction between the despised persons of the ancient period and medieval outcastes, in the sense that discrimination against the former was unrelated to any purity fetish. Nagahara, "The Medieval Origins of the Eta-Hinin," p. 388.

67. Nagahara, "The Medieval Origins of the Eta-Hinin," pp. 386–391.

68. Koyama, "Chūsei senminron," an essay summarizing scholarship on medieval outcastes, cites Kuroda Toshio's definition of them as a social status group consisting of those cast off from society, lacking ties to others, and therefore seldom leaving descendants (pp. 169–170). Kuroda Hideo's work on outcastes is in the same camp as that of Kuroda Toshio in defining them primarily as a social status group. See Kuroda Toshio, "Chūsei no mibunsei to hisen kannen"; Kuroda Hideo, "Shiryō to shite no emakimono to chūsei no mibunsei."

69. Koyama, "Chūsei senminron," pp. 169–170. Koyama points out that in premedieval forms of Buddhism, lepers and beggars were regarded as manifestations of the boddhisatva Monju (p. 174).

70. Ōyama Kyōhei has defined outcastes primarily as an occupational group whose function was purification, a very different characterization from that of Kuroda; see Ōyama, "Chūsei no mibunsei to kokka." Koyama Yasunori calls for a combination of the Kuroda and Ōyama definitions of outcastes ("Chūsei senminron," p. 161). Amino Yoshihiko, whose inclusion of outcastes among nonagricultural occupational groups of the medieval period is widely known, is, according to

Koyama (p. 160), properly seen as part of Ōyama's camp. See, for example, Amino, "Hinin ni kansuru ichi shiryō."

71. Koyama, "Chūsei senminron," p. 165.

72. Noda Tadao summarizes the activities of outcastes affiliated with the Bureau of Capital Police and religious institutions in "Chūsei senmin no shakai keizaiteki ichi kōsatsu," pp. 58–65.

73. Niunoya, *Kebiishi*, p. 57.

74. MBL no. 474 (1523/4/3), *CHS*, vol. 2, p. 135. This strongly suggests that outcastes performed similar functions for the shogunate as for other elite groups.

75. *Honnōji monjo*. This dispute rages through documents dated 1438/11/2, 1438/11/10, 1450/11/28, 1465/7/26, 1486/8/17, 1488/10/23 (the shogun's reconfirmation to Honnōji), and 1491/7/18 (same as previous, by a new shogun). For unknown reasons the bath fell out of use by 1499, for a document dated 1499/10/2 refers to the "remains of the *hinin* (outcaste) bath," indicating disuse. In shogunal reconfirmations of 1501/12/29 and 1525/9/3, the bath is again in use by outcastes.

76. *Inujinin* are depicted as Gion Festival guards in the Machidabon screen. For a discussion of their role, see *Rakuchū Rakugai zu taikan*, pp. 130, 133. For an analysis of the dress of medieval outcastes, including the warrior garb of *inujinin*, see Kawata, "Chūsei hisabetsumin no yosōi." See Part 2 for more on the outcastes' relationships to overlords like temples and shrines.

77. Fujii, "Shinkyū Bukkyō no kyōsen," p. 155. In the fifteenth century, "Ami" became a common name suffix not necessarily connected to the Ji movement. See Varley, "Cultural Life in Medieval Japan," pp. 468–469, and "Ashikaga Yoshimitsu and the World of Kitayama," pp. 188–189.

78. Wayne Farris states that the great diseases of smallpox and measles had become chronic in Japan by the thirteenth century as mainly childhood infections; thus they were no longer major factors in preventing population increase. Farris, *Population, Disease, and Land in Early Japan*, p. 73.

79. Murai, "Heiankyō," p. 42. This rather broad range is based on three considerations: first, that the population of Chang-an, the model for Kyoto, was about one million and Kyoto was only a third its size in space (this could be dismissed as an irrelevant consideration); second, that in the early ninth century there were 540 *machi* in all (only half the number the city was originally designed to hold) and therefore 18,560 household heads (assuming full occupancy of each *machi*); and finally that there were on average five people per household in the ninth century.

80. Population statistics from Takao, "Sekai no naka no Kyōto," pp. 33–41. Kozo Yamamura puts it at 200,000 on the eve of the Ōnin War. Yamamura, "The Growth of Commerce," p. 377.

81. Statistics from *Jinkō daijiten*, p. 326. These figures were also calculated by very rough methods—i.e., how many people Japan's total land area under cultivation could have supported. In the absence of reliable national statistics, even estimating the total arable is risky. Total population statistics for the medieval period use similar methods, which are at least as unreliable if not more so, given the conspicuous lack of comprehensive records for the period. The household registration system was in place only until 824, and in the ninth and tenth centuries was no more than an imperfect way of determining taxes. As a result, records are spotty,

with age and sex statistics unreliable. The very last census was in 1004, for Sanuki province, and its results show far too few men for the number of women, casting doubt on its veracity. Kitō, *Nihon nisennen no jinkōshi*, p. 42. To show how drastically varying estimates can be, this source, using the same method as *Jinkō daijiten*, above—i.e., estimating population by the amount of land under cultivation —arrives at a national population figure of 6,920,000 for the medieval period. See Kitō, *Nihon nisennen no jinkō*, p. 47.

82. Statistical data, however, are lacking. One way of estimating the population of medieval European cities—counting gravestones—is not applicable to Japan because cremation was widespread among the elites from the Heian period and because of generally unmarked burial of commoners. Another method of calculation for European cities, measuring the space inside city walls and calculating according to presumed density, is also useless for Japan because its medieval cities were not walled. However, there are extensive medieval family genealogies, though only for the elite classes.

83. It has been estimated that from the years 567 to 1975, 506 famines large and small ravaged Japan. In the medieval period, major famines occurred in 1181, 1185, 1231, 1259, 1410, 1438, 1460, 1472, and 1512, more than three-quarters of them due to weather or natural disasters. Nakajima, *Kikin Nihonshi*, p. 11.

84. In the late medieval period crop damage during war was not only a matter of the arable land being trampled during fighting. Particularly widespread was the practice of *karita* (harvested field) in which warriors literally stole the enemy's crops off his land, damaging his ability to make war by starving his troops. Arakawa, *Kikin*, p. 28. Scholarly works on famine like this tend to concentrate on the Tokugawa period and treat the medieval period in a summary fashion.

85. Religious observances are recounted in Shimosaka, "Machishū no seikatsu," pp. 81–82.

Part Two: The Lives of the Moneylenders

Chapter One: The Business of Lending Money

1. Kuwayama, "Muromachi Bakufu keizai," pp. 18–20; Hall, "The Muromachi Bakufu," p. 223.

2. There is no known documentation of such a practice, but Kuwayama Kōnen infers it from the prevalent custom of charging the debtor a deposit fee, similar to an insurance premium. Kuwayama, "Muromachi Bakufu keizai," p. 29, n. 21.

3. Kuwayama, "Muromachi Bakufu keizai," p. 20, citing *Kennaiki*, diary of Fujiwara Tokifusa, entry for 1441/9/3.

4. Interest paid by moneylenders on borrowed capital was called *aisen*. See, for example, MBL no. 257 (1457/12/5), *CHS*, vol. 2, p. 89. *Aisen* is mistranslated as interest *charged* by moneylenders in Grossberg, *The Laws of the Muromachi Bakufu*, p. 109.

5. See Nakamura, "Chūsei Kyōto ni okeru shidōsen kin'yū no tenkai," pp. 10–18, on Zen temples loaning to secular moneylenders. On loans among townspeople, a dispute brought before the Muromachi shogunate in 1472 between a moneylender named Sekime and an apparent commoner named Tsuda is illuminating. The

moneylender claimed that a debt amnesty of 1466 should apply to his own debt to Tsuda of 23 *kanmon*. The shogunate decided otherwise, on the ground that the debt contract lacked specific terms. Nos. 924 and 925 (*Yamashinake raiki*, dated 1472/11/24 and 1472/11/25), *Muromachi Bakufu bugyōnin hōsho*, vol. 1, pp. 259–260.

6. An alternate pronunciation of *dosō* is *dokura*. Toyoda Takeshi cites the 1234 *Meigetsuki* entry as the earliest incidence of the term. See Toyoda, "Dosō," in *NRD*, vol. 13, p. 301.

7. An illustration of a *dosō* is found in *Nihon jōmin seikatsu ebiki*, vol. 4, p. 146–147, taken from the *Kasuga gongen kenki*, an early-fourteenth-century illustrated scroll. In this case, a Kyoto home has burned and the family has temporarily taken up residence in its storehouse, which survived the fire unscathed.

8. For a case study of *dosō* tax farming on estates, see Suma, "Dosō ni yoru nengu shūnō." Nakajima Keiichi asserts that financial management of Kyoto area estates, and not moneylending and storage of valuables, accounted for the large number of lenders in medieval Kyoto. Nakajima, "Chūsei Kyōto ni okeru dosōgyō no seiritsu," p. 41. His study is persuasive, but wealthy peasants also performed this function on estates in the Kyoto area, and there is strong evidence that moneylending was a thriving business.

9. See the discussion of the Muromachi shogunate below for more on tax agents (*nōsenkata*) and financial agents (*kubō mikura*).

10. But their role was probably not a direct one; the Muromachi shogunate, the *gozan* Zen network, the shogun's Kyushu deputy, and Kyushu merchants were the parties directly involved. Kyoto products like swords and folding screens were major exports in the trade with China. See Kawazoe, "Japan and East Asia," pp. 440–444.

11. Among the scholars who assume that Kyoto moneylending and *sake* brewing were usually performed by the same entrepreneur are Kuwayama Kōnen, "Sakaya-dosō," in *Chūseishi handobukku*, p. 66, and "Dosō," *KDJ*, vol. 10, p. 369; Toyoda Takeshi, "Dosō," *NRD*, vol. 13, p. 301; Wakita Haruko, "Dosō to bōeki," p. 236; and Yunoki Manabu, "Shuzōgyō," *KDJ*, vol. 7, p. 381. So frequently do *sake* brewers and moneylenders appear in sources as a continuous term (*sakaya dosō* or *dosō sakaya*) that it is likely they were intimately connected. This study accepts this assumption and treats as moneylenders all *sake* brewers affiliated with Enryakuji and its subordinate institutions, including, for example, the malt makers under Kitano Shrine. In other words, I do not assume that all moneylenders were brewers, but that brewers were usually in the moneylending business, and that as a rule moneylenders under Enryakuji's control were both. Kurokawa Naonori refers to both *sake* brewers and warehousers (*dosō*) as moneylenders, but does not necessarily conflate them into a single institution. Kurokawa, "Doikki no jidai," pp. 330–331.

12. Hashimoto, "Dosō no sonzai keitai," p. 21, quoting *Kanmon gyoki* entry for 1420/11/12.

13. Moneylenders were the archetypal *utokunin*. The word is written with characters meaning "person having virtue," but far from indicating virtue, it connoted simply wealth. (The character for virtue, *toku*, is homophonous with *toku*, profit.) It is translated as "the well-to-do" in Hayashiya, "Kyoto in the Muromachi Age," p. 27.

14. A detailed study of land accumulation by moneylenders is found in Suma, "Dosō no tochi shūseki to tokusei," pp. 1–20.

15. *Kitano tenmangū shiryō—monjo* (hereafter cited as *KM*), no. 62, pp. 34–46. Compiled to better enforce the monopoly of malt producers (see Part 2 and Appendix, no. 1), the list is generally considered the most complete available of the medieval Kyoto moneylender-brewers. Noda Tadao based his map in "Chūsei Kyōto ni okeru kōrigashigyō no hatten," pp. 43–44, on the addresses of each in this and in *KM*, nos. 10–61 (1419/10/3), pp. 7–34. The Appendix, no. 1, divides the names on this list into status categories.

16. Yunoki Manabu, "Sakaya," *KDJ*, vol. 6, p. 292, and "Sake," *KDJ*, vol. 6, p. 331.

17. Toyoda Takeshi, "Dosō," *NRD*, vol. 13, p. 301.

18. Yunoki Manabu, "Shuzōgyō," *KDJ*, vol. 7, p. 381. A basic medieval recipe for *sake* follows:

    1. Polish rough rice (*genmai*); wash and soak it in water; then steam it.
    2. Remove a portion of the steamed rice to a malt chamber; add malt to produce rice malt. (In Kyoto a group of brewers held a monopoly on rice malt by the fourteenth century and it was produced at a site apart from the brewery.)
    3. Mix rice malt, steamed rice (and sometimes other grains like barley, depending on the brewer); add water and allow to ferment.
    4. When the fermentation process is complete, strain the *sake* through cloth; the resulting liquid is called "new *sake*" (*shinzake*).
    5. The new *sake* is heated, then placed in casks for storage.

    From about the twelfth century, for nonimperial consumption *sake* would not be strained at the fourth step but would have more rice malt, steamed rice, and water added to it and then be fermented further. By medieval times, then, the fermentation process was lengthy and elaborate, and thus less likely to be done in the home. Hence, a *sake* industry developed. See Katō, "Sake, seishu, Nihonshu," pp. 242–243. In contrast to the cloudy Kyoto *sake,* Nara brewers developed a clear *sake* sought after to the extent that in the sixteenth century it was being brought into Kyoto for sale, threatening the brewers' monopoly there. In 1511 the shogunate put a stop to selling non-Kyoto *sake* in Kyoto by *kenmon* claiming that it was for their personal use. MBL no. 380 (1511/3/23), *CHS*, vol. 2, p. 122.

19. Yunoki, "Shuzōgyō," *KDJ*, vol. 7, p. 381.

20. A list of brewers taxed by the Oshikōji family for the Distillery Office *sake* tax includes many moneylenders, but also lists rice dealers, tofu shops, tea shops, and even a fish monger. No. 5 (*Konishi Yasuoshi shozō monjo*, 1515/1), *SKR*, vol. 4, pp. 307–311.

21. Based on locations in *KM*, no. 62, pp. 34–46. Kurokawa Naonori notes that in the late Kamakura period, 335 Kyoto moneylenders (*dosō*) were taxed for the construction of Hie Shrine's portable shrine, and adds that the number of *sake* brewers would have been about the same. Kurokawa, "Doikki no jidai," p. 332.

22. Illustrations of such *sake* peddlers can be found in *Saigyō monogatari emaki* in *Nihon jōmin seikatsu ebiki*, vol. 3, p. 61, and *Haseokyō sōshi*, in *Nihon jōmin seikatsu ebiki*, vol. 4, p. 94. In the home *sake* was stored in large ceramic con-

tainers. See the *Eshi sōshi*, in *Nihon jōmin seikatsu ebiki*, vol. 4, p. 70, for an illustration of a woman clutching one.

23. Wakita, "Dosō to bōeki," p. 243. Retail shops were called *ukezakaya*.
24. For example, Wakita, "Marriage and Property in Medieval Japan," p. 97.
25. Wakita, "Chūsei ni okeru seibetsu yakuwari buntan," p. 67.
26. Ibid., pp. 86–87.
27. MBL no. 372 (1510/12/17), *CHS*, vol. 2, p. 120.
28. Kurushima, "Sengokuki no shukikuyaku," p. 93. *Muromachi bakufu hikitsuke shiryō shūsei*, vol. 1, p. 531.
29. In the *Eshi sōshi*, in *Nihon jōmin seikatsu ebiki*, vol. 4, p. 70.
30. Wakita, "Chūsei ni okeru seibetsu yakuwari buntan," p. 86, cites drawings of women portrayed as merchants and craftsmen in a collection of illustrations, *Shichijū ichiban shokunin zukushi utaawase*. The aristocrats depicted were participants in a linked-verse party; the recreational nature of the activity might detract from the credibility of this source as a reliable reflector of gender differences in commoners' occupations. On the other hand, one can reasonably presume that they were striving for some degree of authenticity in their game of dress-up. Barbara Ruch, "The Other Side of Culture in Medieval Japan," p. 513, suspects that the professions are paired in the illustrations for religious and poetic reasons that still elude us.
31. Kurushima, "Sengokuki no shukikuyaku," p. 92.
32. Iwasaki, *Shokunin utaawase*, p. 115.
33. This was not the case from about the mid-Edo period, however, when women were excluded from brewing. See Lebra, "Women in an All-Male Industry," pp. 131–132, and Wakita, "Marriage and Property," p. 97.
34. Wakita, "Chūsei ni okeru seibetsu yakuwari buntan," pp. 83–84.
35. Amino, *Shokunin utaawase*, p. 146–147. Amino links, albeit loosely, the fact that women, by virtue of their relative freedom or exclusion from the established order (their *muensei*, to use his terminology), were put in charge of storehouses, to the widespread acceptance of women as moneylenders in the society.
36. *Heian kento 1200nen kinen yomigaeru Heiankyō*, illustration no. 321, p. 168. Obviously in great discomfort, she is supported on either side by two smaller women.
37. Wakita, *Chūsei ni ikiru onnatachi*, p. 187.
38. Amino, *Shokunin utaawase*, pp. 139–149. Amino compares the role of Japanese women in finance and commercial enterprises favorably to that of medieval European women. Illustrations of the latter include key and bell makers, organists and singers, roles that he deems more limited than those held by women in medieval Japan.
39. See Kuwayama, "Muromachi Bakufu keizai," p. 11, on forms of taxation.
40. Kuwayama, "Kaisetsu," in *Muromachi Bakufu hikitsukekata shiryō shūsei*, p. 8.
41. Exceptions to this are so few that they prove the rule. The villagers of Tokuchin-ho in Ōmi province, for example, produced and preserved an extensive collection of documents in the medieval and early modern periods. See Tonomura, *Community and Commerce*. The Kawashima, a warrior-peasant family based on an estate to the southwest of Kyoto, is another exception, though their tie of vassalage to the

Muromachi Bakufu makes the "commoner" label less appropriate. See Gay, "The Kawashima."

42. MBL no. 410 (1520/3/8), *CHS*, vol. 2, p. 130. This law offers proof that the moneylenders used ledgers: it stipulates that in disputes in which there is no pawn ticket (*shichimotsusatsu*), the shogunate will make a decision after examining the moneylender's ledger (*dosōchō*).

43. MBL no. 179 (1425/9/26), *CHS*, vol. 2, p. 66. This refers partly to moneylenders who donate loan contracts to temples and shrines.

44. MBL no. 203 (1431/10/17), *CHS*, vol. 2, p. 73. Moneylenders may claim collateral, according to this law. The purpose of this decree was to prevent moneylenders from freely claiming debtor's property, a widespread abuse that will be discussed further.

45. MBL no. 260 (1459/11/2), *CHS*, vol. 2, p. 90; MBL nos. 262–264 (1459/11/10), *CHS*, vol. 2, p. 91; and last article of no. 17 (no date, probably 1459/11/10), *Ninagawake monjo*, vol. 1, p. 22.

46. Summary of contents of MBL nos. 397–399 (1520/2/12), *CHS*, vol. 2, p. 127; nos. 417–447 (1520/3/8), *CHS*, vol. 2, pp. 131–135.

47. MBL nos. 480–482 (1530/12/19), *CHS*, vol. 2, pp. 139–140; MBL nos. 493–495 (1546/10/30), *CHS*, vol. 2, pp. 143–144.

48. A wall scribbling appeared in Kyoto in the fourth month of 1334, a time of political uncertainty: "armor is pawned and then reclaimed bit by bit . . . " *Gunsho ruijū*, vol. 25, pp. 503–504. Warriors backing the northern or southern court may have found themselves in financial straits.

49. Kurokawa, "Doikki no jidai," p. 332.

50. Ibid., pp. 332–333.

51. MBL no. 261 (1459/11/12, *CHS*, vol. 2, p. 90) decries "selfish demands" for payment, high interest rates, and demands that interest rates be set jointly by moneylenders, suggesting that high and arbitrary interest rates were the norm. MBL no. 267 (1466/5/26, *CHS*, vol. 2, p. 93) decries lenders rewriting loan contracts on the pretext of loss, and then changing the terms of the original loan. According to this decree, loans are considered null and void when twice the original loan amount has been repaid.

52. This type of loan is first mentioned, not in a debt amnesty, but in a 1440 decree on real-estate contracts. MBL no. 211 (1440/10/26), *CHS*, vol. 2, p. 77.

53. MBL no. 211 (1440/10/26, concerning *honmotsugaeshi*), *CHS*, vol. 2, p. 77.

54. MBL no. 215 (1441/intercalary 9/10, concerning *urikishinchi*), *CHS*, vol. 2, pp. 78–79.

55. MBL no. 218 (1441/intercalary 9/10, concerning *nenki kokyakuchi*), *CHS*, vol. 2, p. 97.

56. MBL no. 314 (1497/6/7), *CHS*, vol. 2, p. 103, decries issuing loan contracts disguised as bills of sale.

57. See Hayashima, "Kyōto kinkō ni okeru," for the evolution of shogunal policy on this matter and its effects on the accumulation of such land in the fifteenth century.

58. MBL no. 205 (1433/10/13), *CHS*, vol. 2, p. 74: at the ten-year mark, twice the original loan must be repaid the moneylender; between ten and twenty years four

times the original loan. This law does not apply to debts outstanding for more than twenty years, and so may not necessarily be interpreted as a statute of limitations. MBL no. 210 (1440/10/26), *CHS*, vol. 2, p. 77, is easier on debtors than previous law: now they have up to twenty-one years to repay only twice the original loan amount.

59. Shimosaka, "Machishū no seikatsu," pp. 119–120, in reference to a story in an early Edo period collection of humorous stories. The authority in question, Taga Takatada, was deputy head of the Board of Administration twice, in 1464–1466 and 1484–1486, when he was said to have ruled Kyoto with such a firm sense of justice that people stopped locking their doors.

60. MBL no. 179 (1425/9/26), *CHS*, vol. 2, p. 66.

61. MBL no. 202 (1430/11/6), *CHS*, vol. 2, p. 73.

62. MBL no. 205 (1433/10/13), *CHS*, vol. 2, p. 74.

63. MBL no. 207 (1436/5/25), *CHS*, vol. 2, p. 75. A penalty of one-tenth the debt will be imposed on tardy debtors; forcible collection by the Board of Administration is threatened if debtor does not pay. See also MBL no. 210 (1440/10/26), *CHS*, vol. 2, p. 77: again, the Board of Administration will take on defaulting debtors. Note that twenty years is not an absolute statute of limitations.

64. Grossberg, *The Laws of the Muromachi Bakufu*, p. 96.

65. MBL no. 267 (1466/5/26), *CHS*, vol. 2, p. 93.

66. MBL no. 204 (1433/10/3), *CHS*, vol. 2, p. 74. See also MBL no. 199 (1430/9/30), *CHS*, vol. 2, p. 72: moneylenders are donating loans and collateral to "temples and shrines"; the Bakufu harshly forbids such activities. Again, MBL no. 257 (1457/12/5), *CHS*, vol. 2, p. 89: lenders forfeit all interest if pawned items are stolen. And MBL no. 415 (1520/3/8), *CHS*, vol. 2, pp. 130–131: if loss is proven (by whom is not clear), twice the amount of the loan must be paid to the debtor as compensation. If there is no proof, an investigation will take place. (This also implies that the shogunate will take it out of the hands of the moneylender.)

67. For example, MBL nos. 480–482 (1530/12/19), *CHS*, vol. 2, pp. 139–140.

68. MBL no. 179 (1425/9/26), *CHS*, vol. 2, p. 66.

69. MBL no. 199 (1430/9/22), *CHS*, vol. 2, p. 72. The heading for the group of laws that include this one refers to moneylenders and commoners (*jigenin*); my assumption is that it applies to commoner debtors.

70. MBL no. 200 (1430/9/30), *CHS*, vol. 2, p. 72. Shimosaka Mamoru suggests that moneylending establishments had two tiers: the owner, who provided capital and ultimately reaped the profits, and the employee(s) who operated the business on a day-to-day basis. See Shimosaka, "Chūsei dosōron," pp. 219–220. The Muromachi Bakufu law cited here would bear this out. I am not convinced, however, that all or even most of the hundreds of moneylenders in the city necessarily operated at such a level of complexity. Many, I suspect, were small enterprises.

71. MBL no. 206 (1436/5/22), *CHS*, vol. 2, p. 75.

72. This stipulation is contained in the text following MBL nos. 397–399 (1520/2/12), *CHS*, vol. 2, p. 127; MBL nos. 480–482 (1530/12/19), *CHS*, vol. 2, pp. 139–140; and MBL nos. 493–495 (1546/10/30), *CHS*, vol. 2, pp. 143–144. To speculate— Lotus Sect adherents, in their nighttime carousing, may have menaced money-lenders, though the twelfth and second months would have been chilly indeed for such activities.

Chapter Two: Overlords

1. Endō, "Shokunin no soshiki," pp. 2–4.
2. On *za*, see Sasaki, *Muromachi Bakufu*, p. 136; Sasaki Gin'ya, "Za," *KDJ*, vol. 6, pp. 113–119; Toyoda, *Za no kenkyū*; Wakita, *Nihon chūsei shōgyō hattatsushi no kenkyū*. My analysis of the *za* is political and institutional rather than economic in nature, stressing the relationship between overlord and members. For an economist's account of the emergence, development, and decline of the *za*, see Yamamura, "The Development of Za," pp. 438–465, and "The Growth of Commerce," pp. 361–364. A summary of the scholarly debate over medieval commerce and the *za* is included in Tonomura, *Community and Commerce*, pp. 104–106.
3. Wakita Haruko uses this term (*hōshinoza*: "service" guild) in her analysis. See Wakita, "Ryōshu keizai," p. 276, "Shōgyō to machiza," pp. 215–216, "Towards a Wider Perspective," p. 335, and "Dimensions," p. 307.
4. Sasaki, "Za," *KDJ*, vol. 6, p. 113.
5. Ibid., p. 118. Tonomura, *Community and Commerce*, pp. 104–105. Another theory, formulated by Kuroda Toshio after studying a guild in Yase, a village north of Kyoto, is that *za* referred to the special privileges of communal organizations in villages inhabited by people of the same profession. Thus its members were linked both by locale and by occupation. Sasaki, "Za," *KDJ*, p. 118.
6. Wakita Haruko called these *eigyōnoza*, to distinguish them from the older *hōshinoza*. See Wakita, "Za no seikaku henka," pp. 235–274. This is a refinement of the commercial vs. noncommercial *za* defined by Akamatsu Toshihide, "Za ni tsuite," pp. 1–25. The terms *"honza"* (original guild) and *"shinza"* (new guild) are found in medieval documents and are perhaps more commonly used by historians to distinguish among types of guilds, though interpretations of these terms vary so widely as to make definitive categorization difficult. Toyoda Takeshi's definition of original and new guilds is close to Wakita's service and trade guilds, insofar as the degree of independence from the overlord is the key factor. Toyoda, "Chūsei no shōnin to kōtsū," p. 491. Hitomi Tonomura labels the later type "commercial *za*." Tonomura, *Community and Commerce*, pp. 104–106.
7. See Wakita, "Shōgyō to machiza," pp. 215–216.
8. Wakita, "Dimensions," p. 319.
9. Wakita Haruko put forth this theory in "Muromachiki no keizai hatten," pp. 72–77. An alternative view, based on guilds involved in construction, is that the internal structure of the guild was hierarchical in nature, based on members' age and amount of taxes paid to the overlord. See Sasaki, "Za," *KDJ*, p. 118.
10. Toyoda, *Nihon no hōken toshi*, p. 51.
11. Ibid., p. 53.
12. Ibid., p. 55.
13. Wakita, "Dimensions," p. 310.
14. Wakita, "The Japanese Medieval City," p. 12.
15. Toyoda, *Chūsei no shōnin to kōtsū*, p. 491.
16. Wakita, "Chūsei toshi to nōson," p. 219.
17. Wakita Osamu has pointed out that the policy of Nobunaga and other Sengoku daimyo to abolish guild and market restrictions (*rakuichi rakuza*) applied mainly to castle towns as a way of stimulating the economy. He maintains that Nobunaga's

policy in Kyoto was quite the opposite: not wanting to throw commerce into chaos, he confirmed the major *za* in their privileges. "The Fate of the Moneylenders in the Early Modern Age," below, contains more discussion of this issue. See Wakita, *Kinsei hōkensei seiritsu*, vol. 2, pp. 117–126; Wakita, "Shōgyō, kōtsū seisaku," in *KR*, vol. 4, pp. 375–376.

18. Wakita, "Dimensions," p. 311.

19. Using statistics from a 1315 document in which 280 Hie Shrine *jinin* money-lenders and 55 moneylenders under the Bureau of Police were bound to pay a tax to rebuild the portable shrine, Wakita Haruko has estimated that 280, or about 80 percent, of Kyoto's moneylenders were under Enryakuiji's control. Wakita, "Shōkō-gyōsha no seichō," p. 462.

20. Sources on the history, organization, and activities of Enryakuji include: Sonoda Kōyū, "Enryakuji," in *KDJ*, vol. 2, pp. 427–428; Kageyama, *Hieizanji: sono kōsei to shomondai*; Murayama, "Hieizan no kankyō to soshiki"; Toyoda, "Enryakuji sansō to Hiesha jinin no katsudō"; Tsuji, "Chūsei ni okeru Ōmi Sakamoto no hatten to toshi keikan" and "Chūsei sanmon shūto no dōzoku ketsugō to satobō." In English, the monastery and its organization are discussed in Adolphson, *The Gates of Power*, and Tonomura, *Community and Commerce*, pp. 21–26.

21. See Groner, *Saichō: The Establishment of the Japanese Tendai School*, for more on Enryakuji's founding in the context of Japanese Buddhism.

22. See Shimosaka, "Chūsei jiin ni okeru taishū to 'sōdera,' " on Enryakuji's intra-monastic organization, including its relationship with Hie Shrine in the medieval period.

23. Okada Seiji, "Hiyoshi Taisha," *KDJ*, vol. 11, pp. 1036–1037.

24. For an account of the split between Enryakuji and Onjōji, see McMullin, "The Sanmon-Jimon Schism."

25. Tsuji, "Chūsei ni okeru Ōmi," p. 17.

26. Kageyama, *Hieizanji*, p. 14.

27. Ōta Hirotarō, "Enryakuji," *KDJ*, vol. 2, p. 428.

28. Tsuji, "Chūsei ni okeru Ōmi," p. 2. Fifteen percent of all paddy land in Wakasa province on the Japan Sea belonged to Enryakuji by the twelfth century.

29. Kawazoe, "Japan and East Asia," p. 402.

30. MBL no. 56 (1352/7/24), *CHS*, vol. 2, pp. 28–29.

31. MBL no. 97 (1368/6/17), *CHS*, vol. 2, p. 43. Tsuji, "Chūsei ni okeru Ōmi," pp. 9–20; Kageyama, *Hieizanji*, pp. 14–15.

32. Tsuji, "Chūsei ni okeru Ōmi," pp. 9–20; Kageyama, *Hieizanji*, pp. 14–15.

33. MBL no. 17 (1346), *CHS*, vol. 2, p. 17.

34. Tonomura, *Community and Commerce*, pp. 24–25; p. 216, n. 39.

35. Tsuji, "Chūsei ni okeru Ōmi," p. 18.

36. "Santo Enkaku yuisho no omomuki ni makase . . . ," *ukebumi anmon* (1482/5), *Shinjōin monjo*.

37. Similar patterns of clerical involvement in moneylending could be found in other temples as credit was widely sought in the medieval period. The monk Meisai, an administrator at Tōji, initially enriched himself as manager of Yano Estate in Harima province. Returning to Kyoto in 1396, he simultaneously continued his administrative duties at Tōji and established a moneylending business with wealthy neighborhood merchants. Lending to members of all classes, at the time

of his death in 1413 he had 400 clients of all classes owing him an amount totaling over 1,000 *kanmon*, or more than 10,000 times the daily wages of a carpenter. Itō Toshikazu, "Kin'yūgyō o fukugyō ni suru jisō," pp. 30–31, citing Meisai's list of loans dated 1413/9/16.

38. The term "Gion" itself has profoundly Buddhist origins, referring to the garden in which the Buddha preached. In the late-nineteenth-century forcible separation of Shinto and Buddhism, the name was changed to Yasaka Shrine, and its Buddhist character, present from the beginning, was eradicated. Gion remains the name attached to the adjacent neighborhood, whose merchants were closely affiliated with the shrine from early medieval times.

39. Ōta Hirotarō, "Enryakuji," *KDJ*, vol. 2, p. 428.

40. Nishida Nagao, "Kitano Tenjin Engi," *KDJ*, vol. 4, p. 124. The tenth-century institutional and doctrinal process by which control of Gion Shrine in Kyoto passed from the great Nara temple Kōfukuji to Enryakuji is described in McMullin, "The Enryakuji and the Gion Shrine-Temple Complex."

41. Sources on *jinin* include Toyoda, "Enryakuji sansō to Hiesha jinin"; Nagashima Fukutarō, "Jinin," *KDJ*, vol. 7, pp. 21–22.

42. Sources on *kunin* include Inaba Nobumichi, "Kunin," *KDJ*, vol. 4, p. 847; Inaba, "Chūsei no kunin ni kansuru ichi kōsatsu," pp. 1–37.

43. For example, in 1465 the Muromachi shogunate declared that the wealthy *santo*-lender Shōjitsubō was to stop bringing Enryakuji *kunin* into Kyoto as business assistants, a practice of his for some years. *Chikamoto nikki*, entry for 1465/2/22, in *Zōho zokushiryō taisei*, vol. 10, pp. 212–213.

44. Noda Tadao, "Inujinin," *KDJ*, vol. 1, p. 749.

45. Kuroda Toshio discusses this sectarian rivalry in "Chūsei jisha seiryokuron," pp. 255–259. Nagahara Keiji discusses the outcastes' participation in this violence in "The Medieval Origins of the Eta-Hinin," p. 393.

46. Wakita, "Shōkōgyōsha no seichō," p. 459.

47. Shimosaka, "Machishū no seikatsu," p. 70, quoting *Genpei seisuiki*, vol. 29, chap. 1.

48. In the Kamakura period the majority of the Enryakuji lenders held *jinin* rank at Hie Shrine and usually figured in Enryakuji's struggles with the imperial court. Yokoi Kiyoshi, "Hie jinin," *KDJ*, vol. 11, p. 828.

49. Wakita, "Shōkōgyōsha no seichō," pp. 459–462.

50. Wakita Haruko infers this from the entry for 1278/1/25 in *Yasaka jinja kiroku*, which states that dividing among them the land received as collateral on defaulted debts was the established custom of this group. Wakita, "Toshi kyōdōtai no keisei," p. 272.

51. Wakita maintains that this organization of moneylenders was internally stable, governed by its own customary law even in the Kamakura period. See Wakita, "Toshi kyōdōtai no keisei," p. 276.

52. Yang, "Buddhist Monasteries," p. 175.

53. Ibid., p. 177.

54. This was not aimed at Enryakuji's moneylenders in particular, but was intended to protect warriors and keep their lands intact. Yamamura, "The Growth of Commerce," p. 373.

55. Yamamura, "The Growth of Commerce," p. 373.

56. Ibid., pp. 373–374.

57. Grossberg, *The Laws of the Muromachi Bakufu*, p. 11.
58. Kamakura Bakufu Law no. 662 (1297/3/6), *CHS*, vol. 1, pp. 297. The law encompasses commoners as well, so that the shogunate would not be accused of playing favorites. Yamamura, "The Growth of Commerce," p. 375. This amnesty decree was sent to the Rokuhara *tandai*, Kamakura's Kyoto representative. It forbade selling pawned land and loaning at interest. The moneylenders of Kyoto were surely affected by this decree. See also no. 10, (*Shinpen tsuika*, 1297/7/22), *SKR*, vol. 3, p. 201, for the Rokuhara *tandai's* declaration of this measure in Kyoto.
59. Yamamura, "The Growth of Commerce," p. 376.
60. Yunoki Manabu, "Shuzōgyō," *KDJ*, vol. 7, p. 381; Yunoki Manabu, "Sakaya," *KDJ*, vol. 6, p. 292.
61. See Amino, "Mikinotsukasa," pp. 361–396, which draws upon the *Oshikōji monjo* document collection to reconstruct how the Distillery Office came to tax the moneylenders through the fourteenth century. Amino characterizes this tax as the precursor of the Muromachi shogunate's tax on the moneylenders.
62. No. 35 (*Hiradoki*, 1240/intercalary 10/17), in *SKR*, vol. 3, p. 213.
63. Amino, "Mikinotsukasa," pp. 370–371.
64. Wakita Haruko, "Ryōshu keizai," p. 278, interprets this as a move made with Enryakuji in mind; see also Amino, "Mikinotsukasa," p. 372.
65. No. 37 *Oshikōji monjo* (1302/4/3), in *SKR*, vol. 3, p. 215.
66. Wakita, "Shōkōgyōsha no seichō," p. 462; no. 44 (*Hiesha narabi ni Eizan gyōkōki*, 1330/3, referring to an event in 1301/3/24), in *SKR*, vol. 3, pp. 172–173.
67. No. 11 *Kōfukuji ryakunendaiki* (1305/2/29), in *SKR*, vol. 3, p. 202.
68. Wakita, "Shōkōgyōsha no seichō," p. 462.
69. No. 44 *Oshikōji monjo* (1322/2/19), in *SKR*, vol. 3, p. 217. This document provides some details regarding the collection of the tax on that date; at least at this point, it was calculated not on the amount of malt used but on the number of *sake* casks in the brewery. Amino, in "Mikinotsukasa," pp. 373–374, explains that Godaigo ruled in favor of the Distillery Office over two rival offices of the imperial court vying for the right to tax the Kyoto brewer-lenders and brought the Bureau of Capital Police into the matter by ordering them to investigate anyone not submitting the tax. See no. 45 (*Oshikōji monjo*, 1322/5/9), in *SKR*, vol. 3, p. 217, for this order to the police. Wakita Haruko, on the other hand, asserts that this tax was collected by the brewer-lenders themselves through their own organization and then submitted en bloc to the Bureau of Capital Police. Wakita Haruko, "Shukikuyaku," *KDJ*, vol. 7, p. 321. In English, see Goble, *Kenmu*, pp. 45–55, on Godaigo's commercial policies in Kyoto. He interprets the 1322 policy broadly to mean that *sake* in Kyoto was now produced under imperial jurisdiction, allowing that shrines may have continued to receive some of these taxes, but if so only through the imperial agency that collected them. As will be seen, however, there is much subsequent evidence that the original overlord ties were not so easily broken.
70. Amino, "Mikinotsukasa," p. 375. In "Chūsei toshiron," p. 281, Amino asserts that collection of the tax could not have been completely effective with Enryakuji's opposition.
71. This is not to say that every brewer in Kyoto was regularly assessed taxes by three separate overlords throughout the medieval period. As will be shown, taxes could be avoided through exemptions, bribes, and other devices.

72. Satō Shin'ichi equates in substance the activities of Hie *jinin* and Gion *inujinin*, including seizure of property and debt collection for the moneylenders, to the same violent tactics of the Bureau of Police, as part of their official duties. Satō, "Muromachi bakufuron," p. 34.

73. Wakita, "Shōkōgyōsha no seichō," p. 462.

74. Satō Shin'ichi speaks of "low-ranking officials in the Bureau of Police who seem to have extracted from certain businesses stipend money in return for 'official' protection, and thus enjoyed a private relationship with these guilds that went by a public name." Satō, "Muromachi bakufuron," p. 34.

75. The Tokugawa shogunate had good control over rural revenue early on, making urban commercial taxes less necessary at first, and thus not pursued.

76. Wakita, "Ryōshu keizai," p. 278.

77. Satō, "Muromachi bakufuron," pp. 31–38.

78. Wakita, "Ryōshu keizai," pp. 298–299.

79. Satō, "Muromachi bakufuron," pp. 39–40.

80. Wakita, "Ryōshu keizai," pp. 299–300.

81. This four-stage scheme was first put forth in Satō, "Muromachi bakufuron," p. 35. In English see Gay, "Muromachi Bakufu Rule in Kyoto," pp. 52–60, for an account of the first three stages.

82. Commodities leaving and revenues entering had to pass through these physical barriers (*sekisho* or *sotsubunsho*) at the seven major roadways entering Kyoto. They included, clockwise from the north, Ōhara on the Hokurikudō, Shirakawa on the Higashiyamadō, Awata on the Tōkaidō, Fushimi on the Nankaidō, Toba on the Saikaidō, Tōji on the San'yōdō, and Nishishichijō on the San'indō (see Map 2). Tolls were collected in a variety of ways: at times the stations based the toll on the amount of goods being transported (no. 46, *Daijōin jisha zōjiki*, 1478/1/11, *SKR*, vol. 3, p. 289), while in some cases the duty was determined by the type of commodity (no. 24, *Toki monjo*, 1547/2/28, *SKR*, vol. 3, p. 352; in this case salt was being transported). In other cases, a flat fee or percentage (*sotsubun*) of the value of the goods was collected. Or the amount may have varied according to the occupation of the traveler: in 1404, for example, Tōji charged merchants two *sen* each, while a horse was three *sen*, a traveler one *sen*, and a vehicle (carriage or palanquin) ten *sen* (no. 40, *Tōji hyakugō monjo*, *ku* section, 1404/4/3, *SKR*, vol. 3, p. 288). Attempts were also made to tax those taking secondary roads to avoid the toll (ibid.).

83. These included the *kuraryō*, *tonomoryō*, *saeimonfu*, and *ueimonfu*.

84. Wakita Haruko, "Shōgyō to machiza," p. 209.

85. As an example of such overzealous tolling, in the late fourteenth century Enryakuji set up seven toll stations along Lake Biwa's western shore, snagging boat traffic. Tonomura, *Community and Commerce*, p. 98. On toll stations, see Tsuji, "Chūsei ni okeru Ōmi," and Toyoda, "Chūsei no shōnin to kōtsū," pp. 316–323.

86. See, for example, no. 37 (*Kuramadera monjo*, 1340/2/13), *SKR*, vol. 3, p. 287: the imperial court tells one of its low-ranking officials to stop improper collection (*jiyū no ransui*) of the tolls. According to MBL no. 17 (1346), *CHS*, vol. 2, p. 17, no new toll barriers are to be erected because they hinder travel.

87. See Wakita figures in "Shōgyō to machiza," p. 207.

88. MBL no. 6 (Kemmu Shikimoku, 1336/11/7), in *CHS*, vol. 2, p. 5.

89. MBL no. 18 (1346), *CHS*, vol. 2, p. 17.
90. Wakita, "Ryōshu keizai," p. 279, quoting Ono, *Nihon sangyō hattatsushi no kenkyū*, p. 134.
91. Kurushima, "Sengokuki no shukikuyaku," pp. 60–62.
92. Amino, "Mikinotsukasa," p. 392. In the late Muromachi period the eighteenth scion of the Nakahara family changed their surname to Oshikōji; the *Oshikōji monjo*, used by Amino, is an important source on the Distillery Office.
93. MBL no. 150 (1393/11/26), *CHS*, vol. 2, p. 60. This move is described below.
94. Wakita, "Ryōshu keizai," p. 281. This is inferred indirectly from the fact that Gion Shrine requested exemption from the tax for its clients.
95. Kuwayama, "Muromachi bakufu keizai," p. 11.
96. Ibid., pp. 9, 11.
97. Hall, "The Muromachi Bakufu," p. 223.
98. MBL no. 105 (1370/12/16), *CHS*, vol. 2, pp. 45–46. Specifically, they were accused of invading aristocratic residences near the imperial palace.
99. MBL no. 145 (1386/8/25), *CHS*, vol. 2, p. 59.
100. MBL no. 113 (1372/10/10), *CHS*, vol. 2, p. 49.
101. MBL no. 127 (1379/7/25), *CHS*, vol. 2, pp. 54–55.
102. Satō, "Muromachi bakufuron," p. 37, is an example of the traditional view that Enryakuji lost tax income from the moneylenders with this law. It was challenged by Wakita Haruko in "Ryōshu keizai," pp. 277–285.
103. MBL no. 146–150 (1393/11/26), *CHS*, vol. 2, pp. 59–60.
104. Satō, "Muromachi bakufuron," p. 37.
105. Wintersteen, "The Early Muromachi Bakufu in Kyoto," p. 209.
106. Wakita Haruko has suggested that the moneylenders' guild was internally cohesive even in the Kamakura period and had any growing autonomy nipped in the bud with the 1393 shogunal laws. Wakita, "Toshi kyōdōtai," p. 276.
107. Wakita, "Dosō to bōeki," p. 235, referring to a passage in the *Ōninki*.
108. See Kurushima, "Sengokuki no shukikuyaku," pp. 71–73.
109. Wakita, "Dosō to bōeki," p. 237.
110. Wakita, "Ryōshu keizai," pp. 277–285.
111. Most historians, starting with Okuno Takahiro, consider the *dosōkata isshū* the descendant of the *dosō yoriaishū*, which they agree was the term used when the moneylenders dealt with their overlord Enryakuji in the Kamakura period. See Okuno, "Muromachi jidai ni okeru dosō no kenkyū," and Wakita, "Toshi kyōdōtai no keisei," p. 272. Shimosaka Mamoru disputes this entirely, however, first pointing out a gap of over a century between incidences of the two terms in sources. Then, based on sources documenting a moneylender dispute of 1278, he proposes a different meaning for the term *"dosō yoriaishū"*—namely, that it referred to complicated relations within single moneylending establishments that had several "owners" and employers. (Presumably these would have been the largest moneylending establishments.) He does agree that the large group of Enryakuji moneylenders in Kyoto continued into the Muromachi period to be dominated by the *santo* monk members, many of whom became the shogun's tax agents. Shimosaka, "Chūsei dosōron," pp. 224–232.
112. The Board of Administration, as the administrative office of the shogunal house,

had nominal charge of day-to-day shogunal finances, but in practice many of these tasks were farmed out. Not only moneylenders but the Zen *gozan* institution supplied some financial expertise to the shogun—indeed, the latter became the backbone of Bakufu trade missions to China. Duties of the office of *sōroku* (Registrar General of Monks) included drafting documents for the Ming trade and even mediation between Bakufu and *shugo*. Some Zen monks served as shogunal estate agents (*daikan*). Collcutt, *Five Mountains*, pp. 122, 280.

113. Wakita, "Ryōshu keizai," p. 285, and p. 288, n. 34, cites a 1432 case brought to the shogunate on a bad debt between two temples. Even though no moneylender was involved in the loan itself, the Bakufu called on the moneylenders collectively to dispose of the land involved. Wakita surmises from this case that the Kyoto moneylenders may have acted, possibly as a group, as shogunal agents who disposed of property according to the terms of lawsuits. Given their experience in the area, they would be obvious candidates for such jobs.

114. Kuwayama, "Muromachi Bakufu keizai ," p. 11.

115. Wakita, "Dosō to bōeki," p. 237.

116. Ibid., p. 244.

117. Ibid.

118. Also read *nassenkata*. The major study of *nōsenkata* is Kuwayama, "Muromachi Bakufu keizai." See also Gomi, "Kanreisei to daimyōsei"; Kuwayama Kōnen, "Nōsenkata," *KDJ*, vol. 11, p. 368; Kuwayama Kōnen, "Kubō okura," *KDJ*, vol. 4, p. 855; Ono, "Muromachi Bakufu no sakaya tōsei"; Shimosaka, "Chūsei dosōron." See Terajima, "Inryōken mikura ni tsuite," a study of the financial agents of Shōkokuji who handled disbursements from the *gozan* Zen monasteries to the Muromachi shogunate, but who also seem to have acted as financial agents of the shogun. Terajima characterizes them as hard to distinguish in some respects from the nonclerical (i.e., moneylender) shogunal financial agents.

119. This apparently included overarching responsibility for commercial taxes. See MBL no. 379 (1511/3/23), *CHS*, vol. 2, p. 121, which states that *sake* retailers disobeying the *mikura* by evading taxes will be dealt with through a separate tax office set up for that purpose.

120. Shimosaka Mamoru surmises that all the clerical *mikura* were *santo*-rank moneylenders from Enryakuji employed by the shogun for their financial expertise, while the Momii, conspicuously the only secular name in the early decades, was closely tied to the shogunal house as *mikura* and was not an independent moneylender. Shimosaka, "Chūsei dosōron," pp. 233–234.

121. *Kunin* of the Board of Administration did some direct collecting: Niunoya cites a case in 1442 in which *nōsenkata* were specifically bypassed and instead *kunin* armed with Board of Administration documents collected taxes and then submitted them directly to the *mikura*. But their main responsibility was transmitting official documents to debtors or lenders concerning annulment of debt in the case of conditional debt amnesties or in response to requests for confirmation of credit. Niunoya, *Kebiishi*, pp. 265–267.

122. MBL no. 312 (1497/4), *CHS*, vol. 2, p. 102. Inventory and tax collection would be taken on these dates.

123. A 1451 communication from the shogun's deputy, Hatakeyama Mochikuni, to

Nikaidō Tadayuki, the head of the Board of Administration, states that the shogun's tax agents are allowed 10 percent of the total as their commission. Document dated 1451/4/25 in *Maedake shozō monjo*, *CHS*, vol. 2, no. 161, pp. 220–221.

124. MBL no. 180 (1430/2/30), *CHS*, vol. 2, p. 66, lists confiscation of moneylender property as the duty of the *nōsenkata*.

125. MBL no. 306 (1497/11/14), *CHS*, vol. 2, p. 101. Conceivably, this could refer to violence on either side.

126. This is widely understood to have been the case; an example of it is found in an entry in *Mototsune nikki* for 1442/intercalary 9, cited by Niunoya: income from the moneylenders has dropped due to the debt amnesty of the previous year. Tax agents are exempted, but low-ranking functionaries of the Board of Administration are to go out and collect the tax, submitting it to the *mikura*. Niunoya, *Kebiishi*, p. 265.

127. Shimosaka, in his study of the moneylenders before the Ōnin War, asserts that all the *nōsenkata* were *santo* moneylenders of Enryakuji. Shimosaka, "Chūsei dosōron," p. 232. After the Ōnin War, as secularization accelerated and new moneylenders emerged, a mixture of clerical and secular individuals appeared in the ranks of the tax agents.

128. *Ninagawake monjo*, vol. 2, no. 186 (1485/7/10), p. 276; no. 188 (1485/7/20), pp. 277–279; no. 189 (1485/7/25), 279–282.

129. Upon becoming a *nōsenkata*, the income of a moneylender apparently increased enormously. A Zen monk wrote enviously in this regard to the Enryakuji lender Shōjitsubō, who worked for the shogun. Toyoda, "Za to dosō," p. 181.

130. MBL no. 349 (1508/9/16), p. 114, for example, states that special envoys (*kensekishi*) from the shogun will be sent to collect late taxes. This could be construed as a sign that the tax agents were seen by the shogunate as being too liberal with tax exemptions.

131. Sasaki, *Muromachi Bakufu*, p. 132.

132. Ibid., p. 43.

133. Hitomi Tonomura, for example, in her study of the medieval villages of Tokuchinho, describes a similar arrangement, in which merchant-commoners enjoyed some economic leverage in their relationship with the overlord. Tonomura, *Community and Commerce*, p. 191.

134. Kuwayama, "Muromachi bakufu keizai," pp. 31–33. The image of the Muromachi shogunate conveyed by Kuwayama is that of a multitude of ad hoc arrangements amid a certain disorder. In contrast, Satō Shin'ichi's characterization is closer to that of a highly rational bureaucratic network. Satō, "Muromachi Bakufuron."

135. *Ninagawake monjo*, vol. 1, no. 88 (1476/2(1)/13), pp. 158–160.

136. MBL no. 188 (1428/11/22), *CHS*, vol. 2, p. 69.

137. *Ninagawake monjo*, vol. 2, no. 291 (1494/8/26), pp. 58–60.

138. Wakita, "Ryōshu keizai," pp. 283–290.

139. Ibid., p. 283.

CHAPTER THREE: TRANSCENDING SUBORDINATION

1. *Ninagawake monjo*. See Conclusion for a discussion of this collection.

2. Kuwayama, "The Bugyōnin System," p. 56.

3. Shimosaka Mamoru analyzed tax agent disbursement records to determine what purpose the moneylender tax served and concluded that it covered shogunal house expenses. Shimosaka, "Chūsei dosōron," pp. 245–246.
4. The 1393 laws were reissued in 1408, 1432, and 1460, indicating continuity in shogunal policy. *CHS*, vol. 2, p. 61. Also tax agents, who collected moneylender taxes, are mentioned, in MBL no. 180 (1430/2/20), *CHS*, vol. 2, p. 66, as the ones who confiscated property of moneylenders. This may be construed as more indirect evidence that collection was indeed taking place.
5. *Ninagawake monjo* no. 29 (1441/11/20), vol. 1, pp. 44–45.
6. See "Ikki" section for a detailed discussion of debt amnesties.
7. MBL no. 250 (1455/9/18), *CHS*, vol. 2, p. 87, specifies these terms of tax relief, though one cannot be sure that this was true in 1441. See also MBL no. 233 (1445/9/29), *CHS*, vol. 2, p. 82: moneylenders destroyed by fire will be exempted for several years, evidence of shogunal lenience in special cases.
8. On the other hand, MBL no. 233 (1445/9/29), *CHS*, vol. 2, p. 82, states that moneylenders evading taxes (in this case using peasant invasions and subsequent debt amnesties as excuses for inability to pay) have a very adverse effect on shogunal income. This could be interpreted to mean that in 1445 the Bakufu was already experiencing some decline in moneylender tax income.
9. *Ninagawake monjo* no. 75 (1475/1/30), vol. 1, pp. 138–143.
10. *Ninagawake monjo* no. 79 (1475/1/30), vol. 1, p. 148.
11. Shogunal tax documents list mostly moneylenders and brewers, but some other businesses, such as bean-paste merchants, are also represented.
12. *Ninagawake monjo* no. 78 (1475/1/30), vol. 1, pp. 146–148.
13. *Ninagawake monjo* no. 305, vol. 2, pp. 77–82. The addresses are in both upper and lower Kyoto. This document is undated, but 1495/12/23 is the likely date assuming that it was produced along with those on either side of it, nos. 302–308, pp. 71–86, which are also lists of commercial groups. See Appendix, no. 4, for a transcription of these lists.
14. Mary Elizabeth Berry asserts that brewer-lender taxes to the shogunate came to 22 *kan* per month during this period, a very specific figure given the paucity of documentation and great variation in amounts actually collected each year, but within the general range given here. Berry, *The Culture of Civil War*, p. 92.
15. *Ninagawake monjo* no. 310 (1496/1/31), vol. 2, p. 87.
16. *Ninagawake monjo* no. 399 (1509/1), vol. 2, pp. 188–189. These are suspiciously close figures given the much higher concentration of moneylenders in lower Kyoto.
17. *Ninagawake monjo* no. 377 (1505/intercalary/?), vol. 2, pp. 166–167. Most businesses listed in the tax documents are lender-breweries.
18. *Ninagawake monjo* no. 275 (1490), vol. 2, pp. 38–39.
19. MBL no. 315 (1498/10/16), pp. 103–104, and no. 349 (1508/9/16), *CHS*, vol. 2, p. 114, are examples of this. MBL no. 288 (1485/7), *CHS*, vol. 2, p. 98, specifically mentions that tax evasion leads to frequent and troublesome incidental levies (*rinji kayaku*).
20. MBL no. 349 (1508/9/16), *CHS*, vol. 2, p. 114.
21. See MBL no. 350 (1508/9/16), *CHS*, vol. 2, pp. 114–115. The retail *sake* tax of 100 *hiki* per shop was also widely evaded. See, for example, MBL no. 378, 379 (both dated 1511/3/223), *CHS*, vol. 2, p. 121.

22. Tanuma, "Muromachi Bakufu zaisei," p. 1.
23. MBL no. 233 (1445/9/29), CHS, vol. 2, p. 82.
24. MBL no. 239 (1454/10?/29), CHS, vol. 2, pp. 84–85.
25. *Ninagawake monjo* no. 540 (*ukebumi* dated 1539/12), vol. 3, pp. 60–61. There are problems of interpretation in this document: article one contains the term "*onkuhei*," which could mean that the agents should submit a tax equally to an authority—i.e., a bribe—or it may simply refer to this tax that is due the shogun. The second article refers to the official moneylender tax (*yakusen no gi*), which all will pay except those exempted, within the amount of 7 *kanmon*. Thus two taxes on the moneylenders may be referred to here. Berry, *The Culture of Civil War*, pp. 178–179, cites this matter as noted in the *Chikatoshi nikki* entry for 1539/12/30 to demonstrate the resilience of the shogunate's "continuing alliance" with its moneylender agents.
26. A typical example of a reference to the moneylenders as the "financial pillar" of the Muromachi Bakufu is in Hayashiya, *Chūsei bunka no kichō*, p. 247. The assertion tends to be repeated uncritically in histories of the period.
27. Imatani Akira, for example, dismisses the claim "in high school textbooks" that the tax on the moneylenders was an important source of Muromachi Bakufu income at all, even at 6,000 *kanmon* per year (Imatani, *Sengokuki no Muromachi Bakufu*, p. 25). He sees shogunal income from moneylenders dropping off sharply because of peasant uprisings, though he acknowledges that conditional debt amnesties alleviated the situation somewhat. In his view, the Muromachi Bakufu was especially dependent on the Zen establishment for income (ibid., pp. 59–60). Martin Collcutt also considers the Zen establishment "one of the stronger pillars in a weak economic structure," providing as significant levels of shogunal income as revenues from moneylenders (*Five Mountains*, pp. 236, 280). Kurokawa Naonori, in contrast to Imatani, deems moneylender taxes to have been important to the shogunate and suggests that conditional debt amnesties and currency regulations compensated for any post-Ōnin decline in moneylender tax income—in other words, that the shogunate continued to exploit the moneylenders as a significant source of income, but through different devices. Kurokawa acknowledges, however, that the economy was unstable and therefore that a long-term, deliberate economic policy by the Bakufu was out of the question (Kurokawa Naonori, "Gekokujō no seiji," *KR*, vol. 3, pp. 486–488). Retailers who sold *sake* but did not produce it were another source of Bakufu income in Kyoto, according to Wakita, "Dosō to bōeki," p. 243. More recent scholarship has not continued to debate these particular points.
28. MBL nos. 146–150 (1393/11/26), CHS, vol. 2, pp. 59–61.
29. Kuroda, "Chūsei jisha seiryokuron," pp. 259–262, discusses the Enryakuji-Kiyomizudera-Kōfukuji warfare, while Nagahara, "The Medieval Origins of the Eta-Hinin," pp. 393–394, outlines the role of the outcastes in this religious warfare. MBL no. 105 (1370/12/16), CHS, vol. 2, pp. 45–46, refers to "evil deeds" by Enryakuji's *kunin* regarding debts, not religious conflicts. MBL no. 145 (1386/8/25), CHS, vol. 2, p. 59, deplores the general violence of Enryakuji priests and shrine personnel.
30. Tonomura, *Community and Commerce*, p. 52.
31. Kuwayama, "The Bugyōnin System," p. 62.

32. Murayama, "Hieizan no kankyō," pp. 33–34.
33. Tonomura, *Community and Commerce*, p. 50.
34. Murayama, "Hieizan no kankyō to soshiki," p. 34.
35. Shimosaka, "Sanmon shisetsu," pp. 67–114.
36. See Tonomura, *Community and Commerce*, pp. 31–32, on this Bakufu-*shugo*-Enryakuji triangle. The policy of giving Enryakuji envoys the power to settle land disputes in Ōmi province was in effect from 1350 to 1394. Shimosaka and Tsuji see the envoy system as a way for the Muromachi Bakufu to control Enryakuji, by giving these envoys control similar to that of a *shugo* over Enryakuji holdings, and also by penetrating Enryakuji's military and policing section (Tsuji, "Chūsei ni okeru Ōmi," p. 15, and Shimosaka, "Sanmon shisetsu," pp. 97, 104). The relationship was a stormy one, however: in a long-festering dispute, the antagonistic Yoshinori lured insubordinate envoys to Kyoto in 1435, where he killed them. This was a low point, however, and it is reasonable to characterize the envoy system not simply as a Bakufu control mechanism but as one from which Enryakuji's *santo* enhanced their own position.
37. Shimosaka, "Chūsei dosōron," pp. 229–233, cites two entries, dated 1422 and 1425, in the diary *Kanmon gyoki*, indicating that some of the best-known *santo*-moneylender-*nōsenkata* had appointments to be on duty in a religious capacity at Enryakuji halls of worship. He asserts that Enryakuji controlled many of the Kyoto moneylenders, but not simply as a guild overlord. Indeed, attendance at monastic rituals would indicate a strong religious and institutional bond between the moneylenders and Enryakuji, quite transcending merely a commercial one. How long this continued is unclear, and exactly how many of the moneylenders were *santo* is also not known.
38. Wakita, "Ryōshu keizai," p. 284, suggests that the shogunate might have lacked the power to deny completely Enryakuji's right to tax the moneylenders even if it had tried.
39. Tanuma, "Muromachi bakufu zaisei," p. 14.
40. MBL no. 179 (1425/9/26), *CHS*, vol. 2, p. 66; MBL no. 181 (1427/4/20), *CHS*, vol. 2, pp. 66–67.
41. MBL no. 204 (1433/10/3), *CHS*, vol. 2, p. 74.
42. MBL no. 288 (1485/7), *CHS*, vol. 2, p. 98; MBL no. 315 (1498/10/16), *CHS*, vol. 2, pp. 103–104.
43. MBL no. 346 (1508/8/7), *CHS*, vol. 2, p. 112.
44. MBL no. 347 (1508/8/7), *CHS*, vol. 2, pp. 112–113. Among the recipients of this document were Enryakuji envoys and monks as well as Shōren'in priests, which pretty well covers all major parties at Enryakuji who might have commercial dealings or contact with the moneylenders. Other recipients included Kōfukuji monks, wealthy peasants of Settsu province and Sakai, and several warriors.
45. MBL no. 349 (1508/9/16), *CHS*, vol. 2, p. 114.
46. MBL no. 380 (1511/3/23), *CHS*, vol. 2, p. 122. The two aristocratic families holding the Distillery Office stipend (*mikinotsukasa*) could also be included here, although they were rather minor *kenmon*. This document is problematic and other interpretations are possible: these may be new *sake* brewers/retailers bringing their product into the city in violation of long-established guild monopolies. Logically, Enryakuji would not have undercut its own brewers, but if their number had

diminished during the Ōnin War, the monastery might have sought out new ones to tax. In the post-Ōnin period *sake* retail shops proliferated in Kyoto as the production and retail processes were separated. This became a problem for brewers and overlords alike when non-Kyoto *sake* brewers brought their product into the city.

47. *KM* no. 7 (1419/9/12), pp. 5–6. This controversy is discussed in detail below.
48. Wakita Haruko suggests the latter, doubting that the Bakufu's strength was sufficient to deny completely Enryakuji's control of the moneylenders. Wakita, "Ryōshu keizai," p. 284.
49. Wakita Haruko cites the role of Enryakuji's western branch in the malt disturbance as an indirect sign of the monastery's continuing control over aspects of Kyoto commerce. Wakita, "Ryōshu keizai," p. 284.
50. Kenkei's modus operandi is described in detail in the following section. *Shinjōin monjo*, 1434/12/5, 1453/4/24, 1467/intercalary/15.
51. Gokashiwabara Tennō Nyobō hōsho (1511/6/4), *Tateiri Munetsugu monjo*, pp. 87–88. The entire case is related in this document written by female imperial attendants responsible for such matters. There appears to be no other documentation of the case.
52. See Tateiri family genealogy, *Tateiri Munetsugu monjo*, p. 257.
53. See, for instance, a mid-fifteenth-century document in which Hie Shrine exempts some moneylenders from its festival tax but states that others shall pay as usual. Hie bajōyaku sajō (1453/4/24), *Shinjōin monjo*.
54. Wakita, "Ryōshu keizai," p. 283. The tax was called the *bajōyaku*.
55. See Conclusion for a discussion of these sources, the *Yase dōjikai monjo*.
56. "Kaisetsu, " *Yase dōjikai monjo*, pp. 15–18.
57. *Yase dōjikai monjo* no. 246 (Kosatsukie gusoku tachi chūmon, 1429–1454), pp. 276–284. This is a list of armor and swords submitted to Hie Shrine by Kyoto merchants for the festival.
58. *Yase dōjikai monjo* no. 205 (Hōjubōtō rencho chūshinjō an, 1469/5), p. 258.
59. *Yase dōjikai monjo* no. 239 (undated fragment), pp. 273–274. Four hundred and ninety-four *kanmon* in brewery taxes were collected from thirty-eight individuals, or an average of 13 *kanmon* per business. Of sixteen lenders submitting tax, twelve were small operations submitting an average of 3.5 *kanmon* each, while two large operations submitted 12.5 *kanmon* each and two medium businesses submitted 6.5 *kanmon* each .
60. *Yase dōjikai monjo* no. 237 (Ukezaka chūmon, undated fragment), pp. 272–273. On this roster of eleven branch breweries, taxes range from 500 *mon* to 2.5 *kanmon* each.
61. *Yase dōjikai monjo* no. 244 (Bakufu shōgunke migyōsho addressed to Hie jinin, 1389/4/17), p. 276.
62. *Yase dōjikai monjo* no. 245 (Hie jininshū kishōmon, 1416/4/26), p. 276. There could have been more signatories; the last part of this document is missing.
63. *Yase dōjikai monjo* no. 202 (Inō Eishō hanmotsu, 1445/4), p. 257.
64. *Yase dōjikai monjo* no. 203 (Bōkinseian, 1457/4/20), pp. 257–258.
65. The shogunate was involved in this process, for its confirmation of *jinin* status was accepted by Enryakuji as proof. See *Yase dōjikai monjo* no. 207 (Muromachi bakufu bugyōnin hōsho, 1469/6/15), p. 259. In this document a shogunal official confirms to Hie Shrine that a merchant is affiliated with Kasuga.

66. *Yase dōjikai monjo* no. 226 (Bō mōshijō, undated fragment detailing the case), no. 235 (Hie jinin zaisho sho, undated fragment, stating the case and that Sawamura shall continue to pay Hie's tax).

67. *Yase dōjikai monjo* no. 209 (Bajō isshū zasshō mōshijō an, 1472/intercalary/14), p. 260. Examination of this individual was complicated by the fact that he had taken up residence in a warrior encampment in the city as the Ōnin War unfolded.

68. *Yase dōjikai monjo* no. 203 (Bōkinseian, 1457/4/20), pp. 257–258.

69. See, for example, *Yase dōjikai monjo* no. 291 (Sahō shojikisōchū mōshijō an, 1509/8), pp. 310–311, which states that because of the Ōnin War, for the past forty years it has been impossible to collect the Hie Shrine festival tax. See also no. 294 (Zenjūbō Shōsō shojō, no year/3/14), pp. 311–312, in which one of Zenjūbō's collectors states that the merchants who paid as a group now have no ability to pay (*muriki munō*).

70. *Yase dōjikai monjo* no. 290 (Muromachi bakufu bugyōnin hōsho an, 1493/12/3, 1493/12/9), p. 310. Stressing that the spring festival must be revived, the shogunate decried continued nonpayment of tax by the brewer-lenders and appointed Sawamura and Nakamura, two prominent secular lenders, to the job of collecting. By implication the traditional *santo* tax agents had been ineffective.

71. *Yase dōjikai monjo* no. 287 (Bajō isshū mōshijō an, 1484/6), pp. 308–309. This document detailing claims of exemptions and the lack of supporting documentation mentions both the Hie tax and the Gion tax, payable by the Kyoto lenders.

72. No. 2239 (Muromachi bakufu bugyō hōsho an, 1478/11/16) *Yasaka jinja monjo*, p. 1006. Shogunal officials support Gion's right to tax the brewer-lenders in this document, in which they demand that such merchants stop claiming to be Ōyamazaki *jinin* and pay the tax starting on the fifteenth of the following month.

73. No. 2169 (*Gionshaki*, 1500/6/6), *Muromachi bakufu bugyōnin hōsho*, vol. 1, p. 613.

74. Wakita, "Ryōshu keizai," p. 284.

75. Ibid.

76. Toyoda, "Enryakuji sansō," pt. 2, p. 2, characterizes the monastery as an institution in decline even in the fourteenth century, with the warriors on the rise.

77. Kurushima, "Sengokuki no shukikuyaku," pp. 56–115. Kurushima has meticulously analyzed the *Oshikōji monjo*, documents of the Nakahara/Oshikōji family, and the *Konishi Yasuoshi shozō monjo* to produce a detailed picture of the collection of the Distillery Office tax during the sixteenth century. There is considerable overlap between the two collections of documents, but the latter contains more on the sixteenth century.

78. And rewarding them handsomely: one got one-third of the take and stayed on beyond his three-year term. But in 1512, with shogunal approval, a new collector was installed. (Kurushima, "Sengokuki no shukikuyaku," pp. 81–82). Kamematsu proved a most successful overseer, however, lasting in the job at least until 1540. See entry for 1540/2/29 in *Ōdate Jōkō nikki*, which states that Hayata Kamematsu has been serving as overseer since 1511, in *Zōho zokushiryō taisei*, vol. 15, p. 231.

79. Kurushima, "Sengokuki no shukikuyaku," pp. 86–87.

80. Ibid., p. 96.

81. This possibility is suggested by Kurushima, ibid., pp. 96–97.

82. Ibid., pp. 95, 100, 106. It is not clear what happened between the bankruptcy of 1529 and the family's reappointment in 1538, but the overseer Kamematsu's survival through at least 1540, described above, suggests continuity.

83. Large-scale bribery was one of the few offenses punishable by death under Muromachi law. See article 10 of the *Kemmu Shikimoku* (1336/11/7), *CHS*, vol. 2, pp. 5–6. Apparently, however, this did not apply to the petty, everyday variety.

84. ". . . Even though there may be emergency expenses, the moneylenders are perpetually exempted from emergency levies by temples, shrines, or the Bakufu." MBL no. 148 (1393/11/6), *CHS*, vol. 2, p. 60.

85. Shimosaka, "Chūsei dosōron," p. 247.

86. MBL no. 168 (1422/7/26), *CHS*, vol. 2, p. 64.

87. No. 293: "Ashikaga Yoshitaka genpukura yōkyaku shakuyōsen jōjō jisho" (1494?/11/14?), *Ninagawake monjo*, vol. 2, pp. 60–61. (Yoshizumi was known as Yoshitaka as a youth.) See also MBL no. 305 (1494/11/14), *CHS*, vol. 2, p. 101, on Yoshizumi's coming-of-age ceremony.

88. Kurokawa, "Doikki no jidai," p. 346, quoting a passage in the *Ōninki*, a chronicle of the Ōnin War whose date and author are unknown.

89. Kurokawa, "Doikki no jidai," p. 346. The funeral was for a member of the Takakura family.

90. MBL no. 378 (1511/3/23), *CHS*, vol. 2, p. 121.

91. This is generally understood, though rarely specified in sources, for obvious reasons. It is called *goreimotsu*. (One example is *Shinjōin monjo* [1482/intercalary 7/11].)

92. MBL no. 233 (1445/9/29), *CHS*, vol. 2, p. 82.

93. *Shinjōin monjo* (1434/12/5).

94. *Shinjōin monjo* (1453/4/24).

95. *Shinjōin monjo* (1467/intercalary/15).

96. *Ninagawake monjo* no. 72 (1474/10/6), vol. 1, pp. 135–136.

97. *Ninagawake monjo* no. 305 (undated, probably 1495), vol. 2, pp. 77–82.

98. MBL no. 349 (1508/9/16), *CHS*, vol. 2, p. 114, decries using exemptions as an excuse to evade taxes: *no one* may do this; though it states that a list of exemptees is attached, none survives. MBL no. 379 (1511/3/23), *CHS*, vol. 2, p. 121, decries tax evasion by *sake* retailers.

99. *Ninagawake monjo* no. 540 (1539/12), vol. 3, pp. 60–61.

100. *Ninagawake monjo* no. 540 (1539/12), vol. 3, pp. 60–61, contains the word *"onkuhei,"* which may refer to a bribe. See note 25, above, for a discussion of the possible interpretations of this term.

101. *Shinjōin monjo* (*ukebumi anmon*, 1482/5).

102. *Shinjōin monjo* (1482/6).

103. *Shinjōin monjo* (1482/5).

104. *Shinjōin monjo* (1482/intercalary 7/11).

105. *Tateiri Munetsugu monjo*, nos. 3–10 of gohōsho gechijō section, pp. 87–92. These confirmations and copies of confirmations are dated over the course of the sixteenth century and were issued by shogunal and imperial officials, and Oda Nobunaga.

106. This is not to suggest that bribery as a political problem began in the late medieval period. One of the first laws of the Muromachi Bakufu was to prohibit large-scale

bribery, and it specifies that it is "not a new law," and that the shogun must strongly enforce it (Article 10, *Kemmu Shikimoku* [1336/11/7], *CHS*, vol. 2, pp. 5–6). So concerned was the Bakufu with this problem that officials who took even small bribes were to be excluded from office, while large bribes would be punished with execution. This is one of only four references to the death penalty in all of Muromachi law (see further discussion of the death penalty in my Conclusion). Though enforcement is hard to document, the threat of punishment alone is a good indirect indication that bribery was, indeed, widespread.

107. I am indebted to Anne Walthall for her insightful comments on bribery in other historical contexts: in British India ("old corruption"), in nineteenth-century Germany, and in the Chinese bureaucracy. She also pointed out the correlation between factors like low salary and the lack of a role of birth in official appointments, on the one hand, and the prevalence of bribery, on the other. (The factor of low salary increasingly obtained in late medieval Japanese officialdom, while birth played a role in the sense that officials tended to hold Bakufu office hereditarily.) Likewise, she noted the advantages to the corrupters of the corrupting: bribe-taking officials in the shogunate may have enriched themselves well beyond the level of their stipends (Walthall's comments as discussant, panel on medieval commoners at the Association for Asian Studies Annual Meeting, Chicago, April 8, 1990). Indeed, in late medieval Japan, bribery, as long as it did not proliferate to the point of bankrupting an overlord, benefited the bribe takers (by supplementing their income and extending the life of their weakened institution), the bribe givers (who stayed within the system but got a tax break), and, in a weak way, the system itself (which was not onerous enough for taxpayers to be sufficiently motivated to make a clean break away).

108. MBL no. 350 (1508/9/16), *CHS*, vol. 2, pp. 114–115. Day lenders usually dealt in loans of 100 *mon* or less.

109. I am indebted to Anne Walthall for this insight. This interpretation, emphasizing the moneylenders' long-standing tie to the overlords, downplays without denying the moneylenders' growing independence as townspeople.

110. Information on the Kitano malt guild is derived from Ono, "Kitano kōjiza"; Wakita, "Ryōshu keizai," pp. 284–293, and "Dosō to bōeki," pp. 238–241; Yamamura, "The Development of Za," pp. 451–454, and "The Growth of Commerce," pp. 389–391. In the latter source (p. 389), Yamamura sees the malt guild's fate as an illustration of the effects of changing political circumstances on commerce and on guilds.

111. Yoshimochi issued four decrees prohibiting *sake* consumption between 1419 and 1421. Two were aimed specifically at Zen priests, while another banned consumption of *sake* by all residents in the vicinity of a Zen temple, and the fourth extended the ban to his own vassals, who were not to drink in the presence of his teenaged son, Yoshikazu. The latter became shogun at the age of sixteen in 1423, but died only two years later, supposedly of debauchery. But this commonly accepted character judgment is based solely on Yoshimochi's prohibition decree to his vassals, which may be more a reflection of Yoshimochi's own strong religious leanings than of his son's behavior. This matter is discussed at length in Shimizu Katsuyuki, "Ashikaga Yoshimochi no kinshurei ni tsuite," pp. 36–39.

112. Shibata, "Jinja to minkan shinkō," *KR*, vol. 2, p. 396.

113. *KM* no. 3 (1379/9/20), p. 3. See discussion of the Distillery Office tax in the pre-

vious section. Yamamura dates shogunal "taxation" (characterized in the present study as a bribe) of Kitano in return for shogunal support of the guild from 1388. Yamamura, "The Growth of Commerce," p. 389. Umata Ayako offered me the opinion that a bribe was behind the shogunate's actions, and this seems firmly in line with established medieval practice.

114. *KM* no. 4 (1387/9/16), pp. 3–4.

115. Yamamura, "The Development of Za," p. 452, and "The Growth of Commerce," p. 390.

116. *KM* no. 7 (1419/9/12), pp. 5–6.

117. Ibid.; *KM* no. 8 (1419/9/14), p. 6. The latter is an order addressed to "Isshiki Sakyō Dayu," who was also head of the Board of Retainers, but this title refers to his position as military governor of Yamashiro province.

118. *KM* nos. 10–61 (1419/10/3), pp. 7–34. Many of the pledges were cosigned by townspeople guarantors, who were to see to it that the pledge was not broken. This delegation of responsibility to prominent townspeople by the shogunate suggests that they enjoyed great prestige and respect in the city's social structure. See also Wakita, "Dosō to bōeki," pp. 238–239, for more on this document.

119. Shimizu, "Ashikaga Yoshimochi no kinshurei ni tsuite," p. 41.

120. *KM* no. 62 includes 325 names for 1425/11/10 (pp. 34–46), and twenty-two appended in 1426/2/16 (p. 46). Each entry includes the name of the brewery and its location. See Appendix, no. 1 for the names by categories, and Chapter 1, "The Business of Lending Money," above, for an analysis of the names. As discussed earlier, this is the first documentary indication since the Muromachi shogunate's supposed denial of overlord rights in 1393 that traditional taxation by Enryakuji (in this case by its subsidiary, Kitano Shrine) was continuing. Wakita, "Ryōshu keizai," p. 284.

121. According to the aristocrat Hirohashi Kanenobu, holder of half of the Distillery Office sinecure and therefore in a position to be concerned about the matter, Kitano's monopoly on malt had caused the price of rice in Ōmi province to drop drastically, nearly ruining the packhorse drivers' livelihood (Wakita, "Dosō to bōeki," p. 240, referring to an entry in *Kanenobu kyōki*). Sakamoto is located in Ōmi province, east of Kyoto.

122. Shimizu, "Ashikaga Yoshimochi no kinshurei," p. 42, referring to an entry in *Kanenobu kyōki*.

123. Ibid., p. 43, discusses the possible reasons for the shogunal enforcement of the malt monopoly, tying it to simultaneous prohibitions of liquor consumption.

124. Ibid., p. 47.

125. Kozo Yamamura has interpreted this incident as illustrative of the guilds' growing need for warrior support with the decline of the estate system and its traditional overlords, aristocratic and religious (Yamamura, "The Development of Za," pp. 451–453). This may have been true of some areas of Japan, but in Kyoto warriors, including the shogun, *in addition to* traditional overlords, were demanding taxes of guilds. Yamamura does not mention the actions of the Enryakuji priests in the matter, giving the impression that only the shogunate and the guild were involved (ibid., pp. 451–453). In "The Growth of Commerce," pp. 389–391, Yamamura revised his earlier thesis somewhat, this time to acknowledge that Enryakuji still wielded some influence.

126. *KM* no. 85–99, pp. 75–84. All are either dated 1545 or can be placed roughly in the 1540s.
127. *KM* no. 86 (1545/8/3, order from Saitō of Enryakuji to *jinin* of Kitano Shrine to produce malt only under guild auspices), p. 75; *KM* no. 87 (1545/8/7, order from Muromachi Bakufu administrators to Kitano *jinin* living in western Kyoto), pp. 75–76.
128. *KM* no. 88 (1545/8/7, Bakufu order addressed to brewer-lenders of upper and lower Kyoto), pp. 76–77. Note also *KM* no. 89 (1545/8/7), p. 77, which repeats the same order of no. 88, except to brewer-lenders in the outskirts of Kyoto (Rakugai), possibly subordinate to Zen temples in outlying areas.
129. Document dated 1545 and cited in Ono, "Kitano kōjiza," pp. 21–22.
130. *KM* no. 98 (1546/11/27), p. 83.
131. *KM* no. 112 (1561/9/2), pp. 94–95.
132. Ono, "Kitano kōjiza," pp. 24–25.
133. See discussion of the Nakahara/Oshikōji family's post-Ōnin "comeback" as an overlord earlier in this section.
134. Clouding the picture is a communication from officials of Enryakuji's three branches (east, west, and Yokawa) instructing the Kitano malt guild members that the shogunate has exempted them from all taxes except the Kitano Shrine malt tax (*KM*, no. 96 [1545/10/1], pp. 81–82). This document refers to the malt tax of western Kyoto as the *former* domain of Saitō, the western branch, suggesting that Enryakuji no longer had control over it.

CHAPTER FOUR: RESPONDING TO SIEGE

1. Studies of *tokusei ikki* include: *Ikki* (5 vols.); Hayashiya, *Machishū*; Imatani, *Dōmin gōgō* (on the Kakitsu uprising of 1441); Inagaki, *Nihon chūsei shakaishiron*, pp. 300–310; Kasamatsu, *Tokuseirei*; Katsumata, *Ikki*; Kurokawa, "Chūsei kōki no nōmin tōsō—I. Doikki, "Kuni ikki," "Doikki no jidai," and "Tokusei ikki no takamari"; Murata, "Sō to doikki"; Nagahara, *Gekokujō no jidai*, pp. 99–102; Nakamura, *Doikki kenkyū*; Sasaki, *Muromachi Bakufu*, pp. 178–203; Shimosaka, "Chūsei dosōron" and "Machishū no seikatsu," pp. 70–84; Suzuki, *Nihon chūsei no nōmin mondai*; and Umata, "Doikki no soshikisei to shitokusei." In English, see Berry, *The Culture of Civil War*, pp. 89–93, and Davis, "Ikki in Late Medieval Japan."
2. On terminology, see Katsumata Shizuo, "Tokusei," *KDJ*, vol. 10, pp. 311–312.
3. For a discussion of *sō* in English, see Tonomura, *Community and Commerce*, pp. 42–46.
4. Kurokawa, "Doikki no jidai," p. 411.
5. See Chapter 1, "The Business of Lending Money," above, for a discussion of attempts by the shogunate to regulate interest rates.
6. Kurokawa, "Doikki no jidai," pp. 334–336. See Gay, "The Kawashima," p. 108, on detecting moneylending by season—i.e., winter and spring land accumulation by moneylenders.
7. Nagahara, "Kahei to dosō," pp. 47–53, on the pervasive presence of moneylenders on estates near Kyoto. Monks at landowning temples were typically sent out to do estate duty at some point in their careers. A typical example is Meisai of Tōji,

who returned to Kyoto in 1396 with enough personal wealth to engage in money-lending as well as temple administration. Itō, "Kin'yūgyō wo fukugyō ni suru jisō," p. 30.

8. Nagahara, *Muromachi Sengoku no shakai*, p. 54.

9. Using aristocratic and clerical diary entries, Imatani Akira has listed points of attack by the *ikki* forces around the periphery of the city, asserting that this uprising focused mainly on moneylending by Zen temples, especially Tenryūji. See Imatani, *Domin gōgō*, pp. 125–141. As mentioned earlier, the Kyoto *gozan* establishment was deeply involved in moneylending, but especially to temples more than to individual lenders. Imatani does not dwell on the fact that uprisings, including the one in 1441, invaded Kyoto proper, not just its periphery, attacking moneylenders in the city. Some of the diarists he quotes were writing from villas on the city's periphery; hence their observation of league activities in those areas.

10. Kurokawa Naonori, "Tokusei ikki," *KDJ*, vol. 10, p. 312.

11. Nagahara Keiji acknowledges that direct indebtedness to Kyoto lenders by area peasants may not have been widespread and is in any case very difficult to prove. Nagahara, *Muromachi Sengoku no shakai*, p. 65.

12. Kurokawa, "Doikki no jidai," pp. 288ff., assigns such strategizing acumen to the *ikki*. He also notes (p. 349) that peasant leagues commonly put Kyoto temples and shrines to the torch when amnesties were not forthcoming. He takes this as an indication that their ultimate target was the overlord class.

13. Kurokawa asserts that once storehouses were forced open during league invasions, pawned items were routinely returned not only to peasant debtors but to aristocrats and clerics as well. Kurokawa, "Tokusei kinsei," *KDJ*, vol. 10, p. 313.

14. Kurokawa cites one incident in the Shōchō uprising in which townspeople onlookers, not rural league members, burned a moneylender's premises as the proprietor attempted to negotiate with league members ("Doikki no jidai," p. 262). He presents this as evidence that the leagues themselves were not bent on destroying the moneylenders, but only on procuring an amnesty. There are enough other examples of destruction and looting by leagues, however, to make this characterization of league members as cool-headed strategists hard to accept.

15. Sasaki, *Muromachi Bakufu*, p. 179, quoting *Mansai jugō nikki*, entry for 1428/9/18.

16. On the course of this *ikki*, see Sasaki, *Muromachi Bakufu*, p. 179.

17. On *shitokusei*, see Umata, "Doikki no soshikisei to shitokusei."

18. Sasaki, *Muromachi Bakufu*, pp. 179–180.

19. Kurokawa, "Doikki no jidai," p. 261, quoting *Daijōin nikki mokuroku*.

20. From chronological table in Kurokawa, "Doikki no jidai," p. 411.

21. As part of the *ikki* fallout, some 40 percent of all Bakufu laws concern moneylending—210 out of 542, most of them to regulate lending in response to an *ikki*; 138 of these laws are post-Ōnin, by which time, as discussed below, the shogunate had devised a way to turn *ikki* demands to its own economic benefit.

22. Kurokawa notes that there was no precedent for amnesties at a shogunal, as opposed to imperial, succession and rejects any claim that an amnesty was issued by the shogunate in 1428, which was also the beginning of a shogun's reign. One source, the *Kōya kenkō chō*, refers to an amnesty in that year when the Emperor

Shōkō died and was succeeded by Emperor Gohanazono. No other source corroborates such an occurrence. Kurokawa, "Doikki no jidai," p. 276.

23. The diary *Kennaiki* reports some tens of thousands of *ikki* members, though the citation of such large numbers was most likely a literary flourish made by its shaken author. Kurokawa, "Tokusei ikki," *KDJ*, vol. 10, p. 312.

24. Kurokawa, "Doikki no jidai," quoting *Tōji shigyō nikki*, p. 286. Again, the numbers should be taken taken with a grain of salt. The leagues were attacking temples and shrines as well as neighborhoods.

25. Shimosaka, "Machishū no seikatsu," p. 76.

26. Ibid., p. 77.

27. Sasaki, *Muromachi Bakufu*, p. 182.

28. Murata, "Sō to doikki," p. 146.

29. MBL no. 212 (1441/9/12), *CHS*, vol. 2, p. 78, is the announcement of the amnesty that was posted publicly in Kyoto.

30. MBL nos. 213–221 (1441/9/10), *CHS*, vol. 2, pp. 78–79, contain the terms of the amnesty itself, dated two days earlier than the public announcement of them. The twenty-year loan period was in emulation of a Kamakura Bakufu amnesty for warriors.

31. Zen temple loans were usually set at about 24 percent, a much lower rate of interest than the 60 percent or more charged by moneylenders.

32. *Kinna kōki* (diary of Saionji Kinna, with entries from 1410 to 1468, incorporated into this aristocratic family's chronicle, the *Kankenki*), entry for 1441/intercalary 9/20, records Enryakuji's protest regarding the amnesty's application to land held in perpetuity. *CHS*, vol. 2, p. 307.

33. MBL no. 224 (1441), *CHS*, vol. 2, p. 80. Delinquency meant specifically that the twenty-year loan period had expired before the debt was repaid. The mention of a twenty-year loan was in emulation of the terms of a Kamakura Bakufu debt amnesty for warriors. See Hayashima, "Kyōto kinkō ni okeru eitaibaibaichi no anteika," on shogunal debt amnesty policy regarding such land and the effects on its accumulation in the fifteenth century.

34. Kurokawa makes this point in "Doikki no jidai," pp. 276–277.

35. Ibid., pp. 352–354.

36. Kurokawa, "Ōnin-Bunmei no tairan," p. 310.

37. *Tokusei kinsei*, a decree forbidding *ikki* uprisings and denying an amnesty, was first issued by the shogunate during the 1428 uprising in an attempt to stop the attacks. MBL no. 188(1428/11/22), *CHS*, vol. 2, p. 69.

38. Kurokawa Naonori, "Tokusei ikki," *KDJ*, vol. 10, p. 313.

39. Kurokawa Naonori characterizes this unprecedentedly wanton destructiveness as indicative of laxness creeping into the *ikki* movement. Kurokawa, "Doikki no jidai," p. 359.

40. See Keirstead, "Fragmented Estates," pp. 311–330, on *kajishi* and the split in rural society.

41. Kurokawa, "Doikki no jidai," pp. 362–363, citing a *kishōmon* response to a shogunal communication to Nishigaoka peasants.

42. Kurokawa, "Doikki no jidai," p. 377.

43. Shimosaka, "Machishū no seikatsu," p. 77, quoting *Nobutane kyōki*.

44. The course of this *ikki* is described in Nakamura, *Doikki no kenkyū*, pp. 268–274,

and Kurokawa, "Doikki no jidai," pp. 356–357, both drawing heavily from *Kyōgaku shiyōshō*, a clerical diary.

45. Shimosaka, "Machishū no seikatsu," p. 77, quoting *Yamashinake raiki*, 1457/10/27 entry.
46. Ibid.
47. Ibid., p. 78.
48. Evidence of this dislike is found in the Kyōgen play "Kujizainin," in which a rich man, a moneylender appointed to organize the Gion festival, is ridiculed by Kyoto townspeople. "Kujizainin," pp. 141–151.
49. Kurokawa Naonori insists on the stratification of the townspeople during peasant invasions. That is, the upper stratum of commoners, made up of moneylenders, was threatened by the *ikki* and fought back. The rest of the commoners did not, he maintains, and indeed passively supported the *ikki*, whose demand for debt cancellation was very appealing. Kurokawa, "Doikki no jidai," p. 349. Hayashiya Tatsusaburō is at the other extreme, hailing the cooperative defense of the city by the townspeople as the unifying factor that ended the division between moneylenders and other townspeople. Hayashiya, *Machishū*, pp. 102–104. There is definitive proof for neither viewpoint.
50. Kurokawa, "Doikki no jidai," p. 357.
51. The course of this *ikki* is described in ibid., pp. 370–371.
52. Ibid., p. 371, quoting *Hekizan nichiroku*.
53. Ibid.
54. Hayashiya cites the defense of the city against *ikki* invaders as the occasion for moneylender absorption into the *machi* neighborhoods. Hayashiya, "Kyoto in the Muromachi Age," p. 29.
55. On structures erected by townspeople for self-defense and other purposes, especially from the Ōnin War through the sixteenth century, see Takahashi, "Ōnin no ran to Kyōto no toshi kūkan"; Imatani, "Monzen kendan to kuginuki," in *Sengokuki no Muromachi Bakufu*; and Shimosaka, "Kyōto no fukkō."
56. Berry, *The Culture of Civil War*, p. 91.
57. On *buichi tokusei*, see Kuwayama, "Muromachi jidai no tokusei"; Kuwayama, "Kaisetsu," *Muromachi bakufu hikitsuke shiryōshūsei*, vol. 2, pp. 9–15; and Momose, "Bunmei jūninen tokusei kinsei."
58. *Saitō Mototsune nikki*, 1441/intercalary 9 entry, refers to the cessation of shogunal storehouse taxes as a result of this debt amnesty. *CHS*, vol. 2, p. 307. Kuwayama Kōnen states that these taxes ceased for about six months in "Buichi tokusei," *KDJ*, vol. 12, p. 8. He also links the amnesty-induced reduction of shogunal income from moneylenders to the increasingly frequent incidental levies on them by the shogun. See Kuwayama, "Kaisetsu," *Muromachi bakufu hikitsuke shiryō shūsei*, pp. 8–9.
59. MBL no. 239 (1454/10?/29), *CHS*, vol. 2, pp. 84–85.
60. MBL no. 255 (1455/10/2), *CHS*, vol. 2, p. 88. See also Kuwayama Kōnen, "Tokusei kinsei," *KDJ*, vol. 10, p. 313, for an explanation of this sequence of events.
61. MBL no. 257 (1457/12/5), *CHS*, vol. 2, p. 89.
62. Debt amnesties were issued in 1457, 1480, 1504, 1520, 1526, 1530, and 1546; all contained some type of conditional clause. Kuwayama, "Kaisetsu," *Muromachi bakufu hikitsuke shiryō shūsei*, p. 10.

63. An application accompanied by payment of a portion of the debt had to be submitted to the Board of Inquiry (*hikitsukekata*), the shogunate's organ of adjudication. *Muromachi bakufu hikitsuke shiryō shūsei*, vol. 2, is in large part a collection of such documents pertaining to debt amnesties.

64. Kuwayama, "Kaisetsu," *Muromachi bakufu hikitsuke*, p. 10.

65. And sometimes even when it was not. Mary Elizabeth Berry claims that the debt amnesty of 1480 was unrelated to any uprising (*The Culture of Civil War*, p. 92). There was a large uprising in 1480; a conditional debt amnesty was issued only *after* it was quelled, however, and the sole beneficiary of this amnesty was the shogunate. Kurokawa, "Doikki no jidai," p. 394. Kenneth Grossberg refers to the conditional debt amnesty as "official extortion" (*The Laws of the Muromachi Bakufu*, p. 12).

66. MBL no. 258 (1457/12/5), *CHS*, vol. 2, p. 89.

67. Kurokawa, "Ōnin-Bunmei no tairan," pp. 311–312, referring to MBL no. 257 (1457/12/5), which offers moneylenders themselves an amnesty from their debts. The decree's term *"aisen,"* also pronounced *gōsen* or *gassen*, is interest paid by moneylenders on loans.

68. An example of this is a shogunal ruling in 1472 that a moneylender's debt of 23 *kanmon* was abolished by a debt amnesty. The ruling makes reference to a document of 1466, most likely the debt amnesty of that year. *Muromachi Bakufu bugyōnin hōsho* nos. 924–925 (*Yamashinake raiki*, 1472/11/24–25), vol. 1, pp. 259–260.

69. Figures calculated from *Muromachi bakufu hikitsuke shiryō shūsei*, vol. 2, pp. 6–42, documents recording applications after the 1480 debt amnesty. Pages 5–50 contain the record of debt amnesty applications from debtors during 1481–1486, while pp. 51–82 is a list of applications for the right to pursue debts from creditors from 1480 to 1485. The complexity and expense of the application process presumably account for the fact that some applications were not made until five or even six years after the 1480 debt amnesty. Berry gives a similar figure of 2,032 *kan* for the same period of collection, in *The Culture of Civil War*, p. 92.

70. Katsumata Shizuo, "Tokusei," *KDJ*, vol. 10, p. 312.

71. The first attack began on the twenty-third day of the eighth month and continued until the twentieth of the ninth month; the second stage lasted from the third day of the tenth month until the twenty-first day of the same month.

72. Kurokawa, "Doikki no jidai," pp. 393, quoting *Daijōin jisha zōjiki*.

73. Ibid.

74. Ibid., p. 294.

75. Kurokawa Naonori holds this opinion; see "Doikki no jidai," p. 411.

76. Ibid., pp. 262–263.

77. Ibid., p. 372, quoting the *Daijōin jisha zōjiki*. Kurokawa sees such warrior leadership of the uprisings as an undesirable development for the peasants, potentially subordinating their own goals to those of warriors.

78. Yokoi, "Tairan no naka no seikatsu," p. 333.

79. All examples are from Kurokawa, "Doikki no jidai," pp. 332–333. The refusal of a loan to Tokifusa took place on 1441/9/13. The entry about the shogun is found in *Yamashinake raiki*, entry for 1480/9/29.

80. On the Yamashiro uprising, in English see Berry, *The Culture of Civil War*, pp. 37–44.

81. The extent of damage to moneylenders can be indirectly ascertained. See, for instance, *Yase dōjikai monjo* no. 239 (undated fragment), pp. 273–274. In this document, the tax agent, Zenjūbō, collected Hie Shrine brewer taxes from thirty-eight merchants but storehouse taxes from only sixteen, suggesting that a debt amnesty was recently decreed, forcing lenders to rely on brewing until they recovered.

82. Studies of the Ōnin War include Inagaki, "Ōnin-Bunmei no ran"; Momose, "Ōnin-Bunmei no ran"; Nagashima, *Ōnin no ran*; and Nagahara, *Gekokujō no jidai*. Accounts in English of the Ōnin War include Berry, *The Culture of Civil War* and Varley, *The Ōnin War*. Berry concentrates on the course of the war in Kyoto, primarily from the perspective of aristocratic diarists. Varley's study is a comprehensive account of the war from a warrior perspective, based especially on the *Ōninki*, a chronicle.

83. See Tonomura, *Community and Commerce*, pp. 50–51. The Rokkaku *shugo* of Ōmi province wrested control of land away from Enryakuji during the Ōnin War. In 1491 Shogun Yoshitane reconquered Ōmi as his own land (*goryōkoku*), and he returned some land to the original overlords. Nevertheless, the net loss was considerable.

84. Information specifically on the Ōnin War in Kyoto is drawn from Inagaki Yasuhiko, "Ōnin-Bunmei no ran," *KDJ*, vol. 2, pp. 466–469; Kurokawa Naonori, "Ōnin-Bunmei no ran," *NDJ*, vol. 1, pp. 985–988; Shimosaka, "Machishū no seikatsu" pp. 85–118 and 119–137; Kurokawa, "Ōnin-Bunmei no tairan," pp. 305–332; Yokoi, "Tairan no naka no seikatsu," pp. 333–352.

85. Yokoi, "Tairan no naka no seikatsu," p. 338, referring to a 1467/5/29 entry in *Daijōin jisha zōjiki*.

86. Yokoi, "Tairan no naka no seikatsu," p. 338.

87. Ibid., quoting *Ōninki*. Thirty thousand was probably a way of saying "many," but the chroniclers' hyperbole also conveys a sense of shock at the violent turn of events.

88. Ibid., p. 340, quoting the *Ōninki*.

89. Ibid., p. 347, quoting an entry of 1470/6/10 in the *Chikanaga kōki*.

90. Ibid., pp. 339–340, quoting *Daijōin jisha zōjiki*, entry for 1471/1/1.

91. Ibid., p. 341.

92. Ibid., p. 338, quoting *Gochisokuin Fusatsuguki*, entry for 1467/6/21.

93. Ibid., pp. 340–341, quoting *Tōjishi–yōshū*, entry for 1470/2/26.

94. Ibid., p. 340, quoting *Kyōgaku shiyōshō*, diary of the priest Kyōgaku, entry for 1471/1/2.

95. Shimosaka, "Machishū no seikatsu," p. 122, quoting *Tōji nijūikku kata hyōjō hikitsuke*, entry for 1473/2/16. This incident at Tōji is notable in the context of the Ōnin War for the temple's slow response to a theft, but it is also an example of the arbitrary nature of the medieval "investigation and trial" process. Temple personnel and inhabitants of the precincts were obliged to sign an oath (*kishōmon*) swearing that they had not committed the crime in question. If a certain misfortune befell one of them after signing, it was taken as a indication that he or she had lied under oath and was guilty of the crime. Such misfortunes included, among other things: getting a nosebleed, becoming ill, having a bird defecate on one, choking on food, or bleeding from inside the body (excluding menstruation, hemorrhoids, or bleed-

ing from the mouth). This was in accordance with Kamakura law. See *Kamakura Bakufu Law* no. 73 (1235/intercalary 6/28), *CHS*, vol. 1, pp. 94–95. For more on medieval law, see Amino, *Chūsei no tsumi to batsu*.

96. Yokoi, "Tairan no naka no seikatsu," p. 346. Yokoi characterizes this as a send-off of the war, as well, by the townspeople participants.

97. Ibid., pp. 347–348, quoting the *Tōji shugyō nikki*.

98. Ibid., p. 348, quoting the *Daijōin jisha zōjiki* entry for 1475/7/8.

99. Ibid., referring to entries in the *Sanetaka kōki*.

100. Ibid., p. 351, quoting the 1476/7/8 entry in *Sanetaka kōki*.

101. The culprit in this accidental fire was not a warrior but Baba Yoshirō, a moneylender from whose premises the fire spread, an incident related earlier in the context of the shogunate's tie to the moneylenders.

102. Yokoi, "Tairan no naka no seikatsu," p. 352, quoting the 1477/11/22 entry in *Sanetaka kōki*.

103. See Shimosaka, "Machishū no seikatsu," pp. 128–129, on the post-Ōnin recovery of Kyoto.

104. See Takahashi, *Rakuchū rakugai*, pp. 22–23.

105. *Shinjōin monjo* 1467/4. This document was written before the main fighting of the war, but enough had already occurred, perhaps, to prompt some townspeople to fortify their homes.

106. Shimosaka, "Machishū no seikatsu," p. 129, quoting *Chikanaga kōki*, entry for 1474/8/1, and *Sanetaka kōki*, entry for 1474/8/1, both references to the burning and rebuilding of the Tanaka neighborhood's fortified gate. Some of the wealthier moneylenders now had two-storey houses, as is reflected in the illustrated screens.

107. See Chapter 5, "Urban Affairs."

108. Shimosaka, "Machishū no seikatsu," p. 114, quoting *Gohōkōinki*, entries for 1500/ 6/7, 14.

109. John W. Hall stressed that the Muromachi Bakufu remained a viable though limited governing entity for the rest of the Muromachi period, although the office of shogun went into eclipse. Hall, "The Muromachi Bakufu," *CHJ*, vol. 3, p. 229.

110. Kuwayama, "The Bugyōnin System," p. 58.

111. Ibid., p. 62.

112. *Erizeni* is also pronounced *erisen* or *sensen*. For a discussion of currency regulations (*erizenirei*) and a convenient summary of related literature, see Takizawa Takeo, "Erizeni," *Chūseishi handobukku*, pp. 67–69. The Kamakura Bakufu also regulated currency, though very sporadically. Its actions, like those of the Muromachi shogunate, do not have the appearance of deliberate, long-term policy.

113. MBL no. 320 (1500/10), *CHS*, vol. 2, pp. 105–106.

114. MBL no. 334 (1505/10/10), *CHS*, vol. 2, p. 109.

115. MBL no. 335 (1506/3/2), *CHS*, vol. 2, p. 110.

116. MBL no. 336 (1506/7/11), *CHS*, vol. 2, p. 110–111.

117. MBL no. 344 (1506/7/22), *CHS*, vol. 2, p. 111

118. MBL no. 345 and 346 (1508/8/5), *CHS*, vol. 2, p. 112; no. 348 (1508/8/7, notice to post), *CHS*, vol. 2, p. 113.

119. MBL no. 347 (1508/8/7), *CHS*, vol. 2, pp. 112–113.

120. MBL nos. 360–362 (1509/intercalary 8/7), *CHS*, vol. 2, pp. 117–118; no. 362 contains the comment on prices rising.

121. MBL no. 372 (1510/12/17), *CHS*, vol. 2, p. 120.
122. MBL no. 373 (1510/12/17), *CHS*, vol. 2, p. 120.
123. MBL no. 374 (1510/12/17), *CHS*, vol. 2, p. 120.
124. MBL nos. 385 and 386 (1512/8/30), *CHS*, vol. 2, p. 123.
125. MBL no. 388 (1512/8/30), *CHS*, vol. 2, p. 123.
126. Yamamura, "The Growth of Commerce," pp. 385–388.
127. MBL no. 334 (1505/10/10, on execution and confiscation of residence), *CHS*, vol. 2, p. 109; and no. 389 (1512/8/30, on decapitation of males), *CHS*, vol. 2, pp. 123–124. The death penalty had been abolished in the Heian period, revived during the Hōgen Disturbance, and existed de facto but not de jure in the medieval period. Although rarely ordered by rulers, executions were common at the local level. Thus, regardless of the content of laws, medieval penal practice was arbitrary and brutal.
128. MBL no. 10 (1336/11/7), *CHS*, vol. 2, p. 15, and MBL no. 396 (1516), *CHS*, vol. 2, p. 126.
129. MBL no. 488 (1542/4/8), *CHS*, vol. 2, p. 141.
130. MBL nos. 486–488 (1542/4/8), *CHS*, vol. 2, p. 141; MBL no. 489 (1542/4/20), *CHS*, vol. 2, pp. 141–142; MBL no. 490 (1542/4/22), *CHS*, vol. 2, p. 142.
131. MBL no. 489 (1542/4/20), *CHS*, vol. 2, pp. 141–142.
132. No. 44 (*Daijōin jisha zōjiki*, entry for 1459/9/2), and no. 45 (*Hekizan nichiroku*, entry for 1459/9/7), *SKR*, vol. 3, p. 289.
133. Kurokawa, "Ōnin-Bunmei no tairan," p. 314.
134. Ibid., p. 313.
135. Kurokawa, "Doikki no jidai," p. 392.
136. Ibid., p. 393, quoting *Tōji nijūichi kukata hyōjō hikitsuke*.
137. No. 47 (*Daijōin jisha zōjiki*, entry for 1478/7/11), *SKR*, vol. 3, p. 290.
138. No. 48 (*Shigetaneki*, entry for 1480/9/11), *SKR*, vol. 3, p. 290.
139. Kurokawa, "Ōnin-Bunmei no tairan," p. 314; Wakita, "Shōgyō to machiza," p. 209. In all fairness, Tomiko's husband, Yoshimasa, was an incompetent shogun, and her "interference" probably shored up shogunal financial fortunes. Had the shogun behaved in the same way, he likely would not have been villainized as she has been.
140. No. 51 *Tōji hyakugō monjo*, *wa* section (entry for 1485/5/4), and no. 52 *Daijōin jisha zōjiki* (entry for 1485/5/5), *SKR*, vol. 3, p. 290.
141. No. 54 *Daijōin jisha zōjiki* (entry for 1487/6/22), *SKR*, vol. 3, p. 290.
142. No. *Gohōkōinki* (entry for 1499/9/6), *SKR*, vol. 3, p. 344.
143. No. 14 *Mandokorokata hikitsuke* (entry for 1516/6/2), *SKR*, vol. 3, p. 348.
144. *Hōkyōji monjo* (1498/8/18), vol. 2, no. 6; and *buninjō* (1498/?/?), vol. 2, no. 7, no. 8 of part 3. The tax is called *tana kuji*, literally a tax on the shelves of the cloth merchants. As in the previous case, documentation of this case is incomplete. Hōkyōji preserved the shogunate's judgment only. The dispute was between Minami Gosho and either the merchants themselves or another party with a conflicting claim to the tax.
145. Particularly during heavy fighting, many townspeople might have taken refuge in an encampment. See, for instance, *Yase dōjikai monjo*, no. 205 (Hōjubōtō rencho chūshinjō an, 1469/5), p. 258, which indicates that twelve brewers and two bathhouses (their proprietors, perhaps) were living in an encampment. Similarly, in

Yase dōjikai monjo no. 209 (Bajō isshū zasshō mōshijō an, 1472/intercalary 14), p. 260, Hie *jinin*, probably tax agents, inform the shogunate that a brewer under investigation for tax evasion is currently living in a warrior encampment, having taken refuge there from the warfare plaguing the city.

146. See, for example, a list of five brewers who paid an oil tax to Hie Shrine, in *Shin-jōin monjo* (1473/intercalary). Two of them are listed with Kyoto addresses, but with the notations added that one, Munetsugu, is "now in Kurama," and another, Akisada, is "now in Ichijōji," both northern suburbs where they had presumably fled because of the war. Their presence on Hie Shrine's tax rolls suggests that they were still in business, and also that the shrine, perhaps desperate for cash, was very persistent in pursuing them to their new addresses.

147. Nishimura Hiroko cites this incident, without mentioning a source, to illustrate how adultery by women was treated in medieval times. Nishimura, "Yometorikon e no ugoki," p. 107.

148. *KM* no. 62 (1425/11/10 and 1426/2/16).

149. *Shinjōin monjo* (1467/4), three lists of brewers who paid taxes to Hie Shrine. One is a list of ten brewers (and possibly other merchants) who paid taxes to Sekizan Shrine, a branch of Hie Shrine in Ōmi province. See Appendix, no. 2.

150. *Sō* is a general term implying *biku* status—i.e., having taken all 250 vows. *Shami* is a clerical term applied to one who has taken between 10 and 249 vows. In the late medieval period, the term *shami* described those who took the tonsure and had the appearance of monks, wearing priestly robes but marrying and not living in monasteries. By the time of the Ōnin War, the term *sō* was used so loosely that it could encompass *shami*. Definitions from Ōno Tatsunosuke, "Sō," *KDJ*, vol. 8 (1987), p. 506; "Shami," *KDJ*, vol. 7 (1986), p. 230; and "Zaike shami," *KDJ*, vol. 4, p. 1240.

151. An analysis of petitioners' names is found in the Appendix, no. 3. *Muromachi bakufu hikitsuke shiryō shūsei*, vol. 2, pp. 51–82, contains requests for loan confirmations from lenders, 1480–1485. The shogunal functionaries (*bugyōnin*) who processed these documents evolved over the Muromachi period from scribes or document technicians into, after the Ōnin War, administrators who handled litigation and even military matters for the shogun and deputy shogun. Imatani, "Kaisetsu," *Muromachi Bakufu monjo shūsei—bugyōnin hōsho*, pp. 3–4.

152. *Muromachi bakufu hikitsuke shiryō shūsei* no. 87, p. 71.

153. Ibid., no. 39, p. 61, and no. 69, p. 67.

154. *Ninagawake monjo* nos. 302–308. See Appendix, no. 4.

155. See Appendix, no. 5, for an analysis of names appearing on this list, see *Sakachū-mon* (1511/4/17), in Kurushima, "Sengokuki no shukikuyaku," pp. 75–77, Kurushima allows that this list, like those in the Ninagawa collection cited above, may be a document used by the Muromachi Bakufu's moneylender tax agents to collect shogunal taxes, and that somehow the Distillery Office's tax agent got hold of it. But she also points out that the small amounts collected suggest that it is a list of brewers taxed for the Distillery Office's malt tax. Kurushima, "Sengokuki no shukikuyaku," pp. 80–81.

156. *MBL* no. 317 (1500/9), *CHS*, vol. 2, p. 102.

157. *MBL* no. 350 (1508/9/16), *CHS*, vol. 2, pp. 114–115. This decree asserts that "original" moneylenders especially resented the evasion of taxes by other lenders claiming to be only brewers, bean-paste merchants, or day lenders.

158. MBL no. 379 (1511/3/23), *CHS*, vol. 2, p. 121.
159. Kurushima, "Sengokuki no shukikuyaku," pp. 88 and 92, suggests that new, small brewers tended to be found in upper Kyoto, and larger ones in lower. She interprets this as expansion by powerful large brewers through extended family operations. But she also allows that many new brewers of drastically differing sizes came into being in this age of boom and bust. In the 1511 list of brewers (Appendix, no. 5), there is one brewer, Uwashi, who has sixteen secondary operations run by relatives. This is not necessarily a post-Ōnin phenomenon, but it was only when surnames came into common use after Ōnin that it is clear in sources which brewers had family ties.
160. MBL no. 380 (1511/3/23), *CHS*, vol. 2, p. 122.
161. MBL no. 321 (1504/8/23), no. 352 (1509/4/22), and no. 364 (1510/8/13), *CHS*, vol. 2, pp. 106, 115, 118, decry bypassing the wholesale rice market. See also MBL nos. 393–395 (1516/12/14), *CHS*, vol. 2, p. 126, for an attempt to enforce monopolies of fish guilds.
162. This characterization of the post-Ōnin city can be found in Shimosaka, "Machishū no seikatsu," pp. 128–133.

CHAPTER FIVE: URBAN AFFAIRS

1. Hayashiya, "Kyoto in the Muromachi Age," p. 25.
2. Hayashiya, "Machishū no seiritsu" and *Machishū*; Imatani, *Tenbun Hokke no ran*; Seta, "Kinsei toshi seiritsushi josetsu"; Toyoda, "Toshi ni okeru sōteki ketsugō"; and Wakita, "Chūsei Kyōto no tochi shoyū." On Sakai in English, see Morris, "The City of Sakai and Urban Autonomy," and Watsky, "Commerce, Politics, and Tea."
3. See, for example, the works of Takahashi Yasuo and Niki Hiroshi.
4. See Berry, "The Culture of Civil War," pp. 46–47, for a convenient summary of the principal transitions in Kyoto's government from 1467 to 1568.
5. Tamai, "Toshi no keikaku to kensetsu," p. 77.
6. Shimosaka, "Machishū no seikatsu," p. 132, quoting *Tokitsugu kyōki*, entry for 1550/7/15.
7. The first documented case of *machi* clustering is in 1534, when the so-called six palace neighborhoods (*kinri rokuchōchō*) of upper Kyoto organized themselves. It is thought that others followed, with the phenomenon becoming widespread by mid-century. Tamai, "Toshi no keikaku to kensetsu," p. 74. In 1537 representatives of the five clusters in lower Kyoto brought monetary offerings to the shogun as New Year's greetings. Kawashima, "Chōgumi to kaisho," p. 232, quoting the 1537/1/3 entry of *Nentō gohairei sanpu ranshō no hikae*. Kinoshita Masao's study of the Tachiuri cluster of neighborhoods in upper Kyoto, home to Shōjitsubō and several other prominent moneylenders, asserts that such clusters existed from the Ōnin War. He judges this from the way names of neighborhoods were arranged together in sources at that time and characterizes them as military units, based on their backing of the Hosokawa in 1511. He traces their self-governing activities through the sixteenth century. Kinoshita, "Kyōto ni okeru machigumi no chiikiteki hatten," pp. 21–51. Niki Hiroshi, in disagreement with Kinoshita, Imatani, and others, sees neighborhood units as working together to solve disputes only from the mid-sixteenth century. He characterizes the neighborhood from this point as

an organ of independent self-government based, not on identification with a specific leader or authority, but on the abstract notion of public authority. Niki, "Chūkinsei ikōki no kenryoku to toshi minshū," pp. 41–43.

8. Yamashina Tokitsugu was the aristocrat who took such precautions, and he notes these incidents in his diaries. See Shimosaka, "Machishū no seikatsu," p. 129, quoting *Tokitsugu kyōki*, entries for 1527/11/27, 29, and 1527/12/1.

9. Shimosaka, "Machishū no seikatsu," p. 128.

10. Ibid., p. 130, quoting *Reisenchō kiroku*.

11. Ibid., quoting *Nihon kyōkaishi*.

12. *Rokuōin monjo* no. 60275 (1535/7/10).

13. Dobbins, *Jōdo shinshū*, pp. 112–117.

14. For political and religious background on the Lotus leagues' development and suppression, see Imatani, *Sengokuki no Muromachi Bakufu* and *Tenbun Hokke no ran*; Fujii Manabu, "Shinkyū Bukkyō no kyōsen," "Hokke ikki to 'chōgumi,'" "Hokke Ikki," *NDJ*, vol. 6, p. 184, and "Tenbun Hokke no ran," *KDJ*, vol. 9, p. 1015; Tsuji, *Nihon Bukkyōshi*, medieval vol. 5, pp. 154–163; Iwahashi, "Tenbun Hokke ran."

15. Fujii, "Shinkyū Bukkyō," pp. 134–138, includes details of such conflicts, including the use by Enryakuji of Gion Shrine's outcastes (*inujinin*) to battle the Lotus adherents.

16. Fujii, "Shinkyū Bukkyō," pp. 141–142.

17. For an example of a warrior embracing a "faith" sect, see *Rokuōin monjo* 7–317 (1547?/12/17) letter, which mentions that a vassal of the Isshiki family who died in battle in 1469 had previously given a piece of downtown land to the Ji temple Konrenji to cover his burial costs.

18. See Hayashiya, "Kyoto in the Muromachi Age," p. 31, and Toyoda, "Chūsei no toshi to shūkyō," p. 297, for the first specific assertion that the Lotus sect appealed to merchants particularly. Toyoda makes it clear, however, that merchants also supported non-Lotus temples: quoting the *Yasutomiki*, entry for 1447/6, he notes the substantial contribution of 1,200 *kanmon* from Kyoto merchants, led by moneylenders, for the commissioning of the main image at the Rokkakudō. Toyoda, "Chūsei no toshi to shūkyō," p. 288.

19. Shimosaka, "Machishū no seikatsu," p. 79, quoting the sectarian source *Nichizō monke bunsan yūraiki*.

20. Fujii, "Shinkyū Bukkyō," p. 140.

21. Ibid., p. 141. Such aloofness was unusual among Kyoto temples, which, as we have seen, tended to cooperate as well as compete in the medieval political order.

22. Fujii, "Hokke ikki to 'chōgumi,'" p. 545, quoting an entry in the *Gohōkōinki*.

23. Ibid., p. 541.

24. Ibid., pp. 544, 547.

25. Ibid., p. 547.

26. Yoshiharu's shogunate issued only three decrees during the years 1527 to 1533, a sign that it had ceased to function, for all practical purposes. Imatani, *Sengokuki no Muromachi bakufu*, p. 179. The decrees concern a debt amnesty in Kyoto and are all dated 1530/12/19. MBL nos. 480–482, *CHS*, vol. 2, pp. 139–140.

27. After it was destroyed in Yamashina, the Honganji was rebuilt in Ishiyama on the site of present-day Osaka castle. Harumoto attempted to destroy it again in the early months of 1533 with the aid of Lotus leagues, but he was unsuccessful. The

Honganji's great success in attracting members is sometimes attributed in part to its utilization of the existing self-governing village (*sōson*), the rural equivalent of the *machi* neighborhood unit whose utilization by the Lotus sect in Kyoto is credited by some with its spread.

28. In 1532 Rokkaku Sadayori was the sole supporter of exiled shogun Yoshiharu, and again in 1544 he mediated a dispute between Yoshiharu and Hosokawa Harumoto. In 1536 and 1546, he attempted to mediate disputes between Enryakuji and the Lotus sect. He failed the first time, but succeeded the second.

29. "Paying rent in Kyoto existed in name only when the Nichiren sect [was in control] in Kyoto." *Rokuōin monjo* 7–314 (undated, but probably 1547). This is part of the series of documents in the Seikōin-Rokuōin land dispute discussed below. This reference is quoted by Shimosaka, "Machishū no seikatsu," p. 131, and has been used as a central support of Imatani Akira's contention that the Lotus leagues succeeded in garnering a certain amount of independence from their overlords. Imatani, *Tenbun Hokke no ran*, p. 159. To bolster his case, Imatani cites other incidents of rent withholding during the early 1530s. Imatani, *Tenbun Hokke no ran*, pp. 150–168.

30. Fujii, "Hokke ikki to chōgumi," p. 558, quoting *Tokitsugu kyōki*, entry for 1533/2.

31. Ibid., p. 558.

32. Nishio, " 'Machishūron,' " p. 68.

33. Umata, "Chūsei toshi to shotōsō," p. 146.

34. Nishio, "'Machishūron,'" pp. 67–68.

35. Imatani, *Tenbun Hokke no ran*, pp. 161–162. Imatani interprets this only to mean that withholding of rent was common in Kyoto at this time.

36. Imatani, *Sengokuki no Muromachi Bakufu*, pp. 186–191.

37. Imatani, *Tenbun Hokke no ran*, p. 206.

38. Ibid., pp. 207–208.

39. MBL no. 483 (1536/intercalary 10/7), *CHS*, vol. 2, p. 140.

40. MBL no. 484 (1536/intercalary 10/7), *CHS*, vol. 2, p. 140.

41. MBL no. 485 (1536/intercalary 10/7), *CHS*, vol. 2, p. 140.

42. Fujii, "Hokke ikki to 'chōgumi,'" p. 564.

43. Nishio Kazumi agrees that nonpayment of rent was widespread in the early 1530s and probably continued to some extent after the Lotus leagues were crushed, but rejects the notion that either rent exemptions or half-tax rights were acquired by neighborhoods in a coordinated way en bloc. Nishio, " 'Machishūron,' " pp. 67–68.

44. Hayashiya, "Kyoto in the Muromachi Age," p. 33, characterizes the 1536 crushing of the Lotus leagues as a struggle between the old order and autonomous townspeople.

45. Nishio Kazumi posits that the leagues served the military purposes of Hosokawa Harumoto through the head priest of each Lotus temple, and that once Harumoto no longer needed them, he turned on them. Nishio, " 'Machishūron,' " p. 64.

46. Kawashima, "Chōgumi to kaisho," p. 232, quoting the 1537/1/3 entry of *Nentō gohairei sanpu ranshō no hikae*.

47. Imatani, *Tokitsugu kyōki*, p. 242. On the basis of diary entries alluding to neighborhood management of disputes and dated 1536 through 1551, Imatani concludes that the neighborhood held on to this right long after the Lotus leagues' demise. The neighborhoods in question were all in upper Kyoto; it is by no means

clear that the same was true of lower Kyoto or that the cluster councils of upper and lower Kyoto similarly maintained judicial authority over interneighborhood disputes.

48. *Rokuōin monjo* no. 7–312 (1547/11/6).
49. *Rokuōin monjo* no. 7–314, undated.
50. *Rokuin monjo* no. 7–308 (1544/intercalary 10).
51. See Hayashiya Tatsusaburō, "Machishū no seiritsu" and *Machishū*; Imatani, *Toki-tsugu kyōki*; Seta, "Kinsei toshi seiritsushi josetsu"; Toyoda, "Toshi ni okeru sōteki ketsugō"; Wakita, "Chūsei Kyōto no tochi shoyū."
52. Kawashima, "Chōgumi to kaisho," p. 232, quoting the 1537/1/3 entry of *Nentō gohairei sanpu ranshō no hikae*. This is the first source to use the term "cluster" (*machigumi*).
53. Nishio, " 'Machishūron,' " map on p. 70.
54. Fujii, "Hokke ikki to chōgumi," p. 556.
55. Shimosaka, "Machishū no seikatsu," p. 78, quoting 1532/12/8 entry in *Nisuiki* (1485–1533), diary of Washinō Takayasu, an aristocratic Lotus adherent. Nishi-nokyō, Uzumasa, and Kitayama were the areas raided. Peasant leagues demanding debt amnesties plagued Kyoto occasionally during the first third of the sixteenth century.
56. Nishio, " 'Machishūron,' " p. 58.
57. Hayashiya, "Gion'e ni tsuite." (The shogun's action is recorded in *Gion shugyō nikki*, entry for 1533/6/7, quoted by Shimosaka, "Machishū no seikatsu," p. 117.) Hayashiya places great significance on this event, asserting that it proves the parade of floats had become completely separate from the ritual at the shrine and that the response of the neighborhood officials reflects the self-governing spirit of the townspeople. Seta Katsuya, as indicated above, disagrees that the secular and religious aspects of the festival can be so neatly separated, and at the same time posits a genuine commoner element in the festival as starting much earlier—in the fourteenth century.
58. Lenders' requests for shogunal confirmation of their loans, following a conditional debt amnesty, 1546–1547. *Muromachi Bakufu hikitsuke shiryō shūsei*, pp. 235–288. See Appendix, no. 6.
59. It is doubtful that even these are necessarily Enryakuji priests. They include no. 3 mother of Eirin (p. 238), no. 35 Kōge (p. 270), no. 36 Kōtoku (p. 260–261), no. 37 Gyokuhō (pp. 261–263), no. 40 Kōzen (p. 267), and no. 49 Jōshin (p. 270). Kōge, Kōtoku, Gyokuhō, and Kōzen seem to be big estabishments, with Gyokuhō having especially large outstanding loans. The names are distinctly clerical, though they could have been priests from temples other than Enryakuji.
60. *Chikatoshi nikki*, entry for 1539/12/30, pp. 297–298. See also entries for 1539/7/25 (p. 257), 1539/8/24 (pp. 272–273), 1539/9/4 (p. 275), and 1539/11/11 (p. 287), references to requests by moneylenders of upper and lower Kyoto for a debt amnesty cancellation. Like the letter from the twenty moneylenders, these also suggest business as usual.
61. Hayashiya, *Chūsei bunka no kichō*, p. 248, suggests that Higashiyama culture could not have attained the heights it did without the moneylenders' backing, presumably in the forms of loans and patronage.
62. Hashimoto, "Dosō no sonzai keitai," p. 18, quoting the *Kanmon gyoki*.

63. Hayashiya, "Kyoto in the Muromachi Age," p. 26.
64. Ibid., p. 27, cites terms like *"chatoku"* and *"katoku"*—profit/virtue of tea and poetry.
65. Shimosaka, "Machishū no seikatsu," pp. 134–135, quoting *Tokitsugu kyōki*, entries for 1534/2, 12, 14, 15; 1534/3/13.
66. I am indebted to Anne Walthall for this insight into the relationship.
67. Hashimoto, "Dosō no sonzai keitai," pp. 18–19, has constructed a narrative of aspects of the relationship by analyzing entries in the *Kanmon gyoki*.
68. Yokoi, *Kanmon gyoki*, pp. 217, citing entries for 1417/intercalary 5/14 and 16, and 1417/6/5. Yokoi assumes that the term *"jige otoko"* refers to moneylenders and low-ranking warriors, who then incorporated tea ceremony into their daily lives.
69. Shimosaka, "Machishū no seikatsu," p. 136, quoting *Chikatoshi nikki*, entry for 1538/3/11.
70. Ibid., quoting *Chikatoshi nikki*, entry for 1539/2/19.
71. Ibid., pp. 135–136.
72. Barbara Ruch has postulated that a national literature incorporating elite and common elements evolved during the Muromachi period. See Ruch, "Medieval Jongleurs and the Making of a National Literature" and "The Other Side of Culture."
73. Varley and Elison, "The Culture of Tea," pp. 188–189.
74. *Kemmu shikimoku* no. 2 (1336/11/7), *CHS*, vol. 2, p. 4. "Tea parties" referred to herein are not the tea ceremony of later centuries but gatherings in which participants attempted to identify different types of teas.
75. Yokoi, *Kanmon gyoki*, p. 219.
76. Varley and Elison, "The Culture of Tea," pp. 198–202. A banquet room is a *kaisho*. Examples of this form of socializing include Shogun Yoshimitsu hosting Emperor Goen'yū and provincial governors hosting the shogun. Politics, of course, was the real agenda at these gatherings, if only implicitly, and for a merchant like Hōsen business ties were likely a factor as well.
77. Varley, "Cultural Life in Medieval Japan," p. 474.
78. Keene, "The Comic Tradition in Renga," p. 250.
79. Ibid., p. 261; Varley, "Cultural Life in Medieval Japan," p. 479. Jōha, a sixteenth-century *renga* poet, was the son of a temple servant. Keene, "Jōha, A Sixteenth Century Poet of Linked Verse," p. 114.
80. Carter, "Introduction," *Literary Patronage in Late Medieval Japan*, p. 16.
81. Keene, "The Comic Tradition in Renga," p. 252.
82. Ramirez-Christensen, "Renga and the Popular Dissemination of Classical Literature in Medieval Japan," discusses the phenomenon of linked-verse handbooks.
83. Keene, "The Comic Tradition in Renga," p. 256.
84. Ibid.
85. Tsurusaki, "The Poet Shōkō and the Salons of Sakai," p. 57.
86. Ibid., p. 59, suggests that this, more than linked verse, was a poetic form popular among commoners.
87. Murai, *Sen no Rikyū*, pp. 46–52.
88. Ibid.
89. Berry, *The Culture of Civil War*, p. 261.
90. Ibid., pp. 259–284, analyzes the content and social function of the gatherings recorded in tea diaries.

91. On the mythological origins of the Gion cult and its early history, see McMullin, "On Placating the Gods and Pacifying the Populace."

92. In her study of the Gion festival ("Chūsei no Gion'e") Wakita Haruko has emphasized the important role of rich commoners like moneylenders in the financing of the festival. She distinguishes the procession of floats as the neighborhood-supported, secular element of the festival, from the religious procession of the portable shrine, which was supported by the moneylender tax. Seta Katsuya, on the other hand, insists that, even very early in the medieval period, the shrine was not separate from the surrounding city and concludes that from the beginning the festival tax was perceived by its payers as an occasion for enhancing their own prestige. Seta, "Chūsei no Gion'e goryōe," p. 273.

93. This is the view expressed in Seta,"Chūsei Gion'e goryōe," pp. 275–276. Seta also posits that the shogun's patronage of the festival from this point was another factor in making it a gaudier, more festive occasion.

94. Amino, "Chūsei toshiron," p. 274.

95. This tax is called the *bajōyaku* and was widely levied on merchant groups and individuals. Documents pertaining to the tax dating from 1397 to 1502 can be found in the shrine's collection, *Yasaka jinja monjo*, pp. 286–487.

96. A Gion Shrine document of 1431/9/15 sent to the shogunate lists items the shrine received for the festival from affiliated groups. The names of many clothing shops are included, but prominent moneylenders also contributed heavily (Seta, "Chūsei no Gion'e goryōe," pp. 249–251). Seta is of the opinion that the moneylenders who paid this were not all the Gion Shrine moneylender affiliates (who paid the regular festival tax), but only major moneylenders who hailed from the third rank of Enryakuji priests, like Jōkōbō and Zenjūbō (ibid., p. 267).

97. Seta, "Chūsei Gion'e goryōe," p. 273.

98. Shimosaka, "Machishū no seikatsu," p. 114.

99. Ibid. Shimosaka asserts that the tax on moneylenders had previously financed the floats. This would not seem to be in line with either Wakita's or Seta's research. For that matter, to find any source addressing float finances is difficult. A listing, genealogy-style, of those who contributed to the financing of twelve floats contains names that appear to be twenty-four clerical moneylenders, but no explanatory information is included. *Yasaka jinja kiroku* ("Bajō jūni-hoko sōden keizu," 1414/8/1), vol. 2, p. 513. In this pre-Ōnin period, such individuals may have funded the floats, in contrast to later communal neighborhood financing.

100. Shimosaka, "Machishū no seikatsu," pp. 116–117. See "Kujizainin," pp. 141–152. Lacking pre-Ōnin sources on the organization of the neighborhood floats, the assumption here that this description is of a new, specifically post-Ōnin process may be incorrect. Seta Katsuya sees commoner participation in the festival, though not necessarily communal, from the late fourteenth century. Seta," Chūsei no Gion'e goryōe."

101. See Nakai Shinkō, "Mibudera," *KDJ*, vol. 13, p. 459; Taguchi Kazuo, "Mibu Kyōgen," *KDJ*, vol. 13, p. 457; and Hamada Zenshin, "Yūzū nenbutsushū," *KDJ*, vol. 14, pp. 277–278.

102. Hayashiya, *Chūsei bunka no kichō*, pp. 220–221, asserts that commoners performed in Noh and Kyōgen.

103. See Ruch, "The Other Side of Culture in Medieval Japan," pp. 535–536, for a discussion of this remarkable performance phenomenon.
104. On *otogi zōshi* in English, see Childs, *Rethinking Sorrow*, especially pp. 13–14, for a general introduction to the genre; for a discussion of the role of commoners in this form of literature, see Skord, *Tales of Tears and Laughter*, pp. 3–4.
105. Ichiko Teiji, "Kaisetsu," *Otogi zōshi*, p. 8. Hayashiya, *Chūsei bunka no kichō*, pp. 241–242, posits direct commoner agency in tea, popular song, dance, and companion stories.
106. Ruch, "Medieval Jongleurs and the Making of a National Literature," pp. 282–284. Ruch points out a single case of a Kyoto warrior-turned-priest who was a writer, but notes that he was not necessarily a townsperson. She argues persuasively that the creative impulse for so-called Muromachi culture lay primarily in a rural setting, in which itinerant entertainers, both male and female, produced a largely oral, national literature.
107. Hayashiya, *Chūsei bunka no kichō*, p. 249, quoting the *Inryōken nichiroku*, Shōkokuji's official chronicle.
108. Ibid., pp. 248–249. This work was donated to the Kyoto National Museum in May 1949 from the Gyokuryūin collection.

CHAPTER SIX: THE FATE OF THE MONEYLENDERS IN THE EARLY MODERN PERIOD

1. On Shōjitsubō, see Hashimoto, "Dosō no sonzai keitai," pp. 13–18, 21.
2. No. 423 (Shōjitsubō jōun'ate shuinjō, 1573/11/28) *Zōtei Oda Nobunaga monjo no kenkyū*, vol. 1, pp. 715–716.
3. Kawauchi, "Sengokuki Kyōto no sakaya-dosō"; Hayashiya Tatsusaburō, "Suminokurashi," *KDJ*, vol. 8, p. 152.
4. Kawauchi, "Sengokuki Kyōto no sakaya-dosō," p. 24. Kawashima makes this judgment not only on the basis of geographical location but also because the Suminokura appear in sources to have had business dealings with Daikakuji, including acquiring land as defaulted collateral from the temple. Daikakuji is a Shingon temple that was founded in the late ninth century.
5. Ibid., p. 29.
6. Ibid., pp. 101–104, speculates on the late-sixteenth-century organization of Kyoto's brewers based on the fate of the Distillery Office.
7. Hayashiya, "Kyoto in the Muromachi Age," p. 34.
8. Wakita, "Shōgyō, kōtsū seisaku no tenkai," p. 375.
9. Yasuoka, "Shōgyō no henshitsu," p. 128.
10. Toyoda Takeshi, "Sakaya," *NRD*, vol. 5, pp. 72–73.
11. Yasuoka, "Shōgyō no henshitsu," pp. 128–130. Pawnbroking regulations were issued in 1629/10/18.
12. Miyamoto Mataji, "Kabu nakama," *KDJ*, vol. 3, pp. 522–523; Miyamoto, *Kabu nakama kenkyū*; Hayashi, *Edo toiya nakama no kenkyū*.
13. Sueoka Shōkei, "Ryōgae," *KDJ*, vol. 14, pp. 621–622.
14. Yunoki Manabu, "Sakaya," *KDJ*, vol. 6, p. 292.
15. Wakita Haruko, "Ōtoneri za," *KDJ*, vol. 2, pp. 651–652. *Ōtoneri* was the name of lower-ranking palace officials in the ancient period. Textilers adopted the name for their guild in the medieval period.

16. Wakita Osamu and Wakita Haruko, in "Tokken shōnin no taitō," pp. 421–428, describe the post-Ōnin through early Edo period development of the Nishijin textile manufacturers.

Conclusion

1. Ruch, "The Other Side of Culture," pp. 500–501.
2. Kasamatsu, "Kaidai–Bakufuhō," p. 496.
3. See Grossberg, *The Laws of the Muromachi Bakufu*, pp. 7–13, for a discussion of shogunal law.
4. Ishii Ryōsuke has called the period "the zenith of commoners' legal rights." Ishii, *Nihon hōseishi gaisetsu*, p. 92.
5. *CHS*, vol. 2, pp. 151–292, contains 356 references to laws no longer extant.
6. Grossberg, *The Laws of the Muromachi Bakufu*, p. 13.
7. Kamakura law likewise was explicit regarding punishment of warriors: fines and double fines, detention, confiscation of a percentage of one's property, etc. Mass, *The Development of Kamakura Rule*, p. 143, n. 116.
8. Again, the same applied to the Kamakura period. See ibid., p. 143: "In extreme cases . . . a *jitō* might lose his post; but it is hard to document instances where a defendant was incarcerated or subjected to heavy fines."
9. Torture is referred to as a duty of low-ranking officials in the Board of Retainers. MBL no. 477 (1523/4/3), *CHS*, vol. 2, p. 138.
10. MBL no. 304 (1490/intercalary 8/27), *CHS*, vol. 2, p. 100.
11. On the structure and institutional evolution of the Muromachi Bakufu in English, see Kuwayama, "The Bugyōnin System"; Satō, "The Ashikaga Shogun and the Muromachi Bakufu Administration"; Hall, "The Muromachi Bakufu." In Japanese, see Haga, "Muromachi Bakufu samuraidokoro kō"; Kasamatsu, "Muromachi Bakufu soshō seido"; Fukuda, "Muromachi Bakufu no hōkōshū"; and Imatani, *Sengokuki no Muromachi Bakufu*.
12. The analysis that follows is derived from Takahashi, *Rakuchū rakugai*, p. 192–195. He urges caution in using the screens as historical sources, because their creators were observing artistic conventions and were likely not bound to realistic depiction. It is very difficult, he warns, to claim that a screen represents Kyoto at any given point in time.
13. Reproduced in *Rakuchū rakugai zu taikan—Machidake kyūzōbon*. Takahashi Yasuo speculated to me about the approximate date of this screen.
14. I am indebted to Takahashi Yasuo for these insights.
15. *Yase dōjikai monjo*.
16. Kuwayama, "The Bugyōnin System," pp. 56–62.

Bibliography

Complete publication information for works cited in short form in the Notes is given in this Bibliography. For works published in Japan, the city of publication is Tokyo unless otherwise specified. For Japanese scholars, surname precedes given name.

PRIMARY SOURCES AND REFERENCE WORKS

Chikamoto nikki, vol. 1. *Zōho zoku shiryōtaisei*, vol. 10. Edited by Zōho Zoku Shiryō Taisei Kankōkai. Kyoto: Rinsen Shoten, 1967.

Chikatoshi nikki. *Zōho zoku shiryō taisei*, vol. 13. Edited by Zōho Zoku Shiryō Taisei Kankōkai. Kyoto: Rinsen Shoten, 1967.

Chūsei hōsei shiryōshū, vols. 1 and 2. Edited by Satō Shin'ichi and Ikeuchi Yoshisuke. Iwanami Shoten, 1955, 1957.

Chūseishi handobukku. Edited by Nagahara Keiji. Kondō shuppansha, 1973.

Encyclopedia of Japan. Edited by Itasaka Gen. Kōdansha, 1983.

Gunsho ruijū, vol. 25. Naigai Shoseki Kaisha, 1928.

Hōjōki/Tsurezuregusa. *Nihon koten bungaku taikei*, vol. 30. Edited by Takagi Ichinosuke, Nishio Minoru et al. Iwanami Shoten, 1957.

Hōkyōji monjo. Unpublished documents in *eishabon* form in Kyoto University Archives.

Honnōji monjo. Unpublished documents in *eishabon* form in Kyoto University Archives.

Jinkō daijiten. Edited by Minami Ryōzaburō. Heibonsha, 1957.

Kitano Tenmangū shiryo-komonjo. Edited by Kitano Tenmangū Shiryō Kankōkai. Kyoto: Kitano Tenmangū, 1978.

Kokushi daijiten. Edited by Kokushi Daijiten Henshū Iinkai. Yoshikawa Kōbunkan, 1979–1997.

"Kujizainin." *Kyōgenshū*, vol. 2. *Nihon koten bungaku taikei*, vol. 43. Edited and annotated by Koyama Hiroshi, pp. 141–151. Iwanami Shoten, 1961.

Kyotoshi no chimei. Hayashiya Tatsusaburō, Murai Yasuhiko, and Moriya Tokihisa. Heibonsha, 1979.

The Laws of the Muromachi Bakufu. Edited by Kenneth A. Grossberg. Translated by Kenneth A. Grossberg and Kanamoto Nobuhisa. Tokyo: Sophia University, 1981.

Muromachi bakufu hikitsuke shiryō shūsei, 2 vols. Edited by Kuwayama Kōnen. Kondō Shuppansha, 1980, 1986.

Muromachi bakufu monjo shūsei: bugyōnin hōsho, 2 vols. Edited by Imatani Akira and Takahashi Yasuo. Kyoto: Shinbunkaku, 1986.

Nihon jōmin seikatsu ebiki, 5 vols. Edited by Shibusawa Keizō. Heibonsha, 1984.

Nihon kokugo daijiten. Edited by Nihon Daijiten Kankōkai. 20 vols. Shōgakkan, 1972.

Nihon rekishi daijiten. Edited by Kawade Takao. 22 vols. Kawade Shobō Shinsha, 1956–1961.

Ninagawake monjo, 3 vols. Edited by Tōkyō Daigaku Shiryō Hensanjo. Tōkyō Daigaku Shuppankai, 1981, 1984, 1987.

Ōdate Jōkō nikki, vol. 1. *Zōho zokushiryō taisei*, vol. 15. Edited by Takeuchi Rizō. Kyoto: Rinsen Shokan, 1967.

Rakuchū Rakugai zu taikan-Machidake kyūzōbon. Edited by Ishida Naotoyo et al. Shōgakkan, 1987.

Rokuōin monjo. Unpublished documents in *eishabon* form in Kyoto University Archives.
Sanetaka kōki. Edited by Zoku Gunsho Ruijū Kanseikai. Taiyōsha, 1957.
Shinjōin monjo. Unpublished documents in *eishabon* form in Kyoto University Archives.
Shiryō Kyōto no rekishi, vol. 3. Edited by Kyōto-shi. Heibonsha, 1979.
"Tateiri Munetsugu monjo." In *Tateiri Munetsugu monjo Kawabata Dōki monjo,* pp. 49–286. Edited and published by Kokumin Seishin Bunka Kenkyūsho, 1937.
Yasaka Jinja kiroku. Edited and published by Yasaka Jinja Shamusho, 1923.
Yasaka Jinja monjo. Edited and published by Yasaka Jinja Shamusho, 1939.
Yase dōjikai monjo. Edited and published by Kyōto-shi Rekishi Shiryōkan, 2000.
Zōtei Oda Nobunaga monjo no kenkyu, vol. 1. Edited by Okuno Takahiro. Yoshikawa Kōbunkan, 1969. Reprint 1988.

SECONDARY SOURCES

Adolphson, Mikael S. *The Gates of Power.* Honolulu: University of Hawai'i Press, 2000.
Akamatsu Toshihide. "Za ni tsuite." *Shirin* 37.1 (February 1954): 1–25.
Akiyama Kunizō. "Jōbōsei no 'machi' no hen'yō katei-Heiankyō kara Kyōto e." *Shakaigaku* 10 (September 1968). Reprinted in Akiyama and Nakamura, *Kyōto 'machi' no kenkyū,* pp. 88–169. Hōsei Daigaku Shuppankyoku, 1975.
Akiyama Kunizō and Nakamura Ken. *Kyōto 'machi' no kenkyū.* Hōsei Daigaku Shuppankyoku, 1975.
Amino Yoshihiko. "Chūsei ni okeru tennō shihaiken no ichi kōsatsu." *Shigaku zasshi* 88.8 (August 1972): 1–60.
————. "Chūsei toshiron." In *Iwanami kōza Nihon rekishi,* edited by Asao Naohiro et al., vol. 7, pp. 253–303. Iwanami Shoten, 1976.
————. "Hinin ni kansuru ichi shiryō." *Nenpō chūseishi kenkyū* 1(1976): 92–96.
————. "Mikinotsukasa shukikuyaku no seiritsu ni tsuite." *Zoku shōensei to buke shakai,* edited by Takeuchi Rizō Hakase Koki Kinenkai, pp. 361–396. Yoshikawa Kōbunkan, 1978.
————. *Shokunin utaawase.* Iwanami Shoten, 1992.
Amino Yoshihiko et al., eds. *Chūsei no tsumi to batsu.* Tōkyō Daigaku Shuppankai, 1983.
Arakawa Hidetoshi. *Kikin.* Kyōikusha, 1979.
Atsuta Kō. "Basara no bunka." KR, vol. 2, pp. 528–555.
Berry, Mary Elizabeth. *The Culture of Civil War in Kyoto.* Berkeley: University of California Press, 1994.
Carter, Steven D. "Introduction." In *Literary Patronage in Late Medieval Japan,* edited by Steven D. Carter, pp. 1–17. Ann Arbor: Center for Japanese Studies, University of Michigan, 1993.
Childs, Margaret Helen. *Rethinking Sorrow: Revelatory Tales of Late Medieval Japan.* Ann Arbor: University of Michigan, 1991.
Collcutt, Martin. *Five Mountains: The Rinzai Zen Monastic Institution in Medieval Japan.* Cambridge, MA: Harvard University Press, 1981.
Cooper, Michael, S. J., ed. *They Came to Japan: An Anthology of European Reports on Japan, 1543–1640.* Berkeley: University of California Press, 1965.
Davis, David L. "Ikki in Late Medieval Japan." In *Medieval Japan: Essays in Institutional History,* edited by John W. Hall and Jeffrey Mass, pp. 221–227. New Haven, CT: Yale University Press, 1974.

Dobbins, James C. *Jōdo shinshū: Shin Buddhism in Medieval Japan*. Bloomington: Indiana University Press, 1989.

Endō Motō. "Shokunin no soshiki to shite no 'za' no ichi kōsatsu." *Shakai keizai shigaku* 3.2 (May 1933): 1–30.

Farris, William Wayne. *Population, Disease, and Land in Early Japan, 645–900*. Cambridge, MA: Harvard University Press, 1985.

Fujii Manabu. "Hokke ikki to 'chōgumi,' " KR, vol. 3, pp. 540–568.

———. "Shinkyū Bukkyō no kyōsen." KR, vol. 3, pp. 116–165.

Fukuda Toyohiko. "Muromachi Bakufu no 'hōkōshū.' " *Nihon rekishi* 274 (March 1971): 46–65.

Gay, Suzanne. "The Kawashima: Warrior-Peasants of Medieval Japan." *Harvard Journal of Asiatic Studies* 46:1 (June 1986): 81–119.

———. "Muromachi Bakufu Rule in Kyoto: Administrative and Judicial Aspects." In *The Bakufu in Japanese History*, edited by Jeffrey P. Mass and William Hauser, pp. 49–65. Stanford, CA: Stanford University Press, 1985.

Goble, Andrew. *Kenmu: Go-Daigo's Revolution*. Cambridge, MA: Harvard University Press, 1996.

Gomi Fumihiko. "Kanreisei to daimyōsei." *Kōbe Daigaku Bungakubu kiyō* 4(1974): 27–54.

Groner, Paul. *Saichō: The Establishment of the Japanese Tendai School*. Berkeley: Berkeley Buddhist Studies Series, 1984.

Grossberg, Kenneth. *Japan's Renaissance: The Politics of the Muromachi Bakufu*. Cambridge, MA: Harvard University Press, 1981.

Haga Norihiko. "Muromachi bakufu samuraidokoro kō." *Muromachi seiken*, Ronshū Nihon rekishi, edited by Ogawa Makoto, vol. 5, pp. 25–55. Yūseidō, 1975.

Hall, John W. "Kyoto as Historical Background." In *Medieval Japan: Essays in Institutional History*, edited by John W. Hall and Jeffrey P. Mass, pp. 3–38. New Haven, CT: Yale University Press, 1974.

———. "The Muromachi Bakufu." CHJ, edited by Kozo Yamamura, vol. 3 (medieval), pp. 175–230. London and New York: Cambridge University Press, 1990.

Hara Katsurō. *Nihon chūseishi*. 1906.

Hashimoto Harumi. "Dosō no sonzai keitai." *Shisō* 19 (1961): 8–21.

Hayashima Daisuke. "Kyōto kinkō ni okeru eitaibaibaichi no anteika: jūgo jūroku seiki no hoshō keitai." *Nihonshi kenkyū* 444 (August 1999): 29–53.

Hayashiya Tatsusaburō. *Chūsei bunka no kichō*. Tōkyō Daigaku Shuppankai, 1953.

———. "Gion'e ni tsuite." *Gionsai*. Edited by Minka Kyōto shibu rekishi bukai. Tōkyō Daigaku Shuppankai, 1953.

———. *Kyōwarabe kara machishū e*. Kōdansha, 1974.

———. *Machishū*. Chūō Kōronsha, 1964.

———. "Machishū no seiritsu." *Shisō* 312 (June 1950). Reprinted in Hayashiya Tatsusaburō, *Chūsei bunka no kichō*, pp. 189–285.

Hayashiya Tatsusaburō with George Elison. "Kyoto in the Muromachi Age." In *Japan in the Muromachi Age*, edited by John W. Hall and Toyoda Takeshi, pp. 11–36. Berkeley: University of California Press, 1977.

Hayashiya Tatsusaburō, Mutō Tadashi, and Moriya Tokihisa. "Sōron." In *Kyōtoshi no chimei*, edited by Hayashiya Tatsusaburō, Mutō Tadashi, and Moriya Tokihisa, p. 19. Heibonsha, 1979.

Heian kento 1200 nen kinen: yomigaeru Heiankyō. Edited by Kyōto-shi. Kyōto-shi, 1994.

Ichiko Teiji, "Kaisetsu." In *Otogi zōshi. Nihon koten bungaku taikei*, edited and annotated by Ichiko Teiji et al., vol. 38, pp. 5–23. Iwanami Shoten, 1958.

Ikki. Edited by Aoki Michio et al. 5 vols. Tōkyō Daigaku Shuppankai, 1981.

Imatani Akira. *Domin gōgō*. Shinjinbutsu Ōraisha, 1988.

———. *Muromachi no ōken-Ashikaga Yoshimitsu no ōken sandatsu keikaku*. Chūō Kōronsha, 1990.

———. *Sengokuki no Muromachi Bakufu*. Kadokawa Shoten, 1975.

———. *Tenbun Hokke no ran*. Heibonsha, 1989.

———. *Tokitsugu kyōki-kuge shakai to machishū bunka no setten*. Soshiete, 1980.

Inaba Nobumichi. "Chūsei no kunin ni kansuru ichi kōsatsu-jiin no kunin o chūshin to shite." *Shigaku zasshi* 89.10 (October 1980): 1–37.

Inagaki Yasuhiko. *Nihon chūsei shakaishiron*. Tōkyō Daigaku Shuppankai, 1981.

———. "Ōnin-Bunmei no ran." *Iwanami kōza Nihon rekishi*, vol. 7, pp. 163–202. Iwanami Shoten, 1963.

Inoue Mitsurō and Kawashima Norio. "Rokuhara tandai." KR, vol. 2, pp. 414–417.

Inoue Mitsurō and Nakayama Shūichi. "Nagaoka sento." KR, vol. 1, pp. 193–218.

Ishii Ryōsuke. *Nihon hōseishi gaisetsu*. Sōbunsha, 1971.

Ishii Susumu. *Nihon chūsei kokkashi no kenkyū*. Iwanami Shoten, 1970.

Itō Toshiichi, "Kin'yūgyō wo fukugyō ni suru jisō." In *Tōji hyakugō monjo wo yomu*, edited by Uejima Tamotsu et al., pp. 30–31. Kyoto: Shibunkaku, 1998.

Iwahashi Koyata. "Tenbun Hokke ran." *Rekishi to chiri* 21.6 (June 1928): 8–31.

Iwasaki Kae. *Shokunin utaawase*. Heibonsha, 1987.

Kageyama Haruki. *Hieizanji: sono kōsei to shomondai*. Kyoto: Dōbōsha, 1979.

Kasamatsu Hiroshi. "Kaidai-bakufuhō." *Chūsei seiji shisō*, vol. 1, edited by Ishii Susumu and Ishimoda Tadashi, pp. 479–496. Iwanami Shoten, 1972.

———. "Muromachi Bakufu soshō seido 'iken' no kōsatsu." *Shigaku zasshi* 69.4 (April 1960): 1–28.

———. *Tokuseirei*. Iwanami Shoten, 1983.

Katō Hyakuichi. "Sake, seishu, Nihonshu." *Tabemono no Nihonshi sōran-rekishi yomihon tokubetsu zōkan jiten shiriizu* 17:242–243. Shinjinbutsu Ōraisha, 1993.

Katsumata Shizuo. *Ikki*. Iwanami Shoten, 1982.

Katsuyama Seiji. "Heian jidai ni okeru Kamogawa no kōzui to chian." *Mie Daigaku jinbun gakubu bunka gakka kenkyū kiyō jinbun ronsō* 4 (March 1987): 17–27.

Kawashima Masao. "Chōgumi to kaisho." In *Kyōto shomin seikatsushi*, edited by Hayashiya Tatsusaburō, pp. 232–249. Kyōto Shin'yō Kinko, 1973.

Kawata Mitsuo. "Chūsei hisabetsumin no yosōi." In *Kawata Mitsuo chosakushū*, vol. 2, pp. 2–43. Akashi Shoten, 1983.

Kawauchi Masayoshi. "Sengokuki Kyōto no sakaya-dosō no ichi sonzai keitai-chūsei Suminokura kenkyū no shūi." *Nihon rekishi* 520 (September 1991): 18–30.

Kawazoe Shōji. "Japan and East Asia." CHJ, edited by Kozo Yamamura, vol. 3 (medieval), pp. 396–446. London and New York: Cambridge University Press, 1990.

Keene, Donald. "The Comic Tradition in Renga." In *Japan in the Muromachi Age*, edited by John W. Hall and Toyoda Takeshi, pp. 241–277. Berkeley: University of California, 1977.

———. "Jōha, A Sixteenth Century Poet of Linked Verse." In *Warlords, Artists, and Commoners: Japan in the Sixteenth Century*, edited by George Elison and Bardwell L. Smith, pp. 113–131. Honolulu: University of Hawai'i Press, 1981.

Keirstead, Thomas. "Fragmented Estates: The Breakup of the Myō and the Decline of the Shōen System." *Monumenta Nipponica* 4.3 (Autumn 1985): 311–330.

———. *The Geography of Power in Medieval Japan* Princeton, NJ: Princeton University Press, 1992.

Kiley, Cornelius J. "The Imperial Court as a Legal Authority in the Kamakura Age." In *Court and Bakufu in Japan: Essays in Kamakura History,* edited by Jeffrey P. Mass, pp. 29–44. New Haven, CT: Yale University Press, 1982.

Kinoshita Masao. "Kyōto ni okeru machigumi no chiikiteki hatten." *Nihonshi kenkyū* 92 (July 1967): 21–51.

Kitō Hiroshi. *Nihon nisennen no jinkōshi.* Kyoto: PHP Kenkyūsho, 1983.

Koizumi Yoshiaki. "Nairanki no shakai hendō." In *Iwanami kōza Nihon rekishi,* edited by Asao Naohiro et al., vol. 6, pp. 125–165. Iwanami Shoten, 1975.

Koyama Yasunori. "Chūsei senminron." In *Kōza Nihon rekishi,* edited by Rekishigaku Kenkyūkai and Nihonshi Kenkyūkai, vol. 4, pp. 159–198. Tōkyō Daigaku Shuppankai, 1985.

Kuroda Hideo. "Shiryō to shite no emakimono to chūsei no mibunsei." *Rekishi hyōron* 382 (February 1982): 56–76.

Kuroda Kōichirō. "Chūsei Kyōto no keisatsu seido." *Kyōto shakaishi kenkyū,* edited by Dōshisha Daigaku Jinbun Kagaku Kenkyūsho, pp. 124–159. Hōritsu Bunkasha, 1976.

———. " 'Konjaku monogatari' ni arawareta toshi." *Nihonshi kenkyū* 162 (February 1976): 1–48.

———. "Kyōto no seiritsu." *Nihonshi,* edited by Toda Yoshimi, vol. 2, pp. 15–40. Yūhikaku Shinsho, 1978.

Kuroda Toshio. "Chūsei jisha seiryokuron." In *Iwanami kōza Nihon rekishi,* edited by Asao Naohiro et al., vol. 6, pp. 245–295. Iwanami Shoten, 1975.

———. "Chūsei no kokka to tennō." In *Iwanami kōza Nihon rekishi,* edited by Ienaga Saburō et al., vol. 6, pp. 261–301. Iwanami Shoten, 1963.

———. "Chūsei no mibunsei to hisen kannen." *Buraku mondai kenkyū* 33 (May 1972): 23–57. Reprinted in Kuroda, *Nihon chūsei no kokka to shūkyō,* pp. 351–410. Iwanami Shoten, 1975.

———. "Chūseishi josetsu." In *Iwanami kōza Nihon rekishi,* edited by Asao Naohiro et al., vol. 5, pp. 1–34. Iwanami Shoten, 1975.

———. *Jisha seiryoku-mō hitotsu no chūsei shakai.* Iwanami Shoten, 1980.

———. "Shinto in the History of Japanese Religion." *Journal of Japanese Studies* 7.1 (Winter 1981): 1–21.

Kurokawa Naonori. "Chūsei kōki no nōmin tōsō-I. Doikki, kuni ikki." In *Kōza Nihonshi,* edited by Rekishigaku Kenkyūkai and Nihonshi Kenkyūkai, vol. 3, pp. 227–250. Tōkyō Daigaku Shuppankai, 1970.

———. "Doikki no jidai." *Doikki to nairan, Nihon minshū no rekishi,* edited by Inagaki Yasuhiko and Toda Yoshimi, vol. 2, Sanseidō, 1975.

———. "Ōnin-Bunmei no tairan." KR, vol. 3, pp. 305–332.

———. "Tokusei ikki no takamari." KR, vol. 3, pp. 298–304.

Kurushima Noriko. "Sengokuki no shukikuyaku-'Konishi Yasuoshi shozōmonjo' o chūshin ni." In *Chūsei o hirogeru-atarashii shiryōron o motomete,* edited by Ishii Susumu, pp. 56–115. Yoshikawa Kōbunkan, 1991.

Kuwayama Kōnen. "The Bugyōnin System: A Closer Look." In *Japan in the Muromachi*

Age, edited by John W. Hall and Toyoda Takeshi, pp. 53–63. Berkeley: University of California Press, 1977.

———. "Muromachi bakufu keizai kikō no ichi kōsatsu." *Shigaku zasshi* 73.9 (September 1964): 1–33.

———. "Muromachi jidai no tokusei: tokuseirei to bakufu zaisei." In *Chūsei no shakai to keizai,* edited by Nagahara Keiji and Inagaki Yasuhiko, pp. 497–552. Tōkyō Daigaku Shuppankai, 1962.

Kyōto no rekishi. Edited by Kyōtoshi shihensanjo. Kyōto: Gakugei Shorin. Vol. 1: *Heian no shinkyō* (1970). Vol. 2: *Chūsei no meian* (1971). Vol. 3: *Kinsei no taidō* (1971). Vol. 4: *Momoyama no kaika* (1971). Vol. 5: *Kinsei no tenkai* (1971).

Lebra, Joyce Chapman. "Women in an All-Male Industry: The Case of Sake Brewer Tatsu'uma Kiyo." In *Recreating Japanese Women: 1600–1945,* edited by Gail Lee Bernstein, pp. 131–148. Berkeley: University of California Press, 1991.

Mass, Jeffrey. *The Development of Kamakura Rule.* Stanford, CA: Stanford University Press, 1979.

McMullin, Neil. *Buddhism and the State in Sixteenth Century Japan.* Princeton, NJ: Princeton University Press, 1984.

———. "The Enryakuji and the Gion Shrine-Temple Complex in the Mid-Heian Period." *Japanese Journal of Religious Studies* 14.2–3(1989): 161–184.

———. "On Placating the Gods and Pacifying the Populace: The Case of the Gion Goryō Cult." *History of Religions* 27 (February 1988): 270–293.

———. "The Sanmon–Jimon Schism in the Tendai School of Buddhism: A Preliminary Analysis." *Journal of the International Association of Buddhist Studies* 7.1 (1984): 83–105.

Miyamoto Mataji. *Kabu nakama kenkyū.* Yūhikaku, 1938.

Momose Kesao. "Bunmei jūninen tokusei kinsei ni kansuru ichi kōsatsu." *Shigaku zasshi* 66.4 (April 1957): 1–26.

———. "Ōnin-Bunmei no ran." *Iwanami kōza Nihon rekishi,* vol. 7, pp. 177–217. Iwanami Shoten, 1976.

Moriya Tokihisa. "Rakuchū Rakugai." *Kyōtoshi no chimei,* pp. 44–51.

Morris, V. Dixon. "The City of Sakai and Urban Autonomy." In *Warlords, Artists, and Commoners: Japan in the Sixteenth Century,* edited by George Elison and Bardwell L. Smith, pp. 23–54. Honolulu: University of Hawai'i Press, 1981.

Murai Yasuhiko. "Heiankyō." *Kyōtoshi no chimei,* pp. 31–43.

———. "Heiankyō no keisei." KR, vol. 1, pp. 219–323.

———. "Rokushōji to Toba-dono." KR, vol. 2, pp. 118–143.

———. *Sen no Rikyū.* NHK Books, 1977.

Murata Shūzō. "Sō to doikki." *Iwanami kōza Nihon rekishi,* vol. 7, pp. 135–176. Iwanami Shoten, 1976.

Murayama Shūichi. "Hieizan no kankyō to soshiki." In *Hieizan to Tendai Bukkyō no kenkyū,* edited by Murayama Shūichi, pp. 13–41. Meicho Shuppan, 1975.

———. *Nihon toshi seikatsu no genryū.* Seki Shoin, 1953.

Nagahara Keiji. *Gekokujō no jidai. Nihon no rekishi,* vol. 10. Chūō Kōronsha, 1965.

———. "Kahei to dosō." *Muromachi Sengoku no shakai,* pp. 46–85. Yoshikawa Kōbunkan, 1992.

———. "The Medieval Origins of the Eta-Hinin." *Journal of Japanese Studies* 5.2 (Summer 1979): 385–403.

———. *Nihon no chūsei shakai kōzō no kenkyū.* Iwanami Shoten, 1973.

———. "Nihon zenkindai shakai no tenkai to tennō." *Nihonshi kenkyū* 283 (March 1986): 1–18.

Nagashima Fukutarō. *Ōnin no ran.* Nihon Rekishi Shinsho. Shibundō, 1968.

Nakajima Keiichi. "Chūsei Kyōto ni okeru dosōgyō no seiritsu." *Shigaku zasshi* 101.3 (March 1992): 41–60.

———. "Chūsei Kyōto ni okeru shidōsen kin'yū no tenkai." *Shigaku zasshi* 102.12 (December 1993): 1–33.

Nakajima Yōichirō. *Kikin Nihonshi.* Yūzankaku, 1976.

Nakamura Kichiji. *Doikki kenkyū.* Azekura Shobō, 1974.

Niki Hiroshi. "Chūkinsei ikōki no kenryoku to toshiminshū-Kyōto ni okeru toshi shakai no kōzō hen'yō." *Nihonshi kenkyū* 331(March 1990): 30–54.

Nishimura Hiroko. "Yometorikon e no ugoki to fūfu no jōai." *Nihon josei no rekishi-sei, ai, kazoku,* edited by Sōgō Joseishi Kenkyūkai, pp. 87–97. Kadokawa Shoten, 1992.

Nishio Kazumi. " 'Machishūron' saikentō no kokoromi-Tenbun Hokke ikki wo megutte." *Nihonshi kenkyū* 229 (September 1981): 56–75.

Niunoya Tetsuichi. "Chūsei zenki ni okeru hinin." *Buraku mondai kenkyū* 79 (July 1984): 30–48.

———. *Kebiishi: chusei no kegare to kenryoku.* Heibonsha, 1986.

Noda Tadao. "Chūsei Kyōto ni okeru kōrigashigyō no hatten." *Kyōto Gakugei Daigaku gakuhō* A.2 (August 1952): 31–44.

———. "Chūsei senmin no shakai keizaiteki ichi kōsatsu-toku ni Gionsha inujinin ni tsuite." *Kyōto Gakugei Daigaku gakuhō* A.14 (March 1959): 58–74.

Noguchi Tōru. *Chūsei Kyōto no machiya.* Tōkyō Daigaku Shuppankai, 1988.

Okuno Takahiro. "Muromachi jidai ni okeru dosō no kenkyū." *Shigaku zasshi* 44.8 (August 1933): 44–95.

Ono Kōji (Terutsugu). "Chūsei shuzōgyō no hattatsu." *Shakai keizaishigaku* 6.8(August 1937): 1–36 (pt. 1); 6.9(September 1937): 26–47 (pt. 2); 6.10(October 1937): 55–74 (pt. 3).

———. "Kitano kōjiza ni tsukite." *Kokushigaku* 11 (May 1932): 1–27.

———. "Muromachi Bakufu no sakaya tōsei." *Shigaku zasshi* 43.7 (July 1932): 28–70. Reprinted in Ono, *Nihon sangyō hattatsushi no kenkyū,* pp. 232–266. Shinbundō, 1941.

———. *Nihon sangyō hattatsushi no kenkyū.* Shinbundō, 1941. Reprint Hōsei Daigaku Shuppankyoku, 1981.

Ōyama Kyōhei. "Chūsei no mibunsei to kokka." In *Iwanami kōza Nihon rekishi,* edited by Asao Naohiro et al., vol. 8, pp. 261–313. Iwanami Shoten, 1976.

———. "The Fourteenth Century in Twentieth Century Perspective." In *The Origins of Japan's Medieval World,* edited by Jeffrey P. Mass, pp. 345–365. Stanford, CA: Stanford University Press, 1997.

Ponsonby-Fane, R. A. B. "The Capital and Palace of Heian." *Transactions and Proceedings of the Japan Society* (34th sess.) 22 (1924–1925): 107–228.

Ramirez-Christensen, Esperanza. "Renga and the Popular Dissemination of Classical Literature in Medieval Japan." AAS Annual Meeting, Chicago, April 8, 1990.

Ruch, Barbara. "Medieval Jongleurs and the Making of a National Literature." In *Japan in the Muromachi Age,* edited by John W. Hall and Toyoda Takeshi, pp. 279–309. Berkeley: University of California Press, 1977.

———. "The Other Side of Culture in Medieval Japan." *CHJ*, edited by Kozo Yamamura, vol. 3 (medieval), pp. 500–543. London and New York: Cambridge University Press, 1990.

Sasaki Gin'ya. *Muromachi Bakufu. Nihon no rekishi*. Vol. 13. Shōgakkan, 1975.

Satō Shin'ichi. "Muromachi bakufuron." In *Iwanami kōza Nihon rekishi*, edited by Ienaga Saburō et al., vol. 7, pp. 1–48. Iwanami Shoten, 1962.

———. *Nihon no chūsei kokka*. Iwanami Shoten, 1983.

Satō Shin'ichi with John W. Hall. "The Ashikaga Shogun and the Muromachi Bakufu Administration." In *Japan in the Muromachi Age*, edited by John W. Hall and Toyoda Takeshi, pp. 45–52. Berkeley: University of California Press, 1977.

Seta Katsuya. "Chūsei no Gion'e goryōe." *Rakuchū rakugai no gunzō-ushinawareta chūsei Kyōto e*, pp. 235–288. Heibonsha, 1994. Expansion of "Chūsei Gion'e no ichi kōsatsu-bajōyakusei o megutte," *Nihonshi kenkyū* 200 (April 1979): 15–51.

———. "Kinsei toshi seiritsushi josetsu-Kyōto ni okeru tochi shoyū o megutte." *Nihon shakai keizaishi kenkyū* (medieval volume), pp. 128–136. Yoshikawa Kōbunkan, 1967.

Shibata Minoru. "Jinja to minkan shinkō." *KR*, vol. 2, pp. 390–406.

Shimizu Katsuyuki. "Ashikaga Yoshimochi no kinshurei ni tsuite." *Nihon rekishi* 619 (December 1999): 36–52.

Shimosaka Mamoru. "Chūsei dosōron." In *Chūsei Nihon no rekishizō*, edited by Nihonshi Kenkyūkai and Shiryō Kenkyūbukai, pp. 215–249. Sōgensha, 1978.

———. "Chūsei jiin ni okeru taishū to 'sōdera.'" *Gakusō* 22 (March 2000): 43–85.

———. "Kyōto no fukkō-toimaru, kaidō, sotsubun." *Kinsei fūzoku zufu 3: Rakuchū Rakugai* 1(1983): 128–136.

———. "Machishū no seikatsu." In *Kyōto shomin seikatsushi*, edited by Hayashiya Tatsusaburō, pp. 70–161. Kyōto Shin'yō Kinko, 1973.

———. "Sanmon shisetsu no seiritsu to tenkai-Muromachi bakufu no Sanmon seisaku wo megutte." *Shirin* 58.1 (January 1975): 67–114.

Skord, Virginia, trans. *Tales of Tears and Laughter: Short Fiction of Medieval Japan*. Honolulu: University of Hawai'i Press, 1991.

Suma Chikai. "Dosō ni yoru nengu shūnō no ukeoi ni tsuite." *Shigaku zasshi* 80.6 (June 1971): 1–43.

———. "Dosō no tochi shūseki to tokusei." *Shigaku zasshi* 81.3 (March 1972): 1–20.

Suzuki Ryōichi. *Nihon chūsei no nōmin mondai*. Takagiri Shoin, 1948. Reprint Azekura Shobō, 1971.

Taira Masayuki. *Nihon chūsei no shakai to Bukkyō*. Tachibana Shobō, 1992.

Takahashi Yasuo. *Chūsei Kyōto no tenkai katei ni kansuru toshi shiteki kenkyū*. Privately published, 1979.

———. "Ōnin no ran to toshi kūkan no hen'yō." *Kyōto chūsei toshishi kenkyū*, pp. 291–374. Kyoto: Shibunkaku, 1983.

———. *Rakuchū Rakugai-kankyō bunka no chūseishi*. Heibonsha, 1988.

Takao Kazuhiko. "Sekai no naka no Kyōto." *KR*, vol. 3, pp. 14–41.

Tamai Tetsuo. "Toshi no keikaku to kensetsu." In *Iwanami kōza Nihon tsūshi*, edited by Asao Naohiro et al., vol. 11, pp. 69–106. Iwanami Shoten, 1993.

Tanuma Mutsumi. "Muromachi bakufu zaisei no ichi danmen." *Nihon rekishi* 353 (October 1977): 1–26.

Terajima Masako. "Inryōken mikura ni tsuite." *Chūō Daigaku Daigakuin kenkyū nenpō* 7 (March 1978): 251–265.

Toby, Ronald P. "Why Leave Nara? Kammu and the Transfer of the Capital." *Monumenta Nipponica* 40.3 (Autumn 1985): 331–347.

Tonomura, Hitomi. *Community and Commerce in Late Medieval Japan: The Corporate Villages of Tokuchin-ho.* Stanford, CA: Stanford University Press, 1992.

Toyoda Takeshi. *Chūsei Nihon no shōgyō.* 1937.

———. *Chūsei Nihon shōgyōshi no kenkyū.* Iwanami Shoten, 1944.

———. *Chūsei no shōnin to kōtsū.* Yoshikawa Kōbunkan, 1982.

———. "Chūsei no toshi to shūkyō." *Bunka* 13:1(September 1948). Reprinted in *Toyoda Takeshi Chosakushū,* vol. 7: *Chūsei no seiji to shakai,* pp. 287–308. Yoshikawa Kōbunkan, 1983.

———. "Enryakuji sansō to Hiesha jinin no katsudō." *Hōsei shigaku* 26 (March 1974): 1–16, and 27 (March 1975): 1–20.

———. *Nihon no hōken toshi.* Iwanami Shoten, 1952. Reprint 1976.

———. "Toshi ni okeru sōteki ketsugō no hatten-toku ni Tenbun no Hokke ikki o chū-shin to shite." *Shirin* 41.6 (November 1958): 70–79.

———. *Za no kenkyū.* Yoshikawa Kōbunkan, 1934. Reprint 1982.

———. "Za to dosō." *Iwanami kōza Nihon rekishi,* edited by Ienaga Saburō et al., vol. 6, pp. 153–186. Iwanami Shoten, 1963.

Tsuji Hiroyuki. "Chūsei ni okeru Ōmi Sakamoto no hatten to toshi keikan." *Hisutoria* 88 (September 1980): 1–30.

———. "Chūsei sanmon shūto no dōzoku ketsugō to satobō." *Machikaneyama ronsō* 13 (January 1980): 1–24.

Tsuji Zennosuke. *Nihon Bukkyōshi,* medieval volume 5. Iwanami Shoten, 1951.

Tsurusaki Hirō. "The Poet Shōkō and the Salons of Sakai." *Literary Patronage in Late Medieval Japan,* edited by Steven D. Carter, pp. 45–62. Ann Arbor: Center for Japanese Studies, University of Michigan, 1993.

Umata Ayako. "Chūsei toshi to shotōsō." *Ikki 3: ikki no kōzō,* edited by Aoki Michio et al, pp. 121–168. Tōkyō Daigaku Shuppankai, 1981.

———. "Doikki no soshikisei to shitokusei." *Tachibana Joshi Daigaku kenkyū kiyō* 10(July 1983): 92–106.

———. "Tōjiryō kōsho-shōen ryōshu ni yoru toshi shihai no ichi kōsatsu." *Nihonshi kenkyū* 159(November 1975): 62–86.

Varley, H. Paul. "Ashikaga Yoshimitsu and the World of Kitayama: Social Change and Shogunal Patronage in Early Muromachi Japan." In *Japan in the Muromachi Age,* edited by John W. Hall and Toyoda Takeshi, pp. 183–204. Berkeley: University of California Press, 1977.

———. "Cultural Life in Medieval Japan." CHJ, edited by Kozo Yamamura, vol. 3 (medieval), pp. 447–499. London and New York: Cambridge University Press, 1990.

———. *Imperial Restoration in Medieval Japan.* New York: Columbia University Press, 1971.

———. *The Onin War.* New York: Columbia University Press, 1971.

Varley, H. Paul, and Elison, George. "The Culture of Tea: From Its Origins to Sen no Rikyū." In *Warlords, Artists, and Commoners: Japan in the Sixteenth Century,* edited by George Elison and Bardwell L. Smith, pp. 187–222. Honolulu: University of Hawai'i Press, 1981.

Wakita Haruko. "Chūsei Kyōto no tochi shoyū." *Nihon chūsei toshiron*, pp. 119–180. Tōkyō Daigaku Shuppankai, 1981.

———. *Chūsei ni ikiru onnatachi*. Iwanami Shoten, 1995.

———. "Chūsei ni okeru seibetsu yakuwari buntan to joseikan." In *Nihon joseishi*, edited by Joseishi Sōgō Kenkyūkai, vol. 2, pp. 65–102. Tōkyō Daigaku Shuppankai, 1982.

———. "Chūsei no Gion'e-sono seiritsu to henshitsu." *Geinōshi kenkyū* 4(March 1964): 11–28.

———. "Chūsei toshi to nōson." *Kōza Nihonshi*, edited by Rekishigaku Kenkyūkai and Nihonshi Kenkyūkai, vol. 3, pp. 189–226. Tōkyō Daigaku Shuppankai, 1970.

———. "Dosō to bōeki." KR, vol. 3, pp. 231–268.

———. "The Japanese Medieval City." Unpublished paper presented at the European University Institute, Florence, January 1979.

———. "Marriage and Property in Medieval Japan from the Perspective of Women's History." *Journal of Japanese Studies* 10.1 (Winter 1984): 73–99.

———. "Muromachiki no keizai hatten." *Iwanami kōza Nihon rekishi*, edited by Asao Naohiro et al., vol. 7, pp. 51–98. Iwanami Shoten, 1976.

———. "Nihon chūsei toshi no kōzō." *Nihonshi kenkyū* 139–140 (1974): 15–36.

———. "Ryōshu keizai no henshitsu to ton'yateki shihai." *Nihon chūsei shōgyō hattatsushi no kenkyū*, pp. 275–356. Ochanomizu Shobō, 1969.

———. "Shōgyō to machiza." KR, vol. 3, pp. 186–230.

———. "Shōkōgyōsha no seichō." KR, vol. 2, pp. 445–465.

———. "Toshi kyōdōtai no keisei." *Nihon chūsei toshiron*, pp. 249–301. Tōkyō Daigaku Shuppankai, 1981.

———. "Towards a Wider Perspective on Medieval Commerce." *Journal of Japanese Studies* 1.2 (Spring 1975): 321–345.

———. "Za no seikaku henka to honjo kenryoku." *Nihon chūsei shōgyō hattatsushi no kenkyū*, pp. 235–274. Ochanomizu Shobō, 1969.

Wakita Haruko with Susan B. Hanley. "Dimensions of Development: Cities in Fifteenth and Sixteenth Century Japan." *Japan before Tokugawa: Political Consolidation and Economic Growth, 1500–1650*, edited by John W. Hall, Nagahara Keiji, and Kozo Yamamura, pp. 295–326. Princeton, NJ: Princeton University Press, 1981.

Wakita Osamu. "The Emergence of the State in Sixteenth-Century Japan: From Oda to Tokugawa." *Journal of Japanese Studies* 8.2 (Summer 1982): 343–367.

———. *Kinsei hōkensei seiritsu shiron: Shokuhō seiken no bunseki*, vol. 2. Tōkyō Daigaku Shuppankai, 1977.

———. *Oda seiken no kisō kōzō: shokuhō seiken no bunseki*. 2 vols. Tōkyō Daigaku Shuppankai, 1975, 1977.

———. "Shōgyō, kōtsū seisaku no tenkai." KR, vol. 4, pp. 352–395.

Wakita Osamu and Wakita Haruko. "Tokken shōnin no taitō." KR, vol. 4, pp. 394–434.

Watsky, Andrew M. "Commerce, Politics and Tea: The Career of Imai Sōkyū." *Monumenta Nipponica* 50.1(Spring 1995): 46–65.

Weber, Max. *The City*. New York: The Free Press, 1958.

Wintersteen, Prescott. "The Early Muromachi Bakufu in Kyoto." *Medieval Japan: Essays in Institutional History*, edited by John W. Hall and Jeffrey P. Mass, pp. 201–209. New Haven, CT: Yale University Press, 1974.

Yamamura, Kozo. "The Development of Za in Medieval Japan." *Business History Review* 47.4 (Winter 1973): 438–465.

———. "The Growth of Commerce in Medieval Japan." CHJ, edited by Kozo Yamamura, vol. 3 (medieval), pp. 344–395. London and New York: Cambridge University Press, 1990.

Yang, Lien-sheng. "Buddhist Monasteries and Four Moneyraising Institutions in Chinese History." *Harvard Journal of Asiatic Studies* 13 (1950): 174–191.

Yasuoka Shigeaki. "Shōgyō no henshitsu." KR, vol. 5, pp. 125–144.

Yokoi Kiyoshi. *Kanmon gyoki: ōja to shūsho no hazama ni te*. Soshiete, 1979.

———. "Tairan no naka no seikatsu." KR, vol. 3, pp. 333–352.

Index

Akamatsu family, 151, 156, 166, 202; Mitsusuke, 132, 150
Asakura family, 146
Ashikaga Bakufu. *See* Muromachi Shogunate
Ashikaga family: Takauji, 19; Yoshiakira, 79; Yoshiharu, 179, 180, 182; Yoshihisa, 7, 150; Yoshimasa, 112, 150, 157, 164, 178, 190; Yoshimi, 150; Yoshimitsu, 7, 21, 77, 79, 89, 101, 112, 119, 150, 179; Yoshimochi, 119–123, 134; Yoshinori, 23, 101, 112; Yoshitane, 95; Yoshitsuna, 180; Yoshizumi, 111, 180

Baba Yoshirō, 88
Bajōyaku, 113, 114
Bean-paste merchants, 1, 77, 105, 112, 113
Board of Adjudicants (*hikitsukekata*), 216
Board of Administration (*mandokoro*), 20, 53, 79, 81, 82, 85, 88, 90, 91, 113, 114, 123, 139, 160, 188, 192, 216–217
Board of Retainers (*samuraidokoro*), 31, 77, 160, 164
Bugyōshū. See Corps of administrators
Buichi tokusei. See Debt amnesties, conditional
Bukkōji, 177
Bun'an Disturbance, 122. *See also* Kitano Malt Disturbance
Bureau of Capital Police (*Kebiishichō*), 15, 30–31, 70, 75–76, 78, 146

Capital Office (*Kyōshiki*), 15, 26
Chang-an, 11, 12
Chinkōji, 154
Chō (neighborhood organization). See *Machi*
Commoner (term), 6
Companion stories (*otogi zōshi*), 199
Corps of administrators (*bugyōshū*), 216
Credit, 220–221. *See also* Moneylending
Currency regulations (*erizenirei*), 161–163

Daigoji, 154
Daijōe. See Imperial accession ceremony
Daikakuji, 203
Debt amnesties, 128–148, 213; conditional, 51, 142–144; *Ikki* and, 128–148; Kamakura shogunal policy on, 73; private (*shi-tokusei*), 132

Distillery Office, 44, 74–75, 79, 81, 83, 100, 108, 109, 120, 123, 124, 165, 169, 204, 205
Dosō (earthen storehouses; by extension, moneylenders), 38–39, 206
Dosō yoriaishū (council of lenders), 62, 71, 84
Dosōkata isshū, 83, 84

Eishū, 199–200
Enkaku (lender), 198
Enryakuji: durability as overlord, 100–108; estates of, 64–66; founding of, 62; moneylenders and, 28, 39, 61–62, 71–73; organization and structure, 63, 66–70; portable shrine and, 62, 70, 71, 80; relations with shogunate, 80–81
Erizenirei. See Currency regulations

Frois, Luis, 45, 205
Fujiwara family, 13; Teika, 37; Tokifusa, 37
Fushimi Sadafusa, 49, 103, 190–192, 198

Genpei seisuiki, 71
Genpukuji, 57
Genze riyaku, 28
Gion Festival, 224; cancellation of, 152, 160 (1467), 186–187 (1533); financing of, 197; moneylenders and, 189, 197; organization of, 197; origins of, 197; post-Ōnin revival, 158; taxation for, 107; townspeople's role in, 175, 196–197
Gion Kanjin'in Gionsha, 68
Gion Shrine, 21, 23, 41, 69, 70, 104, 107, 111, 154, 160, 175, 196, 209
Godaigo (emperor), 22, 75, 77
Goen'yū (emperor), 79, 280n. 76
Gohanazono (emperor), 191
Gosanjō (emperor), 70
Goseibai shikimoku, 213
Gotoba (emperor), 15
Goun (lender), 40
Goyō shōnin (designated merchants), 208
Guilds, 24, 26, 56–61, 205–207, 209, 218
Gyokuryūin, 199
Gyokusenbō (lender), 85, 105, 168, 169

Hakubogazake (Kyōgen play), 44
Hanzei, 65

Hatakeyama family, 150, 156, 157; Masa-
naga, 150–151, 154, 157; Mitsuie,
135, 146; Mochikuni, 122, 150;
Yoshimune, 151; Yoshinari, 151,
156
Hayata Kamematsu, 108
Heiankyō, 11, 13
Heijōkyō, 11
Hie Shrine, 62, 63, 67–71, 74, 103–108,
111, 113, 152, 169
Hieizanji, 62
Higashibōjō family, 78
Hinin. See Outcastes
Hino family, 168
Hino Tomiko, 150, 157; control of toll sta-
tions, 78, 144, 164, 165; reputation,
274n. 139
Hirohashi family, 83
Hiyoshi Shrine. See Hie Shrine
Hōdōji, 120
Hōjōji, 140
Hōkanji, 156
Hokke Ikki. See Lotus leagues
Hōkyōji, 165
Hōnen, 73
Hongaku shisō, 198
Honganji, 100, 101, 180, 182, 186
Honkokuji, 183
Honmyōji, 178
Honnōji, 31
Hōsen (lender), 190–192, 193, 198, 199
Hōshōni (lender), 40
Hosokawa family, 150, 152, 157, 179, 202,
204; Harumoto, 180, 181, 182, 184;
Katsumoto, 150, 151; Masamoto, 157,
165; Mochiyuki, 135, 146
Hosshōji, 13

Ikki, 51, 127, 148, 221; decline, 138–147;
etymology, 128; Kakitsu, 134–137;
Kanshō, 141; membership, 128; Shōchō,
131–134; strategy, 130–131; townspeople
and, 131, 174
Ikkō ikki, 180
Illustrated screens of Kyoto, 217–218
Imperial accession ceremony, 20–21,
112
Inari Shrine, 140, 160
Ise family, 111, 164
Ise shrine, 111, 164
Isshiki family, 151
Itakura family, 166; Shigemune, 206

Ji Sect. See Time Sect
Jimon. See Onjōji
Jinin, 62, 68–69, 70, 105–106
Jinnin. See Jinin
Jōkōbō (lender), 85, 86, 105, 201
Jōsenbō (lender), 85, 86, 87, 93, 105, 114

Kabu nakama, 207
Kakitsu Incident (1441), 134, 150
Kamakura shogunate, 73–74
Kamigoryōsha, 151
Kammu (emperor), 11, 13
Kaneyori (Kamakura deputy shugo), 71
Kanmon gyoki, 192
Kasuga Shrine, 105, 106, 209
Kawamura Shinjirō (lender), 83, 86
Kenkei, 103, 104, 115–116, 119, 166, 218
Kenmu shikimoku, 78, 214
Kenmon, 100, 103, 170, 222; system of rule,
4–5, 18–19, 20
Kenninji, 70
Kikutei family, 78
Kitano Malt Disturbance, 103, 119–125,
204, 223
Kitano Shrine, 41, 43, 45, 59, 68, 103, 119–
125, 157, 160, 167, 169, 175, 204, 218
Kiyomizudera, 30, 33, 64, 70, 100
Kōdō, 186
Kōfukuji, 68, 70, 100, 132, 152, 154, 164,
182
Kōgon (emperor), 22
Kokka chingo, 62
Komiyama Shungan (merchant), 28
Kōno family, 152
Konusutto, 192
Kosatsukie, 104
Kōyasan, 182
Kubō mikura, 84, 85
Kujizainin, 197
Kujō family, 129
Kunin, 69–70
Kurahōshi, 140
Kuroda Toshio, 4
Kyōgen, 192, 198, 200, 212, 224
Kyōgi shakubuku, 180
Kyoto: ancient period, 11–15; appearance,
11–13; etymology, 13; founding of, 11;
market economy, 17–18; medieval popu-
lation, 31–33
Kyōshiki. See Capital Office
Kyoto shugō, 15
Kyōwarabe, 26

Lake Biwa pilots, 66
Linked verse, 192–194
Lotus leagues, 124, 174, 177–189, 203
Lotus movement, 173, 174, 177, 179–
180, 223, 224; Lotus Sutra in, 178; self-
governance, 180–182
Lotus Sect, 22, 28, 152, 160, 176, 182

Machi (neighborhood block): components,
24; development, 24–26, 174–176;
leadership (*gachigyōji*); Lotus leagues
and, 185–187; membership, 172, 175,
186; relations with overlords, 185; self-
defense, 141–142, 158–160; self-
governance, 180
Machigumi (neighborhood clusters), 175
Machishū, 26
Madenokōji family, 209; Tokifusa, 147
Malt Disturbance. *See* Kitano Malt Distur-
bance
Meisai (lender), 237nn. 2, 3
Memeko (lender), 40
Mibudera, 198
Mibu family, 78
Mibu Kyōgen, 189, 198
Mikinotsukasa, alternative reading *zōshushi.*
See Distillery Office
Mikura. See Storehouse keepers
Minami Gosho, 165
Minamoto Yoritomo, 15
Miyoshi family, 178, 204; Motonaga, 179
Momii family, 85, 87
Moneylenders: cultural pursuits, 189–200;
decline of, 204–210; as guild members,
59; lists of, 40, 225–235; locations in
Kyoto (map), 40; origins, 37–39, 67–
70; relations with overlords, 99–109;
self-governance, 173, 187; as tax
agents, 85–88; taxation—*see* Taxation of
moneylenders
Moneylending: agricultural, 50–52; by bean-
paste merchants, 1; Buddhism and, 72; in
China, 72–73; clerical, 2, 39; practices,
47–55; role of women, 45. *See also* Credit
Monzeki, 63
Monzenmachi, 203
Mount Hiei. *See* Enryakuji
Munabechisen (munebetsusen), 85, 111
Murata Sōju (tea master), 195
Muromachi Bakufu. *See* Muromachi
shogunate
Muromachi laws, 81–83, 163, 213–214

Muromachi shogun, 21
Muromachi shogunate, 1, 44, 65, 67;
employment of moneylenders as tax
agents, 85–88; in Kyoto, 7, 19–20, 77–
78; policies toward commerce, 78–79,
81; policies toward moneylending, 78,
81–83; relations with Enryakuji, 80–
81; taxation of money-lenders, 84–85,
90–99
Myōhōrenji, 178–179

Nakahara family: role in Distillery Office, 75,
79, 83, 108, 120; Yasutomi, 50, 146. *See
also* Oshikōji family
Nakama, 205, 207
Nakamura (lender), 94, 106, 202
Nakanishi (lender), 86
Nakayama (lender), 189
Nanzenji, 23, 154, 168
Negoroji, 182
Nenbutsu odori, 28
Nichiren, 178, 189, 181, 183
Nichizō, 178
Nihon ryōiki, 44
Ninagawa family, 91, 215–216; Chikamoto,
216; Chikataka, 216; Chikatoshi, 188,
192, 216; Chikayori, 216
Ninnaji, 157, 191
Nishibōjō family, 31
Nishijin textile merchants, 206, 209
Nisshin, 178
Nōsenkata. See Tax agents

Oda Nobunaga, 2, 23, 100, 149, 163, 183,
184, 195, 202, 205, 218
Office of retired emperor (*In no chō*), 13
Ōkurakyō, 202
Ōnin War, 127, 148–149; course of, 150–
157; effects on city life, 149, 157–
160; effects on moneylenders, 96, 166,
171
Ōninki, 112
Onjōji (Miidera), 63, 182
Oshikōji document collection, 169
Oshikōji family (formerly Nakahara), 108–
109, 124, 165, 204; Morokata, 109;
Moroyasu, 109
Otogi zōshi. See Companion stories
Ōtoneri guild, 209
Ōuchi family, 152, 155; Masahiro, 156;
Yoshioki, 108
Outcastes, 29–31, 70

Overlords: as city landlords, 181; decline of, 208–209; rule, 3–5, relations with guilds, 57–59; term, 6
Ōyamagui, 62
Ōyamazaki *jinin,* 105–106
Ōyamazaki oil merchants, 58, 77

Packhorse drivers, 66, 121, 164
Pawnbrokers, 1, 39, 206–207
Pure Land Buddhism, 28, 31, 40, 198

Rai (lender), 40
Rodrigues, Joao, 176
Rokkaku family, 101, 102, 151, 152; role in suppression of Lotus leagues, 100; Sadayori, 180–182
Rokkakudō, 177, 186, 197
Rokuhara deputyship *(tandai),* 16
Rokuōin, 185
Ruch, Barbara, 211
Ryōgaeya (money exchanger), 206, 207
Ryōgen, 62

Saga (emperor), 15
Saichō, 62, 73
Saiji, 12
Saitō (Western branch of Enryakuji), 122, 123, 124
Sakamoto (entrepots at east and west bases of Mount Hiei), 63, 66, 67, 89, 105, 121, 180
Sake brewing, 41, 43–45, 170, 247
Sanbōin, 154
Sanmon (Enryakuji), 63
Sanmon shisetsu (Enryakuji envoys), 101–102
Sano (lender), 189
Santo, 67–68, 94, 101, 106
Satobō, 63–66, 87
Sawamura (lender), 86, 94, 105, 106, 108, 140, 202
Seiganji, 156, 190
Seikōin, 185
Sekime (lender), 245n. 5
Sen'un (lender), 114, 118
Shami, 167–168
Shiba family, 150; Yoshikado, 151; Yoshikane, 146; Yoshimasa, 82; Yoshitoshi, 151
Shichiya (pawnbroker), 206
Shinkei, 194
Shinran, 73
Shirakawa (emperor), 13

Shirakawa leagues, 135
Shōani (lender), 40
Shōhaku, 194
Shōjitsubō (lender), 85, 86, 87, 105, 113–116, 151, 176, 188, 201–203, 205
Shōkō (emperor), 134
Shōkokuji, 129, 137, 154, 157, 168, 199
Shōren'in, 57, 63, 65, 154
Sōchō (poet), 193
Sōgi (poet), 193
Storehouse keepers *(mikura),* 37; for shogun *(kubō mikura),* 84–85
Sugawara Michizane, 68
Suminokura (brewer family), 188, 201, 203–204, 210

Taga Takatada, 52
Taira Kiyomori, 15
Takaya Magojirō (lender), 190–191, 192, 199
Takeda family, 151, 156
Tale of Genji, 194
Tale of the Heike, 191, 193, 199
Tateiri family: Munetsugu, 104, 117; Muneyasu, 104
Taxation of moneylenders: brewer tax, 85, 92, 99; bribery to avoid, 113–119; collection, 85–87; definition, 6; by Enryakuji, 71–72; exemptions, 113–119; by imperial court, 74–76; incidental levies, 111–113; multiple, 99; by overlords, 57–58, by shogunate, 81–85, 90–99; storehouse tax, 92, 99
Tax agents, shogunal, 84–85, 88, 95, 102, 219
Tea ceremony, 189, 195, 196
Temmu (emperor), 11
Tendai Buddhism, 62, 63, 68, 198
Tenji (emperor), 11, 62
Tenryūji, 22, 135, 157, 168
Time (Ji) Sect, 22, 31, 167, 177
Tōdaiji, 57, 182
Tōfukuji, 135, 137, 141
Tōgashi family, 151
Toiya (wholesaler), 207
Tōji, 12, 21, 29, 135, 144–145, 147, 152, 154, 157, 182
Toki family, 151, 156
Tokugawa shogunate, 163, 205
Tokusei. See Debt amnesties
Tokusei ikki, 128, 138–139, 145, 147
Toll stations, 164–165

Townspeople, 24–29, 176–178, 180–181, 184, 186, 192, 196–198
Toyotomi Hideyoshi, 109, 158, 163, 195, 203, 205
True Pure Land Buddhism (Jōdo Shinshū), 100, 180
Tsuda (lender), 245n. 5
Tsugiuta, 194–195

Umegaki (lender), 140

Vilela, Gaspar, 183

Yamana family, 146, 152, 166; Sōzen, 150, 151, 152, 155, 156
Yamashina family, 78, 202; Tokitsugu, 180, 181, 190–191, 199

Yanagi (brewer), 28, 41, 85, 106, 168, 178
Yasaka Shrine, 218. *See also* Gion Shrine
Yase, 57, 66, 218
Yasu (lender), 169
Yasui (lender), 86, 105, 140, 189, 192, 202
Yoriaishū (council of brewer-lenders), 59
Yoshida Munetada (lender), 188, 204
Yun In Bo, 87
Yūzū nenbutsu, 198

Za. See Guilds
Zen institution (*gozan*), 2, 21, 23, 28, 136, 166, 214–215,
Zen'ami family, 31, 152
Zenjūbō (lender), 85, 87
Zenshōbō (lender), 169

About the Author

Suzanne Gay, who holds a doctorate in history from Yale University, is currently associate professor of East Asian Studies at Oberlin College. She is the author of several articles on medieval Japanese political and social history.